Nova & Vetera

Thomas Patrick Halton

Nova & Vetera

Patristic Studies in Honor of

THOMAS PATRICK HALTON

EDITED BY JOHN PETRUCCIONE

The Catholic University of America Press

Washington, D.C.

The paper used in this publication meets the minimum requirements of American National Standards for Information Science—Permanence of Paper for Printed Library materials, ANSI Z39.48-1984
∞

LIBRARY OF CONGRESS CATALOGING-IN-PUBLICATION DATA
Nova et vetera : patristic studies in honor of Thomas Patrick Halton / edited by John Petruccione.
    p.   cm.
    Includes bibliographical references and indexes.
    1. Fathers of the church.   2. Theology—History—Early church, ca. 30–600.   3. Bible—Criticism, interpretation, etc.—History, Early church, ca. 30–600.   4. Christian literature, Early—History and criticsm.   5. Augustine, Saint, Bishop of Hippo.   6. Halton, Thomas P. (Thomas Patrick)   I. Petruccione, John, 1950– .   II. Halton, Thomas P. (Thomas Patrick)
BR67.N68   1998
270.1—dc21
97-40251
ISBN 0-8132-0900-5 (alk. paper)

Contents

⚜

Tom Halton among the Homoousions

Of his three score years and ten
Seventy will not come again,
So if you're keeping Biblical score
That doesn't leave him any more.

But students of the Scriptures know
There's always one more verse to go,
And that no true scholar can find rest
Until he's checked the last-found palimpsest.

Whereas the septuagenarian textual measure,
Acknowledging the decline of bodily function,
Defines the end of sensual pleasure
(Punishment for earlier excess to be eased by Extreme Unction),

The Psalmist offers ten years more
To those with strength to bear pain and labor
And spend the added years refining creeds,
Their failing sight perusing screeds,

To discover who said what first,
Who identified the earliest atheist,
Why Augustine spurned the Manichees
And who were the bishops of Dead Seas.

True doctors of Patristics
Are not shaken by contradictions or statistics,
Nor do they fear to tread
In places even angels dread.

Some stand with Irenaeus and his views
That martyrdom's the sure way to salvation;

Others opt for Athanasius and choose
To make their way by killing heretic and pagan.

Some dare to ask, "Was Leo really number one?"
As was declared at Chalcedon
And draw the line between Homoiousion and Homoousion,
The difference being a vowel or preposition.

Some endorse the grammatical assertion of the Great
That the subject is the predicate (or vice versa)
And accept the conflation of three Marys into one,
Now carried on the calendar as The Magdalen.

Today we start, with Halton, a ten-year wait
For one more wide-eyed Arab spelunker
To dance out of a dry Judaean sepúlcher
With a scroll, ultimate, or perhaps, penultimate,

Revealing that all persons born in County Cavan
Have a head start on the road to heaven.

                                        e.j.mccarthy

Tabula Gratulatoria

The Department of Greek and Latin
The Catholic University of America

Prof. Pier Franco Beatrice
University of Padua

Prof. Maxwell Bloomfield
The Catholic University of America

His Excellency Sean Brady
Armagh

The Rev. Dr. John Hanna Cheikho
St. Thomas Chaldean Parish
West Bloomfield, Michigan

His Eminence Cahal B.
Cardinal Daly
Armagh

Prof. Bruno M. Damiani
The Catholic University of America

Dr. John Dillon
Theological College, Washington

His Excellency Dermot Gallagher
Ambassador of Ireland

Dr. George E. Gingras
The Catholic University of America

Dr. Ellen S. Ginsberg
The Catholic University of America

The Rev. Prof. Patrick Granfield
The Catholic University of America

Prof. Robert M. Grant
The University of Chicago

Prof. Craig L. Hanson
Muskingum College

Prof. Paul B. Harvey, Jr.
Pennsylvania State University

The Rev. Michael Heintz
Fort Wayne, Indiana

Prof. E. Glenn Hinson
Baptist Theological Seminary
at Richmond

The Rev. Dr. David Johnson, S.J.
The Catholic University of America

Prof. Glen M. Johnson
The Catholic University of America

Prof. Kathryn L. Johnson
Louisville Presbyterian Theological
Seminary

The Rev. James F. Kauffmann
St. Mary of the Annunciation
Ladysmith, Virginia

Mssrs. Hugh V. and Brendan Kelly
Kelly's Ellis Island Restaurant and Pub,
Washington

Msgr. John J. Lenihan, V.G.
San José Catholic Church
Jacksonville, Florida

Prof. Kathleen E. McVey
Princeton Theological Seminary

Prof. Virgil P. Nemoianu
The Catholic University of America

Prof. Frederick W. Norris
Emmanuel School of Religion

Sr. Anne M. O'Donnell, S.N.D.
The Catholic University of America

Prof. John J. O'Meara
University College, Dublin

Kristos E. Panayiotis
Ph.D. Cand., Patristics
The University of Edinburgh

The Rev. Prof. Peter C. Phan
The Catholic University of America

Dr. John W. Rettig
Cincinnati, Ohio

Prof. Harry Rosenberg
Colorado State University

Dr. and Mrs. Paul S. Russell, III
Chevy Chase, Maryland

Saint Patrick's College, Maynooth

Prof. Joyce E. Salisbury
University of Wisconsin at Green Bay

Prof. Margaret A. Schatkin
Boston College

The Rev. J. Jayakiran Sebastian
United Theological College

Mr. Tommy Slowey
Cavan

Prof. Michael Slusser
Duquesne University

Prof. Antanas Suziedelis
The Catholic University of America

The Rev. Prof. Leo Sweeney, S.J.
Loyola University

Dr. Efthalia Makris Walsh
Chevy Chase, Maryland

Prof. James Wetzel
Colgate University

Prof. James Youniss
The Catholic University of America

Thomas Patrick Halton

Stella O'Leary

Thomas Patrick Halton was born on February 6, 1925, in the Republic of Ireland, in the small town of Kilnaleck, County Cavan, near the border with Northern Ireland. In the final year of primary school, his teacher, Master Peter Martin, recognizing him as an exceptional student, provided the private coaching in algebra and geometry that culminated in an award of a coveted five-year (1938–1943) scholarship to St. Patrick's College. St. Patrick's was the only boarding secondary school for boys in County Cavan. In his first letter home, Tom, now thirteen years old, reproduced for his mother the Greek alphabet—a harbinger of the scholarly productions to come.

In 1943 Tom entered St. Patrick's College, Maynooth, County Kildare, as a seminarian and an honors student in Ancient Classics. In his first year at Maynooth he was a student of the late Dennis Meehan, then newly appointed. Professor Meehan taught a course in Homer that sparked Tom's interest in Greek literature and archaeology and led in later years to many trips to Greece, the Greek islands, and Troy. In 1987, as editorial director of *The Fathers of the Church*, Tom brought out Dennis Meehan's *Saint Gregory of Nazianzus: Three Poems* as volume seventy-five of that series.

In September 1946, Tom received his Bachelor's degree from Maynooth with first-class honors. He discussed with Professor John Hackett, then the director of Honors Greek at Maynooth, the possibility of pursuing a Master's degree in Greek, but Hackett discouraged the idea on the grounds that the "Authorities" might think that this would interfere with his theological studies. The M.A. had to wait for another decade. Tom's studies in theology (1946–50) led to the Baccalaureate in Sacred Theology in 1949. During these years he was an editor of the student magazine, *The Silhouette*, and a member of his class's debating team.

After ordination at Maynooth on June 18, 1950, Tom spent a year at University College, Dublin, where he completed a Diploma in Higher Education while teaching full-time at the Catholic University School, Dublin. The next year he returned as diocesan inspector of religious education to his native diocese of Kilmore. Then, from 1952 to 1959, he taught Greek, Latin and English at his *alma mater,* St. Patrick's College, Cavan.

During this time he wrote extensively in Irish Catholic journals, including *The Furrow* and *The Irish Ecclesiastical Record,* on such diverse topics as "Contemporary Song," "The Priest on the Stage," and "The Pax Movement in Poland." He read one of his most publicized pieces, "The Catholic Writer," at the twelfth annual congress of the *Christus Rex* Society. This was reported at length in the *Irish Times*[1] and published in the proceedings of the Congress.[2] In this address to "an exclusively clerical audience" the thirty-two-year-old Halton remarked that some Irish authors seemed to write for the tastes of English and American publishers. It was not the actual contemporary Ireland they portrayed but "an Ireland oversupplied with sex and savagery" for "the English market," and an Ireland "mawkishly masquerading in shillelaghs and shamrocks" for the American.[3] The playwright Sean O'Casey took lively exception in a lengthy letter to the *Irish Times.*[4] A week later, in a letter to Brooks Atkinson, the influential drama critic of the *New York Times,* O'Casey reported, "I had a letter in *The Irish Times* replying to a Catholic teacher in a Cavan College, who had lectured about the Catholic writer and the Censorship; a letter that is provoking yelping letters in the same paper."[5] In these articles of Tom's we recognize a challenging and restless intellect and gain a sense of the Irish literary and social climate of the 1950s.

In 1954 Tom enrolled at University College, Dublin, as an M.A. student in Ancient Classics. Two years later he completed and defended, with first class honors, his dissertation, *Theodoret of Cyrus, On Divine Providence, a Translation with Introduction and Commentary.* At University College he had worked under the urbane and exacting direction of Professor John O'Meara, whose charm contrasted with the Olympian aloofness of many of the Maynooth faculty. Some thirty-five years later Tom edited for The Catholic University of America Press his mentor's *Studies in Augustine and Eriugena* (1992). It was O'Meara who encouraged Tom to proceed to doctoral studies. He suggested The Catholic University of America in Washington, D.C., and kindly wrote supporting letters to the graduate school.

With O'Meara's support, Tom won a doctoral scholarship to CUA, which guaranteed free tuition, room, and board for two years. In Fall 1959,

1. April 26, 1957.

2. *Christus Rex* 11 (1957), pp. 707–18.

3. *Ib.,* pp. 707, 712f.

4. V. D. Krause, *The Letters of Sean O'Casey 1955–1958,* vol. 3 (Washington 1989), pp. 431–33.

5. *Ib.,* p. 436.

he entered the Department of Greek and Latin, which has long devoted particular attention to the early Church Fathers. Toward the end of Tom's first year, Professor Martin R.P. McGuire, his dissertation director, called him into his office and told him that the department was very pleased with his work and would like him to join the faculty as assistant professor. In the following September, Tom began a happy career that has continued to the present through promotion in 1965 to associate and, in 1976, to ordinary professor. From 1974 to 1978 he served as Chairman of the Department, and in 1987 he was appointed the Margaret H. Gardiner Professor of Greek.

When Tom began his career of university teaching, the study of Greek and Latin enjoyed, especially at Catholic institutions, what seemed an unassailable security, even in the undergraduate curriculum. The summer before his arrival, the Department had sponsored a well-attended workshop for Latin teachers—mostly secular and religious clergy—whose proceedings McGuire edited and published under the title *Teaching Latin in the Modern World*. Here McGuire made the pronouncement, "As long as Latin remains the official language of the Church, and, especially, of the Liturgy, Latin must have an essential place in Catholic education."[6] Within a few years, Vatican II and the introduction of the vernacular into the liturgy proved him to be, as he laughingly admitted, "the most discredited prophet of the twentieth century." The ancient languages soon lost the privileged position they had enjoyed at CUA, and Tom, like many other classically educated members of his generation, was to face pedagogical challenges arising from their new, entirely elective, status.

He proved to be a most versatile teacher. For decades his department has relied on him to offer the most varied array of courses: undergraduate and graduate, classical and patristic, in Greek and in Latin, on topics literary, archaeological, historical, and philosophical. In recent years he has introduced undergraduates to Greek prose composition, Roman satire, and Plato. He has conducted graduate courses and seminars on Greek epigraphy, Eusebius of Caesarea, Clement of Alexandria, Hibernian Latin texts, and the theme of virginity in Greek and Latin church authors. For the past ten years, he has had sole responsibility for the graduate pro-seminar, "The Introduction to Classical and Patristic Scholarship." In years past he even taught a course on Greek red-figure pottery! He has directed disser-

---

6. "Appendix C: A New Pronouncement from Rome on the Study of Latin," *Teaching Latin in the Modern World: The Proceedings of the Workshop on the Teaching of Latin in the Modern World, conducted at The Catholic University of America, June 12 to 23, 1959*, ed. M.R.P. McGuire (Washington 1960), p. 254.

tations dealing with such diverse topics as classical Greek epigraphy, early Christian homiletics, the tradition of the epithalamium in Greek and Roman sources, and medieval Latin hymnody. For many years Tom's unflagging eagerness to develop new fields of interest has much enriched the instructional offerings available to students not only of his own department but also to those in Early Christian Studies, Church History, and Theology.

Tom's scholarly work has ranged widely in Classics and Patristics and the classical tradition in European literature. One glancing through his list of publications (pp. 263–65 below) will find, among others, Homer and Camus, Eusebius and Hegesippus, Clement of Alexandria and the Pre-Socratics, Isidore of Pelusium, Gregory of Nazianzus, John Chrysostom. He has returned repeatedly to certain fields, authors, and themes: the reception and rejection of classical and pre-classical philosophical notions among the Greek Fathers; the liturgy of the early Church, especially the celebration of the sacraments of baptism and the Eucharist; early and rhetorically elaborated Greek homilies preached at Easter. In all his work, perhaps most especially in his annotated translation of Theodoret of Cyr's *On Divine Providence* (1988), one admires the combination of an enviable philological expertise with broad theological, scriptural, philosophical, and historical erudition.

As bibliographer Tom has rendered exemplary service to the field of classical studies as a whole. His collaborator in updating Martin McGuire's model *Introduction to Classical Scholarship,* I can testify to the magnitude—and the rewards—of that enterprise. We initiated the project with an application for a grant from the National Endowment for the Humanities, which we received in 1978. Eight years later Kraus International published our *Classical Scholarship: An Annotated Bibliography* (White Plains, New York 1986). It was a daunting task and one that at times we felt would never be completed. In 1993 we were at the University of Montpellier, where Tom was collecting material for his projected bibliographical supplement to the first three volumes of Johannes Quasten's *Patrology.* Here we came across a reference to our book in J. Poucet and J.-M. Hannick's *Introduction aux études classiques,* a French bibliographical guide hitherto unknown to us.[7] Under "Bibliographies générales" we read: "On consultera surtout la bibliographie toute récente de Halton, Th. P., O'Leary, St., *Classical Scholarship. An Annotated Bibliography* . . . : bibliographie annotée . . . extrêmement importante et très précieuse, couvrant

---

7. *Introduction aux études classiques: Guide bibliographique* (Louvain-la-Neuve 1988).

l'ensemble du domaine; l'accent y est naturellement mis sur les publications en langue anglaise; remarquable instrument de travail, qui pourrait servir de modèle." Delighted with this review, we cut short our research and celebrated with a lavish dinner of Languedoc food and wine.

It is, of course, in the study of Late Antiquity and early Christianity that Tom's service—again as bibliographer, and also as editor and administrator—has been most influential. Scholars and advanced students have long made use of the survey of a decade of publications in Patristics (1970–79) that Tom and Robert Sider brought out in two issues of the *Classical World* (1979). As editor (1983–87) of the series *The Message of the Fathers of the Church*, Tom saw through the Michael Glazier Press of Wilmington, Delaware, twenty volumes of annotated excerpts of translated patristic texts. Each of these is devoted to a single important theme such as the Fathers' exegetical practices, their discussions of the problem of divine providence and human suffering, their views on war and military service, and their social thought. Tom contributed the volume on patristic ecclesiology, *The Church* (1985), and collaborated with Thomas Carroll on *Liturgical Practice in the Fathers* (1987). Since 1983 Tom has served The Catholic University of America Press as the general editor of its internationally known *Fathers of the Church*, the most extensive series of English translations of the works of the Greek, Latin, and Syriac-speaking theologians and historians of early Christianity. So far twenty-five volumes have come out during his tenure. The high quality of the translations, introductions, and explanatory notes in these recent accessions to the series is testimony to his learning and vigilance. In addition, Tom served for five years (1983–87) on the executive committee and as a section editor of the *Catalogus translationum et commentariorum*, an ambitious and indispensable tool of historical bibliography that lists and analyzes ancient, medieval, and renaissance translations and commentaries of classical and patristic works. From 1980 to 1990 he sat on the editorial board of the *Second Century*, the forerunner to *Early Christian Studies*, which is now the journal of the North American Patristics Society. Tom was president of NAPS in 1981–82.

Many have appreciated Tom's scholarly and professional expertise, but many more—both colleagues and friends—have enjoyed the pleasure of his company. Genial and cheerful in conversation, he has always fostered the increase of collegiality in his department and his field. He is a generous host, an accomplished chef, whose guests can tell of the many and elegant courses of a New Year's brunch or a summer dinner, the good wine, abundant Yeats, and hours of convivial laughter.

   In 1995, at a banquet in County Cavan, on the occasion of his seventieth birthday, Tom was named Cavan Man of the Year. The award was presented by Dermot Gallagher, the Irish Ambassador to the United States, before an international circle of friends, including Richard Riley, the U.S. Secretary of Education, whose own roots go back to County Cavan, and Senator Eugene McCarthy. This volume of essays honoring and celebrating Tom's scholarly achievements also honors and celebrates the heritage and customs of his native Cavan that inspired him. Thomas Halton is preeminently a classicist and a patrologist, but his erudition is always spiced with a distinctively Irish wit and charm.

Editor's Introduction

This volume contains seventeen essays, scholarly tributes to Professor Thomas Halton. The papers do not all address one, even very broadly conceived, theme. When I invited contributions, I suggested only that, in the course of their papers, the authors might wish to offer reflections of a methodological sort: to speak explicitly about the sorts of approaches they find convincing or unconvincing, the kinds of work to which they would guide or from which they would warn their students. Since Tom began his career, the pursuit of fresh interests, the enunciation of new questions, and the proliferation of tools and theoretical approaches have broadened what was usually called "Patristics" into what is now more often indicated by some such phrase as "Early Christian Studies" or "Late-Antique Studies." But I was not hankering after mere novelty. The title of the volume, *Nova et vetera*, referring to the wise scribe of Mt. 13.52, was chosen to emphasize that good work along quite traditional lines would be as welcome as good work following newer approaches.

I would not have been dismayed by controversy. Most often, however, our contributors simply state an issue and set about discussing it without adverting to potentially fractious questions of method. "Just follow my argument," they seem to say, "and you will see what topics I consider important, and how I choose to pursue them." In fact, the very absence of controversy within this rather broad cross-section of English-speaking scholars, the great majority of whom are members of the North American Patristics Society, is, in itself, significant. One may hope that within our profession, the new has received a ready enough welcome from the old, and the old sufficient deference from the new, that the ultimate result will be a broadening of scholarly perspectives rather than the mere substitution of the one for the other.

We have, then, a volume lacking unity of theme as well as unity of topic. In fact, such a diverse collection of essays seems an entirely appropriate tribute to a scholar of such catholic interests. A glance through his bibliography (pp. 263–65) will reveal that Tom's own work as editor, translator, and interpreter includes substantial contributions to at least four of the five subfields represented here: Exegesis, Rhetoric, Augustine, and the Transmission of Texts and Learning. The remarkable command of so much Greek and Latin patristic tradition apparent to readers of his work is even better appreciated by his colleagues and students. Very many of the authors who figure in this volume—from the Greek apologists of the second century to the Irish monastic authors of the early medieval period—have been studied in seminars he has offered to students in our various graduate programs dealing with Late Antiquity and early Christianity. As a junior colleague, I soon learned that in five minutes of consultation Tom would inevitably suggest previously unconsidered approaches to an issue and offer a wealth of pertinent bibliographical advice.

Our selection of authors conveys an idea of the variety and breadth of Tom's bonds to other scholars of this field, at least those within the English-speaking world. The contributors are former students, CUA colleagues past and present, old friends, and fellow members of NAPS. Many fall within more than one of these categories. All are united by their gratitude to Tom: for his erudition, instruction, and friendship.

Patristic literature is always, in some sense, a meditation on the Bible. The first section ("Exegesis") presents three papers dealing with elements of the theory and practice of exegesis from the second through the fifth century and the use of patristic commentaries in the early medieval period. Brian Daley offers an interpretation of Origen's *Peri archon* in which he demonstrates the centrality to the entire treatise of the discussion of scriptural exegesis in the first three chapters of book four, a section often regarded as a loosely integrated appendix. Daley argues that the title should be interpreted as signifying, among other things, "the first principles of a coherent doctrinal system that allows the believing reader to find in the Christian Bible the wisdom that gives life." Daniel Sheerin's essay also focuses on what one might term "patristic methodology of exegesis." It sets out the ways in which the Greek fathers used *synkrisis,* the strategy of comparison, first, as a category of description, to explain the rhetorical structure of passages of the New Testament—especially in the Pauline epistles—referring to the Old and, second, as a hermeneutical tool, to establish correspondences of Jewish type to Christian fulfillment. At times, as Sheerin points out, hermeneutical *synkrisis* was abused in the development of an anti-semitic polemic damaging to the very Christian exegesis it sought to propound. In the third essay Joseph Kelly studies the interpretation of the Matthean and Lucan infancy narratives in a collection of published and unpublished eighth- and ninth-century commentaries attributed to Irish scholars. Though the Irish monks were mainly content to follow patristic authorities such as Jerome and Augustine, they showed flashes of originality in a charming exercise of historical imagination and surprising interpretations of scriptural names. Their exegesis also reveals an effort to draw from the Scriptures lessons of value to the individual's quest for personal sanctity within the contemporary structures of early medieval monasticism. Each of these papers highlights the central role of Christian belief and moral values in determining the meaning of the sacred text.

Section II ("Rhetoric") contains four papers devoted to addresses spoken by Christian bishops of the Greek east probably between the latter second and the early fifth century. William McCarthy studies the structure of the encomium on the Cross embedded in a highly wrought Easter sermon of ps.-Hippolytus, a work typifying the Christian *Kunstprosa* of second-century Asia Minor. McCarthy first breaks the speaker's periods into cola. The identification of complexes of related imagery permits him to divide the encomium into three major sections, of which the second can be subdivided into two halves. Syllable counts of the cola of each section yield a numerical proportion of 4:1:1:4, suggestive of the architectural proportions of the Cross. Having illuminated the spirituality, Christology, and sacramental liturgy of this early Christian rhetor, McCarthy concludes with a suggestion of some interest to art historians: the development of the encomium naturally raises the possibility that the speaker was pointing to what would have been a remarkably early physical representation of the Cross. Ps.-Hippolytus' sermon would have followed the baptism of catechumens; Basil of Caesarea's *Exhortation to Holy Baptism* was spoken at the beginning of the Lenten season, the time when catechumens intending to be baptized the following Easter underwent their most intensive preparation. Everett Ferguson here offers the first study in English devoted to Basil's *Exhortation.* Observing the "deployment of rhetorical devices, use of Scripture, references to contemporary liturgy, and instruction in doctrinal and moral issues," Ferguson then compares this work to the *On Baptism,* whose attribution to Basil remains controversial, and to the *On Holy Baptism* of Gregory Nazianzen and the *Against Those Who Delay Baptism* of Gregory of Nyssa, both of which draw on Basil's *Exhortation.* In all these Lenten discourses Ferguson finds similar techniques of persuasion directed against the hesitations "of catechumens who delayed receiving baptism until the approach of death" and the tergiversations of "those who wanted the status of Christians without the responsibilities." Frederick Norris deals with another Cappadocian work, but this one lacking any apparent reference to an important liturgical moment. In this address, Gregory Nazianzen presents an apologia against the Arian Christians of Constantinople (*Or.* 33), in which he both accuses his enemies of grave crimes of violence and defends himself against defamatory charges of a personal sort. Norris points out that in the first section, dealing with responsibility for manslaughter in an assault on Gregory's church, the Theologian makes use of an argument based on the quality (*i.e.,* the rationality, morality, defensibility), rather than the facts, of the killing; in the second section, dealing with attacks on his appearance, speech, and education, Gregory seeks to redefine the terms of the charge. These, Norris notes, are points of debate defined in the *stasis* theory developed by Hermogenes of Tarsus and other rhetors of the second and subsequent centuries. In an exposition of salient points of Hermogenes' outline of stock arguments Norris lays out the kind of analytical system and compositional pattern available in Late Antiquity to participants in theological as well as judicial disputes. In the last essay of this section Hendrik Stander considers the literary virtues of the five festal sermons of ps.-Epiphanius spoken on Palm Sunday, Easter, and other important occasions of the liturgical year. Here, as in McCarthy's paper, a prior colometric analysis facilitates study of the text. Stander shows how ps.-Epiphanius deploys a wealth of rhetorical strategies to underline important theological doctrines, to hold the attention of his audience, and to adorn his diction. Here, as in the other essays of this section, the rhetorical analysis produces numerous insights into the thought of the speaker, his relationship to his audience, and their shared presuppositions. One may hope that these four contributions will encourage the production of full commentaries on the works here studied.

Recent patristic scholarship has drawn more and more on the insights and methods of the social sciences. The four papers of Section III ("Anthropology: Modern and Ancient") study ancient concepts of individual and social identity in the light of modern sociological and anthropological theory. Elizabeth Clark sets out to reconstruct the position, both her opinions and personal stake, of Melania the Elder in the Origenist controversy of the late fourth and early fifth century. Did Melania and Rufinus find in Origen's notion of the provisional character of the human body and thus of all human social distinctions, a justification for spiritual friendship with ascetics of the opposite sex? Setting out important aspects of Melania's biography and social network, Clark concludes that she likely had access—especially through key works of her friend Evagrius Ponticus—to the "bolder forms" of Origenistic speculation on what Peter

Brown has termed "the fluidity of the human person"; Melania probably shared the optimism regarding the possibility and the propriety of spiritual friendship between males and females that had animated Jerome before his "half-hearted" renunciation of Origenism. Lawrence Hennessey's essay again focuses on the spirituality of Evagrius Ponticus and the social interactions of fourth- and fifth-century ascetics. He inquires into the religious and sociological motivations for *anachoresis* among the Desert Fathers. He shows how insights essential to René Girard's understanding of mimetic violence were anticipated by Origen and Didymus the Blind in their exegesis of the narrative of the Fall in Genesis 3. Hennessey suggests that the desert disciples, who accepted the diagnosis of fallen humanity stated by Origen and Didymus, deliberately deployed mimetic mechanisms of training and learning to reverse the propagation of social violence and to re-establish what they took to be the prelapsarian relationship of humanity to its Creator. The next two papers take us to the Latin West. Thomas Finn reinterprets Augustine's account of his conversion in the *Confessions*. Earlier studies of Augustine's conversion have dwelt on the sudden and dramatic crisis of individual conscience that occurred in 387 in the Milanese garden. Finn, employing a seven-point model of conversion enunciated by a contemporary sociologist of religion, directs our attention to the gradual transformation of belief and, more importantly, of life that culminated in Augustine's baptism, *i.e.*, his becoming a full member of the Catholic Church. This was "a gradual interactive process" that "began with . . . [Augustine's] inscription in the catechumenate as an infant in November 354 and ended when he laid aside his white baptismal garment on the Sunday after Easter [in] . . . 387." Finn concludes that, in Augustine's as in all documented cases of conversion to Christianity in Late Antiquity, ritual was of central importance. Finally, Cynthia White studies the old and the new in late-antique marriage poetry through a prior consideration of Greek myth and initiation ritual. She argues that in the myth of Demeter and Persephone and the rites dedicated to the latter at Locri in southern Italy and to both at Eleusis "the transition from maiden- to womanhood" was presented in terms of "abduction and separation, descent into death (*i.e.*, marriage), . . . union [and] . . . reconciliation." White documents the same "paradigm for marriage" in the structure and themes of pagan epithalamic poetry from Sappho to Statius and Claudian. In her interpretation of Paulinus of Nola's poem celebrating the union of Julian of Eclanum and Titia, White points out how, as Christian and ascetic, Paulinus adverts to, rejects, and transforms paradigmatic elements inherited from traditional Greco-Roman culture. It is in this section that the reader will find the most obvious signs of *nova;* doubtless we can expect to read many doctoral dissertations that will apply modern and ancient theories of human identity and social organization to the interpretation of late-antique literature and documents.

The fourth section contains two essays dealing with Augustine, the first primarily as Christian philosopher, and the second as Catholic churchman. John O'Meara sketches Augustine's progressive rejection or modification of the Platonist view that the body was inessential to human identity. He details the ways in which, despite his early attraction to neo-Platonist immaterialism, Augustine did "more to arrest the influence of Platonism than to pass it on." In the second paper Louis Swift examines Augustine's tense negotiations with the Roman noble Pinianus and his mother-in-law Albina following the mob action in which the Catholic community of Hippo tried to force the wealthy and well-connected young man to accept ordination to the priesthood. Swift shows how Augustine's concern for the integrity and effectiveness of the bishop's office constrained him to insist on the morality and binding character of oaths, even one taken under duress. Both O'Meara and Swift highlight the ways in which pastoral concerns, especially fear of causing scandal to the simple, played a role in forming Augustine's thought.

The last section offers papers concerned with the transmission and manipulation of the cultural achievements, both pagan and Christian, of earlier ages. Our four essayists range from Late Antiquity to the Renaissance to the present. Francis Gignac discusses an important aspect of the textual tradition of John Chrysostom's *Homilies on the Acts of the Apostles,* our only extant commentary on Acts from the first ten centuries. Earlier scholarship has identified three recensions of these homilies, only one of which derives from a transcription of the remarks made by the bishop of Constantinople during the Easter season of 400 A.D. Gignac here illustrates the wide divergence between the purer "rough" and the less reliable "smooth" and "mixed" recensions by citing examples of the different ways in which one or more posthumous editor(s) deliberately revised Chrysostom's work. The next paper deals with early steps at formulating what would become the medieval school curriculum. Here P. G. Walsh studies Cassiodorus' attempt to teach the curriculum of classical antiquity through Christian, rather than pagan, sources. Working on the presupposition, elaborated by the early apologists, that all domains of learning owe their origins to Hebraic sacred teachers from whom the Greeks appropriated a derivative culture, Cassiodorus held that a careful reading of the book of Psalms could "inculcate an understanding of the seven liberal arts and thereby provide an *enkuklios paideia* that . . . [would] absolve the student from the need to have recourse to secular literature." Walsh collects those passages of the *Expositio Psalmorum* where Cassiodorus discovers material exemplifying various forms of the syllogism, the principal tool of the *ars* of dialectic. Next, Robert Sider studies an aspect of Erasmus' philological and historical work within the context of Renaissance scholarly debate. Like his contemporaries, Erasmus viewed the Fathers as arbiters of all questions scriptural, theological, and ecclesiastical. Consequently, he regarded proof of the authenticity or spuriousness of a purportedly patristic work as prerequisite to a determination of its authority. Sider here assembles all the discussions of and references to "writers and writings of the patristic period about which a question of authenticity arises in the *Annotations*," Erasmus' commentary to his various editions of the New Testament. In the process, Sider sets out the external and internal criteria that Erasmus considered in a process of reasoning, itself quite modern and scientific, but whose conclusions were meant to reinforce a reliance on and regard for authority typical of medieval scholarship. The volume ends with an essay by Michael Herren on the best way to train those who will preserve and propagate in the modern academy the language and literature of Hiberno-Latin. Herren first explains why Hiberno-Latin Studies constitute a distinct area of research: "While vernacular influences on vocabulary and word usage occur in other regions, instances of vernacular interference with Latin syntax and orthography are rare in comparison." He then details the sort of philological and historical training the competent Hiberno-Latinist will need: in Latin and Old Irish, in the modern scholarly languages, and in the editorial techniques of constituting a critical text. Herren declares that "the best dissertation as a preparation for this field consists of an edition of a text with *apparatus criticus* and *apparatus fontium,* introduction and a linguistic commentary." Each of these papers raises a question about the exact nature of preservation of traditional learning when that process may involve transformation or, at least, application to quite new uses: some scribes reformulated Chrysostom's commentary as they copied it; Cassiodorus tried to present the traditional liberal curriculum through a new medium; Erasmus separated the authentic from the apocryphal in order to delimit the terms of contemporary textual and theological debate; and the Irish scholars of the seventh and eighth centuries adapted to their own vernacular the scholarly tongue they regarded as the proper medium for book learning of venerable antiquity.

Finally, as editor and a teacher of some future practitioners of Patristic or Late-Antique Studies, I may be permitted several explicit comments on method. I have made it my principal concern to see that the foundations of each argument or exposition are both verifiable and immediately apparent to the alert reader. The reader must be able to retrace all the steps by which an author has reached his conclusions. If conclusions do not bear re-examination, confirmation, or confutation, research is pointless, nothing more than the expression of the author's personality. This conviction has led to editorial choices that may seem to some pedantic or antiquated.

First, I have insisted that wherever authors cite the ancient sources, they supply the ancient text. One might object that much quotation of Greek and Latin will discourage potential readers among graduate and undergraduate students. I hope instead that this will indicate the primary importance of philological competence as a prerequisite to all branches of the study of Late Antiquity that rely upon the written word. Students should not be encouraged to produce doctoral dissertations on authors or works they cannot read. Where practical, the authors have tried to assist students and scholars of other fields by including translations. The source of each translation is scrupulously recorded. One needs to know whose interpretation of Augustine, Origen, or Jerome one is reading. Many excerpts are drawn from works employing a difficult specialized vocabulary; serious students may well be interested to learn, *e.g.,* phraseology drawn from Greek rhetoric (*v.* the papers of Sheerin and Norris) and the Latin equivalents of Greek terms drawn from the field of logic (*v.* Walsh's paper).

Second, I have made certain that every citation of an ancient source follows a reliable critical edition, and that the edition is identified the first time even a single word of Latin or Greek is quoted. Students must be taught to bear constantly in mind the provisional nature of the printed editions of ancient texts, and they should be encouraged to make themselves familiar with the best editions, some of which rank among the great achievements of modern scholarship.

To reduce the length and improve the readability of the notes I have suppressed reference to specific editions where the author has merely alluded to, without quoting, an ancient text. The reader will in these cases consult such works as Quasten's *Patrology,* the *CPG, CPL,* or *BHG* (*v.* pp. xxxiii–xxxv) for appropriate editions. For works of dubious or unknown authorship I have cited the appropriate finding tool and the number under which the work is listed in that source. This will, I hope, spare the reader in search of a good edition unnecessary confusion and loss of time.

Third, wherever possible and appropriate, I have replaced references to English translations of secondary works with references to the edition in the original language. Again, this may seem to erect unnecessary barriers, but it will, I hope, emphasize to students the unavoidable necessity of acquiring at least a reading knowledge of French, German, and Italian, all of which are as indispensable as English for the study of Late Antiquity. Only when the English version constitutes a new or revised edition does it take precedence over the author's self-expression in his native tongue.

Finally, in the body of the papers I have tried to restrict the use of quotation marks to two uses only. The first, and by far the more frequent, is to set apart the words attributed to an identified source. The reader may, therefore, be certain that in virtually all cases where English words are enclosed within quotation marks these words are attributed to a work that has just been or will soon be cited in a note. Excerpts of Latin and Greek are not placed between quotation marks, and the reader may assume that, unless otherwise specified, these constitute direct quotations of the indicated critical edition. An English translation that follows an ancient text and stands within parentheses is set off by quotation marks only if the author is using someone else's translation. Translations of Greek or Latin excerpts, whether the author's own or someone else's, will be set off by quotation marks when not enclosed within parentheses. The second, and very infrequent, use of quotation marks in the body of the essays is intended to highlight a given word or short phrase, as in the following statement: The term "orthodoxy" can be problematical. Thus, the many and ever-proliferating uses of quotation marks, both single and double, to indicate irony, contempt, inexactitude, falsity, or conspiratorial glee have been entirely disallowed. Not all the contributors will thank me for insisting on this policy. It has, however, sometimes encouraged a more explicit and straightforward statement of ideas and has always eliminated the confusion that arises from different uses of single and double marks of quotation on the same page or even in the same paragraph or sentence.

In conclusion, it is my great pleasure to offer public expressions of gratitude to the many people who have assisted in the production of this volume. From the beginning Dr. David McGonagle, Director of The Catholic University of America Press, has shown his interest in this project, which he has now brought to a successful conclusion. The Rev. John Lynch, C.S.P., our Vice Provost for Graduate Studies provided several grants for research assistants. These assistants—Alison Locke, Thomas Berger, and Laurence Pittenger—contributed numerous hours of painstaking effort to every aspect of the planning and editing of the *festschrift.* To the observant eye and cheerful industry of Mr. Pittenger, my principal assistant, the contributors and I owe more than we can ever recompense. Late as this book is, we would still be verifying references if our work had not been much speeded by access to the Dumbarton Oaks Byzantine Library facilitated by Mr. Mark Zapatka, Assistant for Readers' Services. Dr. Michael Meckler of the Yale Classics Department graciously undertook the puzzling task of verifying references to an edition of Chrysostom available in the United States only at the Beinecke Rare Books Library. From the initial planning to the final publication I have relied on the advice and encouragement of my colleague, Dr. Frank Mantello. Finally, I am most grateful to the contributors, who have demonstrated so much patience, good humor, and scholarly expertise in this effort to honor Thomas Halton, an outstanding patrologist and a most genial colleague.

Abbreviations

Biblical Books

OT	*Old Testament*	NT	*New Testament*
Gen.	Genesis	Mt.	Matthew
Ex.	Exodus	Mk.	Mark
Lv.	Leviticus	Lk.	Luke
Num.	Numbers	Jn.	John
1–2Kgs.	1–2 Kings	Rom.	Romans
Ps.	Psalms	1–2Cor.	1–2 Corinthians
Prov.	Proverbs	Gal.	Galatians
Eccles.	Ecclesiastes	Eph.	Ephesians
Wis.	Wisdom	Phil.	Philippians
Sir.	Ecclesiasticus	Col.	Colossians
Is.	Isaiah	1–2Tim.	1–2 Timothy
Jer.	Jeremiah	Heb.	Hebrews
Bar.	Baruch		
Ez.	Ezekiel		
Dan.	Daniel		
Hos.	Hosea		
Zech.	Zechariah		

N.B. In cases where the contributors to this volume cite a passage of the Greek NT not embedded in a quotation from a patristic source, the Greek text follows B. Aland *et al.*, *The Greek New Testament*, 4th revised ed. (Stuttgart 1994). When they translate Latin or Greek passages containing quotations of the Bible, unless otherwise indicated, the translations, including those of the scriptural texts, are their own. Where, however, they cite in English a scriptural text not embedded in a quotation from a patristic source, the translation is drawn from *The Holy Bible: Revised Standard Version . . . An Ecumenical Edition* (New York, *etc.* 1973).

Ancient Authors

Ambr.	Ambrose	Greg. Naz.	Gregory of Nazianzus
Amph. Icon.	Amphilochius of Iconium	Greg. Nys.	Gregory of Nyssa
		Hippol.	Hippolytus of Rome
Apollod.	Apollodorus Mythographus	Ig.	Ignatius of Antioch
		Iren.	Irenaeus of Lyons
Apul.	Apuleius	Jer.	Jerome
Arist.	Aristides	Joh. Dam.	John of Damascus
Aristoph.	Aristophanes	Just. Mar.	Justin Martyr
Arn.	Arnobius of Sicca	Lact.	Lactantius
Ath.	Athanasius	Lucr.	Lucretius
Aug.	Augustine	Max. Taur.	Maximus Taurinensis (of Turin)
Aus.	Ausonius		
Cass.	John Cassian	Men. Rh.	Menander rhetor
Cat.	Catullus	Olymp.	Olympiodorus of Alexandria
Chrys.	John Chrysostom		
Cic.	Cicero	Or.	Origen
Clem. Alex.	Clement of Alexandria	Pal.	Palladius
		Plut.	Plutarch
Cyr. Alex.	Cyril of Alexandria	Rom. Mel.	Romanos Melodos
Cyr. Hier.	Cyril of Jerusalem		
D. H.	Dionysius of Halicarnassus	Soc.	Socrates Scholasticus
Epiph.	Epiphanius of Salamis	Soz.	Sozomen
		Tert.	Tertullian
Eus.	Eusebius of Caesarea	Theoc.	Theocritus
		Theod. Cyr.	Theodoret of Cyr
Evag.	Evagrius of Pontus	Theod. . Mops	Theodore of Mopsuestia
Gen.	Gennadius		
Greg. Mag.	Gregory the Great	Thphr.	Theophrastus

Ancient Works

N.B. The enclosure of an author's name within square brackets indicates doubt concerning the attribution of the work.

Acta Ioh.	*Acta Io(h)annis*
Ad Diog.	*Epistula ad Diognetum*
Ad Gob.	Origen, *Epistula ad Gobarum*
Ad nat.	Tertullian, *Ad nationes*
Ad Pomp.	Dionysius of Halicarnassus, *Epistula ad Pompeium*
Adv. nat.	Arnobius, *Adversus nationes*
Aen.	Virgil, *Aeneid*
Ann. in N.T.	Erasmus, *Annotationes in Novum Testamentum*
Ant.	Athanasius, *Vita Antonii*
Antir.	Evagrius Ponticus, *Antirrheticus*
AP	*Anthologia palatina*
APo.	Aristotle, *Analytica posteriora*
Apol.	*Apologia*
Apostol. dict.	Chrysostom, *Hom. in apostolicum dictum, Nolo vos ignorare, etc. (1Cor. 10.1)*
Ap. pat.	*Apophthegmata patrum*
Apr.	Aristotle, *Analytica priora*
Ars rh.	*Ars rhetorica*
Ath.	Aristotle, Ἀθηναίων Πολιτεία
Bapt.	[Basil], *De baptismo*
Barn.	*Epistle of Barnabas*
Bibl.	Apollodorus, *Bibliotheca*
Bibl. cod.	Photius, *Bibliotheca codex*
Bono vid.	Augustine, *De bono viduitatis*
Brev. in Ps.	ps.-Jerome, *Breviarium in Psalmos*
C.	*Carmen*
C. ac.	Augustine, *Contra academicos*
Cat. ill.	Cyril of Jerusalem, *Catecheses illuminandorum*
Cat. ad illum.	John Chrysostom, *Catecheses ad illuminandos*
Cath.	Prudentius, *Cathemerinon*
Cat. mys.	Cyril of Jerusalem, *Catecheses mystagogicae*
Cat. rud.	Augustine, *De catechizandis rudibus*
C. Cels.	Origen, *Contra Celsum*
C. Crescon.	Augustine, *Contra Cresconium*
C. Hier.	Rufinus, *Apologia contra Hieronymum*
C. Ioh.	Jerome, *Contra Io(h)annem Hierosolymitanum*
C. Iul. op. imp.	Augustine, *Contra Iulianum opus imperfectum*

Civ. dei	Augustine, *De civitate dei*
C. litt. Petil.	Augustine, *Contra litteras Petiliani*
Com.	*Commentarius, ii, etc.*
Conf.	Augustine, *Confessiones*
Conl.	John Cassian, *Conlationes*
Const. app.	*Constitutiones apostolorum*
CP	Theophrastus, *De causis plantarum*
Cup.	Ausonius, *Cupido cruciatus*
Decl. ad cen.	Erasmus, *Declarationes ad censuras Lutetiae vulgatas*
de Gen.	Didymus the Blind, *de Genesi*
de Gen. ad lit.	Augustine, *De Genesi ad litteram*
Deit. f. et sp. s.	Gregory of Nyssa, *De deitate filii et spiritus sancti*
Demonst. ap. pr.	Irenaeus, *Demonstration of the Apostolic Preaching*
De or.	[Evagrius], *De oratione*
Descript. deip.	ps.-Chrysostom, *Hom. in . . . (Luc. 2.1); et in descriptionem deiparae*
de Ser. dom.	Augustine, *De sermone domini in monte*
Dial. Heracl.	Origen, *Dialogue with Heraclides*
Didask.	Albinus (Alcinous), *Didaskalikos*
D. inst.	Lactantius, *Divinae institutiones*
Diem natal.	Chrysostom, *Hom. in diem natalem D.N. Jesu Christi*
D. inst. ep.	Lactantius, *Divinarum institutionum epitome*
Div.	John Scotus Eriugena, *De divisione naturae*
Div. mal. cog.	Evagrius Ponticus, *De diversis malignis cogitationibus*
Doc. christ.	Augustine, *De doctrina christiana*
Eloc.	Demetrius, *De elocutione*
EN	Aristotle, *Ethica nicomachea*
Enc.	Libanius, *Encomia*
Enn. in Ps.	Augustine, *Ennarationes in Psalmos*
Ep(p).	*Epistula(e)*
Ep. ad Mᶜlan.	Evagrius, *Epistula ad Melaniam*
Eph.	Ignatius of Antioch, *Epistula ad ephesios*
Epigr.	Ausonius, *Epigrams*
Exh.	Basil, *Exhortatio ad baptismum*
Exh. virg.	Ambrose, *Exhortatio virginitatis*
Exp.	*Expositio*
Exp. fid.	Ambrose, *Expositio fidei*
Expl. sym.	Ambrose, *Explanatio symboli*
Expl. sym. app.	Erasmus, *Explanatio symboli apostolorum*
Exp. Ps.	Cassiodorus, *Expositio Psalmorum*
Exp. quat. Ev.	ps.-Jerome, *Expositio IV Evangeliorum*
Fide orth.	John of Damascus, *De fide orthodoxa*

Haer.	Irenaeus, *Adversus haereses*
H. E.	*Historia ecclesiastica*
Hebr. nom.	Jerome, *Liber interpretationis hebraicorum nominum*
Her., Mand.	Shepherd of Hermas, *Mandates*
Her., Sim.	Shepherd of Hermas, *Similitudes*
Hist. Laus.	Palladius, *Historia lausiaca*
Hom.	*Homilia, -ae*
Hom. H. Dem.	Homeric *Hymn to Demeter*
Hym.	*Hymnus, -i*
Id.	Theocritus, *Idylls*
in + a biblical book	*homiliae vel sim.* on the respective book; for the abbreviations of the names of the biblical books used in this volume *v.* p. xxvii
In annunt.	ps.-Gregory of Nyssa, *In annuntiatione*
in Evang. hom.	Gregory the Great, *XL homiliarum in evangelia libri duo*
in Or. Greg. Naz.	Elias of Crete, *Com. in orationes Gregorii Nazianzeni*
in Ioh. Ep.	Augustine, *in Io(h)annis Epistulam ad Parthos Tractatus*
in Ios. fil. N.	Theodoret of Cyr, *in Iosuam filium Nave*
in Lc.	Ambrose, *Expositio Evangelii secundum Lucam*
In ss. martt.	Asterius of Apamea, *Hom.* 10 (*in santos martyres*)
Inst.	Cassiodorus, *Institutiones*
Inst. or.	Quintilian, *Institutio oratoria*
Invit. font.	Zeno of Verona, *Invitationes fontis*
IP	ps.-Hippolytus, *in Sanctum pascha*
Isag.	Adrian, *Isagoge in scripturas sacras*
Iud.	John Chrysostom, *Adversus iudaeos*
Keph. gnost.	Evagrius Ponticus, *Kephalaia gnostica*
Laud. s. Dei genetr. Mar.	Proclus, *Laudatio sanctae dei genetricis Mariae*
Leg.	Cicero, *De legibus*
Leuc. et Clit.	Achilles Tatius, *Leucippe and Clitophon*
Liber de ortu	ps.-Isidore, *Liber de ortu et obitu patrum*
Mart.	*Martyrium*
Mend.	Augustine, *De mendacio*
MM	Aristotle, *Magna moralia*
Myst.	Ambrose, *De mysteriis*
Nat.	Pliny the Elder, *Naturalis historia*
OC	Sophocles, *Oedipus coloneus*
Op. hom.	Gregory of Nyssa, *De opificio hominis*
Or.	*Oratio*
Or. cat. mag.	Gregory of Nyssa, *Oratio catechetica magna*
Ord.	Augustine, *De ordine*

Paed.	Clement of Alexandria, *Paedagogos*
Pan.	Epiphanius, *Panarion*
pf.	*praefatio*
pf. Opp. Ambr.	Erasmus, *pf. ad Omnia . . . divi Ambrosii . . . Opera*
Phdr.	Plato, *Phaedrus*
Plot.	Porphyry, *Vita Plotini*
Poen.	Chrysostom, *De poenitentia homilia*
PP	Melito of Sardis, *Peri pascha*
Prak.	Evagrius Ponticus, *Praktikos*
Prin.	Origen, *De principiis*
Procat.	Cyril of Jerusalem, *Procatechesis*
Progym.	*Progymnasmata*
prol.	*prologus*
Protr.	Clement of Alexandria, *Protreptikos*
Prov.	Plutarch, Παροιμίαι αἷς ἀλεξανδρεῖς ἐχρῶντο
Qu. al.	ps.-Athanasius, *Quaestiones aliae*
Quant. an.	Augustine, *De quantitate animae*
Qui diff. bapt.	Gregory of Nyssa, *Adversus eos qui differunt baptismum oratio*
Qu. in Ex.	Theodoret of Cyr, *Quaestiones in Exodum*
Raptu	Claudian, *De raptu Proserpinae*
Ref.	Hippolytus, *Refutatio omnium haeresium*
Rerum nat.	Lucretius, *De rerum natura*
resp.	*responsio*
Resur.	Methodius, *De resurrectione*
Retrac.	Augustine, *Retractationes*
Rhet.	Aristotle, *Rhetoric*
Rom.	Ignatius of Antioch, *Epistula ad romanos*
Ruf.	Jerome, *Apologia adversus libros Rufini*
Sacr.	Ambrose, *De sacramentis*
Sel. in Ps.	Origen, *Selecta in Psalmos*
Sent.	Evagrius, *Sententiae ad virginem*
Ser.	*Sermo(nes)*
Silv.	Statius, *Silvae*
Sim. et An.	ps.-Methodius, *Sermo de Simeone et Anna*
Sp. s.	Basil, *De spiritu sancto*
Stat.	Hermogenes, *De statibus*
Strom.	Clement of Alexandria, *Stromateis* or *Stromata*
Ti.	Plato, *Timaeus*
tit.	*titulus*
Top.	Aristotle, *Topica*

Tract.	*Tractatus*
Trad. apost.	Hippolytus, *Traditio apostolica*
Util. cred.	Augustine, *De utilitate credendi*
Ux.	Tertullian, *Ad uxorem*
Valent.	Tertullian, *Adversus valentinianos*
Vera relig.	Augustine, *De vera religione*
Virg.	Chrysostom, *De virginitate*
Vir. ill.	*De viris illustribus*
Vita s. Ioh.	Palladius, *Dialogus de vita sancti Io(h)annis Chrysostomi*
Vulg.	Vulgate

Modern Works, Series, Editions

AAWM	*Abhandlungen der Akademie der Wissenschaften und der Literatur in Mainz, Geistes- und Sozialwissenschaftliche Klasse*
ACW	*Ancient Christian Writers*
AGWG.PH	*Abhandlungen der (Königlichen) Gesellschaft der Wissenschaften zu Göttingen, Philologisch-historische Klasse*
AHDL	*Archives d'histoire doctrinale et littéraire du moyen age*
AJP	*American Journal of Philology*
AnBib	*Analecta biblica*
AncB	*Anchor Bible*
AncB.D	*Anchor Bible Dictionary*
ANCL	*Ante-Nicene Christian Library*
ANRW	*Aufstieg und Niedergang der römischen Welt*
ArtB	*Art Bulletin*
ASMG	*Atti e memorie della Società Magna Grecia*
At.	*Athenaeum*
AThR	*Anglican Theological Review*
Aug.	*Augustinianum*
AugustinStud	*Augustinian Studies*
BAug	*Bibliothèque augustinienne*
BHG	*Bibliotheca hagiographica graeca,* 3rd ed. (Brussels 1957)
BibPat	*Biblia patristica: Index des citations et allusions dans la littérature patristique*
BICS	*Bulletin of the Institute of Classical Studies of the University of London*
Bijdr.	*Bijdragen: Tijdeschrift voor filosofie en theologie*
BiLe	*Bibel und Leben*
BLE	*Bulletin de littérature ecclésiastique*
BPatr	*Bibliographia patristica*
ByF	*Byzantinische Forschungen*

CChr.SL	Corpus christianorum, series latina
ChH	Church History
ClW	Classical World
CopticChR	Coptic Church Review
CP	Classical Philology
CPG	Clavis patrum graecorum
CPL	Clavis patrum latinorum, 3rd ed. (Steenbrugge 1995)
CSEL	Corpus scriptorum ecclesiasticorum latinorum
DOP	Dumbarton Oaks Papers
DPAC	Dizionario patristico e di antichità cristiane
DSp	Dictionnaire de spiritualité, ascétique et mystique
ECR	Eastern Churches Review
EL.A	Ephemerides liturgicae: analecta historica-ascetica
FlorPatr	Florilegium patristicum
FOTC	Fathers of the Church
GB	Gräzer Beiträge
GCS	Griechischen christlichen Schriftsteller
GRBS	Greek, Roman and Byzantine Studies
JAAR	Journal of the American Academy of Religion
JAC	Jahrbuch für Antike und Christentum
JEarlyChrSt	Journal of Early Christian Studies
JHS	Journal of Hellenic Studies
JMLat	Journal of Medieval Latin
JThS	Journal of Theological Studies
LSJ	N.G. Liddell and R. Scott, A Greek-English Lexicon, 9th ed. rev. H.S. Jones and R. McKenzie (Oxford 1968)
LXX	Septuaginta: vetus testamentum graecum auctoritate Academiae Scientiarum Gottingensis editum (Göttingen 1974–)
Mar.	Marianum
MGH.QG	Monumenta Germaniae historica, Quellen zur Geistes-geschichte des Mittelalters
Muséon	Muséon: Revue d'études orientales
NPNF	A Select Library of the Nicene and post-Nicene Fathers of the Christian Church
OrChr(R)	Orientalia christiana
PG	Patrologia graeca
Ph.	Philologus
PhP	Philosophia patrum
PL	Patrologia latina
PRIA	Proceedings of the Royal Irish Academy
Quasten	J. Quasten, Patrology, voll. 1–3 (Utrecht 1950): The Beginnings

of Patristic Literature; The Ante-Nicene Literature after Irenaeus; The Golden Age of Greek Patristic Literature; A. Di Berardino, *Patrology,* vol. 4, tr. P. Solari (Westminster, Md. 1986): *The Golden Age of Latin Patristic Literature from the Council of Nicaea to the Council of Chalcedon*

RAAN	*Rendiconti dell' Accademia dei Archeologia, Lettere e Belle Arti di Napoli*
RAL	*Atti della Accademia Nazionale dei Lincei, Rendiconti classe di scienze morali, storiche e filologiche*
RAM	*Revue d'ascétique et de mystique*
RBen	*Revue bénédictine*
RDM	*Revue des deux mondes*
RechAug	*Recherches augustiniennes*
RelStR	*Religious Studies Review*
Rh.	*Rhetores graeci*
RHE	*Revue d'histoire ecclesiastique*
RMP	*Rheinisches Museum für Philologie*
ROC	*Revue de l'orient chrétien*
RQH	*Revue des questions historiques*
RSDI	*Rivista di storia del diritto italiano*
RSR	*Recherches de science religeuse*
SBAW.PPH	*Sitzungsberichte der (Königlich) bayerischen Akademie der Wissenschaften in München, Philosophisch-philologisch und historische Klasse*
SC	*Sources chrétiennes*
SE	*Sacris erudiri*
SJTh	*Scottish Journal of Theology*
SLH	*Scriptores latini Hiberniae*
SM	*Speech Monographs*
StAns	*Studia anselmiana*
StMed	*Studi medievali*
StPatr	*Studia patristica*
StRen	*Studies in the Renaissance*
StTh	*Studia theologica*
ThWNT	*Theologisches Wörterbuch zum Neuen Testament*
TLG	*Thesaurus linguae graecae*
Tr.	*Traditio: Studies in Ancient and Medieval History, Thought and Religion*
TrGF	*Tragicorum graecorum fragmenta*
TU	*Texte und Untersuchungen zur Geschichte der altchristlichen Literatur*
VigChr	*Vigiliae christianae*
ZNW	*Zeitschrift für neutestamentliche Wissenschaft*

Nova & Vetera

I. EXEGESIS

ONE

Origen's *De Principiis*

A Guide to the Principles of Christian Scriptural Interpretation

— ✤ —

Brian E. Daley, S.J.

EW SUBJECTS have puzzled and challenged interpreters of Origen more than the structure, the purpose, and even the title of his treatise Περὶ ἀρχῶν. Earlier in this century, both Protestant[1] and Catholic scholars[2] saw the work as essentially a systematic treatise, in Greek philosophical style, on Christian dogma. More recent scholars, led by Henri Crouzel, have stressed its tentative and experimental character.[3] Others today emphasize its repetitions, its lack of cross references, its seemingly fortuitous shape, as evidence that it is not really a single, coherent treatise, but rather a collection of independent lectures or essays on theological themes, arranged according to a loose philosophical or catechetical outline.[4] In 1941, however, Dom Basilius Steidle made the influen-

1. *V.*, *e.g.*, A. von Harnack, *Lehrbuch der Dogmengeschichte*, vol. 1, 5th ed. (1931), note 1, p. 652; F. Loofs, *Leitfaden zum Studium der Dogmengeschichte*, 4th ed. (Halle 1906), p. 193; and F.H. Kettler, *Der ursprüngliche Sinn der Dogmatik des Origenes* (Berlin 1965).

2. *V.* the references in J.-F. Bonnefoy, "Origène théoricien de la méthode théologique," *Mélanges offerts au R. P. Ferdinand Cavallera* (Toulouse 1948), p. 126.

3. *V.* H. Crouzel, "Qu'a voulu faire Origène en composant le *Traité des Principes*," *BLE* 76 (1975), pp. 161–86, 241–60, esp. pp. 247, 257f.; and *Origène* (Paris/Namur 1985), pp. 74f. L. Lies, following Crouzel, also stresses that the system presented in the work is still very much in process: *Origenes' "Peri Archon": eine undogmatische Dogmatik* (Darmstadt 1992), pp. 8, 14.

4. *E.g.*, P. Kübel, "Zum Aufbau von Origenes' De Principiis," *VigChr* 25 (1971), pp. 31–39, esp. pp. 32f. The theory that the work is composed of originally separate lectures is also the position of B. Steidle, "Neue Untersuchungen zu Origenes' Περὶ ἀρχῶν," *ZNW* 40 (1941), pp. 236–43; and C. Kannengiesser, "Origen, Systematician in *De Principiis*," *Origeniana Quinta . . . Papers of the 5th International Origen Congress, Boston College, 14–18 August 1989*, ed. R.J.

tial suggestion that, while the arrangement of *De principiis* does show signs of an overarching plan, that plan does not simply correspond to its traditional division into four books.[5] Steidle recognized that the subjects listed as basic apostolic doctrines in chapters 4–7 of Origen's preface— God as Father, Son, and Holy Spirit; the nature and freedom of created intelligences; and the material world in which they undergo the drama of salvation—are actually dealt with three times: first, in a positive, didactic style in chapters 1.1–2.3, then again, more at length and with a decidedly anti-Gnostic edge in 2.4–3.6, and finally, in a brief concluding summary in the last chapter, 4.4, in which the order is now God, the cosmos, created intelligences.

In the early 1970s, a team of Parisian scholars, who were translating the work into French under the leadership of Marguerite Harl, took Steidle's observation a step further by showing that this seemingly repetitious structure is actually common to many ancient philosophical and technical treatises, in which a general survey of the material is often followed by a discussion of particular questions on the same topics, arranged in the same order.[6] Further, Harl and her pupils contended that the themes and arrangement of Origen's Christian textbook are strikingly similar to treatments of the ultimate source and constitution of the world in contemporary Greek treatises on natural philosophy or physics,[7] and that even the title of the work, *On First Principles,* had parallels in ancient cosmological handbooks, which doubtless would have sprung into the mind of a contemporary reader.[8] In the view of these scholars, Origen was breaking new

Daly (Leuven 1992), pp. 395–405. Kannengiesser sees the second main section of the work, 2.4–4.3, as a collection of essays later added to an original systematic treatise. *Cf.* L. Lies, (note 3 above), pp. 18f.

5. Steidle (note 4 above).

6. *V.* M. Harl, "Structure et cohérence du Peri Archôn," *Origeniana: Premier colloque international des études origéniennes (Montserrat, 18–21 septembre 1973) dirigé par H. Crouzel, G. Lomiento, Josep Rius-Camps* (Bari 1975), pp. 11–32, esp. p. 16. *Cf.* G. Dorival, "Remarques sur la forme du Peri Archon," *ib.,* pp. 33–45. For examples of this bipartite structure in ancient manuals, *v.* M. Fuhrmann, *Das systematische Lehrbuch: Ein Beitrag zur Geschichte der Wissenschaften in der Antike* (Göttingen 1960). Dorival reaffirms his earlier analysis of the structure of the work in "Nouvelles remarques sur la forme du *Traité des Principes* d'Origène," *RechAug* 22 (1987), pp. 67–108.

7. *V.* Harl (note 6 above), p. 21; and Dorival, "Remarques," etc. (note 6 above), pp. 34–36.

8. The only other known ancient treatise actually called Περὶ ἀρχῶν is a lost work of Longinus, a pupil of the Alexandrian Platonist Ammonius Sakkas and a contemporary of Plotinus and Origen; *v.* Porphyry, *Vita Plotini,* ch. 14. Two important second-century handbooks on Platonic philosophy, however, present their treatments of the ultimate structure and origin of the world as discussions of first principles: God, matter, and the intelligible forms. *V.* Albinus (or Alcinous, as the author is named in the manuscripts), *Didaskalikos,* chh. 8–10; Apul., *De Platone,* ch. 5. Justin (G. Rauschen, *S. Iustini Apologiae duae,* 2nd ed. [Bonn 1911] = *FlorPatr,* vol. 2), contrasting what the Stoics have to say "in the treatise on

ground in Christian apologetic and theological literature by putting together nothing less than a biblical physics, a treatise on the origins and ultimate constitution of the world and the human person based not only on observation and analytic reason but also on Christian Scripture and ecclesial tradition.[9]

This way of conceiving *De principiis,* which has become widely accepted in the past two decades, certainly contains much that is persuasive and enlightening. It takes the obvious structure of Origen's treatise seriously and has enabled scholars to see beyond the sometimes bizarre details of the work and grasp more sympathetically its original theoretical focus and speculative character. Nevertheless, to label this remarkable document an essay on the physics or metaphysics of our world, an exposition of a Christian understanding of what God and God's creation really are, seems to me still somewhat too narrow, if only because it still leaves several important features of the work insufficiently explained.

How, for instance, does one account for the important section on biblical hermeneutics (*Prin.* 4.1–3) that precedes the final chapter? For most of the contemporary scholars we have mentioned, it can be understood, if not as a digression, at least as a kind of methodological appendix but no more.[10] Secondly, how is one to give a convincing interpretation of the final chapter, 4.4, which seems to deal briefly with a few of the main subjects yet again, insofar as they are affected by the theme of immateriality? Although this is entitled, in the manuscripts, an ἀνακεφαλαίωσις or summing-up of "what has already been said about the Father and the Son and the Holy Spirit and other things" (*de patre et filio et spiritu sancto ceterisque, quae superius dicta sunt*), book 4.4 is not merely a repetition or synthesis of previously treated material.[11] To see this section, with Steidle and

ethics" (ἐν τῷ περὶ ἠθῶν λόγῳ) with their teachings "in the treatise on first principles and incorporeal things" (ἐν τῷ περὶ ἀρχῶν καὶ ἀσωμάτων λόγῳ, *Apol.* 2.6[7]), apparently alludes to standard divisions in academic tracts on Stoic philosophy. His association of "first principles" with "incorporeal things" will reappear in a different context in Origen's work.

9. On the lack of precedent for such a work in Christian literature, v. Dorival, "Remarques" (note 6 above), p. 34.

10. V., e.g., J.W. Trigg, *Origen: The Bible and Philosophy in the Third-Century Church* (Atlanta 1983), pp. 91f., 120; J. Rius-Camps, "Orígenes y Marción: Carácter preferentemente antimarcionita del prefacio y del segundo ciclo del Peri Archon," *Origeniana* (note 6 above), pp. 297–312, esp. pp. 308–12; and C. Kannengiesser (note 4 above), p. 402. For M. Harl (note 6 above) the section on hermeneutics is not an afterthought (p. 17), but it does represent a change of philosophical direction from the tract on the natural world that precedes it: "après la 'physique', c'est, en quelque sorte, une théorie de la connaissance spirituelle" (p. 24).

11. The titles given to the different sections or treatises of the *De principiis* are probably the work of later editors, rather than of Origen himself; v. pp. 57–67 of M. Harl, "Recherches sur le Περὶ ἀρχῶν d'Origène en vue d'une nouvelle édition: la division en chapitres," *StPatr* 3 (1961) = *TU*, vol. 78.

Harl, as a brief and somewhat sketchy third survey of the range of physical questions treated much more fully in parts 1 and 2,[12] seems to be missing much of what the chapter actually says.

A third, more general problem raised by this dominant contemporary approach to Origen's treatise is the meaning of the title itself: what precisely are the ἀρχαί, the first principles, that Origen intends to expound? Much of the difficulty in interpreting Origen's title comes from the ambiguity of the term ἀρχή, which can denote a source or beginning, but which usually, in ancient academic works, means either the root assumption of a theoretical system, a principle in the logical sense, or the ultimate underlying cause for the existence of some actual thing, a principle in the causal or ontological sense. Most nineteenth- and early twentieth-century interpreters of Origen, who perhaps read Περὶ ἀρχῶν in light of the norms and methods of scholastic theology, tended to understand the word in the first way, as referring to the axioms of a theological system.[13] More recent writers, stressing the parallels between Origen's treatise and Greek natural philosophy, prefer the second approach, interpreting the ἀρχαί of the title as the fundamental causes of being of the world as we know it, or, in the phrase of Endre von Ivánka, "die Grundprinzipien des Seins."[14] I shall argue here that in the context of the work the title, however traditional, bears an ambiguity of reference Origen may well have intended: constructing a cohesive survey of the ontological principles of the world's being, as Christian faith perceives them, also brings together, for him, the logical principles for an understanding of the content of revelation that is both the anchor and starting point of authentic and creative biblical interpretation.[15]

12. V. Steidle (note 4 above) and Harl (note 6 above), pp. 17–20. Dorival, "Remarques," etc. (note 6 above) admits (note 36, p. 43) that he finds the role of this final chapter "mystérieux." Cf. also Trigg (note 10 above), p. 128; and Kannengiesser (note 4 above), p. 399.

13. V. O. Bardenhewer, Geschichte der altkirchlichen Literatur, vol. 2: Vom Ende des zweiten Jahrhunderts bis zum Beginn des vierten Jahrhunderts (Freiburg im Breisgau, etc. 1914) who takes (p. 168) the ἀρχαί to be "the articles of the science of faith" ("die . . . Grundartikel der Glaubenswissenschaft"). For other references, v. J.-F. Bonnefoy (note 2 above), pp. 131–36.

14. Plato Christianus: Übernahme und Umgestaltung des Platonismus durch die Väter (Einsiedeln 1964), p. 110. Ivánka is followed by H. Karpp, in H. Görgemanns and H. Karpp, Origenes: Vier Bücher von den Prinzipien, 2nd ed. (Darmstadt 1985), p. 10. The doxographers of the second century, whose collections of philosophical opinions on the constitution of the world and the human person were used by the Apologists and Clement, and perhaps by Origen as well, distinguished "first principles" from "elements" (στοιχεῖα) in that the latter were the composite, material elements of things and themselves the result of a chain of causes while ἀρχαί were sources of being, which themselves have no prior source: v. ps.-Plut., De placitis 1.3 (H. Diels, Doxographi Graeci [Berlin 1879], pp. 286f.). In the Platonic tradition, the three ἀρχαί of all beings are God, matter, and form (ib. p. 288).

15. In the introduction to Origène: Traité des principes (vol. 1 [Paris 1978]: bkk. 1f. = SC, vol. 252) H. Crouzel and M. Simonetti also suggest (p. 14) that ἀρχαί here should be taken in

The main criticism, in fact, that I would offer of the current tendency to read Περὶ ἀρχῶν as an essay in the genre of Middle Platonic cosmology is that such an interpretation, illuminating as it is, can also be as one-sided and inflexible as earlier conceptions of the treatise simply as a dogmatic handbook. Secondly, it can reinforce a tendency, common to much modern historical criticism of ancient texts, to break the work up arbitrarily into layers of composition and literary units for which, in fact, there is no evidence, internal or external. If we look not just at its constituent parts but see it as an organic whole—that is, if we assume it was intended and constructed by Origen, probably at a crucial point in his career, to be read in the form it now has—and if we seek within the whole text indications of Origen's purpose, we can come to a deeper understanding of what its title means, and how all its parts, including the section on hermeneutics and the final chapter, fit together. With the help of works of Origen's contemporaries, we can even guess, I think, at a wider context for what Origen is doing here, a context that identifies this work both as a defense of his earlier research and as the necessary prelude for what he still hoped to achieve.

The key to understanding *De principiis,* most interpreters agree, is the preface Origen himself wrote for it. Here he makes clear that his real interest in writing the treatise is Christian biblical theology: the interpretation of the whole of Scripture, both Hebrew and Christian, as a way of coming to saving knowledge of the truth revealed by and in Christ. Faith, Origen suggests in the opening lines of the treatise, is the conviction that Christ, as the Truth, is able to communicate "the knowledge that calls men and women to live well and happily" (*scientiam quae provocat homines ad bene beateque vivendum,* 1, *pf.* 1).[16] But learning this saving truth is not simply a matter of gathering Jesus' own instructions from the pages of the Gospels. Since Christ is the Word of God, who was present in Moses and the prophets, His teaching and the truth embodied in His person are available in the whole of Jewish and Christian Scripture (1, *pf.* 1; *cf.* 1.3.1). The problem for the Christian disciple is not so much finding the source of the truth that enables us to live well, but interpreting it correctly: *Quoniam ergo multi ex his, qui Christo se credere profitentur, non solum in parvis et minimis discordant, verum etiam in magnis et maximis, id est vel de deo vel*

---

both its logical and its metaphysical sense. V. E. De Faye, *Origène: Sa vie, son oeuvre, sa pensée,* vol. 1 (Paris 1923), p. 99.

16. I follow the edition of H. Görgemanns and H. Karpp (note 14 above). I cite the Greek wherever reliable fragments exist, elsewhere, Rufinus' translation. Unless otherwise indicated, all translations of this and other ancient works are my own.

de ipso domino Iesu Christo vel de spiritu sancto, non solum autem de his, sed et de aliis creaturis, id est vel de dominationibus vel de virtutibus sanctis: propter hoc necessarium videtur prius de his singulis certam lineam manifestamque regulam ponere, tum deinde etiam de ceteris quaerere (1, *pf.* 2; Many of those who profess belief in Christ disagree, not only about small and insignificant issues but also about great and very important ones, about God, for instance, and about the Lord Jesus Christ Himself and about the Holy Spirit, and not only about these but also about other creatures, such as the principalities or the holy powers. Therefore, it seems necessary first to lay down a sure line and a clear rule on each of these subjects, and then afterwards to investigate the other topics).[17] According to Origen, that "sure line and clear rule" can be found only within the community of the Church. Since all sorts of groups claim to represent the mind of Christ, even though some of them teach novelties, *servetur vero ecclesiastica praedicatio per successionis ordinem ab apostolis tradita et usque ad praesens in ecclesiis permanens, illa sola credenda est veritas, quae in nullo ab ecclesiastica et apostolica traditione discordat* (1, *pf.* 2; let us hold to the Church's proclamation as it has been handed down by the apostles through the order of succession and remains in the churches until the present day; that alone is to be believed as the truth which does not differ in any way from the ecclesiastical and apostolic tradition).

Thus far, Origen's point is similar to the well-known position of Irenaeus in his *Adversus haereses:* the constant teaching of the Christian community, as represented by the official witness of the designated leaders of the apostolic churches, is the only guide the perplexed believer ultimately has for knowing where to find the authentic revelation of Christ the Word.[18] It is in the next paragraph, however, that the particular program of the *De principiis* begins to appear. Origen goes on to say that, in preaching the Gospel of Christ, the apostles followed a strategy that invites the continuing work of the theologian and Scripture scholar: *Illud autem scire oportet, quoniam sancti apostoli fidem Christi praedicantes de quibusdam quidem, quaecumque necessaria crediderunt, omnibus credentibus, etiam his, qui pigriores erga inquisitionem divinae scientiae videbantur, manifestissime tradiderunt, rationem scilicet assertionis eorum relinquentes ab his inquirendam, qui spiritus dona excellentia mererentur et praecipue sermonis, sapientiae et scientiae gratiam per ipsum sanctum spiritum percepissent; de aliis vero dixerunt quidem, quia sint, quomodo autem aut unde sint,*

---

17. On Origen's notion of a κανών or rule, *v.* R.-C. Baud, "Les 'règles' de la théologie d'Origène," *RSR* 55 (1967), pp. 161–208.

18. *V., e.g., Haer.* 1.10.1f.; 3.2.2–3.3.3.

siluerunt, profecto ut studiosiores quique ex posteris suis, qui amatores essent sapientiae (φιλόσοφοι?), *exercitium habere possent, in quo ingenii sui fructum ostenderent, hi videlicet, qui dignos se et capaces ad recipiendam sapientiam praepararent* (1, *pf.* 3). Apostolic tradition, while providing the "line" and "rule" for interpreting Christ's revelation correctly, does not offer the believer a comprehensive body of doctrine, in Origen's view. What everyone needs to know, he suggests here, is taught clearly in Scripture and in the churches, but the reasons for particular doctrines, their implications and modalities, the way they form a cohesive whole that in turn makes each part convincing and fruitful for further thought—all these crucial details the apostolic witnesses have left to the researches of those endowed with special intellectual gifts by the Holy Spirit. Origen emphasizes here that the object of such research, the theological research that is, for him, always centered on scriptural interpretation, is ultimately to enable the researcher to share in wisdom, *i.e.*, the knowledge of God that is also love, and that unites the knower with the One known.[19]

In what follows, Origen develops his well-known list of the contents of the apostolic teaching that is to serve as the guide to scriptural interpretation. The apostles, he writes, clearly taught that there is only one God, who has created all things from nothing, and who is both the God of the patriarchs and prophets and the Father of Jesus; Marcionite or Gnostic distinctions between a supreme and saving God and the Old Testament's Creator and Lawgiver are ruled out of Christian interpretation from the start. The apostles also clearly taught the eternal divine origin of Jesus, the Son, His role in creation, and the reality of His human body and human experiences. Likewise, "they have taught that there is a Holy Spirit, associated in honor and dignity with Father and Son" (*honore ac dignitate patri ac filio sociatum tradiderunt spiritum sanctum,* 1, *pf.* 4), who inspired the holy men and prophets of both Old and New Covenant, although they have not given clear instruction on His exact relationship to Father and Son.

Continuing his catalogue of apostolic doctrines, Origen asserts that

19. For Origen, wisdom is above all identified with Christ, for whom it is the most fundamental and characteristic denomination. Human beings become wise by participating in Christ according to the power of participation proper to each (*in Ioh.* 1.34. 243–46); *cf. C. Cels.* 6.9. In *C. Cels.* 3.72, Origen seems both to accept the Stoic definition of wisdom as "knowledge of things divine and human and of their causes" (ἐπιστήμη "θείων" . . . "καὶ ἀνθρωπίνων" πραγμάτων καὶ τῶν τούτων αἰτίων) and to add the Christian notion that it is "a breath of the power of God" ("ἀτμὶς" . . . "τῆς τοῦ θεοῦ δυνάμεως") and a reflection of "the everlasting light" ("ἀπαύγασμα . . . φωτὸς ἀϊδίου" [Wis. 7.25f.]) of God; *Origenes Werke,* vol. 1 (Leipzig 1899): P. Koetschau, *Die Schrift vom Martyrium, Buch I–IV Gegen Celsus= GCS,* vol 2. *Cf.* also Clem. Alex., *Strom.* 1.28. For a discussion of wisdom in Origen's theology, *v.* H. Crouzel, *Origène et la "connaisance mystique"* (Paris 1961), pp. 457–60.

they clearly taught the substantial reality of the individual human soul, the certainty of our future resurrection and judgment, and the indestructible freedom of the human will in the face of all the dark forces against which we struggle. They have left the origin of each human soul, however, as a question for investigation. They have taught the reality, though not the precise nature or origin, of the powers of darkness as well as of the good angels and powers, and the finitude of the created world, which has both a beginning and an end in time. They have taught, finally, that the Scriptures are written by the action of the Spirit of God, and that they have not only the obvious meaning their words convey but also deeper, hidden spiritual meanings that represent divine mysteries; the whole Church, Origen says, agrees that Scripture has a spiritual meaning, but only those blessed with the charisms of wisdom and knowledge can explain just what that meaning, in each passage, is (1, *pf.* 8). After a brief reference to the notion of God's incorporeality (1, *pf.* 9), Origen concludes his preface by sketching out his project in the work: to form from these doctrines and from the explanations and conclusions that a trained and inspired mind can weave around them a cohesive and convincing whole, "a sequence and a body," that will give the reader a clearer and surer grasp of Truth: *Oportet igitur velut elementis ac fundamentis* [probably = στοιχείοις καὶ ἀρχαῖς][20] *huiusmodi uti secundum mandatum, quod dicit: "Inluminate vobis lumen scientiae"* [Hos. 10.12 LXX], *omnem qui cupit seriem* [= εἱρμός] *quandam et corpus* [= σῶμα] *ex horum omnium ratione perficere, ut manifestis et necessariis assertionibus de singulis quibusque quid sit in vero rimetur, et unum, ut diximus, corpus efficiat exemplis et affirmationibus, vel his, quas in sanctis scripturis invenerit, vel quas ex consequentiae ipsius indagine ac recti tenore reppererit* (1, *pf.* 10).

Although the original Greek of Origen's preface, like that of most of the work, is no longer extant, it seems clear that he is here proposing to form out of the content of traditional apostolic teaching the kind of integrated, demonstrative, logically coherent system of knowledge that in the Aristotelian tradition was called a science (ἐπιστήμη). One of the prime characteristics of such a system, as Aristotle had depicted it in the *Posterior Analytics,* was that it be developed from original premises or axioms proper to itself, axioms that, because of the risk of endless regress, could not themselves be demonstrated within the logic of the system but were grasped simply by intelligence (νοῦς) in the course of continuous and reflective experience in the world and were rooted in sense perception and

---

20. Bonnefoy (note 2 above) suggests (pp. 133f.) simply ἀρχαῖς.

held together by the memory.[21] Aristotle's description of the characteristics of scientific knowledge, as Jonathan Barnes suggests, is not meant to propose an actual methodology of research, but rather "is concerned with the organization and presentation of results of research: its aim is to say how we may collect into an intelligible whole the scientist's various discoveries—how we may so arrange the facts that their interrelations, and in particular their explanations, may best be revealed and grasped."[22] In this context, those propositions about the world of which we are surest, those of which we are not convinced by reasoning from other, surer convictions, but which we accept as undemonstrable axioms, become the first principles (ἀρχαί) of a structure of syllogistic argument about why things happen, which in the end enables us to grasp a whole body of knowledge, a whole discipline, with the same conviction we have about the principles themselves. Through causal explanation, the certainty and clarity of the first principles are communicated to all the experiences and events explained by them; this leads to the formation of a system of sure knowledge or Aristotelian ἐπιστήμη (*APo.* 1.2 [72a30–b4]). In a passage of the *Magna moralia,* Aristotle speaks more generally still and labels the entire body of organized knowledge about any particular branch of human experience "wisdom" (σοφία), the kind of comprehensive understanding of the world that the philosopher pursues, and that includes both principles and reasoned conclusions in one structured whole: ἡ δὲ σοφία ἐστὶν ἐξ ἐπιστήμης καὶ νοῦ συγκειμένη. ἔστιν γὰρ ἡ σοφία καὶ περὶ τὰς ἀρχὰς καὶ τὰ ἐκ τῶν ἀρχῶν ἤδη δεικνύμενα, περὶ ἃ ἡ ἐπιστήμη· ᾗ μὲν οὖν περὶ τὰς ἀρχὰς, τοῦ νοῦ αὐτὴ μετέχει, ᾗ δὲ περὶ τὰ μετὰ τὰς ἀρχάς, μετ' ἀποδείξεως ὄντα, τῆς ἐπιστήμης μετέχει (*MM* 2.34.14 [1197 a 24–29]; Wisdom is put together from both scientific knowledge and intelligence, for wisdom is concerned both with first principles and with what we demonstrate from first principles, those things that are the province of scientific knowledge. So far, therefore, as it concerns principles, [wisdom] participates in intelligence; so far as it deals with what is subsequent to first principles by the path of demonstration, it partakes of scientific knowledge).[23]

This understanding of the character of first principles in human knowing and of their relationship to both scientific knowledge and wisdom underlies, I suggest, both the title of Origen's work and its intellectual agenda. The whole system of Aristotelian logic and scientific theory, after all,

21. V. esp. *APo.* 2.19 (99b17–100b17); cf. *EN* 1.7 (1098a33–b7); 6.6 (1140b31–1141a3).
22. *Aristotle's Posterior Analytics* (Oxford 1975), pp. xf.
23. F. Susemihl, *Aristotelis quae feruntur magna moralia* (Leipzig 1883).

was generally appropriated by the second-century school philosophy we call Middle Platonism,[24] in which Origen also made his intellectual home. For Origen, however, the Christian ἐπιστήμη, which he says he hopes to form into a cohesive whole, is the teaching of Christ the Logos, contained in the whole of Scripture and enunciated with authority in the apostolic tradition. Some of the teachings of Scripture and the apostles, according to the preface to *De principiis,* are important enough, clear enough, and universally enough believed to be regarded as first principles in the system; other points are less clear, and must be discussed, debated, arrived at by reason. But it is only when one has constructed the system, laboriously, through logical reasoning from that basic apostolic kerygma, that one grasps revelation well enough to see the spiritual, saving meaning in every text of Scripture; in other words, it is only when one has grasped the whole structure of revealed truth that one can begin to see the real divine significance of every little word and detail and, in seeing this, to share in what we might call Christian wisdom.

So at the end of the first chapter of his discussion of scriptural interpretation, in *De principiis,* book four, Origen concedes that for the ordinary reader, the "super-human meaning" (τὸ ὑπὲρ ἄνθρωπον τῶν νοημάτων, 4.1.7) in Scripture is just about as elusive as the action of God's Providence in human history; sometimes we see it, often we do not. Since we have been convinced by some texts of God's gracious reality in some events, we look for it patiently in the rest and trust the Holy Spirit to make it clear to us in both cases. Origen seems to be saying that the tenor of his argument, up to this point in the treatise, should be able at least to convince the reader that a sectarian Gnostic interpretation of Scripture is insufficient, and that only the axioms and arguments of the Church's public, apostolic tradition can enable the believer to read the Bible correctly. With a systematic grasp of this ecclesial faith, then, one can begin to find the spiritual meaning of the whole biblical text, because one already knows the shape of the Truth being revealed. Origen continues: διόπερ δυνάμεως ἡμᾶς οὐρανίου ἢ καὶ ὑπερουρανίου πληττούσης ἐπὶ τὸ σέβειν τὸν κτίσαντα ἡμᾶς μόνον, πειραθῶμεν 'ἀφέντες τὸν τῆς ἀρχῆς τοῦ Χριστοῦ λόγον', τουτέστι τῆς 'στοιχειώσεως', 'ἐπὶ τὴν τελειότητα φέρεσθαι', ἵνα ἡ τοῖς τελείοις λαλουμένη σοφία καὶ ἡμῖν λαληθῇ (4.1.7, *cf.* Heb. 6.1; Since, then, a heavenly or even a super-heavenly power compels us to worship only the one who created us [rather than the remote, transcendent source postulated by the Valentinian and Marcionite systems] let us try to 'let go of the prelimi-

24. V. J. Dillon, *The Middle Platonists* (London 1977), pp. 49–51; on Albinus *v.* pp. 276–80 and on Apuleius, pp. 336f.

nary word of Christ,' namely the 'elements' [of doctrine], and 'pass on to perfection,' so that the wisdom proclaimed to the perfect will be proclaimed also to us). Citing Hebrews, Origen here invites his reader, just before the end of his work, to move beyond the "elements" of the Christian science that he has been developing into a cohesive body over the past three books and to share in the "wisdom that will be spoken among the perfect," a wisdom, he notes a few lines later, in words borrowed from several passages in Paul, that "will be formed in us clearly by the revelation of the mystery hidden for long ages but now disclosed through the writings of the prophets and the appearence of our Lord and Savior Jesus Christ" (αὔτη δὲ ἡ σοφία ἡμῖν ἐντυπωθήσεται τρανῶς ʽκατὰ ἀποκάλυψιν μυστηρίου χρόνοις αἰωνίοις σεσιγημένου, φανερωθέντος δὲ νῦν διά τε γραφῶν προφητικῶν [Rom. 16.25f.] καὶ τῆς ἐπιφανείας τοῦ κυρίου καὶ σωτῆρος ἡμῶν Ἰησοῦ Χριστοῦʾ [1Tim. 6.14, 2Tim. 1.10], 4.1.7).

As this passage suggests, Origen's discussion of the Bible and its interpretation in the first three chapters of *De principiis,* book four is clearly not an appendix or even an important footnote to the work, but rather its real goal: the introduction to a deeper way of reading Scripture that will be possible for him and plausible to his readers only after they have mastered the doctrinal structure he has been presenting in books one through three.[25] The tenor of the work is, from the start, both constructive and polemical: Origen sketches out the "series and organic whole" formed by the "single body" of Christian teaching (1, *pf.* 10) as a way of responding to the alternative readings of Christian Scripture and tradition offered by Gnostic sects.[26] The believer who has formed a synthetic Christian ἐπιστήμη rooted in the apostolic tradition can then turn to individual biblical passages, even individual words, and find in them the door to deeper participation in the mystery of divine wisdom, the way toward what Clement of Alexandria would call true γνῶσις.[27] This sense of the internal relationship among doctrinal exposition, anti-Gnostic polemic, and

25. Karpp (note 14 above) remarks justly (p. 14): "Da dieser Sinn [*i.e.,* the deeper, underlying meaning of Scripture] zumal als ein 'System,' im Sinne gedanklicher Einheit, für Origenes zwar hinter und über der Schrift liegt, aber nur durch sie zur Gewißheit werden kann, darf die Hermeneutik in seinem Werk nicht fehlen. . . . Zugleich stellt sich abschließend sein ganzer Systementwurf als ein Beitrag und ein Mittel zu einem vertieften Verständnis der heiligen Schrift dar."

26. For the fundamentally anti-Gnostic character of *Prin., v.* esp. A. Le Boulluec, "La place de la polémique antignostique dans le *Peri Archôn,*" *Origeniana* (note 6 above), pp. 47–61. For a convenient list of passages in the work that explicitly deal with Gnostic theses, *v.* M. Harl, G. Dorival, and A. Le Boulluec, *Origène, Traité des Principes* (Paris 1976), pp. 18f.

27. *V. Strom.* 6.16.146.3: τὴν ἐκκλησιαστικὴν καὶ ἀληθῆ γνῶσιν; *cf. Strom.* 6.1.2.4: γνῶσις ἡ ἀληθής; 6.1.3.2: ἡ . . . ἐξαιρέτως ὀνομαζομένη γνῶσις; 7.15.91.5: τὴν ἀκριβεστάτην . . . γνῶσιν; and 7.15.92.3: ἥ τε ἀκριβεστάτη γνῶσις; O. Stählin *et al.,*

scriptural interpretation makes clear the structure of the whole work far more satisfactorily, it seems to me, than interpretations that assume it to be simply a bipartite treatise on physics, which begins with a general sketch of Christian cosmology, turns then to special questions on the same subjects, and ends with a few important but somewhat marginal appendices.

In what is generally accepted today as the first part of the work (1.1–2.3), Origen gives a fairly straightforward exposition of doctrine, which includes both what he considers the clear and uncontested teaching of the apostles, the first principles of the Christian system of knowledge in the strict sense, and the logical consequences that can be drawn from those principles (v., e.g., 1.7.1). The second part of the work clearly repeats this same sequence of themes—God, intelligent creation, and material creation—but in a distinctly different perspective. It is not that he is discussing less fundamental, more specialized issues than he did in part 1; rather, the treatment here is both more explicitly exegetical—more concerned with the interpretation of particular passages of Scripture and with the relationship of Christ to the Old Testament as the key to that interpretation—and more explicitly anti-Gnostic. The first sentence of *De principiis* 2.4 makes this new perspective clear: *His per ordinem prout potuimus breviter digestis, consequens est secundum id, quod ex initio proposuimus, confutare etiam eos, qui putant alium deum esse patrem domini nostri Iesu Christi praeter illum, qui Moysi responsa legis dabat vel prophetas mittebat, qui est deus patrum Abraham, Isaac et Iacob* (2.4.1; Now that we have briefly treated these subjects in order, as well as we could, the next step, according to the plan we proposed at the start, is to refute also those who think that the Father of our Lord Jesus Christ is a God different from the one who gave Moses the response of the Law or who sent out the prophets, the one who is the God of our ancestors Abraham, Isaac, and Jacob). The subjects treated now under the same general structural headings of the triune God, the history of the salvation of intelligent creatures, and the material cosmos are all presented in refutation of a Gnostic reading of the Bible. It is almost as if he were attempting here to show, on the basis of the body of Christian teaching already presented, how not to interpret the Bible.

Clemens Alexandrinus, vol. 2, 4th ed. (Berlin 1985): *Stromata* bkk. 1–6 and vol. 3, 2nd ed. (Berlin 1970): *Stromata* bkk. 7f. = *GCS*, voll. 15 and 17. For the phrase "true gnosis" in Christian works roughly contemporary with Clement, v. also Iren., *Haer.* 4.33.8: γνῶσις ἀληθής (A. Rousseau *et al.*, *Irénée de Lyon, Contre les hérésies Livre IV*, vol. 2 [Paris 1965]: *Texte et traduction* = *SC*, vol. 100); *Ad Diog.* 12.6: γνώσεως ἀληθοῦς (H.I. Marrou, *À Diognète* [Paris 1951] = *SC*, vol. 33); and Or., *Frag. 2 in Ioh.* (on 1.4): γνῶσιν ἀληθείας (*Origenes Werke*, vol. 4 [Leipzig 1903]: E. Preuschen, *Der Johanneskommentar* = *GCS*, vol. 10).

It is only after this second survey of God, intelligences, and material beings that Origen turns to consider the fourth main topic of his preface, the principles of biblical interpretation. At the start of this section, he remarks that in what has been said up to now he has made use not only of "common concepts and the evidence of visible things" (ταῖς κοιναῖς ἐννοίαις καὶ τῇ ἐναργείᾳ τῶν βλεπομένων), *i.e.,* the matter for empirically grounded first principles that serve, in the Aristotelian epistemological scheme, as axioms for other bodies of human knowledge (*APo.* 2.19 [100a1–b4]), but also of Scripture, the data of God's self-revelation in history (*Prin.* 4.1.1). Now, he suggests, is the time to consider the divine status of the scriptural text itself. Arguing from the pattern of prophecy and fulfilment that links the two Testaments, Origen makes the surprising point that "the divine character of the words of the prophets and the spiritual aspect of the law of Moses came to light when Jesus appeared among us" (τὸ τῶν προφητικῶν λόγων ἔνθεον καὶ τὸ πνευματικὸν τοῦ Μωσέως νόμου ἔλαμψεν ἐπιδημήσαντος Ἰησοῦ, 4.1.6; *cf.* 1.1.2). It is only in the light of the whole body of Christian faith centered on the person of the risen Jesus that the divine meaning and source of each part of the Bible, even its seemingly scandalous aspects, become luminous and incontestably clear (4.1.6f.).[28]

Chapters two and three of book four are meant to offer a way on which one might proceed in reading and understanding Holy Scripture (τῷ τρόπῳ τῆς ἀναγνώσεως καὶ νοήσεως αὐτῶν, 4.2.1) based on "the rule of the heavenly church of Jesus Christ, according to the tradition of the apostles" (τοῦ κανόνος τῆς Ἰησοῦ Χριστοῦ κατὰ διαδοχὴν τῶν ἀποστόλων οὐρανίου ἐκκλησίας, 4.2.2). The problem in both Jewish and Gnostic interpretations, he insists, as well as in the understanding of many simple Christians, is that they read the Old Testament too literally and so either form false concepts and expectations or reject the text out of hand (4.2.1). Most people do assume that the dark passages of Scripture contain "certain mysterious dispensations" for our benefit (οἰκονομίαι τινές εἰσι μυστικαί, 4.2.2), but they are usually at a loss to identify what those dispensations are, either because they lack training or because they do not have "the key of knowledge" to which Jesus refers in Lk. 11.52 (τὴν κλεῖδα τῆς γνώσεως, 4.2.3). Presumably, that key is the sense of the whole of Christian teaching, which Origen has just identified, in books one through three, as the apostolic κανών of faith.

In what follows, Origen does not, as is sometimes suggested, actually set forth a distinctive method of scriptural interpretation. His approach is,

---

28. *V.* also Origen's remarks in 4.3.6–10, arguing that this hidden but central meaning of the Old Testament is meant for the spiritual Israel, whose ancestor is not Adam but Christ.

rather, descriptive and builds on the conviction of the divine origin and saving purpose of Scripture, which he has already expressed. So his famous explanation of the discovery of levels of scriptural meaning in terms of body, soul, and spirit (4.2.4–6) is really simply the observation that the true and important meaning of a passage is not always obvious to a serious Christian reader, and that this meaning, intended by God to be understood for our salvation, must therefore often be searched out studiously by those already advanced in heavenly wisdom and communicated by them to the rest (4.2.4).[29] In laying the foundations for such an understanding in the rest of 4.2, Origen distinguishes three "goals" (σκοποι) or strategies used by God in inspiring the authors of Scripture: first, to instruct human beings about their own situation and future (4.2.7); second, to make the essentials of this knowledge available to those who are not capable of discovering the deepest mysteries for themselves, by including in the Bible instructive historical narrative and moral examples (4.2.8); and third, to "weave into" (συνύφηνεν) this narrative enough that is improbable or scandalous to lead the discerning reader beyond the narrative and even the literal level in search of the saving mysteries (*Prin.* 4.2.9; *cf.* Aug., *Conf.* 12.26.36–32.43). In describing this divine method of scriptural composition, Origen again emphasizes that the main purpose of the Spirit is always to show the whole structure (εἱρμός) or sequence (ἀκολουθία) of the truth being revealed (*Prin.* 4.2.9). Within this structure some things are more basic than others: one cannot understand the promise of salvation for fallen creatures, for instance, without first understanding "the doctrine of God and of His only-begotten Son" (τὰ περὶ θεοῦ ... καὶ τοῦ μονογενοῦς αὐτοῦ), the news of the incarnation of the Word, the status and origin of the invisible powers, and the nature of the material cosmos (4.2.7).

It is with this sense of how God reveals and of what one must understand to interpret Scripture as divine revelation that Origen offers his advice to those who wish to engage in this difficult research (4.3). The method he proposes is little more than common sense: by careful examination of each passage, one must try to discern what, given the meaning of the whole Bible—as that is already known from the rest of Scripture and from Church teaching—can be taken "bodily" as literally true and what is impossible. When something important and obviously true appears in a narrative context that is morally or rationally unacceptable, one must take

---

29. On Origen's understanding of Scripture's various levels of meaning and the connection of the exegetical process with salvation, *v.* esp. K.J. Torjesen, "'Body,' 'Soul,' and 'Spirit' in Origen's Theory of Exegesis," *AThR* 67 (1985), pp. 17–30.

the whole passage figuratively rather than literally. The reason is simple: Διακείμεθα γὰρ ἡμεῖς περὶ πάσης τῆς θείας γραφῆς, ὅτι πᾶσα μὲν ἔχει τὸ πνευματικόν, οὐ πᾶσα δὲ τὸ σωματικόν· πολλαχοῦ γὰρ ἐλέγχεται ἀδύνατον ὂν τὸ σωματικόν (4.3.5; We are, after all, of this opinion concerning the whole of Holy Scripture, that all of it has a spiritual meaning, but not all of it a bodily meaning, for in many places the bodily can be shown to be impossible).

Origen's reflections on Scripture and its correct interpretation, on the role of the "bodily" and the "spiritual," the literal and the more edifyingly figurative, in the communication of truth, lead him inescapably, at the end of the whole work, to discuss a topic he had already touched on at the end of the preface: incorporeal reality.[30] He has conceded in the preface that the term ἀσώματον comes from Greek philosophy, even though he insists that Scripture describes God and rational creatures as incorporeal (1, *pf.* 9; *cf.* 4.3.15). In the final chapter of *De principiis* he returns to the notion and insists that whatever we say about the generation of the Son from the Father or about the presence of the divine Word in the human Jesus must be understood in an "immaterial," and therefore in some sense, an analogical or nonliteral, manner (4.4.1–4). Matter itself, he suggests, is a complex philosophical notion that can be conceived of in a number of plausible ways and must in any case not be understood as an ultimate metaphysical principle (4.4.6f.; *cf.* 2.1.4). Intelligent creatures, on the other hand, share in the "spiritual light" (*intellectuali luce*) of God's eternal and incorruptible reality, because they are themselves not material bodies (4.4.9). This leads to the concluding point of the whole treatise: that as intelligent creatures, made in God's image and likeness, we already share in God's fundamentally spiritual or incorporeal existence in our "inner person" (*interior homo*), and that in developing our ability to know (*intellegere* [probably = γνῶναι], 4.4.9) in an immaterial, spiritual way, we come to share in the qualities of God (4.4.10). Origen refers to this spiritual mode of knowing, built up by the exercise of the virtues in "imitation of God" (*imitationem dei*) and exercised particularly in the spiritual interpretation of Scripture, as the acquiring of a "divine sensibility" (*sensum . . . divinum* [*cf.* Prov. 2.5]).[31] Origen suggests in the last lines of *De principiis* that this transformed intelligence, this divine sense, is both the ultimate product of the

30. On the importance of the idea of incorporeality for the *De prin.* and its connection with Greek philosophical and Gnostic theories, *v.* G. Stroumsa, "The Incorporeality of God: Context and Implications of Origen's Position," *Religion* 13 (1983), pp. 345–58.

31. Origen develops this idea of the senses of the inner person at length in the *Dialogue with Heracleides* 15–24. *V.* also earlier passages in *Prin.*: 1.1.9; 2.11.6f.; and K. Rahner, "Le début d'une doctrine des cinq sens spirituels chez Origène," *RAM* 13 (1932), pp. 113–45.

science whose axioms and implications have been sketched out so pain-stakingly through the whole work and the final judge of its validity. It is only through this immaterial, inner way, of knowing that the intellectual creature comes to genuine communion with both his fellow intellects and God. The final norm Origen offers for regulating the use of this spiritual sense is the "form" of the body of doctrine he has constructed, *i.e.*, the conformity of spiritual knowing and spiritual exegesis with reasoned faith: *Hoc autem sensu intuendum nobis est etiam de his singulis quae supra dix-imus rationabilibus, et hoc sensu audienda sunt ista, quae loquimur, et con-sideranda quae scribimus. Nam divina natura etiam taciti quid intra nos volvamus, agnoscit. De his autem, quae diximus, vel de reliquis, quae conse-quentia sunt, secundum hanc formam, quam supra exposuimus, sentiendum est* (4.4.10).

Throughout this survey of the contents of Origen's *De principiis*, my purpose has been to show both its inner cohesion and its overall plan: that, namely, of constructing an articulated body of Christian teaching, based on Scripture and the principles laid out in the apostolic kerygma, which can serve in turn as the hermeneutical grounding for a more thor-oughgoing spiritual reading of Scripture. In its general lines, the purpose of the work thus appears to be not unlike that of the first book of Augus-tine's *De doctrina christiana* and to offer the reader who wants to discover the riches hidden under the obscurity of Scripture and proclaim them reliably to his fellow believers an ordered sense of the whole of its con-tent, which can act as a starting point for finding the meaning of individ-ual verses. For Origen, the ultimate goal of such intellectual labor seems to be the more unitive and affective knowledge of God he calls wisdom (σοφία).[32]

Origen's conception of the importance of an integrated body of Christ-ian doctrine, scientifically developed from revealed first principles, as the basis of authentic scriptural interpretation, is not, in fact, new with him; hints of the same project can be found in his contemporaries. Irenaeus, for instance, in the first book of *Adversus haereses*, attacks the Valentinians for rearranging authentic pieces of revelation, like the *tesserae* of a mosaic or the half-lines in a Homeric cento, to form a distorted picture of revela-tion. The believer who adheres to the "rule of truth" (τὸν κανόνα τῆς ἀληθείας) on the other hand, "will restore each one of the passages (*i.e.*, the scriptural texts used misleadingly by the Valentinians) to its proper or-

---

32. For Origen's further reflections on the development of an articulated body of reli-gious knowledge, formed from the ἀρχαί present in Scripture, and above all from Christ the ἀρχή, and leading to divine wisdom, *v. in Ioh.* 1.18.106f. (on 1.1) and 13.46.301–04 (on 4.36).

der and, having fit it into the body of the truth, will lay bare their fabrication and show it is without support (ἓν ἕκαστον δὲ τῶν εἰρημένων ἀποδοὺς τῇ ἰδίᾳ τάξει καὶ προσαρμόσας τῷ τῆς ἀληθείας σωματίῳ, γυμνώσει καὶ ἀνυπόστατον ἐπιδείξει τὸ πλάσμα αὐτῶν, 1.9.4).[33]

Clement of Alexandria, too, offers a hint at the start of *Stromateis*, book four, of a planned large-scale theological enterprise of his own, which may offer a clue to the role Origen expected *De principiis* to play within his wider *oeuvre*. Clement says he is about to discuss martyrdom and the ascetical life and then will turn to faith and the role of symbols before concluding his treatment of ethics. Second, he will give a brief apologetic exposition of Scripture to refute the positions of pagans and Jews. Third, he will expound "what has been said by way of natural philosophy about first principles by Greeks and barbarians" (τὰ περὶ ἀρχῶν φυσιολογηθέντα τοῖς τε Ἕλλησι τοῖς τε ἄλλοις βαρβάροις) and refute them. Then he will give "a cursory view of theology" (τὴν ἐπιδρομὴν τῆς θεολογίας) and discuss the prophetic character of Scripture. The purpose of this fourth section of his promised enterprise will apparently be to refute Gnostic Christian theories after establishing the authority of the Scriptures by an ordered (εἱρμῷ) exposition of their contents (4.1.2.2). All four steps, says Clement, must be done carefully and at length, as a kind of practical and apologetic prelude to the heart of his work, which will communicate a deeper kind of knowledge on the same subjects: τότε δὴ τὴν τῷ ὄντι γνωστικὴν φυσιολογίαν μέτιμεν, τὰ μικρὰ πρὸ τῶν μεγάλων μυηθέντες μυστηρίων, ὡς μηδὲν ἐμποδὼν τῇ θείᾳ ὄντως ἱεροφαντίᾳ γίνεσθαι προκεκαθαρμένων καὶ προδιατετυπωμένων τῶν προϊστορηθῆναι καὶ προπαραδοθῆναι δεόντων. ἡ γοῦν κατὰ τὸν τῆς ἀληθείας κανόνα γνωστικῆς παραδόσεως φυσιολογία, μᾶλλον δὲ ἐποπτεία, ἐκ τοῦ περὶ κοσμογονίας ἤρτηται λόγου, ἐνθένδε ἀναβαίνουσα ἐπὶ τὸ θεολογικὸν εἶδος. ὅθεν εἰκότως τὴν ἀρχὴν τῆς παραδόσεως ἀπὸ τῆς προφητευθείσης ποιησόμεθα γενέσεως, ἐν μέρει καὶ τὰ τῶν ἑτεροδόξων παρατιθέμενοι καὶ ὡς οἷόν τε ἡμῖν διαλύεσθαι πειρώμενοι (4.1.3.1–4.1.3.3; We shall pass on then to the truly gnostic doctrine of nature, since we will have been initiated into the little mysteries before the great ones, so that we will not experience any obstacle to the truly divine revelation of sacred things, having been cleansed and formed in advance by the things that must first be narrated and explained.

33. A. Rousseau and L. Doutreleau, *Irénée de Lyon, Contre les hérésies*, bk. 1, vol. 2 (Paris 1979): *Texte et traduction* = *SC*, vol. 264. Like *De prin.*, Irenaeus' *Demonst. ap. pr.* is an anti-Gnostic summary of the central apostolic doctrines that is arranged in a two-part parallel structure and claims (ch. 1) to offer the reader a brief summary of "the body of truth." V. L.M. Froidevaux's translation of the Armenian version in *Irénée de Lyon: Démonstration de la prédication apostolique* (Paris 1959) = *SC*, vol. 62.

An account of nature in the gnostic tradition, given according to the rule of truth or rather, a first-hand initiation into this tradition, begins with a consideration of cosmogony and ascends from there to the genre of theology. Therefore it is right that we develop the beginning of this tradition from the Genesis given us in prophecy, setting the opinions of heretics alongside it and trying, as far as we can, to refute them).

Although it is never easy to understand Clement with absolute clarity on matters of detail, he seems here to be sketching out plans for an enormous theological program, moving from ethical and practical questions to apologetics, to doxographical reporting, to a systematic anti-Gnostic consideration of scriptural doctrine, all as a prelude for a "truly gnostic" account of the cosmos and God, drawn from the Bible and consistent with the "rule of truth."[34] Whether or not Clement's great plan was ever realized,[35] it seems more than likely that Origen would have known about it and at least plausible that he may even have tried to adopt it, with modifications, for his own intellectual projects in Alexandria. We know that Origen's early work there included commentaries on the first twenty-five Psalms and on Lamentations, a collection of *Stromateis,* which perhaps dealt with practical and ethical issues, and a treatise on the resurrection, all probably dating from 222–25. In addition, he wrote two other anti-Gnostic works in Alexandria, *De naturis,* on the nature or natures of the soul, and the *Dialogue with Candidianus,* on the relation of the Son to the Father and on the devil; these also were probably completed before he began his *Commentary on Genesis* in 229.[36] There are hints here of the same sequence Clement outlines in the passage we have quoted: beginning with ethics, basic scriptural study and anti-Gnostic apologetic before moving on to consider the deeper cosmological and theological issues raised by the book of Genesis.

Pierre Nautin has showed, in his outline of Origen's career, that Origen probably wrote the *De principiis* around 229–30, after completing the first few books of his *Commentary on Genesis* and before writing book five.[37] Nautin plausibly suggests that the occasion for his writing the *De principiis* may have been the criticism raised by his spiritual exegesis of Genesis

---

34. *Cf.* this programmatic statement with the briefer ones at *Strom.* 1.1.15.2 and 2.1.1.1–2.2.3).

35. P. Nautin has argued that he did finish it, but that our present *Strom.* represent only the ethics or first part; *v.* "La fin des Stromates et les Hypotyposes de Clément d'Alexandrie," *VigChr* 30 (1976), pp. 268–302.

36. For the chronology of Origen's early works *v.* P. Nautin, *Origène: sa vie et son oeuvre* (Paris 1977), pp. 368–71.

37. *Ib.,* 368f.

and the view of God and the world it implied.[38] In the eyes of many simple Alexandrian Christians, some of them, perhaps, even occupying powerful places among the clergy, Origen's way of reading the biblical creation accounts may have seemed dangerously close to Platonic or Gnostic speculation. In that case, his real purpose in the *De principiis* would be to make a clear statement of the foundations of his hermeneutic in the science of ecclesial faith and to give an anti-Gnostic account of what he regarded as the right way to read Scripture—like the fourth step in Clement's proposed program—before passing on to initiate his readers, as Clement hoped also to do, into the "great mysteries" of Christian cosmogony and theology: the contemplation, through a deeper understanding of Scripture, of what is ultimately real. That next step, hinted at in the discussion of incorporeality and the "divine sense" in the last chapter of *De principiis,* would have been the main concern of his still unfinished *Commentary on Genesis* and of the great *Commentary on John,* which he began to compose a year or so after finishing the *De principiis.*

However much his plans may have been influenced by Clement's intellectual program, Origen's theological method was clearly different: more explicitly based on the text of Scripture, more self-consciously rooted in ecclesiastical doctrine, less concerned with the details and forms of Hellenistic literature, philosophy, and culture. The irony of his writing a treatise Περὶ ἀρχῶν, with all the Middle Platonic resonances of that title, cannot have escaped him. The work does concern physics, the causal principles at the heart of a world of motion and change, the nature of the human person and of our material and spiritual surroundings. Even more, however, it deals with the first principles of a coherent doctrinal system that allows the believing reader to find in the Christian Bible the wisdom that alone gives life.

38. *Ib.,* pp. 370, 423f.

Rhetorical and Hermeneutic *Synkrisis* in Patristic Typology

Daniel Sheerin

This essay charts two roles played by the figure σύγκρισις, or rhetorical comparison, in patristic texts that have to do with types and their fulfillments.[1] We will consider (1) aspects of the treatment of *synkrisis* in rhetorical handbooks, (2) appropriation of features of *synkrisis* derived from the school tradition to rhetorical commentary on typological passages of Scripture, and (3) the employment of *synkrisis* by patristic writers in their exegesis and preaching on issues of typology.

1. Rhetorical *Synkrisis:* Guidelines from the School Tradition

The device of formal *synkrisis,* evaluative comparison, was most explicitly developed in oratory.[2] Though *synkrisis* was adapted to the writing of biography[3] and literary criticism,[4] its true home remained in the schools of rhetoric, where it was the subject of formal instruction and was cultivated

---

1. This is a refinement of a paper delivered at the 1994 meeting of the North American Patristics Society. Unless otherwise indicated, translations are by the author.

2. The various aspects of *synkrisis* are reviewed by F. Focke, "*Synkrisis,*" *Hermes* 58 (1923), pp. 327–68; for its role in epideictic oratory *v.* T.C. Burgess, *Epideictic Literature* (Chicago 1902; rpt. New York 1987), pp. 125f., and T.R. Lee, *Studies in the Form of Sirach 44–50* (Atlanta 1986), pp. 101–3, 179–81. M.H. McCall gives (p. 136) only brief consideration to *synkrisis* in *Ancient Rhetorical Theories of Simile and Comparison* (Cambridge, Mass. 1969), a study concerned rather with rhetorical figures of simile and non-evaluative comparison. For appropriations of *synkrisis* in Byzantine art *v.* H. Maguire, "The Art of Comparing in Byzantium," *ArtB* 70.1 (1988), pp. 88–103.

3. *V.* D.H.J. Larmour, "Making Parallels: *Synkrisis* and Plutarch's 'Themistocles and Camillus,'" *ANRW,* part 2, vol. 33.6 (Berlin/New York 1992): *Allgemeines zur Literatur des 2. Jahrhunderts und einzelne Autoren der Trajanischen und frühhadrianischen Zeit,* pp. 4154–200.

4. Dionysius of Halicarnassus defends his comparative-critical method, τὴν ἐκ τῆς

through set-piece declamatory exercises (προγυμνάσματα).[5] In discussions of the use of *synkrisis* for amplification in encomium and invective, its main traditional use, the rhetoricians often consider the two issues of the relative value of the entities to be compared and the impropriety of vilifying one to enhance the other.

Even early on there is some disagreement about the relative value of objects suitable for comparison in a *synkrisis*. Aristotle recommends that we compare the subject of an encomium to the famous, or, if that is impossible, with people in general: δεῖ δὲ πρὸς ἐνδόξους συγκρίνειν· αὐξητικὸν γὰρ καὶ καλόν, εἰ σπουδαίων βελτίων ... διὸ κἂν μὴ πρὸς τοὺς ἐνδόξους, ἀλλὰ πρὸς τοὺς ἄλλους δεῖ παραβάλλειν, ἐπείπερ ἡ ὑπεροχὴ δοκεῖ μηνύειν ἀρετήν (1.9[1368a]; "One should make the comparison with famous people; for the subject is amplified and made honorable if he is better than [other] worthy ones. ... Thus, even if there is no comparison with the famous, one should compare [the person praised] with the many, since superiority [even over them] seems to denote excellence").[6] Anaximenes, however, maintains the contrary, suggesting that we compare the subject to the least entity of the category: τοὐλάχιστον τῶν ὑπὸ τὴν αὐτὴν ἰδέαν πιπτόντων (3.8[1426a]).[7] But in Hermogenes' (*fl.* 161–80) account, we find the following menu of choices for the relative value of the *comparanda*: Ἐνίοτε μὲν οὖν κατὰ τὸ ἴσον προάγομεν τὰς συγκρίσεις, ἴσα δεικνύντες, ἃ παραβάλλομεν, ἢ διὰ πάντων ἢ διὰ πλειόνων· ἐνίοτε δὲ θάτερον προτίθεμεν, ἐγκωμιάζοντες κἀκεῖνο, οὗ τοῦτο προτίθεμεν· ἐνίοτε δὲ τὸ μὲν ψέγομεν ὅλως, τὸ δὲ ἐπαινοῦμεν, οἷον εἰ λέγοις σύγκρισιν δικαιοσύνης καὶ πλούτου. γίνεται δὲ καὶ πρὸς τὸ βελτίον σύγκρισις, ἔνθα ἀγὼν τὸν ἐλάττονα ἴσον τῷ κρείττονι δεῖξαι, οἷον εἰ σύγκρισιν λέγοις Ἡρακλέους καὶ Ὀδυσσέως (*Progym.*, sec. 8; Sometimes we advance *synkrises* based on equality, showing that the things we are juxtaposing are equal, either in all respects or in most. Sometimes we express a preference for one, but praise the other to which we are

---

συγκρίσεως ἐξέτασιν, in *ad Pompeium*, sec. 754; H. Usener and L. Radermacher, *Dionysii Halicarnasei quae exstant*, vol. 6 (Leipzig 1929; rpt. Stuttgart 1985): *Opusculorum*, vol. 2.

5. G.A. Kennedy, *Greek Rhetoric under Christian Emperors* (Princeton, N.J. 1983) describes (pp. 58, 64) the situation of *synkrisis* among *progymnasmata*, or school exercises, and remarks on use of *synkrisis* in orations by Julian (p. 31), Synesius (p. 41), and Himerius (p. 146). Progymnasmatic *synkrises* could compare persons, activities, or things; *v., e.g.*, Libanius' comparisons of Achilles and Diomedes (pp. 334–38), of Ajax and Achilles (pp. 339–42), of Demosthenes and Aeschines (pp. 342–49), of seafaring and farming (pp. 349–53), of country and city (353–60); R. Foerster, *Libanii Opera*, vol. 8 (Leipzig 1915): *Progymnasmata, Argumenta orationum demosthenicarum*.

6. W.D. Ross, *Aristotelis ars rhetorica* (Oxford 1959). The translation follows G.A. Kennedy, *Aristotle On Rhetoric: A Theory of Civic Discourse* (New York/Oxford 1991), pp. 86f.

7. M. Fuhrmann, *Anaximenis ars rhetorica quae vulgo fertur Aristotelis ad Alexandrum* (Leipzig 1966).

preferring it. Sometimes we completely disparage the one and praise the other, as if one should declaim a *synkrisis* of justice and wealth. There is also *synkrisis* to something superior, in which one strives to show that the lesser is equal to the better, as if you would declaim a *synkrisis* of Herakles and Odysseus).[8] The rhetor Aphthonius, a student of Libanius, offers similar choices and describes a *synkrisis* as either a double encomium or an invective composed of an encomium and an invective. The choice would depend, one presumes, on whether one were comparing entities of equal or disparate excellence.[9]

The comparison of superior to inferior, with attendant depreciation of the inferior, could, of course, be taken to absurd extremes. Aelius Theon (first century A.D.) provides a warning about comparing ἀσύγκριτα: πρῶτον δὲ διωρίσθω, ὅτι αἱ συγκρίσεις γίνονται οὐ τῶν μεγάλην πρὸς ἄλληλα διαφορὰν ἐχόντων· γελοῖος γὰρ ὁ ἀπορῶν, πότερον ἀνδρειότερος Ἀχιλλεὺς ἢ Θερσίτης, ἀλλ᾽ ὑπὲρ τῶν ὁμοίων, καὶ περὶ ὧν ἀμφισβητοῦμεν, πότερον δεῖ προθέσθαι, διὰ τὸ μηδεμίαν ὁρᾶν τοῦ ἑτέρου πρὸς τὸ ἕτερον ὑπεροχήν (*Progym.* secc. 231f.; First, let it be laid down that *synkrises* are made not between entities that are greatly different from one another—thus someone posing the question of who was more courageous, Achilles or Thersites, would be ridiculous—but between similar entites, those about which there is some disagreement as to which to prefer because we can perceive no superiority of one over the other).[10]

There are, moreover, warnings against an excess of depreciation in *synkrisis*. Menander Rhetor (late third century A.D.) provides, in connection with the encomium of the emperor, a specific warning against running down his predecessors: ἥξεις δὲ ἐπὶ τὴν τελειοτάτην σύγκρισιν, ἀντεξετάζων τὴν αὐτοῦ βασιλείαν πρὸς τὰς πρὸ αὐτοῦ βασιλείας, οὐ καθαιρῶν ἐκείνας (ἄτεχνον γάρ) ἀλλὰ θαυμάζων μὲν ἐκείνας, τὸ δὲ τέλειον ἀποδιδοὺς τῇ παρούσῃ (secc. 376f.; "You should then proceed to the most complete comparison, examining his reign in comparison with preceding reigns, not disparaging them [that is bad craftsmanship] but admiring them while granting perfection to the present").[11] And in a treatise of Nicolaus the Sophist, a rhetor of the later fifth century, there is a more

8. H. Rabe, *Hermogenis opera* (Leipzig, 1913) = *Rh.*, vol. 6. On Hermogenes *v.* Kennedy (note 5 above), esp. pp. 58f.

9. *V.* sec. 42, H. Rabe, *Aphthonii progymnasmata* (Leipzig 1926) = *Rh.*, vol. 10: Δεῖ δὲ συγκρίνοντας ἢ καλὰ παραθεῖναι χρηστοῖς ἢ φαῦλα φαύλοις ἢ χρηστὰ πονηροῖς ἢ μικρὰ παραθεῖναι τοῖς μείζοσι. καὶ ὅλως ἡ σύγκρισις διπλοῦν ἐγκώμιόν ἐστιν ἢ ψόγος ἐξ ἐγκωμίου καὶ ψόγου συγκείμενος. On Aphthonius *v.* Kennedy (note 5 above), esp. pp. 59–66.

10. L. Spengel, Θέωνος προγυμνάσματα (Leipzig 1854) = *Rh.*, vol. 2. On Theon *v.* Kennedy (note 5 above), esp. pp. 56–58.

11. All citations and translations of Menander Rhetor follow D.A. Russel and N.G. Wilson, *Menander Rhetor* (Oxford 1981). On Menander *v.* Kennedy, (note 5 above), pp. 25f.

general warning against excessive depreciation of the inferior of the two *comparanda*: ἐκεῖνο δὲ χρὴ μόνον προσθεῖναι, ὅτι, εἴτε ἀγαθῶν εἴτε κακῶν ποιούμεθα ἐξέτασιν, δεῖ μὴ καθαιρέσει τῶν ἀντεξεταζομένων, αὔξειν τὰ ἡμέτερα· οὐ γὰρ οὕτω μεγάλα ταῦτα ἐπιδείξομεν, ἀλλὰ τότε ἔσται τὰ ἡμέτερα μεγάλα, ὅταν μεγάλων μείζονα φανῇ (This point alone needs to be added, *sc.* whether we are making an evaluation of good things or bad, it is necessary not to amplify our subjects by disparaging the things being measured against them, for we do not in this way prove that they are great; rather, our subjects will be great when they appear greater than the great).[12]

Some entities, furthermore, should not be submitted to a comparison of relative value, not because they are incomparable, but because circumstances forbid it. In such a case, one might deploy not a σύγκρισις, an evaluative comparison, but an ἀντεξέτασις, a comparison that considers one entity in the light of the other without pronouncing on their relative worth. In his advice on how to manage encomia of the families of bride and groom in a wedding speech, Menander Rhetor offers two methods: either to combine the praise of both or to praise each family separately. If the first method is to be employed, he warns: γένος γένει συνάψεις οὐ συγκρίνων, ἵνα μὴ δοκῇς τὸ μὲν ἐλαττοῦν, τὸ δὲ αὔξειν, ἀλλὰ κατὰ ἀντεξέτασιν προάγων τὸν λόγον, ὅτι ὅμοιον ὁμοίῳ συνάπτεται (sec. 402; "You may link family with family, not making a comparative evaluation, so as not to appear to disparage one family or overvalue the other, but none the less proceeding by a method of comparison, since like is being linked with like"). So, while the school tradition offers a degree of latitude in the variety of types of comparisons, it warns that the effectiveness of *synkrisis* will be vitiated by naïve comparison of ἀσύγκριτα and vituperative treatment of one of the *comparanda*. It also provides a method of comparison that is an alternative to the evaluative comparison of the *synkrisis*.

2. *Synkrisis* in Rhetorical Criticism of the Bible

It would be surprising if patristic authors well trained in rhetoric failed to make use of *synkrisis* in their panegyric speeches on the saints and other encomia. In the introduction to his edition of John Chrysostom's encomia on St. Paul, Auguste Piédagnel has cited examples of *synkrisis* in encomia and panegyrics by Basil the Great, Gregory the Theologian, Gregory of Nyssa, and John Chrysostom.[13] Patristic use of *synkrisis* in invective is not so well documented. Chrysostom provides an example in *Adversus Iu-*

---

12. *V.* p. 61, I. Felten, *Nicolai Progymnasmata* (Leipzig 1913) = *Rh.*, vol. 11. On Nicolaus *v.* Kennedy (note 5 above), esp. pp. 66–69.

13. *V.* p. 29 of A. Piédagnel, *Jean Chrysostome, Panégyriques de s. Paul* (Paris 1982) = *SC,*

daeos, where he compares Christ to other would-be founders of religious movements. Chrysostom apostrophizes his opponents: Τὰ γὰρ πράγματα ἀπὸ συγκρίσεως μάλιστα φαίνονται. Σύγκρινον τοίνυν, ὦ Ἰουδαῖε, καὶ μάθε τῆς ἀληθείας τὴν ὑπεροχήν (sec. 5.3; The facts become especially apparent from comparison. Compare, then, Jew, and learn the superiority of the truth)![14] Although patristic authors continue the traditional use of *synkrisis* in encomium and invective and find for it some perhaps nontraditional uses as well, in this study we want to focus on the multiplex role of *synkrisis* as category of thought and as rhetorical device in biblical exegesis, and most especially, on the uses made of *synkrisis* in comments upon the relationship of the Old Covenant and the New.[15]

Synkrisis as simple comparison appears in patrisitic exegesis as a rudimentary category of thought when exegetes merely point to an instructive use of comparison in biblical texts. But in many comments authors are clearly drawing on their rhetorical training to identify rhetorical *synkrises* in Scripture and are thus applying rhetorical criticism to the elucidation of biblical texts. So, we find the exegetes commenting on the technique and effectiveness of rhetorical *synkrises* they identify in Scripture.[16] Christ's speeches are analyzed in this way. For example, John Chrysostom's comment on Christ's description of the Judgment in Mt. 25.31–46 provides a catalogue of types of *synkrisis* that could come from a handbook of

vol. 300. Kennedy (note 5 above) identifies (pp. 229–36) instances of *synkrisis* in Gregory the Theologian's *epitaphios* for St. Basil.

14. *PG*, vol. 48, col. 887. *V.* the account M.A. Schatkin has provided (pp. 41f., esp. note 139, p. 41) of Chrysostom's use of *synkrisis* in the *Discourse on Blessed Babylas* and *Against the Greeks,* in *Saint John Chrysostom, Apologist* (Washington 1985) = *FOTC,* vol. 73. *V.* also Kennedy (note 5 above), p. 221.

15. Note, *e.g.,* Chrysostom's use of *synkrisis* in scriptural homilies: comparisons of John the Baptist to the Greek Cynic philosophers (*in Mt.* 10.4), of the apostles to the philosphers and to the generals Themistocles and Pericles (*ib.* 33.4), of the Samaritan woman to Nicodemus (*in Ioh.* 32.1), of the Christian martyrs to Socrates (*in 1Cor.* 4.4), and of the apostles to philosophers (*ib.* 35.4). Chrysostom seems to adapt the set-piece *synkrisis* of the schools of rhetoric in his work in defense of monasticism, Σύγκρισις βασιλικῆς δυναστείας καὶ πλούτου καὶ ὑπεροχῆς, πρὸς μόναχον συζῶντα τῇ ἀληθεστάτῃ καὶ κατὰ Χριστὸν φιλοσοφίᾳ; *PG*, vol. 47, coll. 387–92.

16. In addition to texts cited below, *v.* Or., *Sel. in Ps.* on Ps. 44.3; Cyr. Hier., *Cat. ill.* 3.6 (on Mt. 11.11); *Amph.* Icon., *Or.* 8 *(in Zacchaeum)* sec. 2 (on Lk. 19.1f.); [Basil], *Bapt.* 1.2.19 (on 2Cor. 3.6), 2.2 *resp.* (on Mt. 12.6); Chrys., *in Gen.* 14.1 (on Ps. 18.11); *id., in Mt.* 37.3 (on 11.7–9), 58.3 (on 18.6); *id., in Ioh.* 14.3 (on 1.17), 32.1 (on 4.13f.); *id., in Rom.* 11.3 (on 6.14); *id., in 1Cor.* 22.1 (on 9.13f.); *id., in 2Cor.* 7.4 (on 3.16); *id., in Phil.* 11.1 (on 3.7f.); *id., in Heb.* 8.1 (on 5.1–3), 12.2 (on 7.4), 15.1 (on 9.6–8), 16.2 (on 9.23), 17.1f. (on 9.24–10.9), 19.1 (on 10.19–23), 32.1f. (on 12.18–24); *id., Poen.* 6.4 (on Mt. 5.28); Cyr. Alex., *in Ioh.* 1.9 (on 1.16f.); Theod. Mops., on Heb. 9.1f. (K. Staab, *Pauluskommentare aus der griechischen Kirche* [Münster 1933]); Theod. Cyr., *in 2Cor.* on 3.7f.; *id., in Ios. fil. N., prol.; id., in Heb., passim, e.g., argumentum,* on 1.4, 2.17, 3.5f., 6.20.

rhetoric: Ἵνα γὰρ μὴ λέγωσιν, ὅτι Οὐκ εἴχομεν, ἀπὸ τῶν συνδούλων αὐτοὺς καταδικάζει· ὥσπερ τὰς παρθένους ἀπὸ τῶν παρθένων, καὶ τὸν δοῦλον τὸν μεθύοντα καὶ γαστριζόμενον ἀπὸ τοῦ πιστοῦ δούλου, καὶ τὸν τὸ τάλαντον καταχώσαντα ἀπὸ τῶν τὰ δύο προσενεγκάντων, καὶ ἕκαστον τῶν διαμαρτανόντων ἀπὸ τῶν κατωρθωκότων. Καὶ αὕτη ποτὲ μὲν ἐξ ἴσου ἡ σύγκρισις γίνεται, ὡς ἐνταῦθα καὶ ἐπὶ τῶν παρθένων· ποτὲ δὲ ἐκ τοῦ πλεονάζοντος, ὡς ὅταν λέγῃ, Ἄνδρες Νινευῖται ... καὶ ἰδοὺ πλεῖον Σολομῶνος ὧδε· καὶ ἀπὸ τοῦ ἰσάζοντος δὲ πάλιν, ὅτι Αὐτοὶ κριταὶ ὑμῶν ἔσονται· καὶ πάλιν ἀπὸ τοῦ πλεονάζοντος· Οὐκ οἴδατε ὅτι ἀγγέλους κρινοῦμεν; μήτιγε βιωτικά; Καὶ ἐνταῦθα μέντοι ἀπὸ τοῦ ἰσάζοντος· καὶ γὰρ πλουσίους πλουσίοις, και πένητας πένησι παραβάλλει (*in Mt.* 79.2; In order to keep them from saying: "I could not," he condemns them on the basis of their fellow servants, just as the virgins from the virgins, and the drunk and gluttonous servant from the trusty one, and the one who buried the talent from those who returned the two talents, and in each case the sinners from those who behaved rightly. And this comparison sometimes is to equals, as here and in the case of the virgins, but sometimes to one who is superior, as when he says: "The men of Nineveh will rise up ... and behold a greater than Solomon here" [Mt. 12.41f.], but again also to one who is equal, "These will be your judges" [Mt. 12.27], and again to one who excels, "Don't you know that we will judge angels? Not to mention what pertains to this life" [1Cor. 6.3]! And here too, to an equal, for he sets rich alongside rich and poor alongside poor).[17]

But identification of *synkrisis* in biblical passages and comments upon it occur most commonly in typological contexts. Thus, Cyril of Alexandria clarifies the occasion and motivation of Christ's eucharistic discourse in John 6 by pointing out that it constitutes a *synkrisis* comparing the Eucharist to the manna of old: Ἐπειδὴ δὲ δεδόσθαι τὸ μάννα κατὰ τὴν ἔρημον τοῖς πατράσιν αὐτῶν διαβεβαιούμενοι, τὸν ἄρτον ἀληθῶς τὸν ἐξ οὐρανοῦ καταφοιτήσαντα, τουτέστι τὸν Υἱόν, οὐκ ἐδέχοντο, ἀναγκαίαν τοῦ τύπου πρὸς τὸ ἀληθὲς ποιεῖται τὴν σύγκρισιν, ἵν' οὕτως εἰδεῖεν οὐκ ἐκεῖνον ὄντα τὸν ἄρτον τὸν ἐξ οὐρανοῦ, ἀλλ' ὃν ἡ τοῦ πράγματος πεῖρα τοιοῦτον κατὰ φύσιν ὄντα δεικνύει [Jn. 6.48–50](*in Ioh.* 4.2; But because, with their confident assertion of the gift of manna to their fathers in the desert, they did not accept the bread that truly came down from heaven, *i.e.*, the Son, He makes the required *synkrisis* of the type to its fulfillment, so that in this way they might know that not that [the manna], but the One that experience shows to be such by nature, was the bread from heaven).[18]

17. *PG*, vol. 58, coll. 718f.; *v.* similar treatments of Mt. 12.41f. in *in Mt.* 37.4 and *in Gen.* 25.1.
18. *PG*, vol. 73, coll. 560D–61A.

The juxtaposition of Law and Gospel provides the favored site for *synkrisis* in the Pauline letters. A contemporary rhetorical critic[19] who has described 2Cor. 3.7–18 as a *synkrisis* between the dispensations of Moses and Christ was anticipated in this by a number of patristic authors. For example, Didymus of Alexandria writes: Συγκρίνει ἀμφοτέρας τὰς διαθήκας, τὴν καινὴν καὶ παλαιάν, ἑκατέρᾳ μαρτυρῶν τὸ ἐν δόξῃ τῇ ἐκ θεοῦ δεδόσθαι. ὅμως δὲ εἰ καὶ ἀμφότεραι δεδοξασμέναι, ἡ ἐν πνεύματι πλείονα δόξαν ἔχει. εἰ δὲ ἐκ συγκρίσεως πλείω<ν> ἡ τοῦ πνεύματος δόξα, οὐ ψεκτὴ πρὸς ἣν συγκρίνεται· ἀγαθοῦ γὰρ ἀγαθὸν μᾶλλον ἀγαθόν.... πειρᾶται δὲ ἀπόδειξιν ἐπαγαγεῖν τοῦ ἐν δόξῃ εἶναι τὴν τοῦ πνεύματος διακονίαν, ἐκ τοῦ ἐλάττονος ποιούμενος τὴν ἐπιχείρησιν· φησὶ γὰρ· εἰ ἡ *τῆς κατακρίσεως διακονία* τοσαύτην ἔσχε δόξαν ὡς μὴ πάντας τοὺς υἱοὺς Ἰσραὴλ εἰς τὴν τελείωσιν βλέψαι δύνασθαι—μόγις γὰρ κεκαλυμμένην αὐτὴν ἔφερον—, πόσῳ *μᾶλλον ἡ πνευματικὴ διακονία* ἔσται ἐν δόξῃ; ... εἰ τοίνυν τὸ *καταργούμενον* τὸ τέλος ἔχει ἐν δόξῃ, πολλῷ πλέον *τὸ μένον* πλείονα δόξαν ἔχει· ἡ *καταργεῖται* λέξις οὐ λοιδορικῶς κεῖται (He is comparing the two Covenants, the New and the Old, attesting that each was given in divine glory. But though both are glorious, nonetheless that which is spiritual has the greater glory. Although, on the basis of the comparison, the glory of the spiritual convenant is greater, that to which it is compared is not unpraiseworthy, for what is good is more of a good than another good. . . . He is attempting to provide a demonstration that the ministry of the spirit is glorious and undertakes to do so from the lesser. For he is saying: If the "ministry of condemnation" had such great glory that all the children of Israel could not gaze upon its consummation [for they could scarcely bear to when it was veiled], how much more will "the ministry of spirit" be glorious? . . . If, then, that which was made void had a glorious end, even more will that which abides have a greater glory. The word "is voided" is not used abusively).[20] Brief comments in a similar vein have come down from Severian of Gabala (*in 2Cor.* on 3.10)[21] and Theodoret (*in 2Cor.* on 3.7f.), but Chrysostom's comments on this *synkrisis* are more extensive. The following remark on 2Cor. 3.9f. can serve as an example: Ἐνταῦθα καὶ τὴν ὑπεροχὴν, ὅση, δείκνυσι λέγων, ὅτι Ἐὰν συγκρίνω ταύτην ἐκείνῃ, οὐδὲ δόξα ἐστὶν ἡ δόξα τῆς Παλαιᾶς· οὐχ ἁπλῶς τὸ μὴ εἶναι δόξαν κατασκευάζων, ἀλλὰ τῷ τῆς συγκρίσεως λόγῳ· διὸ καὶ ἐπήγαγε, *Τούτῳ τῷ μέρει*· τουτέστι, κατὰ τὸν τῆς συγκρίσεως λόγον. Οὐ μὴν τοῦτο διαβάλλει

---

19. G.A. Kennedy, *New Testament Interpretation through Rhetorical Criticism* (Chapel Hill, N.C./London 1984), p. 89.
20. Staab (note 16 above).
21. *Ib.*

τὴν Παλαιάν, ἀλλὰ καὶ σφόδρα αὐτὴν συνίστησιν· αἱ γὰρ συγκρίσεις ἐπὶ τῶν συγγενῶν εἰώθασι γίνεσθαι (*in 2Cor.* 7.2; Here too he shows how great the superiority is, saying [in effect] "If I compare this one to that, the glory of the Old Covenant is no glory at all!" not maintaining that there was no glory absolutely, but [that there was none] by way of comparison. For this reason also he added "in this respect," that is, according to the rationale of the comparison. In fact, this does not slight the Old Covenant but commends it highly, for comparisons are customarily made between things of the same sort).[22]

As we should expect, Chrysostom identifies instances of *synkrisis* throughout the Epistle to the Hebrews and analyzes this phenomenon.[23] For instance, he comments on the author's deployment of *synkrisis* at the beginning of the comparison of the levitical priesthood and the priesthood of Christ in Heb. 5.1: Ἔδει μὲν γὰρ ἀπὸ τῶν οὐρανίων τὰ ἐπίγεια πιστοῦσθαι, ἀλλ᾽ ὅταν ἀσθενεῖς ὦσιν οἱ ἀκούοντες, τὸ ἐναντίον γίνεται. Τέως οὖν ἃ κοινά ἐστι, τίθησι πρῶτα, καὶ τότε δείκνυσιν ὅ τι ὑπερέχει. Ἡ γὰρ κατὰ σύγκρισιν ὑπεροχὴ οὕτω γίνεται, ὅταν ἐν μὲν τοῖς κοινωνῇ, ἐν δὲ τοῖς ὑπερέχῃ· εἰ δὲ μὴ, οὐκέτι κατὰ σύγκρισιν γίνεται. Πᾶς γὰρ ἀρχιερεὺς ἐξ ἀνθρώπων λαμβανόμενος. Τοῦτο κοινὸν τῷ Χριστῷ. Ὑπὲρ ἀνθρώπων καθίσταται τὰ πρὸς τὸν Θεόν. Καὶ τοῦτο κοινόν. Ἵνα προσφέρῃ δῶρά τε καὶ θυσίας ὑπὲρ τοῦ λαοῦ. Καὶ τοῦτο, οὐχ ὅλον δέ· τὰ δὲ λειπόμενα, οὐκέτι. Μετριοπαθεῖν δυνάμενος τοῖς ἀγνοοῦσι καὶ πλανωμένοις. Ἐνταῦθα λοιπὸν ἡ ὑπεροχή (*in Heb.* 8.1; He should have argued from the things of heaven to prove the things of earth, but when one's hearers are weak, the opposite is done. So, first, he presents the features that are common and, then, shows what is superior. For superiority appears through *synkrisis* in this way, when in some respects there is community but in others superiority; otherwise it is no longer a *synkrisis*. "For every high priest taken from among men." This is in common with Christ. "Is appointed for men for the things that have to do with God." This too is in common. "To offer gifts and sacrifices for the people." This is too, but not completely, and what is left is not at all. "Who can have compassion on those who are ignorant and err." Here finally is the superiority).[24] Likewise, when commenting on the *synkrisis* of the giving of the Law and the Christian dispensation in Heb. 12.18–24, Chrysostom apparently takes upon himself the *persona* of the author of Hebrews to clarify the nature of the *synkrisis*: Οἱ τὰς συγκρίσεις ποιοῦντες, μᾶλλον ἐκεῖνα αἴρουσιν, ἵνα ταῦτα πολλῷ μείζονα δείξωσιν· ἐγὼ δὲ κἀκεῖνα ἡγούμενος θαυμαστὰ (Θεοῦ γὰρ ἔργα, καὶ τῆς αὐτοῦ δυνάμεως

22. *PG,* vol. 61, coll. 443f.; *cf. in 2Cor.* 7.1.   23. *Cf.* note 16 above.
24. *PG,* vol. 63, coll. 67f.

ἀπόδειξις), ὅμως καὶ ταύτῃ κρείττονα καὶ θαυμασιώτερα τὰ ἡμέτερα δείκνυμι (*in Heb.* 32.2; Those who make *synkrises* exalt some things all the more so as to prove that others are much greater. While I regard these past events too as wondrous [for they are God's works and show forth His might], at the same time, by this I show that our dispensation is greater and more wonderful).[25]

The accumulation of comments on the deployment of *synkrisis* in typological passages led to the identification of *synkrisis* as one of the especially typical tropes (τρόποι γενικώτατοι) of Scripture. In the *Isagoge in scripturas sacras,* Adrian (*fl. c.* 425) defines *synkrisis:* "Κατὰ σύγκρισιν", (ὅταν) τὰ πάροντα τοῖς παλαιοῖς ἐκ τῶν ὁμοίων ἐθέλει εἰκάζειν· (ὡς) τὴν τοῦ βαπτίσματος χάριν τῇ ἐρυθρᾷ θαλάσσῃ, καὶ τὴν τῶν θείων μυστηρίων μετάληψιν τῇ τε τοῦ μάννα καὶ τῷ ἐκ πέτρας ὕδατι (sec. 110; "By *synkrisis*," when it wants to compare the present to the past on the basis of their similarities, *e.g.,* the grace of baptism to the Red Sea and partaking of the Divine Mysteries to the manna and the water from rock [1Cor. 10.2–4]).[26]

This sort of commentary appears in a form partly theological and partly rhetorical when exegetes deny that incomparable things are actually being compared. Thus, in a lengthy comment on Heb. 1.4 (τοσούτῳ κρείττων γενόμενος τῶν ἀγγέλων), Cyril of Alexandria explains many apparent comparisons of ἀσύγκριτα in Scripture.[27] An alternative approach is to maintain that the *synkrisis* is made only by some kind of license, as when Chrysostom suggests that Christ is compared to John the Baptist in Mt. 11.11 (Ὁ δὲ μικρότερος ἐν τῇ βασιλείᾳ τῶν οὐρανῶν μείζων αὐτοῦ ἐστι) and goes on to say: Τί οὖν; φησί· κατὰ σύγκρισιν τοῦ Ἰωάννου μείζων ἦν; Ἄπαγε. Οὐδὲ γὰρ Ἰωάννης ὅταν λέγῃ, Ἰσχυρότερός μού ἐστι, συγκρίνων λέγει· οὐδὲ Παῦλος, ὅταν Μωϋσέως μεμνημένος γράφῃ, Πλείονος γὰρ δόξης οὗτος παρὰ Μωϋσῆν ἠξίωται, συγκρίνων γράφει. Καὶ αὐτὸς δὲ, Ἰδοὺ πλέον Σολομῶνος ὧδε, λέγων, οὐχὶ συγκρίνων φησίν. Εἰ δ᾽ ἄρα δοίημεν καὶ κατὰ σύγκρισιν εἰρῆσθαι παρ᾽ αὐτοῦ τοῦτο, οἰκονομικῶς ἐγίνετο διὰ τὴν τῶν ἀκουόντων ἀσθένειαν. ... Καὶ γὰρ καὶ ἡ Παλαιὰ οἶδεν οὕτω διορθοῦν τὰς τῶν πεπλανημένων ψυχάς, τὰ ἀσύγκριτα κατὰ σύγκρισιν παραβάλλουσα· ὡς ὅταν λέγῃ· Οὐκ ἔστιν ὅμοιός σοι ἐν θεοῖς, Κύριε· καὶ πάλιν, Οὐκ ἔστι θεὸς ὡς ὁ Θεὸς ἡμῶν (*in Mt.* 37.2; "What, then," someone says, "is he greater than John by comparison?" Not at all! For when John says, "He is mightier than I," he is not speaking by way of comparison, nor is Paul writing by way of comparison when, mentioning Moses, he writes, "He was counted worthy

25. *Ib.,* col. 221.
26. F. Goessling, *Adrians εἰσαγωγὴ εἰς τὰς θείας γραφάς* (Berlin 1887).
27. *PG*, vol. 74, coll. 953A–57C.

of a greater glory than Moses [Heb. 3.3]." And He himself is not speaking by way of comparison when He says "Behold a greater than Solomon here [Mt. 12.42]." But even if we should grant that this was said by Him by comparison, this was done by way of accommodation to the frailty of His audience. . . . Indeed, the Old Testament also knows how to direct erring souls in this way, by setting incomparable things against one another by comparison, as when it says: "There is none like you among the gods, O Lord [Ps. 86.8]," and "There is no God like our God [Ps. 76.14]").[28] But as we shall see in the application of *synkrisis* to typology, even the denial of comparability is itself a kind of radical *synkrisis*.

3. Hermeneutical and Rhetorical *Synkrisis*

Another type of comparison was employed in exegesis, a philological procedure that clarified an obscure passage by comparing it to a more obvious parallel. Origen is the most explicit about building much of his exegesis upon a particular interpretation of 1Cor. 2.13 (πνευματικοῖς πνευματικὰ συγκρίνοντες), though the methodology is widespread and, indeed, fundamental to patristic exegesis.[29] As Prinzivalli has observed, the method Origen describes is ultimately an application to Scripture of the philological principle especially associated with Aristarchus and eventually formulated by Porphyry: Ὅμηρον ἐξ Ὁμήρου σαφηνίζειν (to clarify Homer from Homer).[30] In a comment on Mt. 13.52 Origen provides a fuller description and doctrinal justification of this method, for which he finds precedent in Christ's practice. This comment is of specific interest to us, for it describes the method itself in terms reminiscent of the discussions of *synkrisis* in rhetorical manuals: Συναχθήσεται δὲ ταῦτα, ἐπὰν καὶ ἀναγινώσκωμεν καὶ γινώσκωμεν καὶ μεμνημένοι τούτων "πνευματικὰ πνευματικοῖς" εὐκαίρως συγκρίνωμεν, οὐ τὰ ἀσύγκριτα πρὸς ἄλληλα συγκρίνοντες, ἀλλὰ συγκριτὰ καὶ ὁμοιότητά τινα ἔχοντα, λέξεως ταὐτὸν

---

28. *PG*, vol. 57, col. 421. *V.* the similar explanation of impossible comparisons in Scripture in *Iud.* 5.3 and *Exp. in Ps.* 117.8f (LXX).

29. For descriptions of Origen's method and citations of texts where he describes or demonstrates his method, *v.* H. de Lubac, *Histoire et esprit: L'intelligence de l'écriture d'après Origène* (Paris 1950), pp. 308–15, esp. p. 309, note 91; H. Crouzel, *Origène et la "connaissance mystique"* (Paris 1961), pp. 400–405; and note 3, p. 203, of R. Girod, *Origène, Commentaire sur l'évangile selon Matthieu*, vol. 1 (Paris 1970): bkk. 10f. = *SC*, vol. 162. M. Pontet, *L'exégèse de S. Augustin prédicateur* (Paris 1944), describes (pp. 152f.) Augustine's application of this method and its background in earlier biblical exegesis.

30. *V.* p. 406 of E. Prinzivalli, *Origene, Omelie sui salmi: Homiliae in psalmos XXXVI-XXXVII-XXXVIII* (Florence 1991) = *Biblioteca patristica*, vol. 18. For the attribution of this exegetical formula to Porphyry, *v.* R. Pfeiffer, *History of Classical Scholarship from the Beginnings to the End of the Hellenistic Age* (Oxford 1968), pp. 225–27.

σημαινούσης καὶ νοημάτων καὶ δογμάτων, ἵν᾽ "ἐπὶ στόματος δύο ἢ τριῶν" ἢ καὶ πλειόνων "μαρτύρων" τῶν ἀπὸ τῆς γραφῆς στήσωμεν καὶ βεβαιώσωμεν "πᾶν ῥῆμα" τοῦ θεοῦ. Καὶ διὰ τούτων δὲ δυσωπητέον τοὺς ὅσον ἐφ᾽ ἑαυτοῖς τὴν θεότητα διαιροῦντας καὶ διακόπτοντας ἀπὸ τῶν παλαιῶν τὰ καινά, ὡς μακρὰν τυγχάνοντας τῆς πρὸς τὸν οἰκοδεσπότην ὁμοιώσεως, προφέροντα ἐκ τοῦ θησαυροῦ αὐτοῦ καινὰ καὶ παλαιά. . . . Δύναται δὲ καὶ ἁπλούστερον Ἰησοῦς ὁ οἰκοδεσπότης προφέρειν ἐκ τοῦ θησαυροῦ αὐτου καινὰ μὲν τὴν εὐαγγελικὴν διδασκαλίαν, παλαιὰ δὲ τὴν σύγκρισιν τῶν ἀπὸ νόμου καὶ προφητῶν παραλαμβανομένων ῥητῶν, ὧν παραδείγματα ἔστιν ἐν τοῖς εὐαγγελίοις εὑρεῖν (*in Mt.* 10.15; But these [materials from NT and OT] will be brought together when we read and recognize and, mindful [of the scriptural injunction], we compare in an appropriate way "things spiritual with spiritual," not comparing with one another things that are incomparable but things that are comparable and have a certain resemblence when the text has the same meaning both in thought and in doctrine, so that "by the mouth of two or three" or more "witnesses" from Scripture, we may establish and confirm "every word" [2Cor. 13.1] of God. Therefore, we must also confound those who, to the extent they can, divide deity and sunder the New from the Old, for they are far removed from likeness to the householder who brings forth "from his treasure things new and old" [Mt. 13.52]. . . . But in the more basic understanding Jesus the Householder can also bring "forth from his treasure new things," the gospel teaching, "and old," the comparison of texts taken from the law and the prophets, and one can find examples of this in the gospels).[31] Though Origen is concerned here with the juxtaposition and comparison of Old Testament to New Testament texts, the method may also involve the comparison of passages taken solely from the New Testament.[32] But the comparative approach based on 1Cor. 2.13 applies particularly well to the relationship of the Old and the New Testaments, and it came to be applied specifically to typology, to the relationship of Old Testament types to their fulfillments.

Both rhetorical *synkrisis* and the comparative philological approach justified by appeal to 1Cor. 2.13 figure prominently in discussions of the relationships of types (τύπος) and their fulfillments (ἀλήθεια). Here the predominance of one or another sort of *synkrisis* will depend on one's view of the relationship of the type to its fulfillment and of their relative value. If the typology emphasizes the corroboration or clarification of the New Convenant from the Old or the unity of the Old Testament and the New,

31. R. Girod (note 29 above).
32. *V., e.g., in Ioh.* 20.41.381–42.388 (on Jn. 8.52f.).

the *synkrisis,* actual or implicit, will amount to a parallel presentation of common features of the type and its fulfillment without prejudice to the type. If *synkrisis* of type and fulfillment is undertaken to commend, or heighten appreciation for, the fulfillment, the *synkrisis,* if managed correctly, will extol the fulfillment without disparaging the type. But if the goal of the comparison is to assert the incomparability of type and fulfillment or the supersession of type by fulfillment, the *synkrisis* will be of the variety combining encomium and invective.

As one might expect, 1Cor. 2.13 is a text enabling the *synkrisis* of type and fulfillment with a view to corroboration and clarification. A comment of Theodore of Mopsuestia on this text emphasizes the corroborative function of comparison, though it is not clear, due perhaps to the fragmentary state of his comment, what Theodore has in mind as the *comparanda.*[33] Severian of Gabala's comments on the same passage are similarly fragmentary and confusing as to the specific nature of the *comparanda,* but it is clear that he views the comparison of later and earlier revelations as both interpretative and confirmatory.[34] We are on firmer ground with John Chrysostom's comment on 1Cor. 2.13, for he emphasizes the alignment of types to their fulfillment as the proper mode of demonstration in connection with features of the life of Christ: Τί δέ ἐστι, *Πνευματικοῖς πνευματικὰ συγκρίνοντες;* Ὅταν πνευματικὸν καὶ ἄπορον ᾖ, ἀπὸ τῶν πνευματικῶν τὰς μαρτυρίας ἄγομεν. Οἷον λέγω, ὅτι ἀνέστη ὁ Χριστὸς, ὅτι ἀπὸ Παρθένου ἐγεννήθη. Παράγω μαρτυρίας καὶ τύπους καὶ ἀποδείξεις, τοῦ Ἰωνᾶ τὴν ἐν τῷ κήτει διατριβὴν, καὶ τὴν μετὰ ταῦτα ἀπαλλαγὴν, τῶν στειρῶν τοὺς τοκετοὺς, τῆς Σάρρας, τῆς Ῥεβέκκας καὶ τῶν λοιπῶν, τὴν ἐν τῷ παραδείσῳ τῶν δένδρων βλάστην γεγενημένην, οὐ σπερμάτων καταβληθέντων, οὐχ ὑετῶν κατενεχθέντων, οὐκ αὔλακος ἀνατμηθείσης. Τὰ γὰρ μέλλοντα διεπλάττετο καὶ διεγράφετο, ὡς ἐν σκιᾷ, τοῖς προτέροις, ἵνα πιστευθῇ ταῦτα παραγενόμενα. . . . Οὕτω πνευματικοῖς πνευματικὰ συγκρίνω, καὶ οὐδαμοῦ χρείαν ἔχω τῆς ἔξωθεν σοφίας, οὐδὲ λογισμῶν οὐδὲ παρασκευῶν (*in 1Cor. 7.4;* But what does "Comparing spiritual things to spiritual" mean? Whenever a spiritual matter is problematic, we adduce evidence from spiritual matters. As, for example, when I say "Christ is risen," "He was

---

33. Staab (note 16 above).

34. ὅμως οὐχ εὑρίσκομεν λογισμοῖς τὰ ἀποκαλυφθέντα ἡμῖν καλλωπίσαι, ἀλλὰ πνευματικοῖς πνευματικὰ συγκρίνομεν, ὅταν ἡ δευτέρα ἀποκάλυψις ἑρμηνεία καὶ σαφήνεια γένηται τοῦ πρώτου διδάγματος ἢ ὁράματος ἢ θαύματος· τὰ γὰρ δεύτερα τοῖς πρώτοις συγκρίνονται καὶ τὰ αὐτὰ εὑρίσκονται. πληροφορίαν μεγίστην λαμβάνομεν τῆς ἀληθείας ἐκ τῆς συμφωνίας; Staab (note 16 above). Cf. Cyr. Alex., *Explan. ad Rom.* 3.31, which, while not invoking 1Cor. 2.13, suggests the clarification or enhancement of a type by means of its fulfillment: Οὐκ ἀναιρεῖ δὲ τοὺς τύπους ἡ ἀλήθεια, καθίστησι δὲ ἐμφανεστέρους; *PG,* vol. 74, col. 780D.

born of a virgin," I bring forward as evidence types and proofs: Jonah's time in the whale, his subsequent deliverance; births from barren women, Sarah, Rebecca, and the rest; the growth of trees in Paradise without the sowing of seed, without the fall of rain, without the cutting of a furrow. For the things that were to come were modeled and depicted by the earlier things, as in a sketch, so that they would be believed when they did happen. . . . Thus do I compare spiritual things to spiritual, and nowhere have I need of alien wisdom, or arguments, or rhetorical practice).[35] Theodoret makes a similar point when commenting on this passage, but uses the sacraments and their types as his example: "Πνευματικοῖς πνευματικὰ συγκρίνοντες." Ἔχομεν γὰρ τῆς Παλαιᾶς Διαθήκης τὴν μαρτυρίαν, καὶ δι' ἐκείνης τὴν Καινὴν βεβαιοῦμεν· πνευματικὴ γὰρ κἀκείνη. Καὶ γὰρ δεῖξαι βουλόμενοι τῶν ἡμετέρων μυστηρίων τοὺς τύπους, τὸν ἀμνὸν εἰς μέσον φέρομεν, καὶ τὸ αἷμα τὸ ταῖς φλιαῖς ἐπιχριόμενον, καὶ τὴν τῆς θαλάττης διάβασιν, καὶ τῆς πέτρας τὰ νάματα, καὶ τοῦ μάννα τὴν χορηγίαν, καὶ μύρια τοιαῦτα, καὶ διὰ τῶν τύπων δείκνυμεν τὴν ἀλήθειαν (in 1Cor. on 2.13; "Comparing spiritual things to spiritual." For we have the testimony of the Old Testament, and through it we confirm the New, for the former too is spiritual. And when we wish to show the types of our mysteries, we bring forward the lamb and the blood smeared on the doorposts, and the crossing of the Red Sea and the streams from the rock, and the provision of manna, and countless such things, and by means of types we demonstrate the fulfillment).[36]

But the very alignment of type and fulfillment for clarification or corroboration may invite evaluative comparison, for elements of similarity and differentiation are built into the relationship of type to fulfillment. Thus, when he presents the exegetical formula τύπων καὶ ἀληθείας . . . συγγένειαν καὶ διάκρισιν,[37] Gregory the Theologian presupposes that one aspect of the διάκρισις is the superiority of fulfillment over type (Or. 2.97).[38] Synkrisis of type and fulfillment tends, quite predictably, to go in one of two ways: praise of the fulfillment amplified by comparison to the type, but a comparison managed with due respect for the type, or an exaltation of the fulfillment at the expense of the type in a synkrisis that amounts to a

35. PG, vol. 61, col. 59. Chrysostom's comments are echoed in the commentaries on 1Cor. 2.13 of Oecumenius and Theophylact.

36. PG, vol. 82, col. 244D.

37. J. Bernardi, Grégoire de Nazianze, Discours 1–3 (Paris 1978) = SC, vol. 247.

38. This relationship is clearly described by Chrysostom in his homily (Apostol. dict.) on 1Cor. 10.1–10, where he emphasizes (ch. 4) the kinship (συγγένεια) of Old and New Testaments and the prophetic, corroborative role of types but also gives an evaluative assessment of the relationship of type and fulfillment; v. PG, vol. 51, col. 248.

combination of encomium and invective. As Erasmus observed, Chrysostom's works abound with *synkrisis*,[39] and, as his remarks on St. Paul's use of *synkrisis* lead one to expect, Chrysostom, in keeping with his encomiastic project, tends to present the types in positive terms: Φρικτὰ καὶ φοβερὰ τὰ μυστήρια, καὶ πολὺ τὸ βάθος ἔχοντα. Εἰ δὲ ἐν τοῖς τύποις οὕτω φοβερά, πολλῷ μᾶλλον ἐν τῇ ἀληθείᾳ (*in Eph.* 23.2; Mysteries awesome and dread and possessed of great depth of meaning. But if they were so dread in the types, how much more so in their fulfillment)?[40]

Negative *synkrisis* involving invective seems to be triggered by a perceived or potential misappropriation of types by religious adversaries. For example, in Chapter 14 of *De spiritu sancto* St. Basil deals with the claim of the Pneumatomachians that the practice of baptizing in the Spirit does not indicate that the Spirit is God, because, some "were baptized unto Moses" (εἰς τὸν Μωϋσῆν ἐβαπτίσθησαν, 1Cor. 10.2). Basil counters by recourse to the ultimate *synkrisis*, denial of the comparability of types and fulfillments: Τί οὖν; ἐπειδὴ τυπικῶς εἰς Μωϋσῆν ἐβαπτίσθησαν, διὰ τοῦτο μικρὰ ἡ τοῦ βαπτίσματος χάρις; Οὕτω μὲν οὖν οὐδ᾽ ἂν ἄλλο τι μέγα εἴη τῶν ἡμετέρων, εἴπερ τὸ ἐν ἑκάστῳ σεμνὸν τοῖς τύποις προδιαβάλλοιμεν.... Ταὐτὸν τοίνυν ποιεῖ καὶ ἐπὶ τοῦ βαπτίσματος ὁ τῇ σκιᾷ συγκρίνων τὴν ἀλήθειαν, καὶ τοῖς τύποις παραβάλλων τὰ παρ᾽ αὐτῶν σημαινόμενα, καὶ διὰ Μωϋσέως καὶ τῆς θαλάσσης πᾶσαν ὁμοῦ διασύρειν τὴν εὐαγγελικὴν οἰκονομίαν ἐπιχειρῶν.... Τί οὖν συγκρίνεις τὰ βαπτίσματα, ὧν ἡ προσηγορία μόνη κοινή, ἡ δὲ τῶν πραγμάτων διαφορὰ τοσαύτη, ὅση ἂν γένοιτο ὀνείρου πρὸς τὴν ἀλήθειαν καὶ σκιᾶς καὶ εἰκόνων πρὸς τὰ κατ᾽ οὐσίαν ὑφεστηκότα (*Sp. s.* 14.32: What then? Because they were baptized unto Moses in a type, is the gift of baptism for that reason a small one? In this way nothing else of ours would be great, if, that is, by means of the types we create a prejudice against what is sublime in each of them.... This is

---

39. *Ep.* 1800, ll. 174–79: *Metaphoris et collationibus, quoniam plurimum conducunt et ad lucem et ad iucunditatem orationis, frequenter vtitur; in quibus inueniendis quidem mirus est, sed multo mirabilior artifex in tractandis. Tractantur autem ex circunstantiis, a pari, maiore et minore. Hic mirum quos gradus inuenit vel deprimendi vel exaggerandi* (P.S. Allen and H.M. Allen, *Opus epistolarum Des. Erasmi Roterodami*, vol. 6 [Oxford 1926]: 1525–27). For examples of *synkrisis* of type and fulfillment in Chrysostom's works, *v. in Mt.* 1.1: giving of Law and descent of Holy Spirit; *in Ioh.* 14, *passim*: old and new dispensations; 26.2: baptism and exodus; 46.3: blood of Christ and its types; *in 1Cor.* 22.1: apostles and levitical priesthood; 23.2f.: sacraments and their types; 25.4: Paul and OT figures; *in 2Cor.* 7.4: Old and New Covenant; 25.3: Paul's battle with the devil and David's with Goliath; *in Eph.* 23.2: Eucharist and Passover; *in Heb.* 27.3: Joshua (Jesus) and Moses; *Iud.* 3.6: Passover and salvation through Jesus Christ; *Cat. ad illum.* (series tertia) hom. 3, ad neophytos (= CPG, #4467) secc. 23–25: exodus and baptism; *De statuis* hom. 2.9: Christ and Elijah. Many of these are amplifications of *synkrises* he has pointed out in Scripture.

40. *PG*, vol. 62, col. 165.

just what is done in the case of baptism by one who compares the fulfillment to the shadow, and places side by side with the types the things signified by them, and by means of Moses and the Sea undertakes to disparage
the entire economy of the Gospel. . . . Why then do you compare baptisms
that have nothing but the name in common, but, as realities, have as great
a difference between them as the difference between a dream and reality,
between a sketched likeness and things that have real substance)?[41] Basil's
overall view of the types is not nearly so negative as these words would
suggest. In the same chapter he provides a classic account of typology, and
in his *Protreptic to Baptism* he deploys a triple *synkrisis* comparing Christian baptism to the baptism of John (ch. 1), the baptism of Moses (ch. 2),
and the experience of Elijah (ch. 3).

But Basil's words suggest a radical depreciation of types that would
turn a *synkrisis* of type and fulfillment virtually into the "invective composed of an encomium and an invective" mentioned by Aphthonius (*v.* p.
24 above). Such invectives against the types occur infrequently but are
found in texts that emphasize the abrogation of the types of the Old Law
by the coming of the fulfillment of the New. In this approach, most commonly found in anti-Jewish passages in paschal homilies, the types are
presented not as corroborating their fulfillment but as annihilated by it.[42]

The *Peri pascha* of Melito of Sardis is notorious for this technique of invective. Melito argues for the supersession of Judaism by Christianity, and
urges that the types were emptied of their value and significance by the
coming of their fulfillments.[43] Melito has no extended or very explicit
synkrisis, but after what seems to have been a short *synkrisis* of types and
fulfillments in the badly damaged section 4, he manages very adroitly
through implied *synkrisis* in sections 6f. to develop the theme of supersses-
sion: Ἡ γοῦν τοῦ προβάτου σφαγὴ / καὶ ἡ τοῦ πάσχα πομπὴ / καὶ ἡ τοῦ νόμου γραφὴ / εἰς Χριστὸν Ἰησοῦν κεχώρηκεν, / δι' ὃν τὰ πάντα ἐν τῷ πρεσ-
βυτέρῳ νόμῳ ἐγένετο, / μᾶλλον δὲ ἐν τῷ νέῳ λόγῳ. / Καὶ γὰρ ὁ νόμος λόγος
ἐγένετο / καὶ ὁ παλαιὸς καινός . . . / καὶ ἡ ἐντολὴ χάρις, / καὶ ὁ τύπος ἀλήθεια, / καὶ ὁ ἀμνὸς υἱός, / καὶ τὸ πρόβατον ἄνθρωπος, / καὶ ὁ ἄνθρωπος θεός
(Thus the slaughter of the sheep and the rite of the Passover and the inscription of the Law had their outcome in Christ Jesus, for whose sake all
things were done in the earlier Law, and even more so in the new Gospel.

41. *V.* B. Pruche, *Basile de Césarée, Sur le Saint-Esprit,* 2nd ed. (Paris 1968) = *SC,* vol. 17bis.

42. S. Czerwik understates (p. 79) this phenomenon in *Homilia paschalis apud patres
usque ad saeculum quintum* (Rome 1961).

43. For a recent analysis of interpretations of Melito's anti-Jewish bias *v.* M.S. Taylor,
Anti-Judaism and Early Christian Identity: A Critique of the Scholarly Consensus (Leiden
1995), pp. 65–73.

For the Law became the Word, and the old became new, and commandment grace, and type fulfillment, and the lamb a son, and the sheep a man, and the man God).[44] After reviewing the Passover narrative, Melito proceeds with his famous analogy that likens the type to the preliminary sketch of a monumental sculpture and the fulfillment to the completed work. He concludes the typological section of his homily with the assertion that the type has been voided by its fulfillment: ὁ τύπος ἐκενώθη / παραδοὺς τῇ ἀληθείᾳ τὴν δύναμιν ... / καὶ ὁ λαὸς ἐκενώθη ... / καὶ ὁ τύπος ἐλύθη / τοῦ κυρίου φανερωθέντος, / καὶ σήμερον γέγονεν τά ποτε τίμια ἄτιμα / τῶν φύσει τιμίων φανερωθέντων (secc. 42f.; the type was made void surrendering its reality to the fulfillment ... and the people was made void ... and the type was undone at the manifestation of the Lord, and today things once of value have become valueless at the revelation of things really of value).

Not all paschal homilies contain this depreciation of types for which Melito's homily is a byword. The influential third-century pseudo-Hippolytan paschal homily juxtaposes types and fulfillments in a short *synkrisis* that uses the common pattern ἐκεῖ/ἐνταῦθα: ἀμνὸς ἐξ ἀγέλης ἐκεῖ, ἐνταῦθα ἀμνὸς ἐξ οὐρανῶν (2.2; There a lamb from the flock, here a lamb from heaven), and concludes with the rhetorical question: Πῶς οὖν οὐ τὴν καθόλου σωτηρίαν τῶν ὅλων ἐπαγγέλλεται τὰ ἔργα, ὧν καὶ μόνοι οἱ τύποι εἰσι σωτήριοι (3.1; How, then, will they not proclaim the total salvation of all, the realities [*sc.* the fulfillments] whose types alone were salvific)?[45] Later the author asserts the abiding significance of the types rightly understood and even includes a brief encomium of the Mosaic Law.[46]

But later authors of paschal homilies imitated Melito's anti-Jewish tone and dismissal of the types. In a paschal homily often cited for reviving Melito's analogy of model-statue to type-fulfillment, Proclus of Constantinople (d. 446 or 447) offers an extensive juxtaposition of types and fulfillment, and concludes: Οὐ συνῆκαν οἱ δείλαιοι [the Jews], ὅτι μέχρις τότε οἱ τυπικοὶ χρησμοί, ἕως φανῇ ἡ ἀλήθεια. ... πρὶν μὲν φανερωθῆναι τοῖς ἀνθρώποις τὴν ἀλήθειαν, καλῶς τοὺς τύπους ἐφύλαττον, μετὰ δὲ τὸ φανῆναι τὸν Κύριον ἡμῶν Ἰησοῦν Χριστὸν ... μάτην τοὺς τύπους κρατοῦσιν (*Or.*

---

44. O. Perler, *Méliton de Sardes sur la Pâque et fragments* (Paris 1966) = SC, vol. 123.

45. This homily is *CPG*, #4611; *v.* P. Nautin, *Homélies Pascales*, vol. 1 (Paris 1950): *Une homélie inspirée du traité sur la pâque d'Hippolyte* = SC, vol. 27. The formula ἐκεῖ ... ἐνταῦθα is found, *e.g.*, in Chrys., *in Mt.* 43.3 (*PG*, vol. 57, col. 459), Proclus, *Or.* 14.2 (*PG*, vol. 65, coll. 796D–97B).

46. Promising he will examine the hidden mysteries of the divinely given Passover Law, the author declares: τὴν μὲν ἀλήθειαν τῶν γεγραμμένων οὐκ ἀναιροῦντες, τὴν δὲ ἀκρίβειαν τῶν μυστηρίων διὰ τῶν τύπων θεωροῦντες (6.1). The phrase Νόμος ὁ διὰ Μωϋσέως runs like a refrain through sec. 9, which contains the praise of the Law.

14.2; The wretches did not understand that the oracular types were temporary, until the fulfillment should appear . . . [the analogy of the statue].
Until the fulfillment was manifested to humankind, they did well to keep
the types, but after the manifestation of our Lord Jesus Christ . . . they are
unreasonable to maintain the types).[47]

The first of the set of paschal homilies called τὰ σαλπίγγια ("The Little
Trumpets") opens with a *synkrisis* of Jewish and Christian Pascha, and
proceeds to a virtual invective against the types as compared to their fulfillment.[48] The same author, in the second homily, after listing some types
from Exodus, asserts that they have meaning only in Christ and are mean-
ingless in themselves: πάντα γὰρ ταῦτα ἐν Χριστῷ καὶ τῷ τοῦ Χριστοῦ
πάθει συνίσταται καὶ ἀληθῆ καὶ ἀναγκαῖα, καὶ καθ᾽ ἑαυτὰ λόγον ἔχειν οὐδέ-
να δύναται (sec. 1; For all these, as being real and necessary, have their reality in Christ and in the Passion of Christ and in themselves they can have
no meaning).[49]

The author of the fifth homily in this series allows for a connection of
the types with Christ but regards the types manifested in Exodus as mere
shadows of the fulfillments in the Christian dispensation.[50] Furthermore,
he considers the types in themselves unremarkable, paralleled by events
celebrated by the gentiles as well: miraculous cures, liberation from tyranny, migrations, founding of cities, victories, *etc.* Event by event, he sees the
real meaning of the events of Exodus in their Christian fulfillment, and
concludes by asserting that type and fulfillment are ultimately ἀσύγκριτα:
Ὁρᾷς, ὅτι τὸ πάσχα τὸ σὸν οὐδὲ σύγκρισιν ἔχει πρὸς τὸ Ἰουδαϊκόν, ἀλλ᾽
ὁμοίωσιν αὐτοῦ τὴν σκιοειδῆ μόνον εἶχεν ἐκεῖνο (sec.2; Do you see that
there is no comparison between your Pascha and the Jewish one? Rather,
the latter had only a sketch-like similarity to the former)?[51]

The pathology of religious polemic reveals itself in mistaken rhetoric
and mistaken exegesis. In rhetoric, as Nicolaus the Sophist and Menander
Rhetor warned, destructive invective against one of the *comparanda* of a

47. *PG*, vol. 65, col. 797C–D.

48. Ps-Chrys., *In s. Pascha* 1 (= *CPG*, #4606) 1–5. P. Nautin, (*Trois homélies dans la tradition d'Origène* [Paris 1953] = *SC*, vol. 36), suggests (pp. 26–30) that the author of the first
three of these homilies was writing in an Alexandrian theological climate after the conflict
over Arianism and before the emergence of Nestorianism.

49. The second homily is *CPG*, #4607.

50. Ps.-Chrys., *In s. Pascha* 5 (= *CPG*, #4610) 1: Ἐν Ἰουδαίοις οἱ τύποι, παρ᾽ ἡμῖν δὲ ἡ
ἀλήθεια. . . . Οὐδὲ γὰρ τὰ Ἰουδαίων ἀλλότρια Χριστοῦ, τυπικὴν δὲ καὶ σκιώδη τὴν πρὸς
Χριστὸν εἶχεν οἰκείωσιν· ἐτηρεῖτο δὲ τῇ κατὰ πρόσωπον αὐτοῦ παρουσίᾳ ἡ τελείωσις, καὶ ἡ
σαφὴς αὐτοψία τῶν πραγμάτων, ὅτε καὶ ἡ αὐτοψία τοῦ βασιλέως; *PG*, vol. 59, coll. 732f.

51. *Ib.*, col. 734. *Cf.* from much later, the succinct verse of Symeon the New Theologian,
Hymn 51.71: Πῶς ὅλως ἔσται σύγκρισις σκιᾶς καὶ ἀληθείας; J. Koder, *Syméon le nouveau
théologien, Hymnes 41–58* (Paris 1973) = *SC*, vol. 196.

synkrisis ultimately diminishes the subject of praise. Disparaging the types is ἄτεχνον (*v.* pp. 24f. above). At the same time, voiding the types of their proper value, meaning, and significance makes hermeneutic *synkrisis* impossible, for it prevents the types from being propaedeutic, explanatory, and corroborative of their fulfillment. This too, exegetically speaking, is ἄτεχνον. Fortunately, the abusive deployment of *synkrisis* in typology was limited. More often we find that hermeneutic as well as rhetorical *synkrisis*—both derived from the study of public speaking and literature—were effectively applied to the pastoral and scholarly enterprise of the exposition of Scripture.

THREE

The Early Irish Interpretation of
the Infancy Narratives

⁜

Joseph F. Kelly

THOMAS HALTON has spent his professional career elucidating the works of the Church Fathers. His contributions have included not only the explication of texts and themes but service—as editor and bibliographer—to other scholars. He stands in a long tradition of Irish (and later American) patristic scholarship. In this essay, I will examine how his predecessors, the first Irish Christian scholars, both followed the Fathers and made their own contributions to the Christian explication of the gospel infancy narratives.

Patrick and other missionaries brought the Christian faith to Ireland in the fifth century. Little is known about the first century of Irish Christianity, but by the late sixth century Christianity had not only become the dominant form of Irish religious life; it was also changing intellectual life.[1] The Irish achievement was considerable, even this early. It would be no exaggeration to say that the Irishman Columbanus (ca. 540–615) was the most learned Latin Christian of his day. This learned tradition flourished for three centuries after Columbanus.[2]

On the other hand, the Irish did know that many great scholars and theologians had gone before them, men such as Augustine, Ambrose, and Jerome, who were known for sanctity as well as learning. The Irish welcomed the learning of the holy Fathers, especially for the help it could afford in interpreting Scripture; they studied the Fathers primarily as bib-

---

1. *Cf.* Liam De Paor, *Saint Patrick's World: The Christian Culture of Ireland's Apostolic Age* (Notre Dame, Ind./London 1993) for an account of early Christian Ireland.

2. For a valuable catalogue of Irish and other Celtic writings from the early Middle Ages, *v.* M. Lapidge and R. Sharpe, *A Bibliography of Celtic-Latin Literature 400–1200* (Dublin 1985).

lical commentators. For most Irish scholars were monks, who devoted their lives to understanding and living the Scriptures; like the Fathers, they wished to combine doctrine and sanctity.[3] By the late sixth century the Irish had begun producing their own exegetical works, and by the end of the ninth century these had grown to a considerable body of literature. Members of the Western Church, the Irish exegetes wrote in Latin; their collective works are referred to as Hiberno-Latin exegesis.

The study of Hiberno-Latin exegesis has its roots in a 1954 essay by the German scholar Bernhard Bischoff and is thus a comparatively young discipline.[4] Although considerable progress has been made in the decades since Bischoff's article, many significant Hiberno-Latin exegetical texts still await editors.[5] Thus, one cannot at this time speak with confidence about Irish schools of thought, although some texts are clearly related. In this overview of the Irish interpretations of the infancy narratives I shall draw material from a variety of sources, both published and unpublished, that are linked primarily by the Irishness of their authors.

By the time the Irish undertook exegesis, some basic points had long been established. First, it was agreed that the gospels offered a reliable historical account of Jesus' life, including his birth. No less a figure than John Chrysostom had claimed that the exact date of Christ's birth could be verified from census records made by Augustus and kept in Rome.[6] Second, it was generally held that, although the accounts were historical, they contained far more than history. Non-historical exegesis went under a variety of names—figurative, spiritual, allegorical—but, whatever the name, this exegesis sought a meaning beyond the historical.[7] This procedure, for which the monks could find precedent in the works of almost all the patristic figures as well as in those of great contemporary exegetes like Bede, offered great theological and spiritual possibilities. Third, Christmas was a well-established feast by the early Middle Ages.[8] Scholars had studied the first two chapters of Matthew and Luke since the second century, but the

---

3. The greatest authority on Irish monasticism, John Ryan wrote, "It would be difficult to overestimate the place which the Bible held in the monastic system of education"; *Irish Monasticism: Origins and Early Development* (London, *etc.* 1931; rpt. Ithaca, N.Y. 1972), p. 379.

4. "Wendepunkte in der Geschichte der lateinischen Exegese im Frühmittelatler," *SE* 6 (1954), pp. 189–281; reprinted with some addition in Bischoff's *Mittelalterliche Studien: Ausgewählte Aufsätze zur Schriftkunde und Literaturgeschichte*, vol. 1 (Munich 1966), pp. 205–73.

5. Lapidge and Sharpe (note 2 above) chronicle some of this progress. *V.* also J.F. Kelly, "A Catalogue of Hiberno-Latin Biblical Commentaries, I," *Tr.* 44 (1988), pp. 537–71; and "A Catalogue of Hiberno-Latin Biblical Commentaires, II," *ib.* 45 (1989–90), pp. 393–434.

6. *Diem natal.* sec. 2, *PG,* vol. 49, col. 353; *cf.* S.K. Roll, *Toward the Origins of Christmas* (Kampen 1995), p. 193.

7. *Cf.* M. Simonetti, *Profilo storico dell'esegesi patristica* (Rome 1981), esp. pp. 37–52.

8. Roll (note 6 above), *passim.*

importance of Christmas in the liturgical year gave that study added impetus.

I will concentrate on the birth story rather than the associated material, such as the Annunciation and Visitation (Lk. 1.26–56), which generally received less attention from the Irish. This is partly because the Irish commented very frequently upon Matthew's gospel and less so on Luke's.[9] The Irish had a fascination with genealogies, and their fondness for Matthew's infancy narrative derived in part from its genealogy. Indeed, it was not uncommon for the Irish to comment upon the genealogy apart from the rest of the text.[10]

The Irish exegetes all commented upon Jesus' birth from a virgin. Since this was historically true, the thaumaturgical element presented no problem, and the exegetes concentrated upon the theological significance of the event. In general, the Irish followed Jerome's *Commentarii in Matheum,* which listed four answers to the question of why Christ was conceived after, rather than before, Mary's espousal to Joseph (on 1.18).[11]

The Irish accepted that Mary became pregnant when the Holy Spirit overshadowed her, but they wondered how this occurred. Many exegetes simply overlooked the question, but those who did write about it, including an eighth-century commentator on Luke from an Irish circle near Salzburg[12] and a contemporary Matthean commentator, favored *conceptio per aurem.*[13] The Irish also knew the famous formula *ante partum, in partu, post partum,* which appears in an eighth-century collection of homilies from northern Italy[14] and the late eighth-century *Liber de ortu et obitu patrum,* a treatise on biblical figures falsely ascribed to Isidore of Seville.[15]

The question of Mary's perpetual virginity arose in the interpretation of Mt. 1.25. Here Jerome's commentary reads *peperit filium suum primo-*

9. *Cf.* my "Catalogue, II" (note 5 above), #66–87, #91–93.

10. No one has yet identified the source of this fascination or explained why the Irish had rather little interest in Luke's genealogy (3.23–38). The first great genealogical treatise is that of Aileran the Wise (died in 665), now brilliantly edited by Aidan Breen, *Ailerani Interpretatio mystica et moralis progenitorum domini Iesv Christi* (Dublin 1995); *v.* especially the remarkable indices of patristic references, pp. 111–35 and 137–62.

11. D. Hurst and M. Andriaen, *S. Hieronymi presbyteri Commentariorum in Matheum libri IV* in *S. Hieronymi presbyteri opera,* part 1.7 (Turnhout 1969) = *CChr.SL,* vol. 77.

12. On 1.28; J.F. Kelly, *Commentarius in Lucam* in *Scriptores hiberniae minores,* part 2 (Turnhout 1974) = *CChr.SL,* vol. 108C. Henceforth, I shall refer to this work as the Salzburg commentary.

13. *Commentarius in Mattheum* in *Cod. Vind.* 940, fol. 24v; *cf.* my "Catalogue, II" (note 5 above), #77. Henceforth I refer to this as the Vienna Matthean commentary.

14. Verona, Bibl. capit. LXVII (64), fol. 38v; *cf.* Lapidge and Sharpe (note 5 above), #804.

15. *Virgo ante partum, virgo in partu, virgo post partum,* sec. 36; *PL,* vol. 83, col. 1285C. For this text *cf.* Lapidge and Sharpe (note 2 above), #780.

genitum. The issue of whether Mary had other children after Jesus interested the Irish, but probably because it had also interested Jerome, not because it was a serious theological issue among them. Paraphrasing Jerome's comment on Mt. 1.25, a late eighth-century Matthean commentary from southern Bavaria treats the question in a catalogue of heretical opinions: *In hoc loco quidam perversissime suspicantur et dicunt: Ideo primogenitum nominasse eo quod beata Maria alios postea filios habuisset* (For this verse [Mt. 1.25] some very perversely claim that if he [Jesus] is called her firstborn, then she must have had other sons). The interpreter linked this to the question of generation in the Trinity (*ingenitus*) and quickly turned to the heretics who claimed that the Spirit is inferior to the Father and Son. But there is more: *Errant quidam in hoc loco et dicunt: Si Filius de Spiritu Sancto et Maria virgine natus est, ergo Spiritus Pater est Filii* (They err who say for this verse, "If the Son was born from the Holy Spirit and the virgin Mary, therefore the Spirit is the Father of the Son"). Although this spirited defense of orthodoxy wanders at times, it does show a solid knowledge of patristic teaching concerning Christ's birth and the nature of the Trinity.[16] No other early Irish commentary offers so thorough a discussion of *primogenitum*.

As a virgin who had accepted the will of God, Mary had great symbolic significance. An eighth-century primer from the Freising area saw Mary's virginity as an example for others: *In nouo [testamento]* Christus capud uirginum, feminarum *autem* Maria.[17] The Vienna Matthean commentator understood Mary as *ecclesiae gentium figura*,[18] while a mid-ninth-century Lucan commentator from an Irish circle in northern Italy, probably near Bobbio, saw Mary as *figura ecclesiae*.[19]

These interpretations indicate how the Irish viewed Mary in the economy of salvation. She is not the last Old Testament figure but stands firmly in the New. She could have represented the synagogue while her son represented the Church, born from the synagogue, but instead she herself represents the Church and even—in spite of her Jewishness—the Church of the gentiles.[20] The Freising primer relates her to Christian monasticism,

---

16. Clm 6233, foll. 33r–35v; *cf.* my "Catalogue, II" (note 5 above), #72. Henceforth, I refer to this as the south Bavarian commentary.

17. *Prebiarum de multorum exemplaribus* sec. 72 in R.E. McNally, *Scriptores hiberniae minores*, part 1 (Turnhout 1973) = *CChr.SL*, vol. 108B.

18. Fol. 24v; *v.* note 13 above.

19. *In Lucam*, Paris Bibl. Nat. 1841, foll. 137v–138r; *cf.* my "Catalogue, II" (note 5 above), #93. Henceforth, I refer to this as the Bobbio commentary.

20. One late seventh-century Hiberno-Latin commentator, known as ps.-Jerome, did interpret Mary as the synagogue: *v. Exp. quat. Ev.* on Mt. 12.46f. and Lk. 2.46–48.

thus giving her an immediacy to the Irish, whose Christian heroes included the famous abbess Bridget of Kildare (ca. 500–550).

The Gospel of Luke provides the fullest narrative of events surrounding the birth of Jesus: the census, the Holy Family's journey to Bethlehem, the birth of Jesus, the angelic annunciation to the shepherds, and the visit of the shepherds to the Holy Family (Lk. 2.1–20). The Irish produced few Lucan commentaries.[21] These followed patristic practice in commenting on both the historical and spiritual meanings of the text. In its remarks on Lk. 2.1 (*Factum est in diebus illis*) the eighth-century Salzburg commentator draws on Orosius' *Historia adversus paganos* (6.18) to establish the historical background of Jesus' birth. He mentions, for example, among the *magna miracula in aduentu saluatoris* the sudden appearance of a stream of oil in an inn near Rome (*oleum in taberna meritoria promens*) a portent that Orosius places in the mid-30s B.C. The commentary then offers an allegorical interpretation of the name Caesar (possessio principalis) taken from Jerome's *Liber interpretationis hebraicorum nominum* (*de Luca*, C). Some of the allegorizing rests on a metaphorical interpretation of the biblical language. For example, *ascendit autem Ioseph* [to Bethlehem] is interpreted, *bene dicitur* ascendit, *quia ab hac hora ascensio nobis datur in caelum* (on 2.4; [the gospel] well says *ascendit*, because from this hour ascension into heaven is given to us).

The Irish exegete believes it was truly worthy (*Vere dignum*) that the Lamb of God was first made manifest to the shepherds, whose humility appealed to the Irish monks, who also kept flocks. The shepherds represent the *doctores in ecclesia* (on 2.8) who are devoted to the *opus doctrinae* (on 2.20). The Irish interpreter also draws a moral interpretation from the text. When the angel says to the shepherds, "Do not fear," the exegete observes that *Angelus consolationem dat, diabulus disperationem* (on 2.10; An angel gives consolation, a devil causes despair).[22] This exegesis of Lk. 2.8–10 reflects the Irish concern to draw from scholarship lessons relevant to personal sanctity.

Two Augustinian motifs appear here. In his discussion of Lk. 2.7, *Peperit filium primogenitum,* the Irish exegete asserts that Jesus was born sine matre *in caelo,* sine patre *in terra.* This recalls Augustine's formulations *Filius Dei de Patre sine matre, filius hominis de matre sine patre* (*Ser.* 147.1) and *Generatio Christi a Patre sine matre, et a matre sine patre* (*Ser.* 149.4).[23] The exegete also developed (on 2.9) the Augustinian theme of light and dark, the light of the world coming at night to the shepherds.

---

21. *Cf.* Kelly, "Catalogue, II" (note 5 above), #56A, 91–93.
22. *Cf.* Ath., *Ant.* ch. 43.
23. *PL,* vol. 38, coll. 1001, 1006.

A small ecclesiological theme appears. The Holy Family represents the *primitiua ecclesia noui testamenti* (on 2.16). This reinforces the interpretation noted earlier, that Mary—and here Joseph—represent the new, rather than the old, dispensation.

We cannot leave this text without pointing out a charming example of the author's attempt to imagine the historical and psychological circumstances of the appearance of the angels. One angel had appeared to the shepherds to announce Christ's birth (Lk. 2.9). In 2.13 Luke says *Et subito facta est cum angelo multitudo militiae caelestis* (And suddenly there was with the angel a multitude of the heavly host). The Irish exegete observed that *Primo unus angelus aduenit, ut pastores non magnopere timerent, et postea* multitudo (*ad loc.;* First came a single angel, then the multitude came later, in order not to scare the shepherds too much). I find no parallel for this comment.

The mid-ninth-century Bobbio Lucan commentary shows less interest in history but more in allegory. Regrettably, its interpretations are often brief and sometimes difficult to grasp. For example, Caesar is said to symbolize God the Father and Quirinius, the governor of Syria (Lk. 2.2), to symbolize Christ, but no explanations are provided nor are the interpretations obvious. The inn symbolizes the Church (an interpretation favored by the Irish and also used by the Salzburg Lucan commentator [on 2.7]), and the manger an altar. The *pastores* do not represent the *doctores in ecclesia* but rather the believing congregation, which gives witness to the Lamb of God.[24]

This Irish exegete had more concern for theology than the Salzburg commentator. In his comment on Lk. 2.7 the latter had made no reference to Jerome's concern (on Mt. 1.25) to prove that *primogenitum* did not imply that Mary had subsequently borne other children. But this commentator stopped to explain the adjective "first-born" by reference to the Jewish law: *omne masculinum quod aperit vulvam primogenitus est* (*cf.* Ex. 13.2, 12, 15). He also gave the Holy Family a theological interpretation based on biblical typology: as *per tres*—i.e., Adam, Eve, and the serpent—the world was lost, so through these new three the world is saved.[25]

This interpretation of the Lucan infancy narrative demonstrates that the Irish commentators could not match their patristic forebears as theologians or exegetes. They lacked the Fathers' depth of education in philosophy and Latin rhetoric and the Fathers' knowledge of earlier secular and Christian writers. On the other hand, their genuine sensitivity to the

24. Fol. 139r–v; *v.* note 19 above.
25. *Ib.*

biblical text can be seen where they carefully align one word with appearances of that word elsewhere in Scripture, or seek out interpretations of numbers and places, or relate passages of the Old and New Testaments.

When the shepherds returned to their flocks, Christians turned back to Matthew for the story of the Magi and the star they followed. For the star (Mt. 2.2), as for other elements of the infancy narratives, the Irish, rather than looking for a single authoritative interpretation, tried several. Some exegetes interpreted the star within a scheme of biblical typology. Thus, the eighth-century south Bavarian commentary on Matthew views the star as a fulfillment of Balaam's prophecy and suggests a parallel between the stellar apparition granted the Magi and the angelic apparition granted the shepherds in Luke's gospel.[26] A Matthean commentary of the same century preserved in a manuscript at Orléans accepts this parallel and extends the typology further into the New Testament: the star appeared to the Magi who did not have the Law, angels to shepherds who did, and Christ himself to the Apostles. This exegete, who observes that the Jews had to consult the Law to see where the Messiah was to be born while the pagan Magi followed the star, perhaps introduces anti-Jewish polemic into his typology.[27] A late eighth-century exegete reports that the star both fulfilled the prophecy of Num. 24.17—"a star shall come forth out of Jacob"—and presented a parallel to the dove, that is, the Holy Spirit, who descended in the form of a dove when John baptized Jesus at the River Jordan (Mk. 1.10; Mt. 3.16; Lk.3.22).[28] Another late eighth-century commentary written by Irishmen on the continent and preserved in a Würzburg gospel book identifies the star with the Holy Spirit and also draws the comparison to the dove at Jesus' baptism.[29] The *Interrogationes vel responsiones tam de veteri quam novo testamento,* a ninth-century biblical primer, claim that the Magi recognize the star as a fulfilment of the prophecy of Balaam, their distant ancestor.[30]

The anti-Jewish polemic perhaps implicit in the eighth-century Orléans commentary is explicit in the later *Interrogationes.* Following Jerome (on Mt. 2.2), the Irish exegete observes, [*Magi] venerunt ad Hierusalem pro multis causis . . . tertia, ut Iudei, qui prope erant, culparentur, quando Magi*

26. Foll. 37v–38r; *v.* note 16 above.

27. Orléans 65 [2], fol. 34.

28. Clm 6392, fol. 35v; *cf.* Kelly, "Catalogue, II" (note 5 above), #73.

29. K. Köberlin, "Eine Würzburger Evangelienhandschrift (Mp. th. f. 61 s. VIII)" (Doctoral diss., Friedrich-Alexanders-Universität Erlangen 1890; publ. Augsburg 1891), p. 20. Henceforth, I refer to this as the Würzburg commentary.

30. *Interrogationes vel responsiones tam de veteri quam novo testamento,* in Lyons 447 [376], fol. 141r; *cf.* Kelly, "Catalogue, I" (note 5 above), #15C.

Dominum quesierunt; quarta, ut sacerdotes, qui de Christo dixerunt, ubi nasceretur, inexcusabiles essent.[31] In general, the Irish did not espouse anti-Semitism, except when they followed their patristic exemplars, as this exegete does here.

Some of these texts emphasize the importance of the star by insisting on its preternatural qualities. The south Bavarian exegete claims that the wonderful star stood higher in the sky than all the other stars. He also states that the Magi adored it just as they adored Christ the King. He apparently knows little about the ancient Chaldeans and assumes that they worshipped stars.[32] The Vienna Matthean commentary declares that the star outshone the sun and compares the brilliance of the star to that of God Himself.[33] The Würzburg Matthean commentary and the *Interrogationes* agree with the Vienna commentary that the star burned more brightly than the sun.[34]

The Magi fascinated the Irish. Mysterious and romantic—kings traveling a long distance to worship a newborn king—they were also the first gentiles to recognize Jesus.[35] This made them exemplars for virtually all Christian converts after the second century. As noted earlier, the *Interrogationes* traced the descent of the Magi from Balaam and thus linked the gentile sage who recognized God's grace at work among the people of the Old Testament to the gentile sages who recognized God's Son in the New.[36] This is a patristic view, held by Origen (*in Num. hom.* 13.7) and Jerome (on Mt. 2.2; *cf.* on Is. 19.2–4). A ninth-century exegete known as ps.-Bede understood the three sons of Noah as types of the Magi (on 2.4): *Mystice autem tres Magi tres partes mundi significant, Asiam, Africam, Europam, sive humanum genus, quod a tribus filiis Noe seminarium sumpsit.*[37]

The Irish followed the Fathers in numbering the Magi at three, a figure not in the biblical text but inferred from the number of gifts. The patristic tradition had also bestowed names on the Magi, which an eighth-century continental Irish exegete known as Pseudo-Isidore repeated and tried to explain via Hebrew and Greek philology. His results "stand completely outside the patristic tradition."[38] For example, the exegete claimed that

31. Fol. 141r; *v.* note 30 above.

32. Foll. 37v–38r; *v.* note 16 above.

33. Fol. 27r; *v.* note 13 above.

34. P. 20 (*v.* note 29 above); fol. 141r (*v.* note 30 above).

35. Much of my discussion of the three kings depends on R.E. McNally, "The Three Holy Kings in Early Irish Latin Writing," *Kyriakon: Festschrift Johannes Quasten,* ed. P. Granfield and J.A. Jungmann, vol. 2 (Münster 1970), pp. 667–90.

36. Fol. 141r; *v.* note 30 above.

37. *In Mt., PL,* vol. 92, col. 13A; *cf.* my "Catalogue, II" (note 5 above), #82.

38. R.E. McNally, "Three Holy Kings," (note 35 above), p. 671.

Melchior derived from Malgaloth in Hebrew and was Damascus in Greek and Innocens in Latin.[39] By the time the Irish turned to them, many traditions about the Magi had become established. As in so many other matters, the Irish exegetes drew from the Fathers but also made their own contributions.

The Irish also tried to understand the significance of the three gifts. An eighth-century Matthean commentator offered these interpretations: *Aurum regi, tuus Deo, mirra homini. Spiritaliter, autem, aurum cor mundum, tuus sermo bonus, myrra opus bonum; myrra ad fidem pro qua morimur et patimur; aurum ad actum quo ornamur; thus ad theoriam qua ad aeternam [vitam] sublevamur.*[40] Ps.-Bede noted that some preferred to interpret the three gifts as referring to both secular and Christian learning: *Alii tres species philosophiae in his muneribus intelligere volunt: physicam, ethicam, logicam. . . . Alii in auro allegoriam, in myrrha historiam, in thure anagogen, dicunt insinuari* (on Mt. 2.11).[41]

The Magi were distinguished by their homeland as well as by their persons and gifts. After being warned not to return to Herod, the Magi went *in regionam suam* (Mt. 2.12). For this phrase the Irish preferred moral and spiritual, to historical, exegesis. The eighth-century Vienna Matthean commentator offered a moral interpretation: *In regionem suam, id est, in bonum naturae suae.* The late eighth-century Würzburg commentator suggested a spiritual: "In regionem suam," *id est regio nostra paradisus est,* an interpretation favored by other Irish exegetes.[42]

Since so many Hiberno-Latin biblical texts have yet to receive critical editions, we cannot determine precisely how much Irish scholars stood in the patristic tradition and how original they were. But enough evidence exists to draw some conclusions, at least about their exegesis of the infancy narratives. The Irish, like most medieval scholars, preferred to repeat the conclusions of earlier exegesis rather than present novel interpretations. On the other hand, they felt free to offer their own insights when these

39. R.E. McNally, "Der irische Liber de numeris: Eine Quellenanalyse des pseudo-isidor-ischen Liber de numeris" (Doctoral diss., Ludwig-Maximilians-Universität zu München 1957), pp. 69–71.

40. Clm 6302, fol. 36r. Note the alternate spellings, *tuus, thus* and *mirra, myrra;* such orthographical variations are not uncommon in early medieval manuscripts. For this interpretation of the three gifts *cf.* Greg. Mag., *in Evang. hom.* 10.6. There is a delightfully Irish addition to the interpretation. The exegete asked, *Quid dixerunt Magi, invento Salvatore? Glorificamus te. Adoramus te. Magnificamus te; i.e.,* the Magi quote an Irish version of the angels' hymn. *Cf.* F.E. Warren, *The Liturgy and Ritual of the Celtic Church* (Oxford 1881; rpt. Woodbridge, Suffolk and Wolfeboro, N.H. 1987), p. 197.

41. *PL,* vol. 92, coll. 13C–D.

42. Fol. 28v (note 13 above); p. 21 (note 29 above); *cf.* also Clm 6302, fol. 36v.

seemed consonant with orthodox tradition. They clearly followed the Fathers in preferring multiple interpretations where feasible, in relating the Old Testament to the New, and in drawing from the text some inference for Christian living.

The history of scholarship usually centers on the new, and the Irish exegetes can make little claim to that. Like most early medieval exegetes, they looked back at Origen, Ambrose, Jerome, Augustine, and Gregory with a reverence bordering on awe. They knew they could not match their scholarship. Furthermore, as monks, the Irish exegetes had committed themselves to a life of humility, hardly a preparation conducive to challenging the authority of Augustine or Jerome. But we must recall that these Irish scholars lived at time when the lamp of learning burned low in the Western Church, and just conserving patristic tradition was no small achievement.

II. RHETORIC

FOUR

Christ, The *Arbor Mundi*

❖

William J. McCarthy

B Y HIS STUDY of the Περὶ Πάσχα (= *PP*) of Melito of Sardis, A.
Wifstrand enhanced our appreciation of that homily's similarity
to the contemporary *Kunstprosa* of Asia Minor.[1] He showed that
the fondness for parallelism, particularly the frequent use of isocolon,
characteristic of Melito's style, is a prominent feature of the discourses of
Maximus of Tyre and others. Yet, if this scholar, by his comparisons of
Melito's work with that of other second-century figures, stressed the commonplace of the extensive use of parallelism, J.S. Sibinga, by limiting himself to a meticulous study of the *PP*, proved the extent to which the balanc-
ing of the numbers of syllables might become for Melito his "mathemat-
ics, or rather his science of numbers [which he applied] to the *Kunstprosa*
of his homily."[2] The symmetry of Sibinga's syllabically balanced structure
of the entire homily, while perhaps almost prescriptively mathematical is,
nonetheless, convincingly argued and warrants substantial acceptance.[3]
After all, Greek poetic and prosaic composition of every period, from that
of the Homeric epics themselves, has recourse to a panoply of devices that
may lend a pleasing and/or unifying arrangement to a few words or a
few lines or may help to provide symmetry and unity on an even larger
scale.[4]

1. A. Wifstrand, "The Homily of Melito on the Passion," *VigChr* 2 (1948), pp. 201–23.

2. J.S. Sibinga, "Melito of Sardis: the Artist and His Text," *VigChr* 24 (1970), pp. 81–104. V.
also his use of syllabic patterns to determine the structure of 1Jn in "A Study in I John," *Studies in John Presented to Professor Dr. J.N. Sevenster* (Leiden 1970), pp. 194–208.

3. *Cf.* the recondite, Pythagorean structure that P. Maury believed Vergil to have imposed
on his book of poems: "Le secret de Virgile et l'architecture des Bucoliques," *Lettres d'hu-
manité* 3 (1944), pp. 71–147.

4. *V., e.g.*, B.A. van Groningen, *La composition littéraire archaïque grecque*, 2nd ed. (Amsterdam 1960).

Inasmuch as the *PP* and, thanks to the magisterial study by Cantala-messa, the Paschal homily of ps-Hippolytus (= *IP*) have been shown to be products of the Asianic schools of the second century A.D., Sibinga's work on the former may tempt us to probe for similar symmetries in the latter.[5] Indeed, there are passages in the *IP*, in particular the encomium on the cross (section 51 = p. 177, line 7–p. 179, line 9 [N.]), that exhibit extraordi-nary structural symmetries.[6] The structure of this encomium, although it lacks the more precise mathematical neatness discerned in the *PP* by Sibinga and is not founded in the pattern of the isocola, does clearly de-pend on a careful reckoning of the numbers of syllables, which is closely tied to the deployment of the imagery of the cross. The resulting propor-tioned balance among four coherent groups of syllables strongly suggests that the homilist has imposed a kind of cruciform pattern on this part of the homily.

Our two principal guides to the *IP*'s encomium on the cross, a passage that has been much admired for the beauty and power of its ecstatic flour-ish, are Cantalamessa,[7] of course, and Reijners. The latter, in his survey of early Christian terminology for the cross, devoted a valuable appendix to the study of the *IP* and section 51 in particular.[8] While both scholars offer many useful observations and insights, neither devotes sufficient attention to the structure of the passage. And yet, by virtue of its cruciform struc-ture, the encomium of the *IP* stands apart from certain gnosticizing, roughly comparable pieces from the early period of Christian Greek litera-ture, such as the cosmic visions of the cross in the *Acts of John* (98–101), the

---

5. For a review of earlier work on *IP*, v. R. Cantalamessa, *L'omelia "In s. pascha" dello pseudo-Ippolito di Roma: ricerche sulla teologia dell' Asia Minore nella seconda metà del II sec-olo* (Milan 1967). I shall assume that what Cantalamessa strove to demonstrate, *viz.*, that the homily is the product of an unknown Christian rhetor of second-century Asia Minor, re-mains untoppled by more recent attempts to revive old attributions or to argue new ones. *V.* esp. the study of V. Loi ("L'omelia '*In sanctum pascha*' di Ippolito di Roma," *Aug.* 17 [1977], pp. 461–84), who has attempted to revive the attribution to Hippolytus once claimed by C. Martin ("Un Περὶ τοῦ Πάσχα de s. Hippolyte retrouvé?" *RSR* 16 [1926], pp. 148–65) and the monograph of E. Cattaneo, *Trois homélies pseudo-chrysostomiennes sur la Pâque comme oeuvre d'Apollinaire de Laodicée* (Paris 1981). Cattaneo summarizes his conclusions on pp. 225–31. Throughout I cite *IP* according to the text of P. Nautin, *Homélies pascales,* vol. 1 (Paris 1950): *une homélie inspirée du traité sur la Pâque d'Hippolyte* = *SC,* vol. 27. Unless otherwise indicated, all translations of this work are my own.

6. To prevent confusion with the line numbers I use in my own colometric divisions, I shall place the initial "N." after the page(s) and line number(s) whenever I refer to Nautin's text (note 5 above).

7. *L'omelia* (note 5 above), pp. 109–38.

8. G. Reijners, *The Terminology of the Holy Cross in Early Christian Literature as Based upon Old Testament Typology* (Nijmegen 1965), "Appendix II: The Eulogy on the Cross in the Paschal Homily Inspired by Hippolytus' Περὶ τοῦ Πάσχα," pp. 198–214.

Gospel of Peter (10.38–42), and the *Martyrdom of Andrew* (14).[9] Given this care in composition, the artistry of the *IP*, as that of the *PP*, whose ofttimes incantatory style is certainly "reminiscent of the sophist Gorgias or the excesses of Hellenistic Asianism," cannot be so easily dismissed along with the rest of early Christian preaching as "basically 'a projection of the eloquence of Scripture' and not an achievement of the eloquence of the preacher."[10]

Before turning to the encomium itself, we must briefly review an important point concerning the use of parallelism in ancient rhetoric. Derived to a certain extent from a regular Semitic usage, one especially common in Hebrew poetry, which was subsequently transmitted to the Hellenistic world through the LXX, parallelism is a common stylistic device in the rhythmic prose and hymnody of the New Testament and early Christian literature.[11] One particular sort of parallelism, the isocolon, that by which parallel cola in immediate succession are balanced by their numbers of syllables, recurs with considerable frequency. The following example from Paul (1Cor. 15.41–44) will serve in illustration of an especially ex-

9. I refer to the *Mart. Andreae* (= *BHG*, #96). On the Latin side, the *De pascha* of ps.-Cyprian (*CPL*, #1458) is particularly noteworthy for its development of the cross as a cosmic tree of life. Concerning generally such visions of the cross, *v.* E.S. Greenhill, "The Child in the Tree: A Study of the Cosmological Tree in Christian Tradition," *Tr.* 10 (1954), pp. 323–71. Concerning those of the second century in particular, *v.* Cantalamessa (note 5 above), pp. 109–38, esp. ch. 4, part 2: "La croce cosmica in *IP* e nelle fonti ecclesiastiche, apocrife e gnostiche del II secolo," pp. 122–38; and V. Grossi, "La Pasqua quartodecimana e il significato della croce nel II secolo," *Aug.* 16 (1976), pp. 557–71. The personified Σταυρός = the Aeon Ὄρος played a significant role in the cosmology/soteriology of Valentinian Gnosticism; *v.* Iren., *Haer.* 1.3.5 and Hippol., *Ref.* 6.31.

10. G.A. Kennedy, *Classical Rhetoric and Its Christian and Secular Tradition from Ancient to Modern Times* (Chapel Hill, N.C. 1980), pp. 136f. In part, this slighting evaluation of Christian preaching may be attributed to the author's intention (p. xi) to provide "a short introduction to a vast subject, the history of man's effort to accomplish his purposes by speech," to an audience "primarily made up of English-speaking students and nonspecialists in the classics who are interested in discourse in a variety of ways, including religious discourse." The phrase "a projection of the eloquence of the speaker" comes from J.S. Chamberlin, *Increase and Multiply: Arts-of-Discourse Procedure in the Preaching of Donne* (Chapel Hill, N.C. 1976), p. 28.

11. Pursuing work done by E. Norden (*Agnostos Theos: Untersuchungen zur Formengeschichte Religiöser Rede* [Berlin 1923]), J. Kroll covers the problems of the style of composition in *Die christliche Hymnodik bis zu Klemens von Alexandreia* (Darmstadt 1968) = combined reprint of *Verzeichnis der Vorlesungen an der Akademie zu Braunsberg im Sommer 1921,"* part 1, pp. 3–46, and *ib., im Winter 1921–22*, part 2, pp. 47–98. *V.* also R. Deichgräber *Gotteshymnus und Christushymnus in der frühen Christenheit: Untersuchungen zu Form, Sprache und Stil der frühchristlichen Hymnen* (Göttingen 1967); and T. Wolbergs, *Griechische religiöse Gedichte der ersten nachchristlichen Jahrhunderte*, vol. 1 (Meisenheim am Glan 1971): *Psalmen und Hymnen der Gnosis und des frühen Christentums*. This last was reviewed *in extenso* by A. Kehl, "Beiträge zum Verständnis einiger gnostischer und frühchristlicher Psalmen und Hymnen," *JAC* 15 (1972), pp. 92–119.

pert use of a commonplace device: ἄλλη δόξα ἡλίου, (7) / καὶ ἄλλη δόξα σελήνης, (8) / καὶ ἄλλη δόξα ἀστέρων· (8) / ἀστὴρ γὰρ ἀστέρος διαφέρει ἐν δόξῃ. (13) / Οὕτως καὶ ἡ ἀνάστασις τῶν νεκρῶν. (11) / σπείρεται ἐν φθορᾷ, ἐγείρεται ἐν ἀφθαρσίᾳ· (15) / σπείρεται ἐν ἀτιμίᾳ, ἐγείρεται ἐν δόξῃ· (15) / σπείρεται ἐν ἀσθενείᾳ, ἐγείρεται ἐν δυνάμει· (16) / σπείρεται σῶμα ψυχικόν, ἐγείρεται σῶμα πνευματικόν. (18). In this passage, the three-fold anaphora of ἄλλη δόξα and the four-fold anaphora of σπείρεται in conjunction with the recurrence of ἐγείρεται at the beginning of the second part of each colon well exemplifies the manner in which the syllabic balance of the isocolon may be manipulated and intensified by other devices of word and sound repetition.

Greek prose stylists also regularly employ the isocolon. Demetrius expressly indicates this in his discussion of the techniques of the rhetorical art: Εἶδος δὲ τοῦ παρομοίου τὸ ἰσόκωλον, ἐπὰν ἴσας ἔχῃ τὰ κῶλα τὰς συλλαβάς, ὥσπερ Θουκυδίδῃ· ὡς οὔτε ὧν πυνθάνονται ἀπαξιούντων τὸ ἔργον, οἷς τε ἐπιμελὲς εἴη εἰδέναι οὐκ ὀνειδιζόντων ἰσόκωλον μὲν δὴ τοῦτο (Eloc. 25). As P. Chiron points out, in this excerpt from the *archaeologia* of book 1 (5.2), Thucydides balances one colon of sixteen syllables with another of seventeen.[12] As our examination of this and the excerpt from Paul reveals, the phrase "equality of members" normally indicates only a rough parity rather than a precise balance.

If, despite this only approximate equality characteristic of Greek rhetoric, Melito of Sardis uses ἰσόκωλον rather more precisely to compose an impressive, mathematically balanced superstructure for the entire *PP*, we should hardly be surprised to discover in the *IP* a less numerically rigorous parallelism but one that is in complete harmony with the traditional flexibility of the rhetorical device. Let us turn to the encomium in the second major division of the *IP*.[13] The text of section 51 (= p. 177, l. 7–p. 179, l. 98 [N.]), broken down into cola, follows:

12. P. Chiron, Démétrios, *Du style* (Paris 1993). V. Chiron's note 40, p. 91.
13. Nautin (note 5 above) outlines (p. 67) the homily as a whole as follows:

Proem (1–3)
Subject and Plan (4–8)
Part I: The Figures
    A. The Law (9f.)
    B. The Pasch (11–42)
        1. The First Pasch (11–15)
        2. Its Typological Meaning (16–42)
Part II: The Realities
    A. The Ἐπιδημία of Christ (43–48)
    B. The Pasch of Christ (49–61)
Peroration (62f.)

51.1
Τοῦτό μοι φυτὸν εἰς σωτηρίαν αἰώνιον,
τούτῳ τρέφομαι,
τούτῳ συνεστιῶμαι.

51.2
Τούτου ταῖς μὲν ῥίζαις ὑπορριζοῦμαι,
τοῖς δὲ κλάδοις συνεκτείνομαι,   5
τῇ δὲ δρόσῳ φαιδρύνομαι,
τῷ δὲ πνεύματι ὡς ὑπὸ ἀνέμου ἐντρυφῶν γεωργοῦμαι.

51.3
Τούτου τῇ σκιᾷ ὑπεσκήνωσα
καὶ τὸν πολὺν καύσωνα διαφυγὼν ἔνδροσον ἔχω κατάγειον.

51.4
Τούτου τοῖς μὲν ἄνθεσι συνανθῶ,   10
τοῖς δὲ καρποῖς τελείως συνήδομαι,
τοὺς δὲ ἐξ ἀρχῆς μοι τετηρημένους καρποὺς ἀκωλύτως τρυγῶ.

51.5
Τοῦτό μοι πεινῶντι τροφή,
καὶ διψῶντι πηγή,
καὶ σκέπη γεγυμνωμένῳ,   15
οὗ καὶ τὰ φύλλα πνεῦμα ζωῆς,
οὐκέτι μοι φύλλα συκῆς.

51.6
Τοῦτό μοι Θεὸν φοβουμένῳ φυλακτήριον,
καὶ σαλευομένῳ στήριγμα,
καὶ ἀγωνιζομένῳ βραβεῖον,   20
καὶ τρόπαιον νενικηκότι.

51.7
Τοῦτό μοι ἄτραπος ἡ στενή,
τοῦτο ἡ τεθλιμμένη ὁδός.

51.8
Τοῦτο κλῖμαξ Ἰακὼβ
καὶ τῶν ἀγγέλων πορεία,   25
ἐφ' ἧς ἄκρας ἀληθῶς ἐστήρικται ὁ Κύριος.

51.9
Τοῦτο δένδρον οὐρανόμηκες ἀπὸ γῆς εἰς οὐρανοὺς ἀνέβαινεν,
ἀθάνατον φυτὸν στηρίξας ἑαυτὸν ἐν μέσῳ οὐρανοῦ τε καὶ γῆς,
ἔδρασμα τῶν ὅλων,
στήριγμα τοῦ παντός,   30
ἔρεισμα τῆς ὅλης οἰκουμένης,
σύμπλεγμα κοσμικόν,

τῆς ποικίλης καὶ ἀνθρωπίνης οὐσίας συνεκτικόν,
ἀοράτοις γόμφοις τοῦ πνεύματος συνηλωμένον,
ἵνα τῷ θείῳ συναρμοσθὲν μηκέτι λυθῇ.   35
51.10
Ἄκραις μὲν κορυφαῖς τῶν οὐρανῶν ἐπιψαύων,
τὴν γῆν δὲ στηρίζων ποσί,
τὸ δὲ πολὺ καὶ μέσον πνεῦμα τοῦ ἀέρος
πανταχόθεν χερσὶν ἀμετρήτοις περιλαβών,
ὅλος ἦν ἐν πᾶσι καὶ πανταχοῦ.   40

According to the arrangement of the several types of imagery applied
to the cross, this passage may be divided into three parts: first, lines 1–17,
consisting of five sections to which a strictly arboreal imagery, *i.e*, the cross
as a tree, source of sustenance and shelter, is confined; then, lines 18–26,
which consist of two smaller, interrelated sections (18–21 and 22–26), in
which the speaker[14] evokes the tree/cross first through a series of images of
fixity (18–21), then through another series in which he sees it as a means of
passage (22–25) and concludes with a fusion of the two sets of images in
the final line (26); lastly, lines 27–40, where Christ, whose arms are extended on the tree/cross in the gesture of ἐκπέτασις, is arboreally, tectonically,
and anthropomorphically imaged as a cosmic figure in such a way that
tree, cross, and Christ become virtually and appropriately indistinguishable from one another.[15] A powerful justification for this arrangement derives from the pattern that emerges when we compute the numbers of syllables in the three parts. The first and third consist of 181 and 173 syllables
respectively while the second has approximately half the number of either,
viz., 89. This figure, because of the structure of the second part, may be divided into 42 and 47 syllables, so that each half of the second part contains
approximately one quarter of the syllables of the first and third parts. In
the analysis to follow we shall demonstrate that the careful deployment of
the imagery in these three parts is to be taken closely with the numbers of
syllables. As a result, a roughly cruciform pattern is suggested by the ratio
of the syllables, 4:1:1:4.[16]

14. To facilitate discussion of the artistic techniques of the encomium, I distinguish between speaker and homilist.
15. H. de Lubac ("L'arbre cosmique," *Mélanges E. Podechard* [Lyon 1945]) correctly notes
(p. 192) that the imagery accumulates: "la croix est ici d'abord assimilée à un arbre, puis à un
support cosmique, enfin au Crucifié lui-même. Ces assimilations ne sont pas discontinues:
elles se totalisent."
16. These numbers presuppose hiatus rather than elision or crasis. There are, in fact, only
12 cases of hiatus, of which three (ὑπό, l. 7; δέ, l. 12; τοῦτο, l. 23) could admit elision and two

Having identified the cross in the preceding section (50) as an antitype, a new tree of life planted by Christ to replace the one lost in Eden (Καὶ διὰ τοῦτο ξύλον ξύλῳ ἀντιρριζώσας), the speaker begins his laudation of the cross by setting out to portray it as a cosmic tree, which he enjoys as a source of sustenance and shelter, and with which he is united.[17] The arboreal cross portrayed here is uniquely distinguished in that, as Reijners has noted,[18] the *IP* is the first work of Christian literature in which the cross is called a φυτόν. This is, however, more than an interesting lexical datum. Although the word is one of a group of synonyms (such as ξύλον and δένδρον) used of the cross when imagined as a kind of tree, the emphasis on the cosmic, markedly organic character of the tree/cross/Christ, which emerges as the encomium unfolds, indicates that the homilist's choice of φυτόν is deliberate and carefully tailored to his portrayal of the cosmic Christ. We may discern two important sources of influence in this choice, one scriptural and one that may be loosely termed "Platonic."[19]

First, φυτόν, not uncommon in the LXX (18 times), has already moved beyond its prosaic denotation (in *e.g.,* Gen. 22.13) to the threshold of metaphor in the expression φυτὸν εἰρήνης ("plant of peace" = material prosperity) at Ez. 34.29. At Is. 61.3, the use of φύτευμα, which is virtually indistinguishable from φυτόν, applies the arboreal metaphor, in an evocative transference, to those presently afflicted who will, in "the year of favor from the Lord" (ἐνιαυτὸν κυρίου δεκτόν), receive glory from God for having been and proving to be his Φύτευμα ... εἰς δόξαν.[20] The potential of the imagery evolves to the point that φυτόν occurs in the LXX version of Dan. 11.7 and 20 in reference to conquerors whose rise to power is envi-

---

(καί, l. 20; καί, l. 33) crasis. Such slight variations in the count do not affect my argument. For the method of syllable counting *cf.* Sibinga (note 2 above), p. 85.

17. The praise of the cross, to the extent that it is regarded as a beneficent φυτόν, is part of an established tradition of the praise (*laudationes*) of plants; *v.* A.S. Pease, "Things without Honor," *CP* 21 (1926), pp. 27–42, esp. note 7, p. 27 and note 2, p. 33. A significant number of works referred to as *laudationes* were apparently Pythagorean treatises on the powers and properties of plants and, therefore, not purely encomiastic. *V.* H. Thesleff, *The Pythagorean Texts of the Hellenistic Period* (Åbo 1965), pp. 174–77, for a review of surviving evidence. Nevertheless, it seems likely that the fascination with the plant was broadly based. Pliny says (*Nat.* 20.33) that such diverse figures as Pythagoras, Chrysippus, and Cato the Elder composed works on the virtues of the *brassica* (cabbage). More importantly, as concerns the encomium of the *IP,* we must bear in mind that the typical praise of a plant was based partially in fact, partially in religious/superstitious fantasy (*v.* note 28 below), which mixture Libanius' encomium of the palm and the apple (*Enc.* 9) well exemplifies.

18. Reijners (note 8 above) speaks (p. 202) of the word φυτόν as "a stylistic variation."

19. *V.* note 24 below.

20. J.W. Wevers, *Genesis* (1974) = *LXX*, vol. 1; J. Ziegler, *Ezechiel,* 2nd ed. (1977) = *LXX,* vol. 16.1; *id., Isaias,* 3rd ed. (1983) = *LXX,* vol. 14.

sioned.[21] The most significant realization of the arboreal metaphor, however, is the messiah himself, he who is to lead Israel to victory over her enemies, as an ἀνατολή.[22] Although φυτόν itself is not used of the messiah, the image of his appearance like a shoot or branch from a tree occurs in Is. 11.1 and 4.2 (*cf.* Zech. 4.3, 11–14 and Ez. 17).[23]

Secondly, the connotation of growth in the word φυτόν, which is so important in Plato's doctrine of the soul, seems also to be very much at home in, and even necessary to, our understanding of φυτόν in the context of the *IP*.[24] Here the homilist, lending the cosmic epiphany a pointed psychological dimension—*i.e.*, Christ is said to grow back toward heaven in order to join it to earth for mankind's salvation—has inverted the notion of the sad descent of the human soul, the φυτὸν οὐράνιον, which Plato presents in the *Timaeus*: Christ enroots the φυτὸν εἰς σωτηρίαν (= his cross = himself) in the earth. The Christian, in turn, enroots himself in Christ and grows heavenward.[25]

Following the introductory lines 1–3 (26 syllables), in which the heavenward direction of the φυτόν and its provision of sustenance to the

21. J. Ziegler, *Susannna, Daniel, Bel et Draco* (1954) = *LXX*, vol. 16.2. *V.* also 4.7–24 (LXX), where a sort of cosmic tree of life in Nebuchadnezzar's dream (δένδρον ὑψηλὸν φυόμενον ἐπὶ τῆς γῆς, 4.7), is interpreted by the prophet as the king himself. In an effort to identify biblical sources for the portrayal of Nebuchadnezzar as a gigantic tree, L.F. Hartman compares "the allegory of the cypress of Lebanon in Ezekiel 31, where it is applied to the king of Egypt." *V.* p. 176 of *The Book of Daniel: A New Translation with Notes and Commentary on Chh. 1–9* by L.F. Hartman *[and] Introduction and Commentary on Chh. 10–12* by A.A. DiLella (Garden City, N.Y. 1978) = *AncB*, vol. 23.

22. This term has vegetal or arboreal connotations—sprouted shoot—in Zech. 3.8, 6.12, and Jer. 23.5; *v.* G. Kittel, *ThWNT*, vol. 1 (Stuttgart 1933): *A - Γ, sub vocc.* ἀνατέλλω and ἀνατολή.

23. *V.* C.L. Meyers, *Tabernacle Menorah: A Synthetic Study of a Symbol from the Biblical Cult* (Missoula, Mont. 1976), pp. 151–53.

24. Plato's earlier notion of the planting (φυτεῦσαι) of the soul in the body (*Phdr.* 248D) anticipates his definition of the soul in the *Timaeus* as a φυτὸν οὐράνιον (90A). In this phrase he captures quite graphically its movement from τὰ ὄντα to τὰ γιγνόμενα and the soul's partial implication in the processes of φύσις, the constant coming-into-being and passing-away characteristic of becoming. Of course, the homilist may well have understood φύσις to connote vegetal growth in addition to fixity without deriving his conceit concerning Christ as plant from Plato, for the semantic field of φύσις radiates from φύω. Nonetheless, the focus the homilist places on Christ as cruciform world-soul suggests membership in the "Platonic underworld" of the first centuries A.D., that milieu of thought in which it is notoriously difficult to trace Platonic or Platonist influence or to distinguish one sort of influence from the other. *V.* J. Dillon, *The Middle Platonists: 80 B.C. to A.D. 220* (Ithaca, N.Y. 1977), pp. 384–414.

25. Note that, before the term νεοφώτιστος displaced it, νεόφυτος designated the newly baptized Christian who had been "newly planted" or "newly engrafted" into the Church. *V.* 1Tim. 3.6, and J. Daniélou, "La vigne et l'arbre de vie," *Les symboles chrétiens primitifs* (Paris 1961), pp. 33–48.

speaker are introduced, there follow four groups of lines: 4–7 (46 syllables), in which the speaker declares his physical union with the tree; 8f. (30 syllables), in which he describes it as his source of coolness and shelter; 10–12 (40 syllables), in which he paradoxically asserts at once to be in union with it and to eat of its fruits, and 13–17 (39 syllables), in which he summarizes the benefits the tree confers upon him. Note that the demonstrative τοῦτο, serving as a modest sort of overture to the passage, occurs in polyptoton in the introduction and is repeated at the beginning of each group of lines. The antecedent in each instance is φυτόν.

From the speaker's declaration of his union with the tree, a union so complete that, in the manner of a tree, he is "cultivated" by its πνεῦμα (τῷ δὲ πνεύματι ... γεωργοῦμαι, 7),[26] we may infer the key arboreal and spiritual feature of the visionary φυτόν, which is both Christ's cross and ultimately even Christ himself: its πνεῦμα is its vital energy, or rather, its sap. Having recognized that this tree cannot be understood or appreciated in terms of Theophrastean botany, and that it is clearly a part of the vast and often difficult to delimit plantlore of antiquity,[27] we observe that πνεῦμα seems to play a role in the structure of the φυτόν that recalls that of πῦρ in the structure of portentous olive trees found elsewhere in Greek literature. That is to say, fire and the role traditionally attributed to it in the metabolism of certain plants, in particular, the olive, is roughly analogous to πνεῦμα and its role in the metabolism of the new tree of life.[28] The πνεῦμα

26. Thus construing πνεύματι as the dative of agent with γεωργοῦμαι.

27. Because both Christian and non-Christian, in framing thoughts or fantasies about plants, perforce drew on ideas that, at best, were part of a faulty science and, at worst, and more usually, were little more than the ancient superstitious lore of the ῥιζοτόμοι, the term, plantlore, can by no means be strictly reserved for the more transparently fabulous φυτά. V. A. Delatte, *Herbarius: Recherches sur le cérémonial usité chez les anciens pour la cueillette des simples et des plantes magiques*, 3rd ed. (Brussels 1961) = *Académie de Belgique, Classe des Lettres, Mémoires, Collection in-80*, 2nd ser., vol. 54.4. Although a Christian writer might find a number of scriptural precedents for the visionary tree, which scarcely require or even admit an elemental theory of composition, our late Hellenistic Christian homilist was able to draw on the common Greek elemental theory.

28. The role of fire in the metabolism of the olive is mentioned in the second-century romance *Leucippe and Clitophon* (2.14.5f.). Here the flammability of the tree's most important product, oil, is associated with the fiery nature of the soil by which the tree is nourished. Olive oil, the liquid essence of the tree, has inspired the novelist to associate the elemental fire imagined to be present in the soil with that likewise imagined to be present as an element in the oil. Thus, the tree itself draws fire from the soil and passes it on to its fruit. *Cf. Ti.* 59E–60A, where Plato speaks of plant metabolism as a "distillation" (ἠθημένα) of elements from the earth; J. Burnet, *Platonis Opera, tomus IV* (Oxford 1902): *Tetralogiam VIII continens*. This theory is consonant with the perhaps more sophisticated concept of concoction—the process of taking up within the plant the elements of the environment and transforming them into what it requires to reach its τέλος—which one finds in subsequent botanical works, *e.g.*, Thphr., *CP* (2.4).

which "cultivates" the speaker, who declares himself part of the tree, is derived not from the soil but from Christ, he who not only planted the φυτόν but also, as ἡ ζωὴ κρεμαμένη (*cf.* sec. 50), is nailed to it and, in fact, is it.

Though artfully deployed among the three parts of the encomium, the arboreal, tectonic, and anthropomorphic images of Christ are cumulative and ultimately converge, and this compounding of imagery dramatically enriches the homilist's portrayal of the cosmic Christ and his Pasch while at the same time it requires us to discern a certain risk in probing too closely any one sort of image. Nonetheless, our interpretation of the role of πνεῦμα in the tree seems valid because, both as the sap of the tree and as the "bolts" (γόμφοις, 34) that permanently hold together his human self, πνεῦμα is essential to Christ, the God-man, for it is the stuff of divinity. Further, the speaker's pneumatic association with the tree complements the complex portrayal of Christ. He partakes of πνεῦμα through a literal union with the tree, yet at the same time he enjoys its fruit and shade as if not a part of the tree.

The deliberate but not immediately obvious ambiguity of τρέφομαι and συνεστιῶμαι in lines 2f. becomes clear as we ponder this first part of the encomium. Does the speaker mean that he is "fed by" the tree or that he "feasts with it," that he "shares in the feast on it" or "feasts together with it?" These speculations are not as captious as they may seem. Indeed, there is a studied effort to establish a subjective (the speaker's identification with the tree) and an objective aspect (his enjoyment of it as a source of food and shelter). Thus, the subjective aspect of lines 4–7 alternates with the objective in 8f. while the thought of 4–7, when it is resumed in 10–12, has been subtly altered. Both 4–7 and 10–12 detail arboreal features in a purposed sequence: 4–7, roots to branches to foliage (implied by the dew that covers them) and 10–12, blossoms to fruits. But at the end of the former, the speaker is cultivated as the tree, at the end of the latter, he is fed by it. The ambiguity of συνήδομαι (11) is crucial to this transition; as the pivot of the subjective aspect of συνανθῶ (10) and the objective aspect of τρυγῶ (12), it is to be understood not in the sense of "rejoice with" but rather in that suggested by its basic components σύν and ἡδύς. The statement "I am sweet/sweetened with its fruits" is purposefully vague. The speaker is one of the καρποί and yet eats of them at the same time.

In lines 13–17 the various roles of the tree as source of food, drink, and shelter are summarized. Note that line 13 begins as 1, with the demonstrative returned to the nominative case, and that the jingles of initial assonance (οὐ καὶ, οὐκέτι) and homoioteleuton (ζωῆς, συκῆς) in lines 16f. signal the end of the first part of the encomium. While lines 13–15 preserve the speaker's subjective aspect reëstablished in 12, lines 16f. serve both to juxtapose the objective and subjective and to generate, by the echo of φυτόν (1) in φύλλα (17), a frame for the first part. The link between the two words, suggested by an imagined, if linguistically unsound, common derivation from φύω,[29] and the obvious nature of their interrelationship, builds an etymological word-play which permits, and in view of the context of φύλλα, even requires that it mean more than "leaves," just as φυτόν must mean more than "plant."

There existed a Jewish tradition according to which Adam and Eve's use of fig leaves to cover their tragically discovered nakedness (Gen. 3.7) was taken to indicate that the fig was the forbidden fruit that had provided them the knowledge.[30] The φύλλα of lines 16f., whose full meaning is to be appreciated in conjunction with the summary character of 13–15, seem to allude to this tradition and accordingly should not be rendered merely as "leaves" but rather as "foliage and fruit."[31] Φύλλα, then, is to be taken synecdochically.[32] This interpretation will allow us to exploit more fully the etymological play with φύτον by making of the φύλλα, as source of sustenance and shelter, a pneumatic antitype of the foliage and fruit of the fig. Thus, the final lines (16f.) assume an appropriate breadth of meaning by virtue of their ambiguous aspect. By saying "no longer are my foliage and fruit those of the fig" does the speaker mean to indicate that he and the new tree of life are one (as he had claimed in 4–7), or that its foliage and fruit belong to him (as he had claimed in 8–12)? In fact, he means both.

Having matched the fusion of fruit and foliage in the type with a fusion of pneumatic fruit and foliage in the antitype, the homilist effectively evokes the latter's φύλλα, the πνεῦμα ζωῆς, as both the spiritual food of the Eucharist and the spiritual garment of baptism. Both sacraments, but more certainly the former, seem to have been part of the Paschal liturgy at which the *IP* was performed, and both are now clearly linked with the image of Christ as nascent cosmic tree.[33] The Christian becomes a part of

---

29. *Cf.* the phrase, φύλλα φύει in Mimnermus 2.1; M.L. West, *Iambi et elegi graeci ante Alexandrum cantati,* vol. 2 (Oxford 1972): *Callinus, Mimnermus, et al.*

30. V. H.-G. Leder, "ARBOR SCIENTIAE: Die Tradition vom paradiesischen Apfelbaum," *ZNW* 52 (1961), pp. 156–89, esp. 164–89.

31. There is allusion as well to the wondrous, eschatological trees referred to at Ez. 47.12 and Apoc. 22.2

32. Similarly, Sophocles refers to the olive's fruit and foliage through the single word φύλλον: γλαυκᾶς παιδοτρόφου φύλλον ἐλαίας, *OC* 701; R.D. Dawe, *Sophoclis Tragoediae,* 2nd ed., vol. 2 (Leipzig 1985).

33. V. Cantalamessa (note 5 above), pp. 282–333.

Christ the tree growing heavenward (27) by putting on Christ (15) and eating his fruits (11–13), but the pneumatic agencies of baptism and Eucharist, which secure the Christian's spiritual union with Christ, also incorporate him into the cosmic Christ who is emerging as the encomium unfolds. Indeed, by means of the carefully ordered sets of images in its second part, our attention is raised from the speaker's relationship with the tree to the nature of the cosmic Christ as a tree/cross so that the simultaneously spiritual and cosmic presence of Christ, which is at the heart of the homilist's understanding of the Pasch, becomes clearer.

Lines 18–26 may be divided into two groups, 18–21 (42 syllables) and 21–25 (32 syllables), with line 26 (15 syllables, to be added to the count of the latter group) serving to summarize this section of the encomium by uniting the imagery of the two groups (v. Diagram I). The first group opens with Christ's cross, the φυτόν of the first section, described as a φυλακτήριον. The cruciform shape has already been associated with this word in section 15.1f. (ll. 7–end [N.]), where the lamb's blood marking the homes of the Israelites prefigures the baptismal sign of the cross on the soul of the Christian.[34] The recurrence of φυλακτήριον in the encomium adds the cosmic to its already established spiritual aspect, so that, as is the homilist's intention throughout the encomium, Christ and his Pasch begin to assume universal proportions.

The first designation of the tree/cross is paired with στήριγμα, and this pair is in turn balanced against that of πορεία and κλῖμαξ. In either instance a more general is paired with a more specific and concrete noun: "protection" and "prop," "pathway" and "ladder." Φυλακτήριον, the pivotal image between the cruciform pattern drawn with paschal blood and the cruciform tree of life whose vital element is πνεῦμα, opens the catalog of the emblems of fixity, which are all neuter nouns. Πορεία, whose spiritual and cosmic connotations patently intertwine, for it refers to the angels' ladder in Jacob's dream (Gen. 28.10–17), a type of the Christian's paschal path between earth and heaven, closes the catalog of the emblems of passage, which are all feminine nouns.

The remaining nouns, ἄτραπος and ὁδός, also form one smoothly interlocking pair whose transit is from the tree/cross as an emblem of fixity to an emblem of passage. Also, βραβεῖον, fixed in the sense that it is the es-

---

34. F.J. Dölger notes that, to judge from the references in Tertullian and Clement of Alexandria, the sign of the cross played an important catechetical and baptismal role already in the second century; v. "Beiträge zur Geschichte des Kreuzzeichens IV," JAC 4 (1961), pp. 5–17, esp. "Das Kreuzzeichen als Aufnahmeritus," pp. 9–13. The typology of the Pasch and the Exodus date from the beginnings of Christianity; v. J. Daniélou, Sacramentum futuri: Études sur les origines de la typologie biblique (Paris 1950), p. 131.

fixity (18–21)	passage (22–25)
φυλακτήριον	ἄτραπος
στήριγμα	ὁδός
βραβεῖον	κλῖμαξ
τρόπαιον	πορεία

passage and fixity (26)

ἧς = πορεία + ἐστήρικται

DIAGRAM I

tablished goal toward which the competitor strives in a contest,[35] and τρό-παιον, the monument of victory, which is the fixed emblem of success, already imply the interrelationship between the fixity of the tree and its role as provider of passage. The nouns ἄτραπος and ὁδός, which suggest a highway, share with κλῖμαξ and πορεία the notion of movement. All four of these terms are artfully linked with the imagery of fixity by the paronomasia of τρόπαιον and ἄτραπος.

The arrangement of the nouns in this part of the encomium is framed by references to God (18) and to Christ (26). The former is object of its verb, the latter subject. The two types of imagery of movement and fixity are brought together in line 26: Christ is fixed to the apex of the new angelic path, the tree that is the cross. Having placed Christ at the top of the tree/cross, in the final part of the encomium, the homilist endeavors to describe his cosmic stature by imaging him in terms of both the φυτόν and the cross.

At lines 27f. the third part of the encomium begins. The return here to an obviously arboreal (τοῦτο δένδρον ... τοῦτο φυτόν) representation of Christ on the cross, the salvific "growth" of the first part of the encomium (1–17), is marked by a grammatical irregularity.[36] The proper antecedent of στηρίξας (28), the masculine form of the participle, ought to be neither φυτόν nor δένδρον, but rather Christ, whom we might understand as the implied subject of the participle, if we take κύριος, the subject of ἐστήρικ-ται (26), as the antecedent. The noun δένδρον would then be taken as an appositive to κύριος, φυτόν as an appositive to ἑαυτόν. But according to the structure of the encomium we have proposed, lines 18–26 form a discrete unit. Note, in conjunction with Diagram III on page 69 below that τοῦτο δένδρον of line 27 echoes τοῦτο φυτόν of line 1. This procedure is, there-

35. The special Christian redolence of this word is established, of course, by Paul (Phil. 3.14).

36. V. Nautin (note 5 above), p. 97.

fore, neither necessary nor desirable. Indeed, the solecism of στηρίξας should be regarded as an intentional stylistic effect calculated to tinge the arboreal imagery with anthropomorphism. Just as, in the first part of the encomium, the homilist blurs the distinction between the speaker and the pneumatic tree of life, which is Christ, in order to express the union of the two, so, in this final part, he brings together images of the tree, the cross, and the human body in order to represent the epiphany of the crucified Christ as an arboreal/tectonic/anthropomorphic figure of gigantic dimensions.[37]

Once again an outline (by line and syllable count) will prove helpful before we proceed with the discussion:

27   (20): tree/Christ has ascended from earth to the heavens.

28   (21): tree/Christ props himself in the middle region between heaven and earth

29–31   (22): tree/Christ as the universal prop

32–35   (51): cosmic cross as the tectonic symbol of the union of natures in Christ

36   (14): tree/cross/Christ touches the heavens with the crest of his brow

37   (8):   tree/cross/Christ steadies the earth with his feet

38f.   (27): tree/cross/Christ embraces the winds in the air between heaven and earth

40   (10): tree/cross/Christ is universally present (as a kind of world-soul)

The two elaborations, one on the idea of the universal prop (29–31) and the other on the idea of the permanent union, cosmic and psychosomatic, represented by Christ (32–35), are carefully crafted and form a smoothly interlocking pattern. Note the following interplay of assonance and alliteration (v. Diagram II). In this sequence, σύμπλεγμα constitutes, both logopoetically and phanopoetically, the pivotal element. The tree, i.e., Christ, the foundation of the cosmos, has ascended from earth to the heavens and, thus, has taken a position in the intervening space (ἐν μέσῳ, 28). A σύμπλεγμα κοσμικόν (32; "cosmic entwining") because it joins heaven and earth, the tree itself is also a thing entwined because, inasmuch as it is also the cross, its beams are bound together (συνεκτικόν, 33), nailed to-

---

37. On the portrayal of Christ as a gigantic figure in early Christian literature (e.g., Her., Sim. 9.6.1), v. M.G. Mara's comments (p. 185 and note 4) on sec. 40 of the Gospel of Peter in Évangile de Pierre (Paris 1973) = SC, vol. 201.

DIAGRAM II

gether (συνηλωμένον, 34), and fitted together (συναρμοσθέν, 35). Even more than this, however, the tree/cross represents the structure of Christ, the divine incarnate. The arboreal imagery, already somewhat anthropomorphic because of the solecism of στηρίξας, becomes appropriately tectonic in lines 32–35, where the repetition of the words with the prefix συν- helps to amplify the idea of the union of the divine and the human in Christ. The result of the conjunction of imagery, again manifest in the apparent solecisms ἐπιψαύων (36), στηρίζων (37), περιλαβών (39), and ὅλος (40), whose antecedents are all neuter nouns,[38] is that the form of the cross mediates tacitly as a *tertium comparationis* between the forms of the tree of life and Christ in the attitude of ἐκπέτασις.

In the closing lines of the encomium the pneumatic tree of life is resolved into an image of the crucified Christ who, as a world-soul-like figure, embraces and completely interpenetrates the cosmos.[39] This cosmic

38. *V.* Nautin's (note 5 above) *ap. crit. ad* 36–40 for alternative readings of neuter or adverbial forms in certain mss. and in H. Savile's edition (Τοῦ ἐν ἁγίοις πατρὸς ἡμῶν Ἰωάννου ... τοῦ Χρυσοστόμου ... τόμος πέμπτος [Eton 1612], pp. 930–40).

39. The interpretation of πνεῦμα τοῦ ἀερός at l. 38 offers much difficulty. The opening line of sec. 52, Γεμίσας δὲ δι᾽ ἑαυτοῦ τὸ πᾶν, πρὸς ἀερίους ἀρχὰς γυμνὸς ἀνταπεδύσατο (and having filled through himself the whole cosmos, he, naked, wrestled against the powers of the air), should be regarded as a transition from the encomium on the cross to the description of Christ's cosmic passion rather than as a part of the encomium, which Cantalamessa wrongly takes it to be; *v. I piu antichi testi pasquali della Chiesa: Le omelie di Melitone di Sardi e dell' anonimo quartodecimano e altri testi del II secolo* (Rome 1972), p. 79. There is no need, in order to anticipate the mention of the ἀέριοι ἀρχαί in sec. 52, to translate πνεῦμα at l. 38 of sec. 51 as "evil spirits" as do Nautin (note 5 above, pp. 97f., and *ad loc.*) and Cantalamessa (note 5 above, p. 132; and *I piu antichi*, p. 79 and note 88, pp. 123f.). Rather, we should render πνεῦμα as "winds" because, at the close of the encomium, it is the cruciform extension of Christ throughout the cosmos, not his combat against, and subjugation of, the demonic forces, which is foremost in the homilist's mind. Thus, the winds of the atmosphere are embraced by Christ's boundless horizontal extension (*cf.* χερσὶ ἀμετρήτοις at l. 39 with ἀὴρ ἀμετρήτοις βάθεσι καὶ πλάτεσι μετρούμενος in sec. 3.2, p. 121, ll. 12f. [N.]), just as his vertical extension reaches from the earth stabilized by his feet to the heavens touched by his brow.

epiphany of Christ marks the culminating emergence of the human figure from that of the tree and the cross. The vivid unity of the form of the three may be regarded as a rhetorical centerpiece, and the interplay of the imagery is certainly an important key to our understanding of the homily. What is more, the encomium, through which this union of tree, cross, and Christ is presented, seems itself to have been composed in such as way as to suggest the shape of a cross.

By this reading, the lower, earth-established portion of the cross corresponds to the first section (1–17), in which the human union with and enjoyment of the tree are considered. One arm of this cross, the first part of the second section (18–21), is represented by the emblems of fixity both of the cross firmly established on the earth and of Christ himself, fixed at the zenith of the tree/cross (26). The other arm, the second part of the second section (22–26), is represented by the emblems of passage both of the speaker and of Christ as well. Finally, the upper, heavenward-extending portion of the cross corresponds to the third section (27–40), in which the tree/cross and Christ the incarnate divinity imaged thereby are considered in their cosmic aspect. A suggestion of a cruciform pattern may also be detected in the ratio earlier computed among the numbers of syllables: 4 (1–17 = 181 syllables) : 1 (18–21 = 42 syllables) : 1 (22–26 = 47 syllables) : 4 (27–40 = 172 syllables).[40] This reading of the encomium may be diagrammed (by line and syllable count; v. Diagram III).

An exceptionally happy marriage of form and content, and one sufficiently distant from the formal mannerism of the τεχνοπαίγνια,[41] emerges from our recognition of this pattern. Yet, although we ought not to underestimate the abilities of those for whom the piece was originally intended, even a rhetorically sophisticated audience would have had difficulty in savoring the passage unless, at its delivery, there were present as a kind of visual aid a cross, whether of wood, or painted on a wall, or indicated by gestures. The presence of a cross, scarcely inappropriate at a paschal celebration, seems especially likely, since it is the cross that constitutes the very subject of the encomium.[42]

40. Note that the emblems of fixity and of passage, which constitute the inner elements of this ratio, fall into two groups of four each.

41. On the τεχνοπαίγνιον, v. C.A. Trypanis, *Greek Poetry from Homer to Seferis* (London/Boston 1981), pp. 341f. The absence from the encomium of the *IP* of the characteristic obscure words (γρῖφοι) and arcane periphrases as well as its imprecise syllable count indicate a relative freedom from such mannerism.

42. Concerning the extent to which the cross and its symbolism penetrated the minds and habits of second-century Christians, v. F.J. Dölger, "Beiträge zur Geschichte des Kreuzzeichens IX," *JAC* 10 (1967), pp. 7–29; and V. Grossi (note 9 above). P. Stockmeier, *Theologie und Kult des Kreuzes bei Johannes Chrysostomus: Ein Beitrag zum Verständnis des Kreuzes im 4. Jahrhundert* (Trier 1966) treats the import of the cross to the fourth century.

40	(10):	tree/cross/Christ is universally present (as a kind of world-soul)
38f.	(27):	tree/cross/Christ embraces the winds in the air between heaven and earth
37	(8):	tree/cross/Christ steadies the earth with his feet
36	(14):	tree/cross/Christ touches the heavens with the crest of his brow
32–35	(51):	cosmic cross as the tectonic symbol of the union of natures in Christ
29–31	(22):	tree/Christ as the universal prop
28	(21):	tree/Christ props himself in the middle region between heaven and earth
27	(20)	tree/Christ has ascended from earth to the heavens.

= 173 syllables

18–21 (42)   22–26 (47)

the speaker and the tree: the speaker and the tree:
the emblems of fixity   the emblems of passage

τρόπαιον   (κύριος) πορεία
βραβεῖον   κλῖμαξ
στήριγμα   ὁδός
φυλακτήριον (θεός)   ἄτραπος

13–17	(39):	summary: the tree as the speaker's sustenance and shelter	φύλλα
10–12	(40):	the speaker's union with, eating of the tree (blossoms—fruits)	
8f.	(30):	the tree as the speaker's shelter	
4–7	(46):	the speaker's union with the tree (roots—branches—foliage)	
1–3	(26):	introduction: speaker is nourished by, "feasts with" the tree	φυτόν

= 181 syllables

DIAGRAM III

FIVE

Basil's Protreptic to Baptism

Everett Ferguson

MANY EXHORTATIONS to baptism were delivered in the latter half of the fourth century;[1] one of these is Basil of Caesarea's *Exhortation to Holy Baptism*.[2] This work has been less studied than another discourse attributed to Basil, *On Baptism*,[3] perhaps because of the controversy over the genuineness of the latter.[4] The only major recent study of the *Exhortation* I have found is that by Jean Gribomont.[5] Here I purpose first to consider some key elements of the work—its de-

1. In addition to the works of the Cappadocian Fathers discussed in this paper, note the following by Latin authors: Zeno, the eight *Invit. font.* = *tract.* 1.32, 1.49, 2.28, 1.55, 2.23, 1.23, 1.12, and 2.14 in B. Löfstedt, *Zenonis Veronensis Tractatus* (Turnhout 1971) = *CChr.SL*, vol. 22; Max. Taur., *Ser.* 111.3 in A. Mutzenbecher, *Maximi Episcopi Taurinensis Sermones* (Turnhout 1962) = *CChr.SL*, vol. 23; Aug., *Ser.* 132.1 and 216.4, 9.

2. Ὁμιλία προτρεπτικὴ εἰς τὸ ἅγιον βάπτισμα; *PG*, vol. 31, coll. 423–44. In the body of this paper, I shall refer to this work as the *Exhortation*; elsewhere, under the abbreviation *Exh.*, I shall cite texts from the *PG* first by the chapter or section number of the ancient work and then by the number and letter of the column in the printed volume. I follow, with slight revision, the translation of T.P. Halton in *Baptism: Ancient Liturgies and Patristic Texts*, ed. A. Hamman (Staten Island, N.Y. 1967), pp. 76–87.

3. Περὶ βαπτίσματος; *PG*, vol. 31, coll. 1513–1628. In the body of this paper, I shall refer to this work as *On Baptism*; elsewhere, under the abbreviation *Bapt.* I follow, with slight revision, the English translation by M.M. Wagner, pp. 339–430 of *Saint Basil: Ascetical Works* (New York 1950) = *FOTC*, vol. 9.

4. Most scholars now seem to favor authenticity, as a result of the extensive parallels assembled in U. Neri's commentary to accompany his critical edition and translation, *Basilio di Cesarea, Il Battesimo: testo, traduzione, introduzione e commento* (Brescia 1976); his conclusions are summarized on pp. 31–53. Neri's critical text is used by J. Ducatillon in *Basile de Césarée, Sur le Baptême* (Paris 1989) = *SC*, vol. 357.

5. "Saint Basile: Le Protreptique au Baptême," pp. 71–92 of *Lex Orandi Lex Credendi: Miscellanea in onore di P. Cipriano Vagaggini*, ed. G. J. Békés and G. Farnedi = *StAns* 79 (1980). This article is wrongly assigned to *Word and Spirit* in *BPatr* 24/25 (1979/80), p. 84, #1087. There is a brief treatment of the *Exh.* in J. Bernardi, *La prédication des Pères Cappadociens: Le prédicateur et son auditoire* (Paris 1968), pp. 68–70.

ployment of rhetorical devices, use of Scripture, references to contemporary liturgy, and instruction in doctrinal and moral issues—and then to compare it with analogous works by Gregory of Nazianzus and Gregory of Nyssa.

Despite some ancient evidence for other attributions, the genuineness of this work seems generally accepted.[6] The *Exhortation* refers to the approach of the Pasch (1, 424D), and the occasion for the sermon is to encourage catechumens to turn in their names in order to undergo the final preparations for baptism (7, 440A). If we follow the predominant tradition in favor of Basil's authorship, the work likely comes from early in his episcopate, so the date would be prior to the paschal season in the years from 371 to 373.[7]

Rhetorical Features[8]

Basil addresses the problem, which became common after the example of Constantine, of catechumens who delayed receiving baptism until the approach of death.[9] Basil mercilessly exposes all excuses. He exalts the advantages enjoyed by those who receive baptism (3, 429A–431A; 5, 433A), and he repeatedly warns about the dangers of delay (3, 429C; 5, 433B–C; esp. 7f., 441B–444C). Whatever one's age, one should act now, because of the uncertainties of life (5, 432C, 436C). Basil responds to the temptations to procrastinate offered by the devil (6, 437B–C) and answers objections about the supposed difficulty of the Christian life (7, 440B–D). Worthwhile human endeavors such as agriculture, commerce, marriage, and raising children carry the risk of failure, but they are not avoided (7, 441A). Though many who become catechumens spend their lives in pleasure with the idea of giving to God their old age (5, 433B, 436B), Basil urges that the

6. V. P.J. Fedwick, "The Translations of the Works of Basil before 1400," in *Basil of Caesarea: Christian, Humanist, Ascetic: A Sixteen-Hundredth Anniversary Symposium,* Part 2, ed. *id.* (Toronto 1981), pp. 455f. for the attribution of this work to Chrysostom by Augustine and note 89, p. 456 for the same attribution in some Greek manuscripts. V. note 193, p. 478 for an Armenian version that assigns the work to Severian of Gabala.

7. Gribomont (note 5 above) says (pp. 71, 87f.) January 7, 371 or 372; Bernardi (note 5 above) suggests (p. 68) January 6 (Epiphany), 371, but acknowledges (p. 394) that the date is not certain.

8. For Basil's educational preparation, v. T.H. Olbricht, "The Education of a Fourth Century Rhetorician," *Western Speech* 29 (1965), pp. 29–36.

9. Gregory Nazianzen (*Or.* 40, εἰς τὸ ἅγιον βάπτισμα, *PG*, vol. 36, col. 360B) and Gregory of Nyssa (πρὸς τοὺς βραδύνοντας εἰς τὸ βάπτισμα, *PG*, vol. 46, coll. 415f.B) also addressed this subject in discourses influenced by Basil's exhortation. V. the brief comparison at the end of this paper. In the body of this paper, I shall refer to the first work as *Or.* 40 and to the second as *Against Those Who Delay Baptism.*

present is the proper time for baptism and the acceptance of the life it entails (1, 424A–C).

As the Greek title indicates, the work is a protreptic. The rhetorical analysis by Gribomont makes unnecessary a similar undertaking on my part.[10] Gribomont notes some of the features of protreptic found in the speech: the hearers are continually addressed in the second person singular; there are, according to his counts, some fifty imperatives, seventy-six questions, and at least a dozen exclamations underlined by "Oh" (῀Ω + the genitive) or "Woe." (Ἀι μέ).[11]

I want to call attention to some other rhetorical features of the *Exhortation* that are recorded in J.M. Campbell's study of the style of the sermons of Basil. He mentions the frequency of redundancy and especially repetition in the *Exhortation*.[12] Campbell further notes some of the devices for achieving vivacity. Basil is fond of putting imagined speech in the first person into the mouth of the hearers (προσωποποιία).[13] Extended examples occur in chapters five (433B, 436A–B) and eight (444A–B). He often employs the rhetorical question.[14]

Metaphors and illustrations are also frequent. Campbell counts thirty-seven examples of metaphor.[15] Examples of Basil's use of metaphors common among rhetoricians are his illustrations drawn from military life (an army's use of a password, 4, 432B), medicine (a physician who promises to restore youth, 5, 432D), the sea (a ship overloaded, 5, 433C), and athletics (a crown won only by competition, 7, 440B).[16] Among the less common metaphors Basil gives some elaboration to the following: a heifer under the yoke (1, 425C), a distribution of gold (3, 429A), a freeing of slaves (3, 429B), a cancelling of debts (3, 429C–D), objects that are sealed or marked (4, 432C), a person seeking to win another's friendship (5, 433C), a mother

10. Gribomont (note 5 above) gives (pp. 73–86) this outline: *Exordium* (424A8–425A1), *Narratio* (425A1–428A15), *Argumentatio I. Exempla et hypotheseis* (428A15–433B1), *Argumentatio II. Refutatio* (433B1–440A6), *Argumentatio III. Conclusio et confirmatio* (440A6–444B7), *Peroratio* (444B7–C8).

11. *Ib.*, p. 73. V., e.g., 3, 429B–C; 8, 444A.

12. J.M. Campbell, *The Influence of the Second Sophistic on the Style of the Sermons of St. Basil the Great* (Washington 1922), chh. 4 and 5.

13. *Ib.*, pp. 58–60. He counts (p. 60) six examples in the *Exh.*

14. Campbell's (*ib.*) count (p. 52) of 35 may differ from Gribomont's (note 5 above) 76 interrogations (p. 73), because the latter is counting all questions and Campbell only what he considers rhetorical questions.

15. Campbell (note 12 above), pp. 96–109.

16. Among the most common metaphors in rhetoric Campbell (*ib.*) counts (p. 107) the following in the *Exh.*: military (3), athletics (4), hippodrome (2), sea (1), debt (3), agriculture (1), heavenly bodies (1), roads (2), court (5), personification (1), and theater (0). I have not attempted to verify these.

bird that distracts hunters from her young (7, 437C–440A), enrollment in an army, or in athletic contests, or on the citizen list (7, 440A). Campbell concludes that Basil does not use the four common metaphors of rhetors—war, athletics, the hippodrome, and the sea—as often as other speakers did, but all do appear in this work. Campbell, who uses the term "comparisons" for "similes," records fewer of these in the *Exhortation:* to the sea (2), animals (3), and war (1).[17]

Basil makes much use of a practice dear to ancient rhetoricians, comparisons (σύγκρισις), especially those involving persons of the past.[18] In the *Exhortation* he draws lessons from John the Baptist (1, 425A), Moses and Israel (2, 428B), Elijah (two different episodes: 3, 428C–429A), Eve (3, 429C), and Cain (5, 436B). The rhetorical handbooks provide parallels also to his references to the ages of life (youth, prime of life, and old age: 5, 432C, 436C)[19] and to the times and occasions suitable for different activities (1, 424C).[20]

Use of Scripture

As with Basil's other writings, the *Exhortation* contains frequent quotations and allusions to Scripture, both the Old and New Testaments. The persons named in his historical comparisons are biblical. Biblical, rather than secular, history provides the common history for Basil and his hearers.

The *Exhortation* begins with a quotation of Eccles. 3.1f.: "For everything there is a season, and a time for every matter under heaven: a time to be born, and a time to die." This leads into the declaration that every time in man's life is a time for baptism, but especially fitting is the day of the Pasch (1, 424C–D). The application of this passage to baptism occurs first in Cyril of Jerusalem, who also anticipates Basil in suggesting that the reversed order, "to die and to be born," is more appropriate to baptism (*Cat. mys.* 2.4). This is one of the indications that Basil knew the work of Cyril.[21]

17. *Ib.*, pp. 110–27, esp. p. 125.

18. *V.* Men. Rh. secc. 376f.; D.A. Russell and N.G. Wilson, *Menander Rhetor* (Oxford 1981). Subsequent reference to Menander Rhetor follows this edition.

19. *V.* ch. 6, secc. 265f. of the *Ars rh.* passed down under the name of Dionysius of Halicarnasus; H. Usener and L. Radermacher, *Dionysii Halicarnasei quae exstant*, vol. 6 (Leipzig 1929; rpt. Stuttgart 1965): *Opusculorum*, vol. 2. Subsequent reference to ps.-D. H. follows this edition.

20. *V.* Men. Rh. sec. 408 and ps-D. H., *Ars rh.*, ch. 3, secc. 243f.

21. Gribomont (note 5 above), p. 74. Ecclesiastes received much study in the Cappadocian theological tradition; commentaries were written by Gregory Thaumaturgos, Gregory of Nyssa, and Evagrius of Pontus.

Basil moves into the body of his discourse by quoting four passages that had occurred in the day's Scripture readings: Is. 1.16; Ps. 33.6; Acts 2.38; and Mt. 11.28 (1, 425A–B). These references, appropriate to baptism and Basil's exhortation, reflect the liturgical practice of Scripture readings from the prophets supplemented by the Psalms, from the apostles (the Epistle), and from Jesus in the Gospel.[22]

Liturgical Matters

In addition to the liturgical readings and the liturgical calendar, Basil refers to vigils of prayer, fasting, and psalmody (7, 440D). Other liturgical information, as is to be expected, has to do with baptismal practice, but nothing exceptional is revealed. Baptism was preceded by catechesis (1, 425A).[23] For some this was a lengthy period lasting from their youth (1, 425B), even for those born into Christian families like Basil himself, since they delayed submitting to the instruction that led immediately to baptism (6, 437A). The candidate entered that period of preparation by turning in his or her name and being enrolled (7, 440A).

The allusions to the baptismal ceremony imply that the person receiving baptism was of responsible age. Repentance was required (7, 441A). The ceremony itself involved speaking "the saving words" (τὰ σωτήρια ῥήματα), lifting the hands to heaven while standing, bending the knee in worship, being taught and making confession, giving adherence to God, and renouncing the Enemy (5, 436C).[24]

These allusions occur in the context of sick-bed or death-bed baptism when the person may not be conscious. Basil emphasizes how undesirable it is not to be able to follow the initiation, not to experience what is happening, and for those present to be in doubt (5, 436D–437A). Evidently clinical baptism was an accepted practice, but these remarks seem to indi-

---

22. Gribomont (note 5 above), p. 75. Basil prefers the phrase "kingdom of heaven" to "kingdom of God" ; this indicates the influence of the Gospel of Matthew. The same preference appears in *Bapt.*, except that there ἡ βασιλεία τοῦ θεοῦ is dictated a few times by its occurrence in biblical quotations. Where Basil determines his own terminology, he chooses ἡ βασιλεία τῶν οὐρανῶν.

23. I have surveyed the different contents of catechetical instruction in "Irenaeus' *Proof of the Apostolic Preaching* and Early Catechetical Instruction," *StPatr* 18.3 (1989), pp. 119–40.

24. Basil, speaking to those not yet initiated, perhaps consciously does not give details or reflect the exact order, but the items to which he refers may be compared with the preliminary and initiatory ceremonies described in Cyr. Hier., *Procat.* 8–16; *id., Cat. mys.* 1–3; and *Const. app.* 7.22, 41–44, which included acts of repentance, confession of sins, renunciation of Satan, reciting the creed to associate oneself with Christ, and baptismal confession (τὴν σωτήριον ὁμολογίαν, Cyr. Hier., *Cat. mys.* 2.4) at the triple immersion.

cate uncertainty concerning its validity. Later in the treatise, Basil refers again to the practice of death-bed baptism and warns that delay may mean the absence of anyone to administer it (7, 441C).

Basil interprets Elijah's act of pouring water three times on the altar (1Kgs. 18.33–35) as prefiguring baptism in the three-fold name of the Trinity (3, 429A). This may indicate a triple pouring in baptism, but the use of water in the biblical story was sufficient to suggest baptism, and the three-fold action of Elijah is related to faith in the Trinity, not expressly to the baptismal action. It would, therefore, be dubious to build an argument for the baptismal procedure from this allusion.[25] His references to Israel drinking from the spiritual rock (1Cor. 10.4) and eating the bread of angels (Ps. 78.25) and to Christians eating "the living bread" (τὸν ζῶντα ἄρτον; cf. Jn. 6.51) allude to the baptismal Eucharist (2, 428B).[26] There are statements about being sealed (σφραγισθεὶς, 2, 428C; τὴν σφραγῖδα, 4, 432C; 6, 437A) but not about an anointing (e.g., a form of ἀλείφω) or chrism (e.g., some such word as χρίω, χρῖσις, χρῖσμα), and the references to a seal seem to indicate the baptism itself and not a particular part of the ceremony.[27]

Doctrinal Points

Basil in his *Exhortation* mentions some of the fundamentals of Christian faith: the Trinity (3, 429A), God as Creator (1, 424C; 3, 429C), salvation through the death and resurrection of Christ (1, 424C–D; 2, 428A), the Spirit as a seal (6, 437A), the Church as mother (1, 425A), human free will (1, 425C; 5, 432C–436C), the value of the soul (3, 429C), the human propensity to sin and its harmful effects (5, 433B, 436A), resurrection and judgment (8, 441D–444C). The greatest doctrinal value of the treatise, naturally, pertains to the importance given to baptism.

Quite basic for Basil was the idea of baptism as death to sin and resurrection to life, the thought with which he begins (1, 424B–C).[28] The benefits ascribed to baptism are numerous: illumination (1, 424C; 3, 429A, C),

25. A triple immersion is explicit in Cyr. Hier., *Cat. mys.* 2.4 (*cf. Cat. ill.* 17.14 for immersion) and Basil, *Sp. s.* 15.35.

26. *Cf.* Theod. Cyr., *Qu.* 27 *in Ex.;* Ambr., *Sacr.* 5.1.

27. *V.* Gribomont (note 5 above), pp. 83, 91, and *v.* my discussion (pp. 76–77 below) of the seal under the doctrine of baptism. It is possible, however, that the phrases τοῖς μυστικοῖς συμβόλοις, τὸ φῶς τοῦ προσώπου Κυρίου, τὰ γνωρίσματα, πρόβατον ἀσημείωτον, and ἐὰν μὴ σημειωθῇ of 4, 432C allude to the chrism. There were both pre- and post-baptismal anointings in the different baptismal rites of the fourth century. These were often, but not consistently, associated with the Holy Spirit; *v.* G.W.H. Lampe, *The Seal of the Spirit,* 2nd ed. (London 1967), esp. pp. 215–22.

28. *Cf.* his use of Rom. 6.2 (7, 440B); 6.5 (2, 428A); 6.13 (436B).

adoption as children of God (1, 425A; *cf.* 3, 429B), perfection (1, 425A), likeness or union with God (1, 425A; 3, 429A), forgiveness of sins (4, 432A), spiritual rejuvenation (5, 433A). The metaphors in chapter 3 are pertinent here: the benefits of baptism are likened to a distribution of gold (429A), a release from slavery (429B), and a forgiveness of debts (429C–D). Hence, Basil calls baptism "the grace" (*v., e.g.,* τὴν χάριν, 4, 432A; τῆς χάριτος, τὴν χάριν, 5, 437A), a common usage in Christian inscriptions.[29] An encomium was a part of speeches on many subjects, and Basil here pronounces an encomium on baptism: "Baptism is the ransom of captives, the remission of debts, the death of sin, the rebirth of the soul, the shining garment, the unbreakable seal, the chariot to heaven, the guarantee of the kingdom, the grace of adoption" (βάπτισμα αἰχμαλώτοις λύτρον, ὀφλημάτων ἄφεσις, θάνατος ἁμαρτίας, παλιγγενεσία ψυχῆς, ἔνδυμα φωτεινὸν, σφραγὶς ἀνεπιχείρητος, ὄχημα πρὸς οὐρανὸν, βασιλείας πρόξενον, υἱοθεσίας χάρισμα, 5, 433A).

Inasmuch as Basil was so important for defining the doctrine of the Holy Spirit, it is fitting that he says much about the Holy Spirit in relation to baptism. This is enunciated in his opening typologies of baptism. As Israel was figuratively baptized in the cloud and the sea (*cf.* 1Cor. 10.2), so baptism is accomplished in the reality of water and the Spirit (2, 427B).[30] Likewise, as Elijah ascended to heaven in the chariot of fire, one can "ascend to heaven through water and the Spirit" (δι' ὕδατος καὶ Πνεύματος ἀναβαίνειν εἰς τὸν οὐρανόν, 3, 428D).[31] The subsequent language comparing to baptism the water and fire on Elijah's altar at Mount Carmel may also be intended to refer to the water and Spirit. The activity of the Spirit in baptism is related to Basil's favorite imagery of the seal. One is "sealed by baptism" (σφραγισθεὶς τῷ βαπτίσματι, 2, 428C), and baptism is called "the seal" (τὴν σφραγῖδα, 4, 432C), but it is the "seal of the Spirit" (τὴν σφραγῖδα τοῦ Πνεύματος, 6, 437A). This provides the proper understanding for this statement by Basil: "A Jew does not postpone circumcision. . . . But you postpone a circumcision not done by hand in the stripping off of the flesh [Col. 2.11], which circumcision is performed by baptism" ('Ο

29. G.W.H. Lampe's (*A Patristic Greek Lexicon* [Oxford 1968], *sub voce,* χάρις I.C.1) "almost = baptism" does not do justice to the common equation of baptism with grace. For the inscriptions see my "Inscriptions and the Origin of Infant Baptism," *JThS* n.s. 30 (1979), pp. 41f.

30. This typology was thoroughly traditional; *v.* J. Daniélou, *Sacramentum Futuri: Étude sur les origines de la typologie biblique* (Paris 1950), pp. 152–76. For Basil's treatment, *v.* also *Sp. s.* 14.31–33.

31. This was not a common baptismal image, but *cf.* Cyr. Hier., *Cat. ill.* 3.5, for the explanation that Elijah crossed the Jordan before he was taken up to heaven.

'Ιουδαῖος τὴν περιτομὴν οὐχ ὑπερτίθεται. ... σὺ δὲ τὴν ἀχειροποίητον περιτομὴν ἀναβάλλη ἐν τῇ ἀπεκδύσει τῆς σαρκὸς, ἐν τῷ βαπτίσματι τελειουμένην, 2, 428A). Baptism is not the spiritual circumcision, as a superficial reading might suggest, but the spiritual circumcision takes place in baptism. In keeping with early Christian interpretation, Basil does not equate circumcision with baptism, but with the activity of the Spirit in baptism.[32]

Moral Concerns

One is born to the Spirit by dying to the flesh (1, 424B), a favorite description with Basil. This expresses his rigorist moral concerns, which are so evident in his discussions of baptism that the treatise *On Baptism* may be classed among his ascetic works.[33] Basil exhorts, "Take instructions, learn the constitution of the Gospels" (Μάθε, διδάχθητι εὐαγγελικὴν πολιτείαν, 7, 440A).

Basil puts into the mouth of his hearer who delays receiving baptism the following representative list of sins: "I will use my body to enjoy what is shameful, I will wallow in the mud of pleasure, I will bloody my hands, I will plunder what belongs to others, I will walk in wickedness, I will curse and swear. And I will receive baptism when I finally cease from sin" (ἀποχρήσωμαι τῇ σαρκὶ πρὸς τὴν ἀπόλαυσιν τῶν αἰσχρῶν, ἐγκυλισθῶ τῷ βορβόρῳ τῶν ἡδονῶν, αἱμάξω τὰς χεῖρας, ἀφέλωμαι τὰ ἀλλότρια, δολίως πορευθῶ, ἐπιορκήσω, ψεύσωμαι· καὶ τότε τὸ βάπτισμα, ὅταν λήξω ποτὲ τῶν κακῶν, ὑποδέξομαι, 5, 433B). It is especially sinful pleasures that receive strong rebuke from Basil: "Pleasure is the hook of the devil, luring us to destruction. Pleasure is the mother of sin" (Ἡδονὴ ἄγκιστρόν ἐστι τοῦ διαβόλου πρὸς ἀπώλειαν ἕλκον. Ἡδονὴ μήτηρ τῆς ἁμαρτίας, 5, 436A). Basil sees pleasure as the main reason for the delay of baptism (3, 429C), as the principal enticement of the devil for the present (6, 437C), but as causing exhaustion (7, 440C), and as bringing eternal torment (8, 444B).

Basil appeals to the fear of punishment and the hope of reward in his

32. E. Ferguson, "Spiritual Circumcision in Early Christianity," *SJTh* 41 (1988), pp. 485–97. I remain unconvinced by J. Daniélou's simple and unsubstantiated equation of spiritual circumcision with baptism in "Circoncision et baptême," *Theologie in Geschichte und Gegenwart: Michael Schmaus zum sechzigsten Geburtstag*, ed. J. Auer and H. Volk (Munich 1957), pp. 755f. For the Spirit given in baptism according to Basil, *v.* Lampe (note 27 above), pp. 198, 211, 240. Basil, *Sp. s.* 12.28–15.35 discusses the relation of the Spirit to baptism and offers numerous parallels to the *Exh.*

33. As is done by M.M. Wagner (note 3 above). For the moral teachings of the *Exh.*, see Gribomont, (note 5 above), pp. 88–91.

stirring peroration. He exhorts, "Fear hell, or strive to gain the kingdom" (ἢ τὴν γέενναν φοβήθητι, ἢ τῆς βασιλείας ἀντιποιήθητι, 8, 444B). The glory of the righteous and the grief of sinners (8, 444A) make the struggles of the Christian life worth it. Basil anticipates the modern principle, no pain, no gain: "One does not bring off the prize without running the race" (Οὐδεὶς μὴ δραμῶν ἀνείλετο τὸ βραβεῖον, 7, 440B). Moreover, the works of the devil bring their pain in this life too. "The happpiness to be enjoyed in heaven succeeds these tribulations [of the righteous], while the suffering and sorrow of hell perpetuate the pains of sin" (Ταύτας μὲν τὰς θλίψεις ἡ ἐν τῇ βασιλείᾳ τῶν οὐρανῶν μακαριότης ἐκδέχεται· τοὺς δὲ τῆς ἁμαρτίας καμάτους τὸ τῆς γεέννης ἐπίπονον καὶ σκυθρωπὸν ἀναμένει, 7, 440B–C).

In one of his vivid rhetorical appeals, Basil challenges his readers: "Now think as if your soul were in a balance, drawn in opposite directions by angels and devils. To which side will you give the impulse of your heart? Who will be victorious in your regard? Carnal pleasure or sanctification of soul?" (Νῦν ὥσπερ ἐπὶ τρυτάνης ἑστάναι νόμιζέ σου τὴν ψυχὴν, ἔνθεν ὑπ' ἀγγέλων, κἀκεῖθεν ὑπὸ δαιμόνων διελκομένην. Τίσιν ἄρα δώσεις τὴν ῥοπὴν τὴν καρδίας; τί παρὰ σοὶ νικήσει; ἡδονὴ σαρκὸς, ἢ ἁγιασμὸς ψυχῆς, 4, 432B). Although the imagery of the scale is Roman, the picture of angels and demons contending for the soul is Jewish. Having come into Christian thought, it was particularly elaborated by Origen.[34] This picture of angels and demons drawing the soul in different directions but the person choosing which influence to follow coincides with Basil's definition of virtue: "To avoid evil and do good" (ἔκκλισις ἀπὸ κακοῦ, καὶ ποίησις ἀγαθοῦ, 5, 436B).

Corresponding to Basil's list of sins is a statement of some of the qualities that constitute virtue. The way of life according to the gospel involves "vigilance of the eyes, control of the tongue, mastery of the body, humility of mind, purity of thought, and an end to anger" (ὀφθαλμῶν ἀκρίβειαν, γλώσσης ἐγκράτειαν, σώματος δουλαγωγίαν, φρόνημα ταπεινὸν, ἐννοίας καθαρότητα, ὀργῆς ἀφανισμόν, 7, 440B). One must take "the narrow road [of self-control] that leads to salvation" and not "the broad road of sin" (τὸ στενὸν τῆς ἐπὶ σωτηρίαν φερούσης, τὸ εὐρύχωρον ... τῆς ἁμαρτίας, 7, 440C).

34. For Jewish thought: *Scroll of the Rule* secc. 3f (a spirit of perversity and a spirit of truth allotted to each person); for Christianity: *Her., Mand.* 6.2 (an angel of righteousness and an angel of wickedness with each person) and *Barn.* 18 (plural angels of God and angels of Satan set over the two ways of life). Origen (*Prin.* 3.2.3f. and esp. 3.3.4: good spirits and evil spirits competing for control of the soul) stresses the role of free will in determining which influences one will follow. V. E. Ferguson, "Origen's Demonology," *Johannine Studies: Essays in Honor of Frank Pack,* ed. J.E. Priest (Malibu, Calif. 1989), pp. 54–66, esp. pp. 62–64.

Comparison with *On Baptism*

A rapid survey of some points of comparison between the two works will not reveal any decisive considerations relative to authorship nor suggest any content inconsistent with Basilian authorship of *On Baptism*. The similarities and differences of the *Exhortation* and *On Baptism* are largely accounted for by their common subject and different purposes: the *Exhortation* is a protreptic to candidates for baptism, *On Baptism* perhaps a guide for catechists who instructed candidates for baptism.[35]

Both works make extensive use of Scripture; *On Baptism* more so, for it is almost a continuous string of quotations.[36] It takes as its basis Mt. 28.19, and its theme may be stated as "to live according to the Gospel" (κατὰ τὸ Εὐαγγέλιον ζῆν, 2.1, 1580C; cf. 1.2, 1565B–1569A). The terminology is different, but the idea is the same as the *Exhortation's* "constitution of the Gospels" or "evangelical way of life" or "way of life according to the gospel" (εὐαγγελικὴν πολιτείαν, 7, 440A). Fundamental texts for *On Baptism* are Rom. 6.1–11 and Jn. 3.5 with the accompanying ideas of crucifixion, death, planting, resurrection, and newness of life or new birth. Both texts are used in the *Exhortation* (2, 428A), but the theme of death to sin is even more prominent in the longer *On Baptism*.[37] Otherwise, there is very little overlap in the scriptures cited.

Both works contrast the superiority of Christian baptism to the baptisms of John and Moses, but the comparison is different in each case.[38] Both works consider catechesis important; *On Baptism* says that instruction is necessary before one is worthy to receive baptism (1.2, 1525C and 1569B; cf. *Exh.* 1, 425A, B). Both *On Baptism* 1.2 (1556B–C) and *Exhortation* 5 (433A) provide lists of benefits accomplished by the death of Christ and conferred in baptism, but the contents are completely different, because the list in the *Exhortation* draws on the metaphors that precede it.[39] The

---

35. U. Neri (note 4 above), p. 53, says the hearers were for the most part priests or other persons with the care of souls.

36. For the doctrine of Scripture reflected in the work, v. Neri's introduction (note 4 above), pp. 54–64.

37. *V.* 1.2, 1553A, 1540B, 1541C–D, 1544A; 1.3, 1577D; 2.1, 1580C. The moral teaching is similar to that of the *Exh.* and Basil's other works; v. Neri (note 4 above), pp. 69–97.

38. The *Exh.* contrasts John's baptism with that of Christ as only repentance instead of adoption as sons, only preliminary instead of accomplishment, only a break with sin instead of union with God (1, 425A); it contrasts Moses' baptism as type with Christ's reality (2, 428A–B). *Bapt.* presents Moses' baptism as recognizing a difference between sins and being a seal of purification; John's made no distinction among sins and offered pardon; Christ's, accompanied by the Holy Spirit, brings glory beyond all hope and a preëminence of grace (1.2, 1532C–1533C). The treatment in *Sp. s.* 14.31–15.36 is different from both.

39. *Bapt.* 1.2, 1556B–C: From the death of Christ flow λύτρωσις ἁμαρτημάτων, ἐλευθερία τοῦ . . . θανάτου, καταλλαγὴ τῷ θεῷ, δύναμις τῆς πρὸς θεὸν εὐαρεστήσεως, δικαιοσύνης δωρεά,

use of the analogy of circumcision is similar and in both cases based on
Col. 2.11f.: "If one who has been circumcised in any part of the body, according to the circumcision of Moses, is a debtor to the whole law, how
much greater is the obligation when one is circumcised according to the
circumcision of Christ, whereby he puts off the whole body of sinful flesh"
(Εἰ . . . ὁ περιτμηθεὶς μέρος τι τοῦ σώματος, τὴν κατὰ Μωϋσῆν περιτομὴν,
ὀφειλέτης ἐστὶν ὅλον τὸν νόμον ποιῆσαι, πόσῳ μᾶλλον ὁ περιτμηθεὶς τὴν
κατὰ Χριστὸν περιτομὴν ἐν τῇ ἀπεκδύσει ὅλου τοῦ σώματος τῶν ἁμαρτιῶν
τῆς σαρκός, 2.1, 1580D; cf. Exh. 2, 428A). Once more, the consequences for
moral living are paramount, an emphasis not inconsistent with the concerns of the *Exhortation* but not so prominent there because of its different occasion.

Comparison with the Two Gregories

Approximately a decade later, both Gregory of Nazianzus and Gregory
of Nyssa addressed the same problem as Basil, the delay of baptism, at the
same season of the year, Epiphany. Nazianzen's *Or.* 40, *On Holy Baptism*, is
in scope and style much more ambitious than the related works of his fellow Cappadocians.[40] The Nyssene has two works on baptism, as does Basil,
but only his *Against Those Who Delay Baptism*, a work closely approximat-
ing Basil's *Exhortation*, will be considered here.[41]

The discourse of Gregory Nazianzus offers several exact parallels, indicating a direct indebtedness, to that of Basil. In keeping with his fuller
treatment, he elaborates the use of Ecclesiastes 3, and makes the point that
every time is appropriate for the work of salvation. In the same context, he
rebukes the attitude of procrastination that yields to the Evil One's enticement: "Give to me . . . the present, and to God the future; to me your
youth, and to God old age" (Ἐμοὶ δὸς τὸ παρὸν, θεῷ τὸ μέλλον· ἐμοὶ τὴν
νεότητα, θεῷ τὸ γῆρας, 14, 376C; cf. Exh. 5, 436B; 6, 437C). Like Basil, Gregory develops the theme of the devil's deceit in inducing people to delay

---

κοινωνία τῶν ἁγίων ἐν τῇ αἰωνίῳ ζωῇ, βασιλείας οὐρανῶν κληρονομία, καὶ μυρίων ἄλλων ἀγαθῶν
βραβεῖον. The list in *Exh.* 5 is quoted in the text of p. 76.

40. *PG*, vol. 36, coll. 359–428. I cite, with occasional modification, the translation in
NPNF, 2nd series, vol. 7 (New York, *etc.* 1894; rpt. 1989): *S. Cyril of Jerusalem, S. Gregory
Nazianzen*, pp. 360–77. A full-scale comparison of the three Cappadocians' works on bap-
tism is beyond my intentions here. V. my "Preaching at Epiphany: Gregory of Nyssa and
John Chrysostom on Baptism and the Church," *ChH* 66 (1997), pp. 1–17, and "Exhortations
to Baptism in the Cappadocians," *StPatr* 32 (1997), pp. 121–29.

41. *PG*, vol. 46, coll. 415–32. Since this text provides no chapter divisions, reference will be
solely by column, *i.e.*, number and letter. *Cf.* note 2 above. Translations from this work are
my own. The second work, "On the Baptism of Christ" = *CPG*, #3173.

baptism (chh. 14, 16). In addition, the warnings about the uncertainties of life are parallel, although Gregory multiplies the specific examples (*cf.* 14, 376D–377A with *Exh.* 5, 436C).[42] Gregory also deals with the concern of not living up to the requirements of the Christian life: "Do you fear the seal because of the weakness of nature?" (δέδοικας τὴν σφραγῖδα διὰ τὸ τῆς φύσεως ἀσθενές, 17, 380D–381A; *cf.* ch. 16 and *Exh.* 7, 440B–D). Like Basil, he stresses the appropriateness of baptism for the different ages (ch. 17; *cf. Exh.* 5, 432C) and conditions of life: "There is no state of life and no occupation to which baptism is not profitable" (οὐκ ἔστιν οὐ βίος, οὐκ ἐπιτήδευμα, ᾧ μὴ τοῦτο λυσιτελέστερον, 18, 381C). Gregory too is of the opinion that pleasure is the chief deterrent to accepting baptism (*e.g.,* 20, 384D).

Acts 8.36, "Here is water! What is to prevent my being baptized?" (Ἰδοὺ τὸ ὕδωρ· τί κωλύει με βαπτισθῆναι;) lent itself admirably to the needs of both preachers to encourage immediate baptism (*cf.* 26, 396A with *Exh.* 6, 437A). There is an incidental agreement in their use of the parable "of the Unforgiving Servant" in Mt. 18.23–35 (31, 404B–C; *cf. Exh.* 3, 432A).[43] More striking is Gregory's use of the "seal" (σφραγίς, σφραγίζω) in the same sense as Basil (10, 372A; 15, 377A–B; 17, 380D), even to the detail of the unmarked sheep being easily stolen (15, 377B; *cf. Exh.* 4, 432C). Furthermore, Gregory closely approximates Basil's words about being baptized while not so sick as to be unable to say the confession.[44] Again the borrowing extends even to a detail. Elaborating the death-bed scene, he repeats the incidental comparison of the person baptized *in extremis* to the one-talent man of Mt. 25.25 (11f., esp. 373B–C; *cf. Exh.* 5, 436C–437A; 7, 441C).

Gregory of Nyssa's *Against Those Who Delay Baptism* is dense with parallels to Basil's *Exhortation* but is nonetheless a work of originality. Gregory's work, while making frequent use of Scripture, has fewer explicit quotations and refers to the Bible more allusively than does Basil's *Exhortation*. The quotations offer some exact parallels to Basil's work: the combination of Ps. 33.6 and Is. 1.16, but in this reversed order (417C; *cf. Exh.* 1.425A), Acts 8.27–39 (more elaborated, 421C–D; *cf. Exh.* 6, 437A), and Jn. 3.5 (424A; *cf. Exh.* 2, 428A).

Basil's brother repeats his exhortation not to delay the reception of baptism (417D–420A). Death may intervene before baptism is received (417D; *cf. Exh.* 7f., 441B–444C). Life is uncertain (420B), and death may come at any age (417D–420A; *cf. Exh.* 5, 432C, 436C). Gregory too feels he

---

42. *Cf. Or.* 40.13, 376A: Πᾶς σοι καιρὸς ἐκπλύσεως, ἐπειδὴ πᾶς ἀναλύσεως.

43. This is the title given by the editors of *The Greek New Testament* (*v.* Abbreviations, p. xxvii above).

44. *Or.* 40.26, 396A: Ἅρπασον τὸν καιρόν· ... καὶ εἰπών, βαπτίσθητι, καὶ βαπτισθεὶς σώθητι.

must answer the objection that, because of the weakness of human nature, one may easily sin after baptism, so it is better to "delay the grace of regeneration" (πρὸς τὴν χάριν τῆς παλιγγενεσίας βραδύνω, 425B; cf. Exh. 7, 440B–441A). He enlarges on a strategy borrowed from Basil in order to show the speciousness of this argument: If the catechumens are living blameless lives now, there is nothing to fear from baptism; if they are living impure lives, they show that they do not want to give up the life of sin (425C–D; cf. Exh. 4, 432A–B).

The Nyssene uses some of the same metaphors as his brother, but not brought together in the same way. Some are less developed, and others more elaborated: release to those in bonds and settlement for debtors (417A; cf. Exh. 3, 429B, C–D), healing (a favorite of Gregory's, 417B; cf. Exh. 5, 432D), distribution of royal gifts (417B; cf. Exh. 3, 429A), the newly enrolled soldier (429C; cf. Exh. 7, 440A).

Gregory of Nyssa, like Basil, urges his hearers: "Give me your names in order that I may inscribe them" (Δότε μοι τὰ ὀνόματα, ἵνα ἐγὼ μὲν αὐτὰ . . . ἐγχαράξω, 417B; cf. Exh. 7, 440A). Otherwise, there are fewer allusions to liturgical practice. This makes all the more striking the description—similar to those of his namesake and his brother—of the sick-bed and the tumult and disorder of the last hours of life when there is the hurried search for "the sacred vessels, the water, the priest, the word that makes ready for grace" (τὰ σκεύη, τὸ ὕδωρ, ὁ ἱερεὺς, ὁ λόγος ὁ πρὸς τὴν χάριν προευτρεπίζων, 425A; cf. Exh. 5, 436C–437A; 7, 441C). It is better in "leisure and calmness" (ἐν σχολῇ καὶ γαλήνῃ) to make the arrangements to be numbered "in the list of those adopted as sons" (τῷ καταλόγῳ τῶν υἱοθετουμένων, 425B).

Gregory, like the other Cappadocians, refers to baptism as the "seal" and uses the analogy of the sheep that is sealed (τὴν σφραγῖδα, 417B; cf. 424B). Like Basil and Gregory Nazianzus, he also appeals to the "one talent" of Mt. 25.25 in his exhortation to baptism; Gregory urges his hearers not to bury it, by deferring baptism to a last-minute decision, but to put it to work (429A–B). Like Basil, he equates baptism and grace (424D; cf., e.g., Exh. 4, 432A). Gregory of Nyssa gives a much shorter list of the benefits of baptism: adoption, participation in grace, cleansing of sins (416C).

Gregory of Nyssa shares Basil's concerns with the threat offered by the appeal of pleasure. He presents baptism as "a hindrance of pleasures" (ἡδονῶν κώλυμα, 425D). He tells his hearers, "Many times you gave yourself to pleasure; give also time to philosophy" (i.e., to the disciplined ascetic life; πολλοὺς χρόνους ἐχαρίσω τῇ ἡδονῇ· δὸς καὶ τῇ φιλοσοφίᾳ σχολήν, 420B–C).

Conclusion

It is a measure of how far the church and its situation in society had changed that authors in the third century wrote exhortations to martyrdom, whereas preachers in the last half of the fourth century delivered exhortations to baptism. The danger to the church was no longer members who apostatized in face of persecution. Now there were those who wanted the status of Christians without the responsibilities.

The Theologian and Technical Rhetoric

Gregory of Nazianzus and Hermogenes of Tarsus

Frederick W. Norris

I N RESEARCH for my commentary on Gregory Nazianzen's *Theological Orations,* a project suggested to me by Thomas Halton, my most unexpected discovery was that of the influence of philosophical rhetoric on the Theologian's work.[1] The term "philosophical rhetoric" was in use at least as early as Dionysius of Halicarnassus, centuries before Gregory was born.[2] George Kennedy, the modern student who perhaps best explains the concept, does not deny that so-called sophistic rhetoric was a significant model in the schools. Handbooks show that professors of rhetoric taught techniques that could be applied to nearly any topic. Some rhetoricians offered their skills on either side of a debate, not merely to entertain people but also to move an audience through carefully crafted orations toward the desired result. Both philosophical and technical rhetoric provided assistance in reaching that end, but philosophical rhetoric looked deeply into the possibilities of how people came to know what they did. Its debate with Platonic idealism was more weighty. It was not the kind of sophistry, dedicated only to feathering one's own nest, that is now

---

1. V. F.W. Norris, *Faith Gives Fullness to Reasoning: The Five Theological Orations of Gregory Nazianzen,* trans. L. Wickham and F. Williams (Leiden 1991), particularly the section of the introduction entitled "Christian *Paideia:* Philosophy, Rhetoric and Theology," pp. 17–39.

2. V. *Ad Pomp.,* sec. 757 (τῆς φιλοσόφου ῥητορικῆς) and sec. 784 (τὴν φιλόσοφον ῥητορκήν); H. Usener and L. Radermacher, *Dionysii Halicarnasei,* vol. 6 (Leipzig 1929; rpt. Stuttgart 1965): *Opusculorum,* vol. 2. Dionysius here describes philosophical rhetoric as the comparison of various kinds of good literature at least in terms of style (sec. 757). It also includes the historical study of both Greek and barbarian customs, laws, forms of government, and biographies in the search for justice, piety, and other virtues (sec. 784).

despised as immoral or trivial and wrongly regarded as typical of all rhetoric.[3]

Though a practitioner of philosophical rhetoric, Nazianzen felt no compunction in employing some of the small, intricate devices developed by the so-called sophistic rhetoricians of the period, particularly those admired by Neoplatonists because of their logical quality.[4] But any good philosophical rhetorician also looked for larger persuasive structures, ones that would provide the ways in which lengthy arguments could be developed and set in order within treatises. Kennedy notes that the works by, or attributed to, Hermogenes of Tarsus were important in the education of fourth-century rhetoricians, both pagan and Christian.[5] Elias of Crete, a twelfth-century commentator on Gregory, insisted that the Theologian's arguments were influenced not only by the understanding of logic and rhetoric found in Aristotle but also by the views on those subjects developed by Hermogenes.[6] John Siceliotes, an eleventh-century rhetorician, wrote a commentary on Hermogenes' Περὶ ἰδεῶν. Poynton shows that Siceliotes used nearly 800 passages from Nazianzen to illustrate Hermogenes' points.[7]

Here I do not attempt to argue that any particular words or phrases establish that Gregory Nazianzen had read Hermogenes of Tarsus. What I am suggesting is that Elias' observation can help the reader understand the basic structure of the arguments in Gregory's *Oration* 33. Looking for the influence of Hermogenes' *stasis* theory, one of the major contributions of this great second-century rhetorician, opens up an avenue for understanding another way in which the Theologian practiced the art of persuasion.

Hermogenes' Περὶ στάσεων is appealing because of its "dialectical qual-

---

3. G.A. Kennedy, *Classical Rhetoric and Its Christian and Secular Tradition from Ancient to Modern Times* (Chapel Hill, N.C. 1980), pp. 18–40.

4. For detailed accounts of the ways in which Gregory employed various small tactics of rhetoric in his writings, particularly his orations, *v.* M. Guignet, *S. Grégoire de Nazianze et la rhétorique* (Paris 1911); E. Fleury, *S. Grégoire de Nazianze et son temps* (Paris 1930); J. Plagnieux, *S. Grégoire de Nazianze Théologien* (Paris 1952); and R.R. Ruether, *Gregory of Nazianzus: Rhetor and Philosopher* (Oxford 1969).

5. G.A. Kennedy, *Greek Rhetoric under Christian Emperors* (Princeton, N.J. 1983), pp. 52–54.

6. Latin translation by J. Leunclavius, *Operum Gregorii Nazianzeni tomi tres. Aucti nunc primum . . . Eliae Cretensis Episcopi . . . et ipsius Gregorii librorum aliquot accessione* (Basel 1571); *v.* Elias' remarks (vol. 1, pp. 94–122, esp. 118f.) on parts of *Or.* 3 and 4.

7. *V.* John Siceliotes, *ΕΞΗΓΗΣΙΣ ΕΙΣ ΤΑΣ ΙΔΕΑΣ ΤΟΥ ΕΡΜΟΓΕΝΟΥΣ*, pp. 56–504 in C. Walz, *Rh.*, vol. 6 (Stuttgart, *etc.* 1834; rpt. Osnabrück 1968); and A.B. Poynton, "Gregory Nazianzus and the Greek Rhetoricians: A Supplement to the Index of Walz, *Rhetores Graeci*, vol. 9," typescript donated to the Library of Congress, April 26, 1934.

ities . . . : the formal validity, systematic method, and clarity of his treatment."[8] *Stasis*, as used in this type of rhetorical literature, refers to a "stock
issue," "a question that acts as a focus or center for opposing contentions
in a controversy."[9] Hermogenes seeks to develop such a question in stock
ways "if there are persons and acts to be judged, or at least one of these, if
plausible arguments are available, and if the decision is uncertain."[10] For
oratory in most juridical, political, and ecclesiastical institutions, *stasis*
theory proved to be central. Because Aristotle did not discuss it in his
Rhetoric, technical handbooks that did treat it became the more important
influences in the study of rhetoric.[11]

Hermogenes' treatise appears to be less than systematically organized.
Thus I have ordered his comments in what seems to me a better outline.
He offers separate examples for nearly each one of his points.[12] Because
those examples do not indicate how a rhetorician would deal with the
same case in different circumstances, they clarify only the individual principles, not the system itself. Therefore, within the following description of
Hermogenes' treatise, I have created in all but one instance my own illustrations, imaginary situations involving the same deed. I provide one hypothetical case adjusted to each rule, save the one, in the hope that the
character of the whole system will be more clearly represented.

According to Hermogenes, there are questions, such as the nature of
justice, honor, or expediency, that are not open to the use of the *stasis*
method. There are also circumstances that may militate against its employment.[13] Even if there is to be "a reasoned disputation on a particular

8. Kennedy (note 5 above), p. 74.

9. R. Nadeau, "Hermogenes *On Stases:* A Translation with an Introduction and Notes,"
SM 31 (1964), p. 369.

10. Kennedy (note 5 above), p. 82. This is a paraphrase of material in Περὶ στάσεων, p. 32,
H. Rabe, *Hermogenis Opera* (Leipzig 1913) = *Rh.*, vol. 6. All citations of Περὶ στάσεων follow
the text and page numbers of Rabe's edition. V. also J. Kowalski, *Hermogenes De Statibus*
(Wroclaw 1947). My translations follow, with slight modification, Nadeau (note 9 above), pp.
361–424.

11. V. O.A.L. Dieter, "Stasis," *SM* 17 (1950), pp. 345–69, and R. Nadeau, "Classical Systems
of Stases in Greek: Hermagoras to Hermogenes," *GRBS* 2 (1959), pp. 51–73.

12. Nadeau (note 9 above) sets Hermogenes' teaching on *stasis* in its lineage. M. Patillon,
*La théorie du discours chez Hermogène le Rhéteur: Essai sur les structures linguistiques de la
rhétorique ancienne* (Paris 1988), offers a critical assessment of Hermogenes and his work,
particularly the treatise On Ideas (Περὶ Ἰδεῶν). G. Kustas, *Studies in Byzantine Rhetoric*
(Thessaloniki 1973) gives considerable attention to Hermogenes in Byzantine tradition.

13. Hermogenes (*Stat.*, pp. 29f.) offers seven types of designations for the defendant that
would allow in greater or lesser measure the application of his method. Personal names (τὰ
ὡρισμένα καὶ κύρια) like Pericles and Demosthenes give most scope while "simple descriptions" (τὰ ἁπλᾶ προσηγορικά) like "general" or "orator" give the least. V. ib., p. 32, for cases
that are not open to the development of an argument based on one of his *staseis*.

item from the standpoint of the laws ... or from the customs arising from ordinary notions of justice, honor, or expediency" (ἀμφισβήτησις λογικὴ ἐπὶ μέρους ἐκ τῶν παρ᾽ ἑκάστοις κειμένων νόμων ἢ ἐθῶν περὶ τοῦ νομισθέντος δικαίου ἢ τοῦ καλοῦ ἢ τοῦ συμφέροντος, p. 29), the focus will be on persons and deeds. Further, it is a specific person or a definite deed capable of being defended that is most open to the development of a *stasis* argument. A particular *stasis* can be employed if the character or the act of a person "is uncertain in judgment and not prejudged before the trial but capable of being judged" (τὸ τῆς κρίσεως ἀφανὲς καὶ μὴ προειλημμένον δυνάμενόν τε πέρας λαβεῖν συνέστηκε). It is also important to be dealing with "arguments which are not only apt for persuasion but also strong in proofs" (τοὺς ... λόγους σὺν τῷ πιθανῷ διαφόρους τε καὶ ταῖς πίστεσιν ἰσχυρούς, p. 32). If these conditions are met, argument for different plausible explanations may be presented. The first thing to do is to identify the subject or the act under investigation: *e.g.,* Aphrodite has been killed. Did Apollo do it? If it is not certain who the perpetrator was, (*e.g.,* as yet we do not know that Apollo killed her), then the so-called facts of the case should be ascertained. We need to know "whether [each fact] is uncertain or certain" (εἰ ἀφανές ἐστιν ἢ φανερόν, p. 36).

If, however, both the doer and the deed are certain (*i.e.,* we know that Apollo killed Aphrodite), then the one pleading the case for the defense might ask whether the understanding of the circumstances surrounding the act "is complete or incomplete" (εἰ τέλειόν ἐστιν ἢ ἀτελές). If it is incomplete, then perhaps a different definition of the act might be presented "first from the standpoint of what has been done and, then, from what is needed to reach a perfect term [for the definition of the act]" (ἔστι γὰρ στάσις ὁρικὴ ὀνόματος ζήτησις περὶ πράγματος, οὗ τὸ μὲν πέπρακται, τὸ δὲ λείπει πρὸς αὐτοτέλειαν τοῦ ὀνόματος, p. 37). For instance, Aphrodite is dead; some say she died of a broken heart because Apollo left her. "He did it," they say. But leaving a lover does not constitute murder.

If the understanding of the facts is complete (*e.g.,* Apollo did indeed kill Aphrodite), and the situation in which the act took place appears to be certain, then the orator should look into "the quality of the act" (τὴν ποιότητα τοῦ πράγματος, p. 37). Is it a legal act? Perhaps there is a conflict (ἀντινομία) in the very laws that govern this particular deed, one denying what another permits (pp. 41, 83). Thus, although one is not normally allowed to kill his wife, this event should be viewed in light of customary practice in cases of marital infidelity. Apollo had the right to kill Aphrodite, because she had committed adultery.

Perhaps there is an ambiguity (ἀμφιβολία) in the law or the legal docu-

ment itself. Because Greek texts were often written without punctuation
or word separation, there were times when what was inscribed was remarkably ambiguous. It might be that in this case there is an ambiguity in
the particular passage, one that can become the basis of an argument in
defense of Apollo. I did not find an imaginative illustration for this principle that would be in line with the other examples I have provided. Thus
the actual cases Hermogenes offers must suffice. They are interesting and
show what a rhetorician should search for in constructing this aspect of a
defense. The first deals with an accent. The law seems to say that if a cour-
tesan inappropriately wears ornaments of gold, those ornaments become
state property. One woman wears such jewelry, is arrested, and concedes
that the gold ornaments belong to the state. The word δημοσια, when ac-
cented on the antepenult, is neuter and refers to the jewelry. But if accent-
ed on the penult, it is feminine and thus indicates that the woman herself
has become state property because of her disobedience. The inscribed law
has no accent marks, so the debate ensues over what actually belongs to
the state, the ornaments or the woman. In a culture where slavery was
common, the answer was not obvious. The second example deals with the
separation of words. There are two sons in the family: Allleo (Πανταλέων)
and Leo (Λέων). The will reads: "My possessions shall be ALLLEO'S"
(ἐχέτω τὰ ἐμὰ πανταλεων). If it is one word, then Πανταλέων receives
everything. If, however, it is two words, then Λέων receives eveything. Because the written will contains no accent marks, word divisions, or differentiation between upper- and lowercase letters, the meaning must be debated (pp. 41f).

If there is no ambiguity in the written text, and both the doer and the
deed are certain, and the understanding of the situation complete, then
the one pleading for the defense might suggest grounds other than the
written legal grounds for finding Apollo innocent or at least reducing the
punishment. Is the deed rationally defensible (p. 37)? The law might be examined in terms of its framers' intent (διάνοια), which may not fit this
case (pp. 82, 84–86): e.g., Apollo killed Aphrodite, but those who framed
the law under which he is charged did not mean to condemn a hero who
defends his city against a traitor. Aphrodite's evil powers of seduction
could have destroyed the state. The act might be examined in terms of
the perpetrator's intent (διάνοια) or "alternative motive" (μετάθεσις τῆς
αἰτίας, p. 49); perhaps the act was unpremeditated and/or unintentional:
e.g., Apollo killed Aphrodite, but it was accidental (pp. 58f., 72f., 82). He
had aimed his spear at Eutrophos, the traitor, who jumped out of the way
at the last moment. The issue could also be debated in terms of the "letter

and intent" (ῥητὸν καὶ διάνοια) of some pertinent document other than the laws applying to the case (pp. 40, 49, 82). *E.g.*, does the epistle Apollo sent to his friend Trypho literally express his intention to kill Aphrodite? Or is the language so ambiguous that we cannot tell if the act was premeditated?

Perhaps one should take into consideration some special "inference" (συλλογισμός) drawn from the facts of the particular situation (pp. 35, 40, 66, 81f., 84, 88f.). *E.g.*, Apollo found Aphrodite's spear in his dead father's chest and jumped to the conclusion that she had killed him. It seemed logical at the time, but the inference was wrong. Yet Apollo should be judged less harshly because he thought he was taking proper revenge as the law allowed.

It might be that, though intentional, the act was caused by the opponent or someone else. In such a case the defense offers a "counter argument" (ἀντίθεσις, pp. 38, 72). *E.g.*, Apollo intentionally killed Aprodite, but in self-defense. In a rage she attacked him, and he was only defending himself.

"Shifting-the-blame" (μετάστασις) is another option (pp. 39, 75). *E.g.*, seated astride his horse Apollo threw his spear at Eutrophos, the traitor. The horse reared, Apollo lost his balance, and his throw was faulty. The horse caused Aphrodite's death.

The deed might be intentional but in itself a "benefit" (εὐεργέτημα, pp. 38f.). *E.g.*, Aphrodite was a traitor. Apollo killed her, but he rid society of a dreaded threat. He deserves praise, not condemnation.

Finally there is a possibility that accountability for the act must be accepted and the one arguing the case for the defense should plead for leniency (συγγνώμη, pp. 39, 75). *E.g.*, in a rage Apollo has killed Aphrodite; now he is deeply distraught with remorse, for she was his lover. Can those making the judgment in this case be anything but lenient when the greatest loss to anyone still living is to Apollo himself?

Hermogenes' system is more complex than here represented. I have used only what is needed for the following comparison with the structure of Gregory's *Or.* 33 and thus have left out the treatment of issues including dual charges in which two acts are involved (pp. 55f.), a plea for a lesser charge (p. 62), or the question of which style should be used in presenting a case: forensic, deliberative, or panegyrical (pp. 34f.). But the good sense and sensitivity of the whole is evident. I am often amused that lawyers know little about ancient rhetoric and nothing of Hermogenes.

The structure of Gregory's *Or.* 33 does not slavishly follow Hermogenes' system of *stases*, but the outline of the oration shows a masterful sense of how *stasis* theory can be employed as a tool that cuts in two different directions. According to Nazianzen, the Constantinopolitan Eunomians had attacked him and his small community in two ways. First, they physically disrupted the services held at the chapel called Anastasia. Gregory even accuses them of having shed blood in a massacre.[14] Second, they belittled the Theologian as one whose origins, looks, accent, and education gave him away as a country bumpkin (secc. 6–12).

Gregory chooses the conduct of these non-Nicenes as the first subject for discussion. Although part of the debate concerns later Arian Trinitarian doctrine (*i.e.*, in the Theologian's view they try to measure the godhead), their ethics receive most attention. Only the final two sections are devoted wholly to what modern theologians recognize as Trinitarian issues (secc. 16f.).

Modern historians of ancient Christianity are struck by how often those considered heretics are also accused of wrong conduct. Thus skepticism about whether or not the Neo-Arians actually were disruptive to the point of manslaughter, if not murder, seems appropriate. But what in the eyes of many a historian of Christian doctrine seems to be either a misplaced argument about ethics or another standard charge about heretics lacking virtue would be for Gregory a reason to employ the intricacies of Hermogenian *stasis* theory. He never separated theology and ethics as the modern discipline of historical theology regularly does. He looks at his antagonists' deeds, which to his mind reveal their theology, and develops his oration in a proper Hermogenian pattern.

The so-called facts behind the charge that the non-Nicenes have attacked his congregation are considered certain. Apparently the Theologian anticipates that his opponents will not now contest the reality of the acts, because their attempt to charge him with the deaths that their mob action brought about has already failed before the magistrate.[15] Had he thought that they would argue that the so-called facts of the case were uncertain, he would have employed a different aspect from the Hermogenian system to confront their position. Then his approach would have been to ascer-

14. *Or.* 33.3. All references to *Or.* 33 follow the section numbers of C. Moreschini and P. Gallay, *Grégoire de Nazianze: Discours 32–37* (Paris 1985) = *SC*, vol. 318. In contrast to the Maurists and Moreschini (p. 24 and note 4, p. 161), I read these statements, not as references to earlier problems in Alexandria, but as veiled allusions to recent events in Constantinople, which I connect with those described in *De seipso*, ll. 652–78 and *Epp.* 77f.

15. The appearance before the magistrate, which he mentions in the autobiographical *De seipso* ll. 668–78, has taken place prior to the speaking of this oration. He was charged with murder, and the charge was refuted. The statement ὑπ' αὐτῶν τῶν ἀρχόντων ἀπανθρωπίαν ἐνεκλήθησαν, τῶν τὰ τοιαῦτα χαριζομένων (*Or.* 33.4) refers to earlier Arian deeds, but may be phrased in this way in order to remind his audience of this recent judicial hearing.

tain whether what the later Arians believed to be the facts were indeed true. He does not make such a move. He understands that even the Eunomians, whom he believes to be ready once again to disrupt the service, have been rebuked in their attempt to prove that he and his party were responsible for the deaths (sec. 1). He suspects that they would be unlikely to bring such charges again in a case they have already lost. Yet he also entertains the thought that they may not be of a mind to admit any responsibility that they or their henchmen had in the killing. Neither side will contest the fact that manslaughter has occurred, and thus in this instance the case will be argued on the basis of the quality of the acts.

Serving here as a prosecutor, the Theologian tries to make the case that his antagonists' attacks were neither legal nor rational under the conditions of normal daily life. He argues that their actions are more like those undertaken in war, the kind that the Roman and barbarian armies wage; they do not represent the way members of a family treat each other (sec. 2). There is nothing legal or rational about besieging a group in prayer, stopping their singing with the blast of trumpets, desecrating their sanctuary by killing. In describing the Constantinopolitan later Arians' actions as illegal and irrational, he further intertwines their deeds with those who left saints' bodies to be eaten by animals and who opposed their burial as criminal. Such folk ripped the flesh from an old bishop and caused the death of eighty priests by burning them in a ship. These Constantinopolitan Eunomians are like the Alexandrian Arians who had earlier defiled the throne of the orthodox hero Athanasius. Gregory also compares them with those who gave sacred vessels to Nebuzaradan or Belshazzar, Israel's enemies from biblical times. They are without excuse (secc. 3f.).

This is doubtless the weakest link in Gregory's argument, for he is bringing to bear analogies that may not be directly connected to the deeds of his opponents. We do not know if they dishonored bodies or tortured an old bishop. They were not responsible for the death of eighty priests in a fiery vessel; that happened off the coast of Nicomedia. They did not attack Athanasius in Alexandria. Whether any in his audience gave up liturgical silver during times of persecution is not known. Although this type of rhetorical ploy was common in his era, it does not stand up to scrutiny.[16] Gregory has not even made a case for the dubious charge of guilt by association, because he has demonstrated no association.

16. Socrates notes (*H. E.* 4.14f.) that in the 370s Constantinopolitan Arians had continually made life miserable for the Nicene Christians. Although it is improbable that Gregory was not told of such events by his congregation, he does not mention them. He selects situations in which killing took place, or a great leader was threatened and deposed.

We may suppose that the later Arians would have fought the charges that they gave up liturgical vessels, set the priests' ship ablaze, tortured an elderly bishop, and desecrated bodies. It would be interesting to know what they would have chosen to do with the charge that their forebears persecuted Athanasius. Some might have vigorously denied that they were to be seen as descendants of Arius. Some surely would have insisted that the Alexandrian bishop richly deserved attack.

In Gregory's eyes, the persuasiveness of *Or. 33* derives from the certainty and completeness of his charges. His opponents could not prove to the magistrate that he was the murderer; they either were not allowed or chose not to reargue the case publicly. He is convinced that they do actually know that some of their group were the perpetrators of the deeds he describes. If, however, they accept the certainty and completeness of the charges—that some of his party were killed, and some of their party were responsible—he thinks they will have difficulty defending themselves. Indeed his case is well-argued along the Hermogenian lines accepted by both his followers and his antagonists.

If his opponents were to answer the charge on the ground of the quality of the act, they would have to argue that their attacks were either legal or rational. Arguing for transferring the blame, due to lack of intention or to accidental circumstances, both appear less likely avenues of persuading any audience whether composed of magistrates or of ordinary citizens. Unintentional harm or accidental circumstances might also have been pursued as lines of defense. Rocks were thrown to disrupt the services; they missed Nazianzen and evidently hit and killed some worshippers. Perhaps there was no intention to kill. Perhaps that was an accidental result. Perhaps manslaughter, not murder, would have been the charge.[17]

Reference to the continued hostility of these non-Nicenes suggests that they are not ready to repent and accept responsibility for the previous conduct, to throw themselves on the mercy of the court and ask for leniency (sec. 1). These later Arians may instead believe that their intentional acts were beneficial and thus only appeared to be illegal or irrational. From their perspective, their deeds may seem both premeditated and good for

17. *Or.* 33.1–4. In *De seipso* ll. 665–72, Nazianzen speaks of trouble with a mob, but again the references are cryptic: Λίθους παρήσω τὴν ἐμὴν πανδαισίαν, / Ὧν ἔν τι μέμφοιμ' οὐ γὰρ ἦσαν εὔστοχοι, / Τούτων τυχόντες, ὧν τυχεῖν κενὸς φόνος. / Ἔπειθ' ὑπάρχοις, ὡς φονεὺς, εἰσηγόμην, / . . . Ὁ δεινὸν οὐδὲν πώποτ' οὐδ' εἰργασμένος, / Οὐδ' ἐννοήσας, ὡς μαθητὴς τοῦ Λόγου; *PG*, vol. 37. My guess is that the phrase κενὸς φόνος means that some persons who were quite vulnerable, old, female, very young, ill, *etc.*, died. The irony, of course, is that the magistrate had to hear a charge that Gregory was the perpetrator when he and his group were the ones attacked.

the Christian community and for the city. In ecclesiastical disputes the killing of a heretic was a defensible action. Exile was more common, but some evidently argued that immediate death was more appropriate.[18] A sentence of banishment or exile to a severe climate often resulted in slower death. Those viewed as heretics from a perspective, either Nicene or non-Nicene, backed by state power were often sent, sometimes repeatedly, to harsh surroundings. They were isolated from power and separated from those who cared for them. If death came more quickly, it would stop their meddling letters and occasional visits with powerful friends. Gregory's opponents are not without their own Hermogenian *staseis*. They can mount a defense based on the quality of the act.

The Theologian has another challenge to face: the slurs directed at him by the Constantinopolitan Eunomians. He must now take the other side and contest these charges as if he were the attorney for the defense. In terms of the Hermogenian analysis, Gregory considers the subject certain, but incomplete. In regard to certainty, Gregory offers no rebuttal to the fact that he grew up in a small town. Everyone knows that the provincial character of Nazianzus cannot be compared favorably with the majesty of Constantinople (secc. 6f.). The Theologian evidently was accused of foolish appearance, unpolished speech, and deficient education. He admits that his appearance is unprepossessing, and that Constantinopolitans might consider his speech rustic (sec. 8). Without making direct comments, he answers the charge that he is not well educated by constructing the oration to indicate his education; one need only listen or read to know that he is learned.

He expressly concentrates on a *stasis* that concedes the certainty of the charges of provincialism, poor pronunciation, and ugliness yet insists that the case is incomplete because its definition has not been settled. Arguing from Scripture, he notes that Ramah became honored because Samuel lived there, not the other way round. Saul, David, Amos, Joseph, Elijah, John the Baptist, even Jesus, came from small towns. Furthermore, the apostles went to foreign lands and talked with those people in their strange speech (doubtless with a foreign accent). They accomplished God's will (secc. 10f.). He now provides the major redefinition that, in his view, should lay to rest the charge that he is just a country bumpkin: every Christian is a citizen of only one city, the heavenly Jerusalem. Constantinople and Nazianzus are not the issue (sec. 12). All believers are both no-

18. Gregory alludes to Athanasius and other exiles in *Or.* 33.5. Socrates mentions the eighty priests burned at sea by the emperor Valens in *H. E.* 4.16, and Gregory alludes to them in *Or.* 33.4.

ble and ignoble, beloved of God and sinful. Christians are those who live a life of virtue. Gregory claims, now with the overtones of a prosecutor, that he and his community have virtuously endured tyranny and attack. He has been accused of strange gentleness (τὴν ἐπιείκειαν ἐνεκλήθην ὡς ἄνοιαν), indeed of being foolish, but in fact he and his community have attempted to be like Jesus (sec. 14).

His opponents might be prepared to contest his definition through further redefinition. The biblical and traditional examples he employs are common to his own congregation and to those of the Neo-Arians, yet his enemies might well have other points to make. They might reply that it is no vice to point out that the representative of a dangerous group is himself uneducated. Hermogenian redefinition of the case could be accomplished by adopting the Aristotelian rhetorical principle of arguing against the *ethos* of a speaker.[19] There is no question that some biblical heroes came from small towns, but coming from a small town does not automatically qualify one as a virtuous leader. Indeed even Nazianzen's redefinition is itself no incontestable answer. Of course the citizenship of Christians is in the New Jerusalem. The question for these non-Nicenes could still be whether or not Gregory and his group are Christians to whom such a redefinition would apply. Within Constantinople the so-called orthodox are considered on political, social, cultural, and theological grounds a small and dangerous sect that ought to be suppressed.

In *Or. 33* Gregory argues that the charges of unethical conduct against his antagonists are certain and complete, supported by recent history and biblical examples. He then argues that the charges against him are certain but incomplete. He overturns these by redefining them in Christian terms and connecting them with scriptural *exempla* and recent events. Within a Hermogenian context, his arguments are well-founded. On this basis Gregory then claims that the later Arians should not be followed in their riches and numbers, in their power and vice, because their actions are not defensible: his opponents are to be followed neither in action nor in thought. Their views of the Trinity are also indefensible.

Yet the power of the Theologian's efforts is still much more dependent upon basic beliefs within a particular community than upon the application of the Hermogenian system as a logical, objective set of rules that defines the issues persuasively for all involved. He argues well and perhaps compellingly. But as a Christian theologian he closes *Or. 33* with an appeal that his hearers remember their confession and their baptism into the Fa-

19. Aristotle, *Rhet.* 1.2.3–5, 1356A.

ther, the Son, and the Holy Spirit. His non-Nicene antagonists have a different confession and a different baptism. As a philosophical theologian, he knows that there is no neutral, public court of appeal in which one foundational logic accepted by everyone decides the issues. The point is to argue as cogently as possible, to speak well for one's position using all the means at one's disposal. His poetic talents, his eloquence, will do much to carry the day.

We can conceive of the Eunomians continuing their struggle, even through the persecution and killing of their opponents. They could employ parts of the Hermogenian *stasis* theory to make their own defense, for the killing of heretics was lawful. They would certainly be most vulnerable on the point of killing in the defense of belief rooted in a Savior who had died for others. But that is the lesson that Christian winners who have taken power in every age and region have found the hardest to learn. Nicenes would too seldom be different.

A number of the Theologian's orations could be analyzed for their use of Hermogenian *stasis* theory both in their larger outlines and in the selection of specific arguments. That analysis would show how this philosophical rhetorician employed to his advantage his command of technical rhetoric. He argued well within the confines of rhetorical systems normally accepted within his place and time. Yet in terms of twentieth-century categories, Gregory Nazianzen as a Christian theologian and a philosophical rhetorician expressed his understanding of Christian ethics and doctrine from an antifoundationalist perspective now rather common.[20] He lived and thought within a community of shared beliefs, a position compatible with that taken by Alasdair MacIntyre.[21] The confession and the practice of his community formed him. Both his participation in the life of worshipping congregations and his education in rhetoric taught him that even the investigation of the so-called facts of the case only began the serious consideration of appealing to the judgment of others. His is therefore not only a voice that should be heard in our era but also one that sounds more postmodern than modern.

20. R. Rorty, "Two Meanings of 'Logocentrism,'" *Essays on Heidegger and Others: Philosophical Papers*, vol. 2 (Cambridge 1991), p. 110: "Most philosophers nowadays *are* antifoundationalists." They are dissatisfied "with ideas like 'self-validating truth,' 'intuition,' 'transcendental argument', and 'principles of the ultimate foundation of all possible knowledge.'"

21. A. MacIntyre, *Whose Justice? Which Rationality?* (Notre Dame, Ind. 1988) and *Three Rival Versions of Moral Enquiry: Encyclopaedia, Genealogy, and Tradition* (Notre Dame, Ind. 1990).

SEVEN

Stylistic Devices and Homiletic Techniques in Ps.-Epiphanius' Festal Sermons

Hendrik F. Stander

MOST PATRISTIC STUDIES deal with theological, historical, exegetical, archaeological, or social issues. Fewer studies have been devoted to the literary qualities of early Christian writings. It is surprising how often works of reference make general statements about the style of an early theologian, when no literary study of the author in question has ever been undertaken.[1] Often these statements are based merely on a general perception or a traditional point of view that has never been properly examined. Professor Halton, however, is one of our well-respected scholars who has ventured to explore the stylistic qualities of early Christian writings.[2] I have therefore decided to express my appreciation for his valuable contribution to our field of study with this modest attempt to analyze the stylistic devices and homiletic techniques in the five festal homilies of ps.-Epiphanius.[3] I hope that this article will encourage the student and the reader to look upon the patristic writings also as forms of art, and not only as sources for the theology of the early Church.[4]

1. V., e.g., Quasten, voll. 1–4, passim.

2. V. T.P. Halton, "Stylistic Device in Melito, ΠΕΡΙ ΠΑΣΧΑ," Kyriakon: Festschrift Johannes Quasten, ed. P. Granfield and J.A. Jungmann, vol. 1 (Münster 1970), pp. 249–55.

3. This article forms part of a larger project on the five festal sermons of ps.-Epiphanius. My fellow researchers are Prof. J.H. Barkhuizen and the Rev. R. Loots. I take this opportunity to acknowledge their contributions to this project, which have led, inter alia, to this article.

4. In the letter in which we were invited to contribute to this Festschrift, we were asked to submit papers that "offer reflections of a methodological sort . . . the sorts of things in which graduate students should be schooled or from which they should be warned." When writing this article, I therefore regarded students as among the intended readers of this publication.

The homily is one of the genres of early Christian literature that can be singled out for its high artistic quality. One should not be surprised to find that the ancient preachers relied on rhetoric, since the latter deals primarily with the art of persuasion: "Rhetoric recognizes the importance of how something is said or written as well as what is argued."[5] Rhetorical principles are therefore most valuable in the hands (or mouth!) of the preacher. Frederick Norris correctly explains that the term "rhetoric" is popularly used today to refer to talk without substance, particularly in comments about political issues. But as Antonio Quacquarelli points out, scholarship has rediscovered rhetoric "come il nesso di contenuto e forma determinante per valutare i fenomeni dell' espressione artistica, la letteraria e la figurativa."[6] He refers to well-known German scholars, from Curtius to Arbusow and Lausberg, who have stressed the literary importance of theological and liturgical texts and the importance of linguistic phenomena in the public life of antiquity.[7]

Norden is indeed correct when he says that "die Beeinflussung der Predigt durch die sophistische Rhetorik erreichte im vierten Jahrhundert ihren Höhepunkt."[8] The cultured people of the day went to church with some of the same expectations they brought to the lecture rooms of the sophists: they wanted to be entertained by the sermon. These homilies can still give much pleasure to modern readers who have an educated literary taste. In this article I hope to share with students and other scholars some of the delight of a literary reading of the sermons of ps.-Epiphanius. I shall show how rhetorical techniques are used (1) to highlight the contents, *i.e.*, the important theological truths; (2) to captivate the attention of the audience; and (3) to adorn the work. I shall focus on these topics in consecutive order, though, as will be immediately apparent, many of the passages I discuss could be used to illustrate all three.

The five homilies are entitled *On the Feast of the Palms* (*Hom.* 1), *On the Great Sabbath* (*Hom.* 2), *On the Resurrection of Christ* (*Hom.* 3), *On the Ascension of Christ* (*Hom.* 4), and *On the Praises of Saint Mary, the Mother of*

---

5. F.W. Norris, "Rhetoric," *Encyclopedia of Early Christianity,* ed. E. Ferguson (New York/London 1990), pp. 788–91, esp. p. 788.

6. A. Quacquarelli, "Retorica," *DPAC* (Casale Monferrato 1983), vol. 2, pp. 2985–88, esp. p. 2985.

7. L. Arbusow, *Colores rhetorici: Eine Auswahl rhetorischer Figuren und Gemeinplätze als Hilfsmittel für akademische Übingen an mittelalterlichen Texten,* 2nd ed., H. Peter (Göttingen 1963); H. Lausberg, *Elemente der literarischen Rhetorik,* 1967; *id., Handbuch der literarischen Rhetorik,* 2 voll. (Munich 1960).

8. E. Norden, *Die Antike Kunstprosa vom VI. Jahrhundert v. Chr. bis in die Zeit der Renaissance,* vol. 2 (Leipzig 1898), p. 550.

God (*Hom.* 5).[9] Though initially ascribed to Epiphanius, they are no longer believed to be his. Epiphanius was bishop of Salamis (Constantia) in Cyprus from 367. Quasten regards his treatises as "hasty, superficial and disorderly compilations of the fruits of his extensive reading." He characterizes their style as "careless" and "verbose" and endorses Photius' remark likening Epiphanius' style "to that of one who is unfamiliar with Attic elegance."[10] This judgment definitely does not hold good for our five festal homilies. Nonetheless, the theology of these homilies suggests that the author probably lived about the time of Epiphanius of Salamis and probably came from the same region.

I. Techniques for Highlighting Theological Truths

A. *The Superiority of Christianity*

We know that the true Epiphanius reckoned the Greek philosophical schools among the heresies and believed that the philosophers had nothing of value to offer to Christians. Similarly, ps.-Epiphanius shows that Christianity superseded both Judaism and the cults and philosophies of classical antiquity. In an apostrophe to the Church of Christ (Χριστοῦ Ἐκκλησία), he declares,

1 οὐκέτι χήρανδρος,
     ἀλλὰ θέανδρος ἐξανθοῦσα·
3 οὐκέτι ἐξ εὐωνύμων Θεοῦ διὰ τὴν εἰδωλολατρείαν,
     ἀλλ' ἐκ δεξιῶν παρισταμένη, καὶ κεκοσμημένη διὰ τὴν
     θεογνωσίαν·
5 οὐκέτι αἵματι δουλικῷ φυρωμένη,
     ἀλλὰ αἵματι θεϊκῷ σφραγιζομένη·
7 οὐκέτι τὸν Ὠβὴλ,
     ἀλλὰ τὸν Ἐμμανουὴλ σέβουσα·
9 οὐκέτι τὴν Τρωάδα,
     ἀλλὰ τὴν Τριάδα δοξάζουσα·
11 οὐκέτι τιμῶσα τὸν Πλάτωνα,
     ἀλλὰ τὸν παντοκράτορα Θεὸν ἡμῶν·

9. I cite the Greek text of these homilies according to the edition in *PG*, vol. 43, first by the number of the homily, then by the number and letter of the column in the printed volume. I have, however, restructured the Greek text on the basis of syntactical markers. The translations are my own.

10. Quasten, vol. 3, p. 385. *V. Bibl. cod.* 122: Τὴν δὲ φράσιν ταπεινός τε καὶ οἷα εἰκὸς Ἀττικῆς παιδείας ἀμελέτητον τυγχάνειν; *PG*, vol. 103, col. 404.

13 οὐκέτι ᾿Ηρακλῆ τὸν ἀλεξίκακον,
    ἀλλὰ τὸν Παράκλητον καὶ πάντων ποιητήν.
15 Οὐκέτι προσκυνεῖς ᾿Αριστοτέλην σοφίσαντα,
    ἀλλὰ Θεὸν τὸν εἰς τέλη τῶν αἰώνων σε σώσαντα (1, 432B–C).

1   No longer are you <u>deprived of your husband,</u>
    but you blossom as <u>bride of God.</u>

3   No longer are you standing <u>on the left hand</u> of God <u>because of your</u>
       <u>idolatry,</u>
    but <u>on His right hand,</u> adorned, <u>because of your</u>
    <u>knowledge of God.</u>

5   No longer are you <u>defiled</u> with the blood of slavery,
    but <u>sealed</u> with the blood of God.

7   No longer are you worshipping <u>Bel,</u>
    but <u>Immanuel.</u>

9   No longer do you glorify <u>Troy,</u>
    but the <u>Trinity.</u>

11 No longer do you honor <u>Plato,</u>
    but our <u>almighty</u> God;

13 no longer <u>Heracles</u> who fends off ill,
    but the <u>Paraclete</u> and the Maker of everything.

15 No longer do you worship <u>Aristotle in his wisdom,</u>
    but <u>God who has saved you for all eternity.</u>

This section consists of eight pairs of well-balanced sentences, and each pair consists of two contrasting statements. The first clause of every pair describes the situation before the Advent, and the second, the situation thereafter. The juxtaposition of the contrasting phrases is emphasized by the use of anaphora, the repetition of the same word[s] at the beginning of successive clauses. The first four antithetical pairs are concerned with the semitic, and the latter four with the greco-roman, world. In all eight instances, prominent features of these two worlds are contrasted with important truths of Christian theology.

In the first pair (ll. 1f.) reference is made to the OT image depicting Israel as the wife of God (*cf.* Is. 54.6 and Ez. 16.8). In the NT, the term "bride" is used as a metaphor referring to the Church (*cf.* 2Cor. 11.2). Because of sin, this marital relationship was broken, but now Christ has come to heal it again. Note the beautiful paronomasia, or wordplay, between the two key words in this pair of clauses: χήρανδρος (deprived of one's husband) and θέανδρος (bride of God). To heighten the contrast, these two opposing terms are juxtaposed with only the adversative conjunction ἀλλά between them. The next pair of lines (3f.) states that Israel fell into disfavor with God, because of her idolatry, and therefore stood at His left hand. Now, however, Christ has adorned her with the knowledge of God and caused her to be seated at His right hand. Note that the phrases ἐξ εὐωνύμων (left hand side) and ἐκ δεξιῶν (right hand side) are placed in the initial position while the concluding phrases are διὰ τὴν εἰδωλολατρείαν (because of idolatry) and διὰ τὴν θεογνωσίαν (because of knowledge of God). Thus the four key ideas are placed in the two most emphatic positions. Note also the rhyme at the end of the sentences.

The two clauses in the next pair of lines (5f.) are parallel in structure. The initial words are αἵματι δουλικῷ (blood of slavery) and αἵματι θεϊκῷ (blood of God), and the final words φυρωμένη (defiled) and σφραγιζομένη (sealed). Again we have end rhyme. In this pair, the allusion to the slavery in Egypt suggests the deeper meaning of being enslaved to sin; the "sealing with the blood of God" alludes to the sealing of door-posts that ensured the salvation of Israel and refers to our salvation through the blood of Christ.

The fourth pair of clauses (ll. 7f.) states that those who formerly worshipped Ὠβήλ (Bel) now worship Ἐμμανουήλ (Immanuel). Bel, the Akkadian deity, is mentioned in both the OT (cf. Is. 46.1; Jer. 50.2, 51.44) and the Apocrypha (Bar. 6.41; Dan. 14). Immanuel is, of course, the name given to Christ (Mt. 1.23). Note that, in each case, the homilist chooses words that rhyme at the end.

The most beautiful examples of paronomasia are found in the second section, where ps.-Epiphanius compares classical antiquity with Christianity. Note how he plays (ll. 9f.) with the key words representing each of these two worlds: the people no longer glorify the Τρωάδα (Troy), but the Τριάδα (Trinity). The ancient city of Troy and the Trinity are almost synonymous with the classics and Christianity. This is also true of the names Πλάτωνα (Plato) and παντοκράτορα (all-sovereign, ll. 11f.).[11] Ps.-Epiphanius continues in the same vein (ll. 13–16): they no longer worship the hero Heracles (Ἡρακλῆ), but rather the Paraclete (Παράκλητον). No longer do they honor Aristotle, who displayed wisdom (Ἀριστοτέλην σοφίσαντα), but rather the One "who has saved you for all eternity" (τὸν εἰς τέλη τῶν αἰώνων σε σώσαντα). The last word in line 16, σώσαντα (saved), functions as a climax of this whole section: The goal of Christ's coming to the world was indeed to save us.

The rhetorical devices in the excerpt above were not intended merely to embellish the text. Rather, they were used very effectively to highlight the

11. This epithet of God was much used in anti-Arian polemic.

differences between the Church, on the one hand, and the greco-roman and semitic worlds, on the other. According to the homilist, Christianity has superseded both Judaism and pagan philosophy.

B. The Two Natures of Christ

Elsewhere in the same sermon ps.-Epiphanius again makes use of antitheses dramatically to illustrate the contrast between the divine and the human natures of Christ:

1 Χθὲς Χριστὸς ἐκ νεκρῶν ἤγειρε Λάζαρον,
  καὶ σήμερον ὁ αὐτὸς ἐπὶ τὸν θάνατον ἔρχεται.

3 Χθὲς ἄλλῳ, ὡς ζωὴ, ζωὴν ἐχαρίσατο,
  καὶ σήμερον ζωοδότης ἐπὶ τὸν θάνατον ἔρχεται.

5 Χθὲς Λαζάρου τὰ σπάργανα ἔλυσε,
  καὶ σήμερον ὁ αὐτὸς ἐν σπαργάνοις δεσμευθῆναι ἑκὼν
    παραγίνεται.

7 Χθὲς ἐν σκότοις ἐξήγαγεν ἄνθρωπον,
  καὶ σήμερον ἐν σκοτεινοῖς τεθῆναι καὶ σκιᾷ θανάτου ἔρχεται
  διὰ τὸν ἄνθρωπον.

9 Χθὲς πρὸ ἓξ ἡμερῶν τοῦ Πάσχα διὰ τῶν πέντε αἰσθήσεων τὸν
    τετραήμερον
  ὁ τριήμερος ταῖς δυσὶ τὸν ἕνα χαρίζεται ἀδελφὸν,

11 καὶ σήμερον ἐπὶ τὸν σταυρὸν ἔρχεται (1, 429B–C).

1 Yesterday Christ raised Lazarus from the dead,
  and today the same Christ is going to His death.

3 Yesterday He, being Life Himself, granted life to another,
  but today the Life-giver is going to His death.

5 Yesterday He loosened the burial clothes of Lazarus,
  but today He Himself comes voluntarily to be wrapped in grave
    clothes.

7 Yesterday He led a man out of the darkness,
  but today He comes to be buried in darkness and
  in the shadow of death for the sake of man.

9 Yesterday, six days before the Pasch [Jesus] restored [Lazarus] with all
    his five senses—Lazarus who had been dead for four days He
    who was Himself dead for three days restored: to the two
    sisters their one brother.

11 But today He comes to the cross.

The antitheses, heightened by anaphora, describe the divine and human natures of Christ. One must keep in mind that the words χθές (yesterday) and σήμερον (today) are not merely rhetorical devices to play off the passion of Jesus against the raising of Lazarus. This excerpt comes from ps.-Epiphanius' homily for Palm Sunday, the second of the seven days ending with Good Friday. Thus, the homilist reminds his readers of the event celebrated on the previous day, when Christ raised Lazarus, and looks forward to future events of Holy Week.

There is much movement and progression in ps.-Epiphanius' description of the miraculous raising of Lazarus (cf. Jn. 11): Christ raises Lazarus from the dead (ll.1f.); He grants him life (ll. 3f.); He orders the people to untie Lazarus' grave clothes; He leads him out of the darkness (ll. 7f.), and finally hands Lazarus over to his two sisters (ll. 9f.). The movement in this miraculous event is also suggested by the placing of the words of movement (ἔρχεται and παραγίνεται) at or near the end of each pair of antithetical sentences. This description thus provides an excellent example of dramatic irony. Here the homilist shows that everything happening to Christ in the course of His passion was completely incongruous with His divine nature: Christ had authority over the realm of the dead, yet He was subjected to death; He who was the Giver of life died.

A most striking play on words appears in the final paragraph: The Holy Week begins with the Saturday before Easter, called Lazarus Saturday, six days before the Pasch (cf. Jn. 12.1). As if in a countdown to a critical event, ps.-Epiphanius is counting backward from the Pasch: He says that six days before Good Friday, Jesus restored Lazarus in complete physical integrity (i.e., with all his five senses)[12] to his sisters, though Lazarus had been dead for four days and Jesus Himself was dead for three. Jesus gave to the two sisters their one brother. One should not underestimate the dramatic effect of this countdown on those who listened to the preacher. Far from mere adornments, these stylistic devices were homiletical techniques calculated to underline the paradox of the hypostatic union.

Finally, it is noteworthy how in one passage ps.-Epiphanius combines two distinct images in such a way as to suggest the complexity of Christ's mission deriving from the hypostatic union: kingship from His divinity, obedient suffering from His humanity. Describing Jesus' triumphal entry into Jerusalem the orator declares: ἰδοὺ ὁ σὸς νυμφίος ἐπὶ πώλου καθήμενος ἔρχεται (1, 428B; Behold! Your bridegroom is coming sitting on a foal). The reference to the foal recalls the prophecy of Zechariah—"Rejoice greatly, O daughter of Zion! . . . / Lo, your king comes to you; / tri-

---

12. I take διὰ τῶν πέντε αἰσθήσεων as an extension of the use of διά with the genitive to indicate the material out of which something is made; cf. the examples from Diodorus, Plutarch, Athenaeus, and Dioscorides Medicus cited by LSJ sub voce, διά A.III.c.2.

umphant and victorious is he, / humble and riding on an ass, / on a colt the foal of an ass (9.9)—and thus emphasizes the kingship of Christ (*cf.* Mt. 21.4f.; Jn. 12.14f.). In fact, early Byzantine art depicts Christ, not sitting astride the foal, but rather with both legs on one side as though he were seated on a royal throne.[13] Ps.-Epiphanius reinforces this tone of triumph by simultaneously depicting Jesus as bridegroom, another biblical image suggestive of Christ's transcendent kingship (Mt. 25.1–13). The image of bridegroom, however, would also remind the listeners of the imminence of the passion: of the time when the bridegroom would be taken away, and it would be appropriate for His disciples to fast and mourn (Mk. 2.18–20; Mt. 9.14f.; Lk. 5.33–35). Ps.-Epiphanius' composite picture of Jesus as king and bridegroom thus states in a vivid and economical way the mystery of the suffering Messiah.

C. The Virgin Birth and the Theotokos

In his praise of Mary, ps.-Epiphanius concentrates on the mysteries of the virgin birth and her motherhood of God. In *Homily* 5 he asks in a series of rhetorical questions whether it is possible for mortal beings really to understand the mystery of the virgin birth (488A):

1 Τίς γὰρ ἱκανὸς τοιοῦτο
   φράσαι μυστήριον;
   ποῖον δὲ φθέγξασθαι στόμα,   a - b
3 ἢ ποία γλῶσσα λαλήσει;   b - a

For who is capable of explaining
such a mystery?
What mouth can talk about it,
or what tongue can declare it?

On a syntactical level, the last two clauses are chiastic: φθέγξασθαι (verb) στόμα (subject) γλῶσσα (subject) λαλήσει (verb) = a-b-b-a. But on a semantic level, they are parallel. This pair of semantically identical clauses also offers examples of synecdoche, where both the mouth and the tongue signify the whole person, the τίς of line one. This elaborate structure emphasizes how difficult it is to understand and explain the mystery of the virginal birth.

Since it is an almost impossible task to speak about this mystery, ps.-

13. *V.*, *e.g.*, the representations of the triumphal entry into Jerusalem on fol. 1v. of the sixth-century Rossano Codex of the gospels and on fol. 196v. of the ninth-century codex of the *Homilies* of Greg. Naz., Paris, Bibl. Nat. gr. 510. For convenient reproductions, *v.* D.T. Rice, *Art of the Byzantine Era* (London 1963), fig. 45, p. 57 and fig. 70, p. 83.

Epiphanius has to resort to the use of images. He asserts that Mary is heaven and temple and throne: Αὕτη γὰρ οὐρανὸς καὶ ναὸς καὶ θρόνος εὑρίσκεται (5, 488D). God dwells in heaven and in the temple, and He sits on a throne; the Blessed Virgin performed the function of these three places when she carried Christ in her womb. Note the downward development from the spacious heaven to the more confined space of the temple and then the throne. This highlights the paradoxical nature of God's indwelling in the womb of a woman.

In the next section ps.-Epiphanius heaps up images characterizing Mary as Theotokos:

1 Χαῖρε, κεχαριτωμένη
   τοῦ νοητοῦ ἀγκίστρου τὸ δέλεαρ·
   ἐν σοὶ γὰρ ἄγκιστρον ἡ θεότης.

4 Χαῖρε, κεχαριτωμένη,
   ἡ νοερὰ τῆς δόξης κιβωτός.

6 Χαῖρε, κεχαριτωμένη,
   ἡ στάμνος ἡ χρυσῆ,
   τὸ οὐράνιον ἔχουσα μάννα.

9 Χαῖρε, κεχαριτωμένη,
   ἡ τὴν γλυκεῖαν τῆς ἀεννάου πηγῆς τοὺς διψῶντας ἐμπλήσασα.

11 Χαῖρε, κεχαριτωμένη,
   νοερὰ θάλασσα,
   τὸν οὐράνιον ἔχουσα μαργαρίτην Χριστόν·

14 Χαῖρε, κεχαριτωμένη,
   ὁ λαμπρὸς οὐρανός,
   ἡ τὸν ἀχώρητον ἐν οὐρανοῖς ἔχουσα θεόν.

17 Χαῖρε, κεχαριτωμένη,
   ἡ τὸν χερουβικὸν θρόνον τῆς θεότητος ἐξαστράπτουσα.

19 Χαῖρε, κεχαριτωμένη,
   κύκλον ἔχουσα οὐρανοῦ,
   καὶ Θεὸν ἀχώρητον,
   ἐν σοὶ δὲ χωρητὸν,
   καὶ ἀστενοχώρητον.

24 Χαῖρε, κεχαριτωμένη,
   στυλοειδὴς νεφέλη,
   ἡ τὸν Θεὸν ἔχουσα,

27 τὸν ἐν τῇ ἐρήμῳ τὸν λαὸν καθοδηγήσαντα (5, 489D–492A).

1 *Hail, O favoured one,*
   Bait of the spiritual fishhook,
   because the Godhead is in you as a fishhook.

4   *Hail, O favoured one,*
     you who are the spiritual covenant box of glory.
6   *Hail, O favoured one,*
     you who are the golden jar,
     containing the heavenly manna.
9   *Hail, O favoured one,*
     you who fill the thirsty with the sweetness of the ever-flowing
          fountain.
11   *Hail, O favoured one,*
     you who are a spiritual sea,
     containing Christ, the heavenly pearl.
14   *Hail, O favoured one,*
     you who are the shining heaven,
     you who are holding God who cannot be held in heaven.
17   *Hail, O favoured one,*
     you who make flash the cherub-throne of divinity.
19   *Hail, O favoured one,*
     you who hold the sphere of heaven,
     and the God who is not to be contained,
     but is contained in you,
     and who is unconstricted.
24   *Hail, O favoured one,*
     you who are the cloud in pillar form,
     which contained God,
27   as He guided the people in the desert.

Not all these images were ps.-Epiphanius' invention; he borrowed
many from theological tradition. But in this short eulogy of the Blessed
Virgin he has piled up the images, both his own and those he has borrowed, in a most effective way. Since he provides so little explication, we
conclude that his audience probably knew the theology of their times
sufficiently well to enjoy rather complex images derived from Platonic
philosophical ideas and biblical typology.[14]

14. Gregory of Nyssa indicates that the people of the fourth century were well-informed
in matters of contemporary theology. He says that even sellers of clothes, money changers,
grocers, bakers, bath managers, in fact, people from all spheres of life, were talking about
controversial theological issues of the day (*Cf. Deit. f. et sp. s.; PG*, vol. 46, col. 557A–C). Note
also that the term Χαῖρε, based on Lk. 1.28, is a common element in eulogies of the Blessed
Virgin. *Cf., e.g.,* Rom. Mel., *Hym.* 9.1, 13.8 (J. Grosdidier de Matrons, *Romanos le Mélode,
Hymnes,* vol. 2 [Paris 1965]: *Nouveau Testament (IX–XX) = SC,* vol. 110); ps.-Greg. Nys., *In
annunt.* (CPG, 3214) ll. 9, 19, 22, 59, 62, 66f., 71, 85f. (D.M. Montagna, "La lode alla Theotokos
nei testi greci dei secoli IV–VII," *Mar.* 24 [1962], pp. 536–39); ps.-Chrysos., *Descript. deip.,
PG,* vol. 50, col. 796A.

In line two, ps.-Epiphanius refers to Mary as τοῦ νοητοῦ ἀγκίστρου τὸ δέλεαρ (Bait of the spiritual fishhook). Behind this image stands a wide-spread *topos* of patristic theology: Satan expected a just recompense for the human race he had held in thrall since the sin of Adam and Eve. Rather than compel the devil to release humanity by an exercise of might that could seem tyrannical, God offered Satan the man Jesus as a ransom. Knowing that Christ was born of a virgin and renowned for miracles, Satan gladly accepted the offer. Only when he grasped at the outward garment of the flesh, did he encounter the concealed divinity and realize that he could not hold Christ; outwitted by this trap, Satan was caught like a fish that swallows the concealed hook along with the bait.[15] Here Mary is hailed as the "Bait of the spiritual fishhook," for she carried within her human womb the divinity that was hidden from the devil. By giving birth to Christ, she confirmed the devil's belief that Jesus was merely a man.

Mary is also called ἡ νοερὰ τῆς δόξης κιβωτός (l. 5; the spiritual covenant box of glory).[16] With this image the homilist wishes to convey that Mary's womb contained God's presence just as the covenant box contained God's presence in OT times. Mary is also ἡ στάμνος ἡ χρυσῆ, τὸ οὐράνιον ἔχουσα μάννα (l. 7; the golden jar containing the heavenly manna).[17] Together with the previous image, this is a reference to Heb. 9.3f., where we are told that the Holy of Holies housed the golden altar of incense and the gold-covered ark of the covenant, in which stood the golden jar of manna. There is reference also to Ex. 16.33, where God orders Moses and Aaron to put manna in a jar in order to preserve it for their descendants. Just as the jar contained manna, Mary's womb contained Christ, the real Bread (manna) from heaven (*cf.* Jn. 6.25–59).

In line 10 ps.-Epiphanius says that Mary is ἡ τὴν γλυκεῖαν τῆς ἀεννάου πηγῆς τοὺς διψῶντας ἐμπλήσασα (she who fills the thirsty with the sweetness of the ever-flowing fountain). The background of this image is to be found in the account of Moses striking the rock (Ex. 17.1–7 and Num. 20.1–13). This narrative is frequently encountered in early Christian art and writings, where it conveys various meanings.[18] In the *Sermon concern-*

---

15. *V.* Greg. Nys., *Or. cat. mag.* 24; Olymp., *in Job* 40.25 (LXX) (ἄξεις δὲ δράκοντα ἐν ἀγκίστρῳ; J. Ziegler, Iob [1982] = *LXX*, vol. 11.4); Joh. Dam., *Fide orth.* 3.27; and ps.-Ath., *Qu. al.* (= *CPG*, #2261) 20.*resp.* Cf. J.N.D. Kelly, *Early Christian Doctrines,* 4th ed. (London 1968), pp. 382f.

16. Proclus (*Or.* 6.17: *Laud. s. Dei genetr. Mar.*) also refers to Mary as ἡ ... κιβωτός, *PG,* vol. 65, col. 753C.

17. Proclus also refers (*ib.,* 756A) to Mary as ἡ στάμνος.

18. *Cf.* H.F. Stander, "The Patristic Exegesis of Moses Striking the Rock (EX 17.1–7 & NUM. 20.1–13," *CopticChR* 12 (1991), pp. 67–77.

ing Simeon and Anna passed down with the works of Methodius of Olympus, the rock is interpreted as a foreshadowing of the motherhood of Mary. Addressing praise to the Virgin mother, the homilist recalls that "that hard and rugged rock, which imaged forth the grace and refreshment which has sprung out from thee for all the world brought forth abundantly in the desert out of its thirsty sides a healing draught for the fainting people" (Στερέμνιος δ᾽ αὖ καὶ πέτρα ἀκρότομος τὴν παγκόσμιον ἐκ σοῦ πηγάσασαν χάριν καὶ ἀνάψυξιν προεξεικονίζουσα, παραμύθιον ἴαμα ἐκλείποντι λαῷ ἐκ λαγόνων ξηρῶν ἐν ἐρήμῳ δαψιλῶς προήγαγεν, sec. 9).[19] Mary is also called νοερὰ θάλασσα, τὸν οὐράνιον ἔχουσα μαργαρίτην Χριστόν (ll. 12f.; the spiritual sea containing Christ, the heavenly pearl). Christ is frequently referred to as a pearl in patristic writings.[20]

God was considered to have His abode in heaven, so Mary was referred to as a heaven since she had accommodated God in her womb: ὁ λαμπρὸς οὐρανὸς, ἡ τὸν ἀχώρητον ἐν οὐρανοῖς ἔχουσα Θεόν (ll. 15f.; the shining heaven, holding God who cannot be held in heaven).[21] In the following lines, ps.-Epiphanius enlarges on this image and calls Mary: ἡ τὸν χερουβικὸν θρόνον τῆς θεότητος ἐξαστράπτουσα (l. 18; she who makes flash the cherub-throne of divinity). The background of this image is to be found in Psalm 80.2, where we read that God sits upon a throne formed by the cherubim. Note the play on the words ἀχώρητον, χωρητὸν and ἀστενοχώρητον with which ps.-Epiphanius works out the consequences of the image representing Mary as a heaven:

20 κύκλον ἔχουσα οὐρανοῦ
    καὶ Θεὸν <u>ἀχώρητον</u>
    ἐν σοὶ δὲ <u>χωρητὸν</u>
23 καὶ <u>ἀστενοχώρητον</u>

you who hold the sphere of heaven,
and the God who is not to be contained,
but is contained in you,
and who is unconstricted.

The last image of Mary is based on the Exodus narrative: στυλοειδὴς νεφέλη, ἡ τὸν Θεὸν ἔχουσα, τὸν ἐν τῇ ἐρήμῳ τὸν λαὸν καθοδηγήσαντα (ll.

19. *PG*, vol. 18, col. 369B. This may be a work of the fifth or sixth century; *v. CPG*, #1827. The translation is that of W.R. Clark, *ANCL*, vol. 14 (Edinburgh 1869): *The Writings of Methodius, etc.*

20. *Cf. Acta Ioh.* 109; Or., *in Mt.* 10.8 (on Mt. 13.45f.).

21. Hesychius bases (*Ser.* 5 [*PG*, vol. 93, col. 1464D]) his image of Mary as a heaven on a somewhat different argument: since Christ is a sun, Mary must be a heaven.

26f.; you are a cloud in pillar form, containing God, who guided the people in the desert). Mary was similar to the cloud, since she too contained the Godhead.

II. Techniques for Captivating the Audience

Ps.-Epiphanius hints that it was quite difficult to hold the attention of his congregation. For example, he introduces his sermon *On the Ascension of Christ* with a plea to his audience to listen:

1   Καὶ εἰ βούλεσθε μαθεῖν, ἀνεξικάκως συντείνατέ μοι τὸν νοῦν.
      Μόνον μοι δι᾽ εὐχῶν συνεργήσατε, παρακαλῶ·
3   καὶ τὰς μολιβδώδεις αὔρας καταστείλατε·
      καὶ τὰ κύματα τῆς φλυαρίας γαληνιάσατε·
5   καὶ σχολάζουσάν μοι τὴν ἀκοὴν παράσχητε.
      Κατὰ γὰρ τὸν σοφὸν Σολομῶντα, λόγοι σοφῶν ἐν ἀναπαύσει ἀκούονται
      (4, 477D).

But if you want to learn, patiently pay attention to me.
I urge you, just coöperate with me with your prayers;
and suppress the leaden breezes;
and calm the waves of foolish talk;
and lend me a receptive ear,
for according to the wise Solomon, the words of the wise are heard in
        quiet [Eccles. 9.17].

Ps.-Epiphanius asks his congregation to support him with their prayers. It is a common ancient Christian *topos* that man, without divine aid, is unable to speak about God.[22] The homilist's request to repress the leaden breezes betrays a realization that his audience finds it difficult to keep awake. They also seem to be busy with idle talk in the church, and ps.-Epiphanius has to call them to order. He cites the witness of Solomon that silence is a prerequisite to learning. To preach on the ascension of Christ to such an inattentive and sleepy congregation is no easy task. One needs to employ all possible rhetorical techniques.

Ps.-Epiphanius immediately turns to something his congregation knows very well: the chariot races. He says that those who enjoy watching the speeding charioteers should watch the chariot race between Jesus and Beliar:[23]

22. *Cf. Ad Diog.* 1; 4.6.
23. This title of Satan occurs in the NT only at 2Cor. 6.15; *cf.* T.J. Lewis, "Belial," *AncB.D,* vol. 1 (New York, *etc.* 1992), pp. 654–56.

1 Ποῦ εἰσιν οἱ περὶ τὰ ἱπποδρόμια ἀσχολούμενοι,
  καὶ ἡνιόχων ἀγαπῶντες ὀξύτητα;

3 Δεῦτε, ἴδετε παράδοξον ἱπποδρόμιον·
  τὸν τῆς κτίσεως Δημιουργὸν ἐν ἀνθρωπίνῳ ἐποχούμενον ἅρματι,

5 οὐκ ἐπὶ γῆς ἀτάκτως ἐλαύνοντα,
  ἀλλ᾽ αἰθερίους δρόμους καινοπρεπῶς ἀναστέλλοντα,

7 καὶ τὸν οὐράνιον καμπτῆρα καταλαμβάνειν ἐπειγόμενον,
  καὶ τὸν παρατρέχοντα Βελίαρ δυνατῶς καταστρέφοντα (4, 480C–D).

1 Where are those who frequent the chariot races,
  and those who love the speed of the charioteers?

3 Come, look at this remarkable chariot race!
  The Demiurge of the creation is riding in the chariot of human flesh;

5 He is not driving on the earth in a disorderly manner,
  but ascending in a novel way to ethereal courses.

7 Hurrying forward to reach the heavenly turning point,
  He powerfully overturns His opponent Beliar.

Ps.-Epiphanius vividly describes Christ's ascension to heaven as a chariot-race in which Satan competes with Jesus. One can feel the tension: Christ and Satan are racing alongside each other on this ethereal course, but Jesus wins the race and overturns Satan.

To make sure that he does not lose his audience's attention ps.-Epiphanius now employs another stylistic device to enhance the vividness of his sermon. Switching to direct speech, he presents Satan bewailing his defeat:

1 σήμερον ὁ διάβολος θρηνεῖ λέγων, Τί ποιήσω, ὁ ἄθλιος;
  Πάντας τοὺς ἀπ᾽ αἰῶνος ὡς ἱέραξ ὀξυπετὴς ἁρπάξας παρ᾽ ἐμοῦ,

3 ἔρημόν με κατέστησε,
  καὶ πανταχόθεν με πτεροκοπήσας εἰς γῆν κατέρραξεν.

5 Ἠπάτησέ με ὁ τῆς Μαρίας υἱός.
  Οὐκ ᾔδειν, ὅτι Θεὸς ἐν ἀνθρωπίνῳ κρύπτεται σώματι.

7 Ἔβλεπον αὐτὸν σῶμα ἀνθρώπινον περικείμενον,
  καὶ ἄνθρωπον αὐτὸν νομίσας ψιλόν,

9 κατ᾽ αὐτοῦ τοὺς Ἰουδαίους ἐκίνησα·
  καὶ ἅπερ δι᾽ ἑαυτοῦ μὴ ἐτόλμων διαπράξασθαι,

11 ταῦτα διὰ Ἰουδαίων ἐνήργησα.
   Μυρίας συκοφαντίας ἐφεῦρον·

13 πᾶν εἶδος ὕβρεως εἰς αὐτὸν ἐπενόησα·
   καλάμῳ καὶ σπόγγῳ αὐτὸν ἐπότισα·

15 ἀκάνθαις τὴν κεφαλὴν αὐτοῦ ἐστεφάνωσα·
   ῥαπίσμασιν αὐτὸν ἠτίμωσα,

17 σταυρῷ διὰ ἥλων προσήλωσα·
θανάτῳ τέλος ὑποβαλών,

19 ὡς νικήσας, μετὰ Ἰουδαίων ἑόρταζον.
Θεασάμενος δὲ αὐτὸν ὅτι τῇ τρίτῃ ἡμέρᾳ ἐγήγερται, καθὼς προεῖπον,

21 ὡς ξίφος κατὰ καρδίας ἀθρόως δεξάμενος κατέπεσον·
θεασάμενος δὲ αὐτὸν ὅτι ἐσθίει καὶ πίνει,

23 πάλιν ἕτερον σταυρὸν κατεσκεύαζον.
Ἀλλ' ὡς ταῦτα ἐνεθυμούμην πρὸς ἑαυτὸν,

25 ὁρῶ αὐτὸν μετὰ δόξης εἰς οὐρανὸν ἀνερχόμενον,
ὅθεν ἐγὼ μετ' αἰσχύνης ἐξέπεσον (4, 481C–484A).

1 Today the devil is lamenting and says: "What shall I do wretch that I
am?
Like a swift-flying hawk, He has snatched from me all those I have ever
held in my power

3 and has made me destitute.
He has clipped both my wings and dashed me to the earth.

5 The son of Mary has deceived me.
I did not know that God was hidden in a human body.

7 I saw Him wearing a human body,
and I reckoned Him a mere man,

9 and I incited the Jews against Him.
What I durst not do on my own,

11 I accomplished through the Jews.
I invented countless calumnies;

13 I conceived every form of outrage against Him;
I gave Him to drink with a reed and a sponge;

15 with thorns I crowned His head;
I slapped Him in the face and dishonored Him,

17 with nails I nailed Him to a cross;
finally I subjected Him to death;

19 Thinking I had conquered, I rejoiced with the Jews.
When I saw that He was raised on the third day, as they had said
beforehand,

21 I suddenly fell down as one stricken to the heart by a sword-thrust.
When I saw that He was eating and drinking,

23 I began again to prepare another cross.
But while I was laying these plans,

25 I saw Him ascending into heaven with glory,
whence I fell with shame."

Our homilist acts the part of the omniscient narrator who knows every-thing going on in the mind of Satan. Thus he can give a graphic descrip-tion of the distress of the devil, whose staccato utterances underline his bewilderment.

A diatribe against the Jews, such as we have in this excerpt, was a very common *topos* in early Christian writings. Satan mentions all the evil done to Jesus and discloses that he planned these misdeeds. Thus ps.-Epipha-nius implies that the Jews collaborated with Satan. The last two sentences (ll. 25f.) serve as a climax of the excerpt and are also ironical: Satan fell from the very heaven to which Christ has ascended. This underscores Christ's victory over Satan.

In the second homily the preacher again arrests the attention of his au-dience in a marvellous way. He dramatizes the interview in which Joseph of Arimathea asked Pilate for the body of Jesus. Like some modern-day preachers, ps.-Epiphanius embroiders the biblical account; he gives his congregation a detailed report of a conversation of which we have only the briefest notice (Mk. 15.43–45; Mt. 27.57f.; Lk. 23.50–52; Jn. 19.38):

1 οὐδὲ λέγει πρὸς αὐτόν·
   Δός μοι τὸ σῶμα τοῦ Ἰησοῦ,
3 τοῦ πρὸ βραχέως τὸν ἥλιον σκοτίσαντος,
   τὰς πέτρας ῥήξαντος,
5 καὶ τὴν γῆν δονήσαντος,
   καὶ τὰ μνημεῖα ἀνοίξαντος,
7 καὶ τὸ καταπέτασμα τοῦ ναοῦ σχίσαντος.
   Οὐδὲν τοσοῦτον πρὸς Πιλᾶτον λέγει.
9 Ἀλλὰ τί;
   αἴτησίν τινα οἰκτρὰν,
11 καὶ τοῖς πᾶσι μικράν.
   Ὦ κριτὰ,
13 αἰτούμενος παρὰ σοῦ ἐλήλυθα αἴτησιν πάνυ μικράν.
   Καὶ οὕτως·
15 Δός μοι νεκρὸν πρὸς ταφήν·
   τὸ σῶμα ἐκείνου τοῦ παρὰ σοῦ κατακριθέντος Ἰησοῦ τοῦ Ναζαρινοῦ,
17 Ἰησοῦ τοῦ πτωχοῦ,
   Ἰησοῦ τοῦ ἀοίκου,
19 Ἰησοῦ τοῦ κρεμαμένου,
   τοῦ γυμνοῦ,
21 τοῦ εὐτελοῦς,
   Ἰησου τοῦ τέκτονος υἱοῦ,

23 Ἰησοῦ τοῦ δεσμίου,
     τοῦ αἰθρίου,

25 τοῦ ξένου,
     καὶ ἐπὶ ξενίᾳ ἀγνωρίστου,

27 τοῦ εὐκαταφρονήτου,
     καὶ ἐπὶ πᾶσι κρεμαμένου.

29 Δός μοι τοῦτον τὸν ξένον·
     τί γάρ σε ὠφελεῖ τὸ σῶμα τούτου τοῦ ξένου;

31 Δός μοι τοῦτον τὸν ξένον (2, 445B–C).

1   And he does not say to him:
     "Give me the body of Jesus,

3   of Him who recently darkened the sun,
     who shattered the rocks,

5   who shook the earth,
     and opened the tombs,

7   and tore in two the curtain of the temple."
     He does not say anything like that to Pilate.

9   But what does he say?
     Just a mournful request,

11 and a small request for anybody:
     "Judge,

13 I have come to make of you a very small request."
     And like this:

15 "Give me the dead man to be buried;
     the body of that man who was condemned by you, Jesus of Nazareth,

17 Jesus the poor man,
     Jesus the homeless one,

19 Jesus the one who is hanging,
     the naked one,

21 the lowly one,
     Jesus the son of a carpenter,

23 Jesus the prisoner,
     the outsider,

25 the stranger,
     and unknown alien,

27 the scorned one,
     who was hanged in the presence of all.

29 Give me this stranger.
     Of what use is the body of this stranger to you?

31 Give me this stranger."

By telling his audience what information Joseph failed to give to Pilate, the homilist effectively highlights Christ's authority over nature. He then continues with his imaginative account of the conversation by telling his audience what type of information Joseph did give Pilate. The short epithets describing the humiliating state of Jesus are most effective in arousing the audience's sympathy and empathy. Immediately thereafter, as though he were interviewing Joseph, our homilist asks him whether he realizes whom he has received:

1 Ἄρα γὰρ, ἆρα, ὦ Ἰωσὴφ,
   αἰτήσας καὶ λαβών,
3 οἶδας ὃν εἴληφας;
   ἆρα προσελθὼν τῷ σταυρῷ,
5 καθελὼν Ἰησοῦν,
   οἶδας τίνα ἐβάστασας;
7 Εἰ ὄντως οἶδας ὃν κρατεῖς,
   νῦν γέγονας πλούσιος.

Do you, Joseph,
you who have asked and received,
do you know whom you have received?
Now that you have approached the cross,
and have taken down Jesus,
do you know whom you have carried?
If you do indeed know whom you hold,
you are now rich (2, 448C).

III. Techniques for Adorning the Work

Ps.-Epiphanius uses various sorts of wordplay to adorn his work. These devices are never, however, merely cosmetic. A notable example of wordplay involving the repetition of the same words and word stems appears in the homily on Palm Sunday (1, 428D): βασιλικῶς τῷ Βασιλεῖ τῶν βασιλέων ἀπαντήσωμεν (Let us meet the King of Kings in a kingly way); δεσποτικῶς τῷ Δεσπότῃ τῶν δεσποτῶν προσκυνήσωμεν (let us worship the Lord of Lords in a lordly way); τῷ Θεῷ τῶν θεῶν θεϊκῶς ἀναμέλψωμεν (let us praise in song the God of gods in a godly way). The parallel structure of these three sentences helps to bring to the fore the three key words βασιλεύς, δεσπότης, and θεός. Each of these words occurs three times, always in a different form: genitive, dative, and adverbial. With this stylistic device, the homilist highlights the royal, lordly, i.e., divine qualities of Christ.

Sometimes he pushes this device to extravagant lengths, as in this passage where he plays variations on a single word stem: ἐπειδὴ ἐν αὐτῇ ὁ θάνατος διὰ θανάτου τὸν θάνατον θανατώσας, καὶ ζωὴν ἀθάνατον τοῖς θανοῦσιν ἐπήγαγεν (4, 480B; since on this [day] He who was dead gave a deathblow to death through His death, and gave life that is not subject to death to those who were dead). The repetition of θάνατος or its derivatives emphasizes that the death of Christ is the focal point of God's plan of salvation.

At other times, ps.-Epiphanius uses different words with a similar pronunciation. Note, for example, the assonance in the following line: οὐρανὸς τοῦ ὁρωμένου οὐρανοῦ ὡραιότερος (3, 465B; [the Church] is a heaven which is more beautiful than the heaven that we see). The beauty of the assonance underscores the beauty of the Church here.

He also plays with words having the same spelling but completely different roots and meanings: ἑορτάζει ἑορτὰς, ὡς κρίνον ἐαρινὸν παραδείσου ὑπάρχουσα· ἐν ᾗ Χριστός, τὸ ὄντως εὐθαλὲς κρίνον, τὸ μὴ κρῖνον, ἀλλὰ σῷ-ζον τὸν κόσμον (1, 429D–432A; [the Church] is celebrating feasts as a spring lily of paradise; Christ is in her the true flourishing lily, not judging, but saving, the world). The word κρίνον (lily) is a noun, while the word κρῖνον is a present participle of κρίνω (judge). Ps.-Epiphanius places these two contrasting keywords close to each other, almost in the middle of the sentence, in order to highlight the contrast: Though Christ is a κρίνον (lily), He is not κρῖνον (condemning) the world.

Conclusion

The excerpts I have cited from the five festal homilies, the entire extant corpus of the works of this author, are characteristic of the homilies as a whole. There are, of course, more loosely structured sections. They serve important stylistic functions, not the least of which is to throw into relief the more artfully constructed passages on which I have concentrated. The sermons of ps.-Epiphanius are interesting to read, but it must have been positively exciting to hear them delivered. Prominent even among the stylistically excellent sermons of the fourth- and fifth-century Antiochenes, the festal sermons of ps.-Epiphanius figure among the best examples of ancient rhetoric.

III. ANTHROPOLOGY:
MODERN AND ANCIENT

EIGHT

Melania the Elder and the Origenist Controversy

The Status of the Body in a Late-Ancient Debate

⁜

Elizabeth A. Clark

ESCRIBING THE Western version of the Origenist controversy, Peter Brown notes the difficulties that the dispute posed for Jerome: Jerome's own "model of the human person"—"austerely spiritual"—had been drawn from the writings of Origen, a model that "enabled him to live at ease with gifted and influential women such as Marcella at Rome and, then, with Paula at Bethlehem."[1] When Jerome at last recognized the dangers stemming from his earlier enthusiasm for Origen, "he came down firmly on the side of views that stressed the lasting differences between the sexes and the irremovable risk of sexual temptation between men and women." Thus, Brown continues, "with all the sharpness of a man disowning a part of his own past," Jerome "turned away forever from the prospect of a limitless fluidity of the human person" that lay at the center of Origen's thought. Jerome and his supporters, Brown concludes, "did not wish their own bodies, and, with their bodies, the landmarks of their own society, to be rendered evanescent by the vertiginous immensity implied in Origen's notion of the slow transformation of all created spirits."[2]

What, we may ask, about Jerome's opponents in this controversy? Were attitudes toward the body at the heart of their struggle, too? Did those whom Jerome now considered enemies posit views of the body that implied "the limitless fluidity of the human person?" Although the writer we

---

1. P. Brown, *The Body and Society: Men, Women, and Sexual Renunciation in Early Christianity* (New York 1988), p. 373.
2. *Ib.*, pp. 379f.

most expect to represent the opposing view is Rufinus of Aquileia, whose translation of Origen's *On First Principles* sparked the debate among Latin-speaking Christians, I propose rather to turn to Melania the Elder, Rufinus' monastic companion, to test the views on bodies here described by Peter Brown. I suggest that both the ascetic practice and the theology of Melania the Elder and her fellow Origenists were undergirded by a belief in the transformability of the body. Moreover, even the limited transformation possible here and now encouraged friendships between the sexes unusual for antiquity. That Jerome renounced the theoretical model provided by Origenism while maintaining the relationships it had facilitated only reinforces the view that his renunciation of Origenism had been half-hearted.

From the early fourth century onward, Origen's theology had been attacked for its denigration of material creation in general and of the human body in particular. Thus Methodius had mounted a major assault on Origen's spiritualized notion of the resurrection.[3] Joined to the critique of Origen's deficient understanding of the resurrection body was an attack upon his views of bodily existence in general, for these reputedly denigrated marriage and reproduction: Epiphanius appears to have originated this argument, and his approach was followed by Theophilus of Alexandria.[4] Moreover, by the late fourth century, pro- and anti-Origenist monks in Egypt were debating whether Genesis 1.26, the story of human creation in the image of God, implied an incorporeal or corporeal nature of God.[5] By the turn of the fifth century, the controversy over Origen's approach to bodiliness had manifestly expanded beyond anthropological and eschatological concerns; it influenced the discussion of ascetic theory and practice and had touched on the very doctrine of God. The status of the body is surely at the center of the Origenist debate.

Of Melania the Elder's life, family background, and ascetic renunciations, I have written elsewhere.[6] More important for my present purpose is

3. *V.* Methodius' treatise on the resurrection, as preserved in Epiph., *Pan.* 64. 12–62.

4. For the charges, *v.* J.F. Dechow, *Dogma and Mysticism in Early Christianity: Epiphanius of Cyprus and the Legacy of Origen* (Macon, Ga. 1988), chh. 11f.

5. For sources and discussion, *v.* my "New Perspectives on the Origenist Controversy: Human Embodiment and Ascetic Strategies," *ChH* 59 (1990), pp. 146–49, and my book, *The Origenist Controversy: The Cultural Construction of an Early Christian Debate* (Princeton, N.J. 1992), ch. 2.

6. *V.* Clark, *The Origenist Controversy* (note 5 above), pp. 20–25, "Ascetic Renunciation and Feminine Advancement: A Paradox of Late Ancient Christianity," *AThR* 63 (1981), pp. 240–57, and "Authority and Humility: A Conflict of Values in Fourth-Century Female Monasticism," *ByF* 9 (1985), pp. 17–33. Both articles are reprinted in Clark, *Ascetic Piety and Women's Faith: Essays on Late Ancient Christianity* (Lewiston, N.Y./Queenston, Ont. 1986), pp. 175–228.

to note that Melania's connections with the supporters of Origenism began long before the outbreak of the controversy at the end of the fourth century. She herself was well versed in Origen's works: Palladius reports that among the books that she had read—and not just once, but "seven or eight times over" (οὐχ ἁπλῶς οὐδὲ ὡς ἔτυχε διελθοῦσα, ἀλλὰ πεπονημένως ἕκαστον βιβλίον ἕβδομον ἢ ὄγδοον διελθοῦσα)—were those of Origen, of whose works she had read three million lines (μυριάδας τριακοσίας, *Hist. Laus.* 55). According to Palladius, when Melania visited the community of monks at Nitria in the 370s, she met some of the "Tall Brothers," four monks and priests who later would suffer for their Origenist views.[7] When during Valens' persecution of Nicene Christians in Egypt, Melania fled to Diocaesarea in Palestine with some of the desert monks, Evagrius Ponticus' friend Ammonius "the one-eared" (ὁ παρώτης), one of the "Tall Brothers," was among them (*Hist. Laus.* 46).[8] She and Rufinus were also on best of terms with John of Jerusalem, bishop of the city since 386, whose rebuff to and mockery of Epiphanius of Salamis enraged Jerome and touched off some unpleasant scenes at the beginning of the Origenist controversy in Palestine.[9] As a religious mentor of the wealthy heiress Olympias of Constantinople, Melania was drawn into the circle of John Chrysostom, to whom the "Tall Brothers" and their fellow Origenist supporters fled after their ouster from Egypt by Theophilus of Alexandria in 399.[10]

Another important connection of Melania the Elder to Origenist circles was through Palladius, who visited her Jerusalem monastery and with whom she travelled to Egypt (*Hist. Laus.* 55). That Palladius was suspected of Origenist sympathies early in the controversy is shown by the warning with which Epiphanius concluded his letter of 394 to John of Jerusalem: "see to it that he [Palladius] doesn't lead astray any of those entrusted to your keeping into the devious route of this false teaching" (*caue, quia Origenis heresem praedicat et docet, ne forte aliquos de populo tibi credito ad peruersitatem sui inducat erroris*).[11] That Palladius also provides a link be-

7. For the nickname οἱ μακροί *v.* Soz., *H. E.* 8.12, *PG*, vol. 67, col. 1545.

8. *V.* E.C. Butler, *The Lausiac History of Palladius: A Critical Discussion Together with Notes on Early Egyptian Monasticism*, vol. 2 (Cambridge 1904; rpt. Hildesheim 1967). All references to the *Hist. Laus.* will follow Butler's text and chapter divisions.

9. In 394 Epiphanius preached in Jerusalem a sermon against Origenism, which was apparently mocked by John of Jerusalem and his clergy (Jer., *C. Ioh.* 11 and 14). John allegedly insinuated that Epiphanius was an Anthropomorphite (Jer., *ib.* 11, *PL*, vol. 23, col. 364B). That Epiphanius had allegedly claimed to have read 6,000 volumes of Origen was another point for mockery (Jer., *Ruf.* 2.13 and *ep.* 82.7).

10. *V.* Pal. *Hist. Laus.* 56; Soc., *H. E.* 6.7, 9, 15, 17; Soz., *H. E.* 8.12f.

11. *V.* sec. 9 of *Epistula Epiphanii Cypri missa ad Iohannem Episcopum a sancto Hieronymo translata* = Jer., *Ep.* 51. All citations of Jerome's letters follow I. Hilberg, *Sancti Eusebii Hi-*

tween the alleged Origenists and John Chrysostom is revealed in his *Dialogue on the Life of St. John Chrysostom*.[12] And in his *Lausiac History*, Palladius reports that on his trip to Rome to plead the cause of the ousted John Chrysostom, he was shown hospitality by the granddaughter of Melania the Elder (*Hist. Laus.* 61). Perhaps most important, he may have carried letters and treatises between Evagrius Ponticus and the Jerusalem monasteries of Melania and Rufinus.

The decisive Origenist contact of Melania the Elder, however, was with Evagrius Ponticus, now recognized as the prime theoretician of later fourth-century Origenism. According to Palladius' account in the *Lausiac History*, Evagrius met with difficult circumstances in the early 380s: he fell in love with a married woman of the highest social class in Constantinople. After an alarming vision, in which he was incarcerated by angels, Evagrius decided to escape the city and fled to ascetic retreat in Jerusalem and the monasteries on the Mount of Olives. Yet he reverted to his former proud manner of speech and dress and, as a penalty, fell into a fever for six months. When the doctors found no treatment for him, he was approached by Melania, who saw that his sickness stemmed from spiritual causes and extracted from him the story of his love affair. She further extracted from him a promise to adopt the ascetic life; according to Palladius, she even presented him with his new monastic garb. Journeying to Egypt to join the desert monks, he stayed first at Nitria and then went further into the desert to "the Cells" (ἐν τοῖς λεγομένοις Κελλίοις, *Hist. Laus.* 38). From the Egyptian desert, he wrote dozens of letters to his former associates, including Melania and Rufinus, and penned numerous treatises on asceticism and speculative theology, the latter of which, in 553, would bring down upon him the Church's condemnation.[13]

Despite Palladius' association of Melania with known Origenists, he consistently represents her as a paragon of orthodoxy. This is the import of his story detailing Melania's support of the Catholic monks during the Arian persecution of Nicene Christians in Egypt during the mid-370s (*Hist. Laus.* 46). He also suggests that Melania's fear that her granddaughter, Melania the Younger, and her family might "be destroyed by evil teaching or heresy or bad living" prompted her return to Rome in 399–400

eronymi Epistulae, vol. 1 (Vienna 1910): *Epp. 1–70* = *CSEL*, vol. 54. Unless otherwise noted, translations from Greek and Latin texts are my own.

12. Pal., *Dial. de vita s. Ioh. Chrys.* ch. 7, describes the flight of the Egyptian monks from Theophilus, their journey to Palestine, and their subsequent appeal to John Chrysostom for help.

13. For the fate of Evagrius, *v.* A. Guillaumont, *Les 'Képhalaia Gnostica' d'Évagre le Pontique et l'histoire de l'Origénisme chez les Grecs et chez les Syriens* (Paris 1962), pp. 143–59.

(φοβηθεῖσα μήποτε περιρραγῶσι κακοδιδασκαλίᾳ, ἢ αἱρέσει ἢ κακοζωίᾳ, *Hist. Laus.* 54). Given the time and place, there could be only one theological problem about which Melania the Elder would have worried: whether her relatives might come under the influence of anti-Origenists (*i.e.,* Jerome's circle) at Rome.[14]

The link between Melania the Elder and Origenism appears even more clearly from a consideration of the relationship she and Rufinus enjoyed with Evagrius Ponticus after his departure from Palestine and settlement in the Egyptian desert. One of the go-betweens linking Egypt and Palestine was Palladius himself. In Egypt, Palladius had met Evagrius, whom he calls his teacher (23), as well as other Origenists (*Hist. Laus.* 11, 23, 35). That Palladius was back in Palestine at least briefly in 393 we know from Epiphanius' warning against him, cited above. It has been suggested by Gabriel Bunge that Palladius was the person who carried the literary remains of Evagrius, who died probably in 399, to Jerusalem after the monks were expelled from their desert retreat by Theophilus in the summer of 400; it may even have been in the monastery of Rufinus that some of Evagrius' writings were copied and preserved.[15]

A second go-between connecting Evagrius with Rufinus and Melania has been posited by Bunge: one Anatolius, to whom Evagrius' trilogy of the *Praktikos, Gnostikos,* and *Kephalaia gnostika* was sent, and who resided on the "holy mountain" (τοῦ ἁγίου ὄρους, *Prak., prol.* 1) in Jerusalem.[16] Anatolius appears in the Coptic, though not the Greek, version of the *Lausiac History* in Egypt, where he is visiting Melania the Elder's friend Pambo.[17] Like Melania, he was a Spaniard and had earlier associated with the family of a Roman named Albinus,[18] who emerges in the Greek version of the *Lausiac History* as an acquaintance of both Palladius and Evagrius Ponticus (26, 47). Perhaps, Bunge suggests, Evagrius may have met Anatolius during his stay with Rufinus and Melania the Elder in the early 380s.[19] If

14. Also noted by E.D. Hunt, "Palladius of Helenopolis: A Party and Its Supporters in the Church of the Late Fourth Century," *JThS,* n.s. 24 (1973), pp. 477f.

15. *Evagrios Pontikos, Briefe aus der Wüste,* trans. G. Bunge (Trier 1986), pp. 175f., 52f.

16. V. the dedication to the works (*Prak. Prol.* 1) and Bunge (note 15 above), pp. 34f.

17. V. Bunge (note 15 above), pp. 33f. and Pal., *Hist. Laus.,* Coptic version, ed. E. Amélineau, *De historia lausiaca: quaenam sit hujus ad monachorum aegyptiorum historiam scribendam utilitas* (Paris 1887), pp. 100f. Melania the Elder is the source of some of the information for Palladius' discussion of Pambo (*Hist. Laus.* 10).

18. Amélineau, (note 17 above), pp. 99f. V. Bunge (note 15 above), p. 33. This Albinus may be the same person who appears as Ἀλβάνιος in the company of Evagrius in the Greek version (*Hist. Laus.* 47); he does not, however, appear in the Greek version of the chapter on Pambo (10).

19. Bunge (note 15 above), p. 35.

Bunge's hypothesis is correct, not only some of Evagrius' letters, but also several of his most important theoretical books, were probably known by the community of the Mount of Olives.

In the six letters of Evagrius that Bunge thinks were definitely addressed to Melania and Rufinus (*Epp.* 22, 31f., 35–37), we encounter nothing that be-tokens Origenist speculation.[20] Rather, these epistles express thanks to the monastic pair for their generous hospitality and spiritual support throughout the years; Evagrius twice refers to letters that he had received from them or to monastic visitors they had sent from Jerusalem to visit him (*Epp.* 22.1; 37.1). If, however, we add to this collection of six letters the nine others that in the Syriac text are assigned to them as recipients (*Epp.* 1, 5, 7f., 10, 19, 40, 44, 49), we encounter some noticeably Evagrian ideas. In these letters, we find references to the notion of *apatheia,* which is an important Evagrian value (1.2, 40.3), to Evagrius' theory of "pure prayer" that disallows any images to enter the mind or passions to disturb the heart at the time of prayer (1.4, 40.3), to warnings against "thoughts of lawlessness," which Evagrius considers demonic temptations, and to complaints about the "images" that disturb his own mind (7.1).[21] Also in these epistles, there are allusions to letters that Evagrius has received from Rufinus and Melania, letters we no longer possess (*Epp.* 5.1; 44.1).

Besides these short and not very informative letters of Evagrius to Melania and Rufinus, we have two Evagrian works that some scholars posit were written for Melania. One is a work often called, in translation, *The Mirror for Nuns.*[22] That title is, however, inexact in more than one respect. The Greek title, Παραίνεσις πρὸς παρθένον, indicates that it is one nun who is addressed. Joseph Muyldermans has argued that the *parthenos* to whom the work was directed was Evagrius' old friend, Melania the Elder.[23] Muyldermans' hypothesis is strengthened by the additional information that it was probably Rufinus himself who translated the work into Latin.[24]

---

20. All references to these letters, which survive only in Syriac, will follow the German translation by Bunge (note 15 above).

21. For short accounts of Evagrius' teaching on the "evil thoughts" (*logismoi*), *v.* Clark, *The Origenist Controversy* (note 5 above), pp. 67, 75–80, 82f.; and I. Hausherr, *De doctrina spirituali christianorum orientalium: quaestiones et scripta,* ch. 3: "L'origine de la théorie orientale des huit péchés capitaux," *OrChr(R)* 30, num. 86 (1933), pp. 164–75.

22. "Nonnenspiegel"; note 26 below. *V.* S. Elm's informative discussion, "Evagrius Ponticus' *Sententiae ad Virginem*," *DOP* 45 (1991), pp. 97–120.

23. J. Muyldermans, *Evagriana Syriaca: Textes inédits du British Museum et de la Vaticane* (Louvain 1952), p. 30.

24. For the clues *v.* Jer., *Ep.* 133.3, Gen., *Vir. ill.* 17, and D.A. Wilmart, "Les versions latines des sentences d'Évagre pour les vierges," *RBen* 28 (1911), pp. 143f.

This may be the Evagrian book written for a nun or nuns that is mentioned by Socrates (παρθένον, *H. E.* 4.23), by Gennadius (*virgines, Vir. ill.* 11), and, with complaint, by Jerome himself (*virgines, Ep.* 133.3). I propose to call the work by its Greek title, *Exhortation to a Virgin.*[25]

The *Exhortation,* which exists in three versions,[26] contains much general advice of an ascetic nature: pray constantly, drive out the vices, keep vigil, embrace humility. Embedded in this advice, however, are some distinctively Evagrian themes. For example, Evagrius believed that the evil "thoughts" (*i.e.,* temptations) that befell humans advanced in a certain order. These eight *logismoi,* which turn into "seven deadly sins" in Latin theology,[27] commence with the temptation to gluttony: for Evagrius, the conquest of gluttony prepares one for the extirpation of other evil *logismoi* such as fornication, avarice, and anger (*Div. mal. cog.* 1; *Antir.* 2.48f.; *Prak.* 15). In the *Exhortation,* the nun is urged to fast in order to reduce evil desires: hunger and thirst will break them, Evagrius counsels (40). Both ἐπιθυμία (26, 34, 40) and θυμός (8, 41) are mentioned throughout, with θυμός being explicitly linked to the vice of ὀργή (8, 41) as is characteristic in Evagrius' writings.[28] The virgin is also warned against λυπή and ἀκηδία, two other important Evagrian vices (39; *cf. Antir.* 4, 6 and *Prak.* 10, 12).[29] Injunctions to sharing—"Do not say 'this is mine and that is yours,' for in Christ Jesus, everything is in common" (μὴ εἴπῃς· ἐμὸν τοῦτο καὶ σὸν τοῦτο. / ἐν γὰρ Χριστῷ Ἰησοῦ τὰ πάντα κοινά)—represent the monastic caution against the *logismos* of avarice (30; *cf. Prak.* 9, *Antir.* 3). Study is recommended to the nun; this suggests an intellectual form of asceticism suitable for a woman such as Melania (4). The Evagrian notion of "pure prayer" is here encapsulated in the injunction to "flee the company of men, lest they become images in your soul and be stumbling blocks at the

---

25. For Socrates *v. PG,* vol. 67, col. 516B; and for Jerome (note 11 above), *pars* 4: *Epp.* 121–54 (Vienna 1918) = *CSEL,* vol. 56.

26. The Exhortation exists in Greek, Latin, and Syriac. For the Greek, *v.* H. Greßmann, "Nonnenspiegel und Mönchsspiegel des Euagrios Pontikos," *TU* 39 (Leipzig 1913), pp. 146–51; for the two distinct Latin recensions, *v. PG,* vol. 40, coll. 1283–86 and pp. 148–51 of Wilmart (note 24 above); for the Syriac, *v.* W. Frankenberg, "Euagrius Ponticus," *AGWG.PH,* n.f. 13 (1912), pp. 562–65. All citations will follow Greßmann's text.

27. *V.* esp. *Prak.* 6–14 and *Antir.; cf.* Cass., *Conl.* 5. *V.* also I. Hausherr (note 21 above), pp. 165f.

28. *Cf. Keph. gnost.* 1.53. Epithumia (desire) is a negative quality for Evagrius, as is *thumos* (the seat of anger).

29. *Lupe* is the sadness that can weaken an ascetic's spiritual purpose. *Akedia* is not easy to translate: in the work of Evagrius, "boredom" or "ennui" seems closer than "sloth" as it is often translated. For a complete discussion, *v.* G. Bunge, *Akedia: Die geistliche Lehre des Evagrios Pontikos von Überdruß* (Cologne 1983).

time of prayer" (Συντυχίας ἀνδρῶν παραιτοῦ, / ἵνα μὴ γένηται εἴδωλα ἐν σῇ ψυχῇ / καὶ ἔσται σοι πρόσκομμα ἐν καιρῷ προσευχῆς, 6). Evagrius' distinctive phrase, "pure prayer" (καθαρὰν προσευχήν) is also mentioned (38). Last, *apatheia* is recommended as one goal of the ascetic's life (51).

It is of great interest for our discussion of so-called orthodoxy, however, that the Latin version contains two expansions that seem designed to correct any misgivings about the propriety of Evagrius' beliefs. One concerns the Trinity; the other, more central for our purposes, is omitted in the Greek, but is found in both the Latin and the Syriac versions of the *Exhortation*. Whereas the Greek text merely mentions that the author sees men who are trying to corrupt virgins ἐν δόγμασι (54), the Latin sharpens the warning: they try to corrupt virgins *in doctrinis haereticis*.[30] The Greek text moves directly to advise the virgin that she should heed "the teachings given in the church of the Lord . . . for the righteous shall inherit the light while the wicked shall dwell in darkness" (ἄκουε . . . δογμάτων ἐκκλησίας κυρίου, / . . . δίκαιοι γὰρ κληρονομήσουσι φῶς, / ἀσεβεῖς δὲ οἰκήσουσι σκότος, 54). The Latin text, however, expands upon the differences between these teachings, here called *decreta ecclesiae,* and those of the heretics: it explicitly affirms the creative power of God as maker of the universe and the good natures of all created things, including originally the demons. The Latin text continues: *Sicut homo ex corpore corruptibili et anima constitit rationali, sic et Dominus noster natus est absque peccato, manducans vere manducabat et cum crucifigeretur vere crucifigebatur, et non erat fantasma mendax in oculis hominum. Erit certa resurrectio mortuorum et mundus iste transibit et nos recipiemus spiritalia corpora; iusti haereditabunt lumen, impii autem haereditabunt tenebras.*[31] Whereas Wilmart's Latin text gives no indication that this passage may be interpolated, Greßmann in his Greek text relegates all but the last sentence (*iusti . . . tenebras*) to his apparatus.[32] Again, it is unclear whether what Greßmann takes to be an expansion in the Latin text is Rufinus' own attempt to bring Evagrius' view on the resurrection body into greater conformity with Church teaching than Evagrius himself admitted in other writings,[33] or whether it is the addition of a later commentator. In either case, the addi-

30. Wilmart (note 24 above), line 81.

31. *Ib.,* ll. 86–93.

32. *V. ap. crit. ad* 54 and Greßmann's discussion on p. 144. On the other hand, Muyldermans (note 23 above) considers (p. 30) the Greek text incomplete here, since the Syriac version of the work, like the Latin, contains the passage that Greßmann believes to have been interpolated.

33. *Keph. gnost.* 4.86, 6.34, 2.77, 3.66, 1.26.

tion suggests that someone thought Evagrius' approach to the body might be improved: the fleshly reality of both our lives and Jesus' is here underscored, and the notion of a bodily resurrection—albeit in a "spiritual body"—upheld.

A second writing of Evagrius ostensibly directed to Melania is one of the primary speculative works in the Evagrian canon, *i.e.*, the so-called *Letter to Melania*. Only the first part of the letter was known through the Syriac text from which Frankenberg worked in making his edition;[34] the second part of the letter was subsequently discovered and published with a French translation in 1964,[35] and an English translation of the entire letter was published in 1985.[36] Doubts have been voiced, however, as to whether the work was actually written for Melania. In the manuscript used by Frankenberg, was it, perhaps, a copyist who inserted the superscriptions giving the names of addressees?[37] In the manuscript used by Vitestam in his 1964 edition of the second part of the letter, however, the letter remains "completely anonymous"; even in the text, "nothing suggests that it was written to a woman." Most difficult for those who favor the hypothesis that the work was directed to a woman is the fact that in Syriac, the forms of the verbs, pronouns, and suffixes are masculine, and the addressee is called "lord" (*mar*).[38]

Yet other evidence militates against abandoning the thesis that the work may have been addressed to Melania the Elder. It was, for example, very common for the Church Fathers to speak of ascetic women as "manly" and even address them as men.[39] Moreover, Melania's own name is masculinized by various writers, including Paulinus of Nola (*Melani, Ep.* 29.5, *C.* 21.285; *Melanius, Ep.* 31.1) and Jerome (*Melanium, Ep.* 39.5).[40] Gabriel

34. Frankenberg (note 26 above), pp. 612–19.

35. G. Vitestam, "Seconde Partie du traité, qui passe sous le nom de 'La Grande Lettre d'Évagre le Pontique à Mélanie l'Ancienne,'" *Scripta Minora* 1963–1964 (Lund 1964), pp. 3–29.

36. All references to this letter, which survives only in Syriac, will follow M. Parmentier, "Evagrius of Pontus' 'Letter to Melania,' I" *Bijdr.* 46 (1985), pp. 2–21. *V.* also *id.*, "Evagrius of Pontus' 'Letter to Melania' II: Summary and Contents," *ib.*, pp. 21–38.

37. *V.* Bunge (note 15 above), p. 194; *cf.* pp. 174–77 for a general discussion of Melania's relation to the *corpus* of letters. *V.* also Vitestam (note 35 above), p. 4.

38. Vitestam, (note 35 above), p. 4.

39. Parmentier, (note 36 above), pp. 5f. Also note the comment (p. 51) of Guillaumont (note 13 above): "Toute cette lettre donne l'impression qu'Évagre s'adresse à quelqu'un en qui non seulement a pleine confiance, mais avec qui il se sent en pleine sympathie intellectuelle."

40. *V.* W. Hartel, *Sancti Pontii Meropii Paulini Nolani Epistulae* (Vienna 1894) = *CSEL*, vol. 29; and *id.*, *Sancti Pontii Meropii Paulini Nolani Carmina* (Vienna 1894) = *CSEL*, vol. 30. *Cf.* N. Moine, "Mélanie l'Ancienne," *DSp*, vol. 10 (1980), col. 959.

Bunge attempts to resolve the dilemma by positing that the letter was in reality directed to Rufinus, not to Melania.[41] But whether we argue that the letter was never addressed to a woman; that it was addressed to a woman to whom personal references have been masculinized; or that it was addressed originally to a man but later re-assigned to the woman who had played such an important role in Evagrius' life,[42] its contents remain startling from the point of view of later Christian orthodoxy, which would condemn the letter's views on the status of the body.

Neither Evagrius' other letters to Melania and Rufinus nor his *Exhortation to a Virgin* contains the kind of cosmological speculation for which Jerome faulted the Origenists. Yet the central theological letter of Evagrius' epistolary *corpus*, the *Letter to Melania*, contains just such speculation.[43] If this letter was received on the Mount of Olives by 397, we would have strong evidence that both Rufinus and Melania probably knew the bolder forms of Origenist speculation that were stirring up the monks of the Egyptian desert in the late 390s.

In the *Letter to Melania*, Evagrius teaches that the created world is a revelation of the divine nature (sec. 2); it is, in effect, the "letters" through which we learn "the intention, the power and the wisdom" of the Creator (sec. 3, ll. 63f.; *cf. ib.*, ll. 87f.). The human mind serves as a "body" for the Son and the Holy Spirit and possesses the same nature as the divine mind (sec. 4). Evagrius believes that "there will be a time when" all plurality will be dissolved, the human body and soul will be raised to the level of mind, and "God will be all in all" ([1Cor. 15.28], sec. 5, ll. 158–65). Plurality and "names" came into existence as a result of the "movement," Evagrius' word for the fall of the pre-existent minds (sec. 5, l. 177). The original minds were "naked" (another distinctively Evagrian phrase), but when they fell through their own free will, they descended to the level of soul and then to bodies (sec. 6, ll. 192–201). Thus they lost the "image of God" and acquired the "image of the animals" (*cf.* Rom. 1.23); having become bestial in their habits, they are unable to raise the body because they themselves are corrupt (sec. 9, ll. 357–64). In the end, however, after souls and bodies again

41. Bunge (note 15 above), pp. 199f. V. pp. 193f. for the following arguments that Melania could not have been the addressee: the addressee is called "lord" (*mar*); nothing in the letter suggests that it was written to a woman; the letter is unlike other letters of Evagrius to Melania; a second Syriac manuscript does not have the superscription to Melania.

42. Vitestam (note 35 above), note 4, p. 5.

43. Bunge tries to rescue Evagrius for orthodoxy. V. his "Origenismus-Gnostizismus: Zum Geistesgeschichtlichen Standort des Evagrios Pontikos," *VigChr* 40 (1986), pp. 24–54; "Hénade ou Monade? Au Sujet de deux notions centrales de la terminologie évagrienne," *Muséon* 102 (1989), pp. 69–91.

become minds, all minds will flow back into God the Father "like torrents into the sea" (sec. 6, l. 210). Then the nature of all rational beings will be "mingled" with that of the Creator and become one with him "in all respects" for ever and ever (sec. 12, ll. 496f.). Bodily nature is thus eradicated and human existence resumes its original incorporeal status; indeed, at the end, it is blended with divinity.

In this letter's brief epitome of Evagrian theology, we find some of the very points that Jerome and other opponents of Origenism had decried: the pre-existence of rational beings, the secondary status of the material creation, the fall from mind to soul to body, the ultimate transformation of the body so that there will be no resurrection of the flesh, and humans' loss of the image of God. Even if Melania and Rufinus knew only this one writing of Evagrius—and I would argue that they knew more—they would have encountered a type of Origenism that developed more explicitly than had Origen himself the theme of the transformability of the body.

We shall probably never know whether or not Melania accepted such views. Nor do we know if Melania was among the Origenist women whom Jerome mocked for their question, "What good will it be to us if this frail body rises again? If in the future life we are to be like the angels, will we not have the nature of angels" (*Quid nobis prode est, si fragile corpus resurget? Futurae angelorum similes angelorum habebimus et naturam, Ep. 84.6*)?[44] That Rufinus accepted such Origenist views in a more cautious form is likely.[45] The positions here expressed, in any event, certainly privilege "fluidity of the human person"—to return to Peter Brown's phrase. This transformability of the human personality ensured that even in the highly stratified society of late antiquity, women could be deemed worthy intellectual partners of men. Exemplified both in the ascetic lives of Melania the Elder and Rufinus, and in the theology of their Origenist friends, the transformed body enjoyed a brief and bright career before being abandoned in favor of a more materialist version of the Christian faith.

44. As Rufinus was quick to note (*C. Hier.* 1.24f.), Jerome himself had encouraged such views in his early work, the *Commentary on Ephesians*. Cf. my "The Place of Jerome's *Commentary on Ephesians* in the Origenist Controversy: The *Apokatastasis* and Ascetic Ideals," *VigChr* 41 (1987), pp. 154–71.

45. For the argument that Rufinus espoused a modified approach to Origenism, v. Clark, *The Origenist Controversy* (note 5 above), ch. 4.

NINE

The Mimesis of *Agape*
in Early Christian Monasticism

Taking on the Non-Violent Identity of Jesus

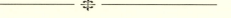

Lawrence R. Hennessey

ONTEMPORARY RESEARCH on fourth-century Christian monasticism has helped clarify many layers of motivation behind the
remarkable movement of individuals and small groups of men
and women into the deserts of Egypt, Cappadocia, and Syria. In the literature spawned by this movement, the migration came to be called *anachoresis*, the withdrawal or separation from the world of ordinary life into
another world of intentional solitude conducive to virtue.[1] The motives
behind this migration were mixed: some, men and women alike, were attempting to escape social restrictions and confinement arising from status,
wealth, or gender;[2] some fled persecution, and, having tasted solitude,
stayed to become examples for others;[3] and some were motivated by a
mixture of these motives, to which they added idiosyncratic impulses of
their own.

A common thread united these various motivations: in each instance,
the *anachoresis* involved withdrawal from some explicit pattern of vio-

1. G.W. Lampe, *A Patristic Greek Lexicon* (Oxford 1961), *sub voce*, 3b. In this study, unless
otherwise indicated, all translations are my own.
2. P. Brown, *The Making of Late Antiquity* (Cambridge, Mass./London 1978), pp. 82–84.
3. D.J. Chitty, *The Desert a City* (Crestwood, N.Y. 1966), pp. 6f.

lence. Much of this violence occurred in the context of everyday relationships. In Egypt, for example, social tensions in the villages along the Nile were aggravated by "singularly abrasive small farmers, for whom violence of body and tongue alike were normal."[4] The literature of the desert disciples suggests that this everyday violence was symptomatic of a deep crisis rooted in the very structures of late-antique culture. It is important to remember that patterns of violence—like almost all human behaviors—are learned by imitation. The same is true of the patterns of desert discipleship. The crisis revealed by the desert literature of the fourth century is this pervasive violence. *Anachoresis* can be understood as an attempt to escape this violence and to provide a clear alternative to a violent way of life.

The present study will propose an interdisciplinary conversation. Beginning with Genesis 3, the story of humanity's fall and the text essential for subsequent Christian understanding of sin and death, the conversation presents two perspectives, one anthropological and the other historical: first (Part I), the contemporary theory of mimetic anthropology, which provides valuable insights into the interpersonal dynamics of societal violence and a systematic exposition of the progress of sin,[5] and second (Part II), the exegesis of the Genesis story by Origen and Didymus the Blind, which contains remarkable anticipations of these modern anthropological formulations, and which we know to have been studied by fourth-century monks. This exegesis supports my contention that the desert disciples could recognize the mimetic mechanisms by which societal violence is propagated and deliberately adopted a way of life that would reverse its progress. The conversation will be carried forward in a brief assessment, also conducted from the perspective of mimetic anthropology, of the cross of Jesus as the reversal of the fall (Part III). The desert disciples join and complete the conversation (Part IV); their voices will be heard in various apophthegms and the more systematic work of Evagrius. The purpose of setting these diverse perspectives in conversation is not to retrieve or construct normative theological definitions for contemporary ecclesial life.

---

4. Brown (note 2 above), p. 83; cf. *Ap. pat.*, Matoes 13.

5. The contemporary theory of mimetic anthropology has been expounded principally by René Girard. I am not convinced that Girard's proposals provide a convincing theory of the origin of culture and religion, as is often claimed, but central aspects of his theory can shed light on the motives behind the desert *anachoresis*. Girard's theory of mimetic anthropology is set out in several works, of which I shall use: *Mensonge romantique et vérité romanesque* (Paris 1961); *La violence et le sacré* (Paris 1972); *Things Hidden Since the Foundation of the World: Research Undertaken in Collaboration with J.-M. Oughourlian and G. Lefort*, trans. S. Bann and M. Metteer (Stanford 1987); and *Le bouc émissaire* (Paris 1982).

What the conversation finally reveals is a consciously chosen pattern of non-violent *agape* that appears central to the earliest Christian monastic experience.

I. Mimesis, Deformed Desire, and Rivalry in Genesis 3

The starting point for mimetic anthropology "is a quality of desire called mimesis."[6] Almost all human behavior is mimetic. We learn to be human by imitation (μίμησις), and all learning is based on imitation. Almost all discussion of mimesis, beginning with Plato, is limited to "representation," what is presented as thought or action by one person is then represented as another's thought or action by imitation. This includes ordinary types of behavior such as social conventions, personal habits, and language. What is missing from the discussion is a consideration of mimesis as "appropriation": when one person expresses a desire for an object, the desire for that object may be appropriated by another. This "appropriation" can be called "acquisitive mimesis";[7] it is rooted in human desire.

Acquisitive mimesis consists in one person copying another's desire for an object. Human beings learn what is desirable from others, who are taken as models, or mediators, of what is desired.[8] Acquisitive mimesis has an innate propensity to overreach. But even if it does not overreach, it still places the person desiring in a "double bind," which is a contradictory double imperative or even a whole network of contradictory imperatives. A person has no sooner responded to that universal human injunction, "Imitate me!" than the baffling counterorder is given, "Don't imitate me!" The counterorder really means, "Don't appropriate my object."[9]

In other words, models want to be imitated, but when they are imitated, the imitators threaten their position and become rivals. When the model's thoughts are imitated, the pattern is generally representational mimesis, and relations with the model are most often harmonious. When the model's desires are imitated, the pattern is always acquisitive mimesis, and the model most often becomes an obstacle and rival. This rivalry does not arise because the desires of the imitator and the model converge on a single object; rather, the imitator will desire an object simply because his

6. R.G. Hamerton-Kelly, *Sacred Violence: Paul's Hermeneutic of the Cross* (Minneapolis, Minn. 1992), p. 19.

7. Girard, *Things Hidden* (note 5 above), pp. 7f.

8. Girard, *Mensonge* (note 5 above), p. 16.

9. Girard, *Violence* (note 5 above), p. 219.

rival wants it.[10] By imitation, human beings learn this rivalry rooted in the human desire deformed by overreaching acquisitiveness. In this sense, acquisitive mimesis may be termed mimetic rivalry.

Considered from this perspective, Genesis 3 is a story about the corruption of human desire. Adam and Eve personify desire, the snake represents the propensity of desire to become overreaching acquisitive mimesis, and in the prohibition of Gen. 2.17, God issues a clear warning about the propensity of mimesis to overreach.[11] In the garden in which God placed humanity, He prohibited access to the fruit of one tree, the tree of the knowledge of good and evil (Gen. 2.9, 17), as a warning against desire's propensity for overreaching acquisitiveness. In their original state, Adam and Eve accepted this primal prohibition as the proper limit to their desire. But then, Adam and Eve freely corrupted their desire: they chose the snake's offer of acquisitive desire, and overreaching the prohibition, became mimetic rivals with God. The infraction arose from rivalry, because Adam and Eve's corrupted desire represented the primal prohibition, not as a warning against the propensity of human desire to engage in overreaching acquisitiveness, but as God's own desire for the forbidden object. Their desire imitated what they mistakenly took to be God's desire.[12]

Adam and Eve's move from free human desire to deformed desire is sin. Sin has an observable progression, and it intensifies. It is "an activity": their "rivalry with God," is expressed as envy (φθόνος). Sin is also "an attitude," a deformed desire, expressed as concupiscence (ἐπιθυμία). Finally, this sin is "a state of affairs," expressed in scapegoating and its attendant violence (ἁμαρτία).[13]

Sin is, in other words, a process of self-corrupting desire. The process begins when the snake, speaking to Eve, extends the primal prohibition to all the trees (Gen. 3.1, *cf.* 2.16f.); this inflames Eve's desire. Even as she corrects the snake's exaggeration, she adds her own prohibition; not only the fruit, but even the tree, is not to be touched. Eve's "feeling of exclusion" has been aggravated; so too, is her propensity to overreach. The snake now fans the flames of desire by convincing Eve that God gave the prohibition to protect His own claim to the object (Gen. 3.5). Only after the snake deceives her into believing that God's beneficent prohibition is actually an expression of envious desire does Eve imitate what she takes to be God's

11. Hamerton-Kelly (note 6 above), p. 92.
12. *Ib.*
13. *Ib.,* p. 88. In his analysis, Hamerton-Kelly uses these Greek terms to help track the progress and intensification of sin.

envy and conceive a desire for the fruit (Gen. 3.6).[14] In other words, Eve learns rivalry by imitating an envious desire she has wrongfully attributed to God: human desire corrupts itself into envy.

Envy toward God is particularly corrupting because it transforms the Creator into a rival. In its most radical form, envy, as the expression of corrupt desire, makes God both a model and an obstacle. This means that the primal prohibition, having been twisted into a means by which God restricts human self-realization, is no longer perceived as a life-giving warning against overreaching acquisitive desire.[15] Envy is driven by a profound feeling of lack: the snake persuades Eve that she lacks something God has, and she cannot have it because God forbids it. The ontological foundation for this profound feeling of lack is the creature's contingency, his dependency on the Creator. The rivalry between humanity and God arises from God's alleged envy in preventing the creature access to the coveted mystery of being.[16]

The activity of sin called envy precipitates a devastating progression:[17] (1) The envious misrepresentation of God as an obstacle preventing the fulfillment of human desire becomes the paradigm for the misapplication of every human desire. Every sense of deficiency tends toward acquisitive mimesis. (2) The envious rejection of contingency inflames mimetic rivalry; it implies that God's desire, like all human desire, is envious and maliciously withholds access to the coveted mystery of being. Every other may become a model, or an obstacle, or a rival. (3) In the progress of sin, the activity of envy (φθόνος) becomes the attitude of concupiscence (ἐπιθυμία) by corrupting the relationship between the sexes. The proper relationship of generous love (ἀγαπή) is deformed into eros (ἔρως). Eros denotes "lack, a desire for what is missing"; one craves what one does not have.[18] The woman is denied her original equality with the man (Gen. 2.23), subordinated to him, and further separated from him by the painful burden of childbearing. This pattern is reinforced by the woman's erotic desire for the man (Gen. 3.16). Concupiscence (ἐπιθυμία), in the usual sense of sexual lust, thus becomes one of the first indications of deformed desire. (4) By transforming the call to life embedded in the primal prohibition into a principle of deep and insatiable need, concupiscence tends toward an infatuation with death. This happens when eros violates the in-

---

14. *Ib.*, pp. 92f.
15. Hamerton-Kelly (note 6 above), p. 93.
16. *Ib.*
17. *Ib.*, pp. 94f.
18. A. Carson, *Eros the Bittersweet: An Essay* (Princeton, N.J. 1986), p. 10.

tegrity of the other; "there is no mutual giving . . . only mutual taking." In a futile attempt to fill the lack, sexuality becomes corrupted into erotic exploitation. (5) The final stage in the progress of sin is reached when the deformed attitude of concupiscence (ἐπιθυμία) becomes "a state of affairs (ἁμαρτία)." This occurs when Adam and Eve blame God, each other, and the snake for their transgression (Gen. 3.12f.). In mimetic anthropology, this "state of affairs" is called "scapegoating."[19]

Scapegoating results from the ancient idea that guilt is almost a palpable thing; it can be passed from one person or community to another, or from a person to an animal, or even from a person to an inanimate object.[20] The scapegoat is the person, animal, or thing to which the guilt is transferred. It is driven out, killed, or otherwise put out of sight as a concrete way of rationalizing personal or communal responsibility for transgressions and as a means of purging the guilt and restoring the person or community to social harmony.[21] In fact, after the scapegoat is excluded or destroyed, a certain peace characteristically settles on the group; mimetic rivalry is temporarily stilled, and the scapegoat acquires an aura of holiness for supposedly bringing the conflict to an end.[22]

Adam and Eve choose conflict: Eve, by believing that God is envious; Adam by blaming God for his own transgression. Adam and Eve make God their scapegoat. The transference of guilt is double: from Eve's mimetic rivalry and from Adam's blaming. The disorder provoked by their mimetic rivalry with God results in the false order of scapegoating: God the victim becomes both the cause of the sin and its exculpation. This double transference works through the victim, God, and transforms the scapegoat into a sort of god, in fact, an idol. God becomes both "accursed" as the reputed cause of sin, and "holy" as the source of sin's exculpation.[23]

In Genesis 3, Adam and Eve's sin is concealed in the myth of divine envy and the original sin of turning God into an idol. Myth, in this context, always implies deception.[24] The mythologizing process begins with

19. *V.* Hamerton-Kelly (note 6 above), p. 94.

20. In classical usage, μίασμα almost objectifies guilt in the same sense of "stain, defilement" or "taint of guilt." A μιάστωρ is one who taints others with guilt; *v.* H.G. Liddel, R. Scott *et al.*, *A Greek-English Lexicon* (Oxford 1968), *sub vocc.* This is also, of course, a biblical idea underlying the ritual of the Day of Atonement (Lv. 16.20–26).

21. *Cf.* Hamerton-Kelly (note 6 above), pp. 36f.

22. Girard, *Things Hidden* (note 5 above), p. 33, 27.

23. Hamerton-Kelly (note 6 above), p. 27.

24. Myth, as used in mimetic anthropology, always entails mendacity: the purpose of myth is to conceal and help us forget the violence hidden in societal structures. In this sense, myth carries the voice of the perpetrators, not the victims, of violence; *v.* Girard, *Things Hidden* (note 5 above), pp. 119f.

the snake, described as "the most cunning of all the animals on earth which God had made" (φρονιμώτατος πάντων τῶν θηρίων τῶν ἐπὶ τῆς γῆς, ὧν ἐποίησαν κύριος ὁ θεός, Gen. 3.1).[25] The snake thus manifests, but then conceals, the fact that temptation arises in human desire, not in God. The snake now represents the renunciation of human freedom and responsibility that is the basis of scapegoating.[26] In the myth of the snake, despite God's clear assessment of responsibility (Gen. 3.14–19), the fundamental seriousness of the violence involved in the original sin tends to be relegated to the background and treated as if it had emanated from outside the human couple. In fact, the myth hides the sin from consciousness behind forces that seem genuinely exterior to Adam and Eve.[27]

By assigning responsibility equally, God exposes the human propensity toward conflict and scapegoating and its attendant violence. Genesis 3 is thus "the first demythologization": God claims His own voice and reveals the true state of affairs. The text also begins the long dialectic between the violence embedded in social structures and the possibility of reclaiming human freedom and seeking to be reconciled with God.[28]

6. The final consequence of the progress of sin is the expulsion of Adam and Eve from Paradise (Gen. 3.23f.). They are not scapegoats; God is not a mimetic rival. Although Adam and Eve are guilty and are offered a chance to repent, they refuse to acknowledge their guilt. In renouncing their responsibility, they surrender their freedom and are thus unfit for life in Paradise. It seems that Adam and Eve, but for their unrepentant transgression, would have been permitted to eat the fruit of the tree of life. By their sin, they incur death.[29]

II. Genesis 3 in the Exegesis of Origen and Didymus the Blind

The desert disciples considered Origen and Didymus of Alexandria two of the most insightful scriptural commentators. The work of Didymus provides a good indication of Origen's great influence on early Christian monasticism.[30] His Scripture commentaries are in constant and explicit dialogue with Origen. Little is known of Didymus' life, which spanned the fourth century; Palladius' evidence (*Hist. Laus.* 4) indicates that he led a

25. J.W. Wevers, *Genesis* (1974) = *LXX*, vol. 1. Unless embedded in extracts from Didymus' *de Gen.*, and therefore italicized, all quotations of Genesis in Greek follow this edition.

26. Hamerton-Kelly (note 6 above), p. 95.

27. Girard, *Violence* (note 5 above), p. 91.

28. Hamerton-Kelly (note 6 above), p. 96.

29. *Ib.*

30. For a concise study of Origen's influence on early monasticism, *v.* H. Crouzel, "Origène, précurseur du monachisme," in G. Lemaître, *Théologie de la vie monastique: Études sur la tradition patristique* (Paris 1961), pp. 15–38.

monastic life, and that monks were the audience to which he directed his many writings.[31]

The exegesis of Genesis 3 by both Origen and Didymus uncovers the pattern of violence embedded in the primordial human condition; they trace the progress of sin from pride, through envy, to concupiscence and the scapegoating driven by this concupiscence. The context of the drama is set by God's prohibition concerning the fruit of the tree in the middle of Paradise: "You shall not eat from it; on the day you eat from it, you will die by death" (ἀπὸ δὲ τοῦ ξύλου τοῦ γινώσκειν καλὸν καὶ πονηρόν, οὐ φάγεσθε ἀπ᾿ αὐτοῦ· ᾗ δ᾿ ἂν ἡμέρᾳ φάγητε ἀπ᾿ αὐτοῦ, θανάτῳ ἀποθανεῖσθε, Gen. 2.17). And so, Origen notes, the snake tempts Eve, who in turn tempts Adam: Cur praecepit vobis Deus, ut non comederetis de omni ligno paradisi? ... *Non solum mulier serpentis interrogationi respondit, sed et mandati mysterium, quod Deus viro ejus Adae dederat, publicavit[. A]dhuc mulier plasmata non fuerat, quando Deus Adae legem hujus decreti constituit. Unde intelligitur ab Adam mulieri proditum fuisse hoc Dei mandatum; ideoque et Scriptura commonet dicens:* A conjuge tua te custodi. (*Ad Gob.* frag. 2; "Why did God command you not to eat of any tree in Paradise?" [Gen. 3.1] ... Not only did the woman answer the snake's question, she also divulged the mystery of the command that God had given to her husband Adam [Gen. 3.2f.]. The woman had not yet been formed when God established this decree as a law for Adam. This means that Adam gave God's command to the woman. And so, the Scripture also warns him: "Protect yourself from your spouse").[32]

According to Didymus, Adam had no excuse, for he was created and received God's prohibition before the creation of Eve. Adam had to know that God gave her to him for his own good. She was not given to teach him, but to follow his example. In fact, God said nothing to Eve about the prohibition, which she learned from Adam. Because she was weak, Adam taught her to be careful and not touch the fruit (*de Gen.* 93).[33]

Nevertheless, as Origen notices, when confronted by God, Adam

---

31. E.C. Butler, *The Lausiac History of Palladius: A Critical Discussion Together with Notes on Early Egyptian Monasticism*, vol. 2 (Cambridge 1904; rpt. Hildesheim 1967). All references to the *Hist. Laus.* will follow Butler's text and chapter divisions. *Cf.* P. Nautin, "Didimo il Cieco d'Alessandria," *DPAC*, vol. 1 (Casale Monferrato 1983), coll. 950–52.

32. Citations of Origen's *Epistula ad Gobarum de undecima* follow, with slight repunctuation, J. Pitra, "*Sanctus Victor capuanus episcopus: Scholia veterum patrum a Victore episcopo capuae collecta,*" *Spicilegium solesmense*, vol. 1: *in quo praecipue auctores saeculo V antiquiores proferuntur et illustrantur* (Paris 1852), p. 267. Pitra points out (note 5, *ib.*), that the last line is not a recognizable citation but, perhaps, a conflation of the many Scripture passages warning about woman; *v. e.g.,* Sir. 26.10.

33. *V.* P. Nautin and L. Doutreleau, *Didyme l'aveugle, sur la Genèse*, voll. 1 (Paris 1976) and 2 (Paris 1978) = *SC*, voll. 233 and 244. Quotations of this text will omit the papyrological sigla indicating line divisions and the restoration of missing and doubtful letters.

blamed Eve, who blamed the snake: *Poenitudinis satisfactione relicta, [in] mulierem culpa[m] convertit. Rursus mulier transtulit in serpentem. Transgredientes ergo mandatum, facti ... sub dominatione Diaboli; ut propterea morti subjecti, ac de paradiso expulsi, in laboriosam terrae sunt operam deputati. Odium felicitatis alienae, unde nascitur, satis in promtu est. Amando enim quisque excellentiam suam, vel paribus invidet, quod ei coaequentur; vel inferioribus, ne sibi coaequentur; vel superioribus quod eis non coaequetur. Superbiendo igitur invidus, non invidendo quisque superbus est. Merito initium omnis peccati superbiam Scriptura definivit, dicens: Initium omnis peccati superbia.* (*Ad Gob.* frag. 3; Instead of offering amends in repentance [Gen. 3.8–11], the man blamed the fault on the woman. She in turn blamed the snake. They therefore broke the commandment and came under the power of the Devil. For this reason, subjected to death and expelled from Paradise, they were assigned the toil of cultivating the earth. Where does hatred of another's happiness arise? It is clear enough. Favoring one's own preëminence, a person envies either his peers, because they are equal to him, or his inferiors so that they may not be regarded as equal to him, or his betters because he is not equal to them. And so, a person is envious by being proud, not proud by being envious. Rightly has Scripture defined pride as the beginning of all sin, when it says: "The beginning of all sin is pride" [Sir. 10.15 *Vulg.*]).[34]

Origen reflects on the role of the Devil in the fall. The Devil tempted Adam and Eve, because he was envious of their happiness, and the human couple imitated the Devil's envy. Origen understands the Devil's envy as an act of pride; because the Devil is above all prideful, he is envious of everyone.[35] Didymus concurs in this judgment. When questioned by God, Eve blames the snake. The snake, however, is not asked a comparable question, for the snake, the Devil, is a liar and the source of evil (*de Gen.* 94).

Both exegetes trace the progress of Adam and Eve's sin from envy to concupiscence: First, there is disorder in their sexual lives, which they come to see as shameful. Then, there is Adam's turn to scapegoating and Eve's to envying God. Origen noticed this corruption setting in during the conversation between Eve and the snake; Eve disclosed to the snake a divine mystery she had learned from her husband, who now had reason to protect himself from her. Because of Eve's indiscretion, Adam's attitude toward her would now have to be guarded. But the shame over their sexuality was a direct result of their mutual sin (*Ad Gob.* fragg. 1f.).

34. I print the text as emended by P. Nautin, *Origène: sa vie et son oeuvre* (Paris 1977), note 80, p. 175.

35. *Ib.*, note 81, p. 176.

Origen remarks "that where there is no sin, there is no shame"; shame pursues Adam and Eve immediately upon their transgression (*ubi peccatum non est, neque confusio; mox enim ut sunt transgressi mandatum, eos sequuta confusio est, Ad Gob.* frag. 1). Adam, says Didymus, is ashamed of his nakedness (Gen. 3.10) because he has lost the virtue that was his protection (τὴν ἀρετήν, ἥτις ἦν σκέπασμα). Virtue is actually a divine garment (*de Gen.* 92). To get Adam to think about what he has done, God asks how he knows he is naked, something he cannot know unless he has transgressed God's prohibition (Gen. 3.11). This is God's word of clemency (Φιλάνθρωπος ὁ λόγος): God's response to the sinner is to invite reflection on the commandment (*de Gen.* 92).

Adam responds to God's invitation to repentance by blaming his wife (Gen. 3.12). This scapegoating is a clear sign of evil. Evil, says Didymus, is fond of fault-finding (Φιλαίτιον ἡ κακία). In fact, scapegoating is characteristic of sinners who avoid confessing their sins and make up excuses for their fall (*de Gen.* 93).

Didymus also notices how Eve's desire is inflamed. The snake effects the deceit by distorting the prohibition with a flattering promise (Gen. 3.5), thus reversing the prohibition and setting the stage for Eve's deception. Eve's blaming the snake is characteristic of those who are deceived; the perception of evil is hidden by pleasure, so they fail to recognize their deception until they have committed the evil. In an allegorical exegesis, Didymus uncovers a psychology of sin rooted in pleasure (ἡδονή), the satisfaction of desire: the snake is pleasure, which first arises in sensation (αἴσθησις), which is the woman; in turn, sensation serves the mind (νοῦς), which is the man (*de Gen.* 95). In other words, the genesis of sin is in desire.

Didymus adds an important observation on this story. Commenting on Gen. 3.5—"God knows that on the day you eat of it, your eyes will be opened and you will be like gods, knowing good and evil" (ᾔδει γὰρ ὁ θεὸς ὅτι ἐν ᾗ ἂν ἡμέρᾳ φάγητε ἀπ᾽ αὐτοῦ, διανοιχθήσεται ὑμῶν οἱ ὀφθαλμοί, καὶ ἔσεσθε ὡς θεοὶ γινώσκοντες καλὸν καὶ πονηρόν)—he observes that Adam and Eve have now become outcasts. In a remarkable anticipation of a key insight of modern mimetic anthropology, he points out that "because the Devil wants this outcome, he tricks the woman, and leads her into thinking that God is envious, and he promises her great things" (τούτων ὁ διάβολος ἔχων τὸ θέλημα σοφίζεται τὴν γυναῖκα, φθόνον εἰσάγει Θεοῦ ἐννοεῖν αὐτήν, ἐπαγγέλλεται δὲ μεγάλα, *de Gen.* 82).

When God deals with the consequences of humanity's fall (Gen. 3.14–19), the possibility of His envy is explicitly rejected and responsibility is carefully attributed: to the snake, "Because you have done this" (ὅτι ἐποίησας τοῦτο, de Gen. 95 on Gen. 3.14) and to Adam, "Because you have listened to the voice of your wife" (ὅτι ἤκουσας τῆς φωνῆς τῆς γυναικός σου, de Gen. 101 on Gen. 3.17). The punishments God metes out have nothing to do with envy and scapegoating; God confronts each perpetrator with the consequences of freely chosen actions.

The progress of Adam and Eve's sin is toward complete corruption. In his comment on Gen. 3.22—"Adam has become like one of us" (Αδὰμ γέγονεν ὡς εἷς ἐξ ἡμῶν)—which is attributed to God speaking to His angels, Didymus, rejecting the majority opinion, interprets ὡς εἷς ἐξ ἡμῶν not as "like one of us," but as "like one who has gone out from among us." He sets up a comparison between the Devil and Adam (de Gen. 108). Didymus follows Origen's insistence (Prin. 1.5.4; in Ioh. 2.13.97–99; and C. Cels. 4.65.31) that the Devil is not evil by nature or substance, but by a free choice rooted in pride. This angel of God, having made his choice, separates himself from the angelic ranks and is "thrown to earth because of the pride he conceived in himself" (ριφεὶς ἐπὶ γῆς διὰ τὴν ὑπερηφανίαν, ἣν ἑαυτῷ ἐπενόησεν). Now, "as one who has gone out from among us," this angel becomes the Devil. Similarly, Adam, "knowing good and evil" (ὡς εἷς ἐξ ἡμῶν . . . τοῦ γινώσκειν καλὸν καὶ πονηρόν), has rejected virtue, which consists in "choosing the good and fleeing the evil" (αἱρεῖσθαι μὲν τὸ ἀγαθόν, φεύγειν δὲ τὸ κακόν). Like the Devil, Adam by his own choice becomes "as one who has gone out from among us." This is why Adam and Eve are expelled from Paradise (de Gen. 109).

Again, when God prohibits Adam from extending his hand, taking from the tree of life, and living forever, His motive is not envy, which cannot exist in God. Eternal life is not appropriate for one who has scorned it. The purpose of this new prohibition is to reverse Adam's trespass of the first. By being denied eternal life, Adam will also be denied the everyday teaching of the tree of life.[36] This prohibition will stir up in Adam a desire to find out how bad his condition really is. But even if it does not, it is far better for Adam to live in the misery of his choice than in contempt of divine things, which he would improperly approach. "Evil becomes chronic in one who scorns the good, and as a result, one comes to hate the good" (πολυχρόνιον γὰρ τὸ κακὸν γίνεται, τοῦ ἀγαθοῦ καταφρονηθέντος, ἐξ οὗ συμβαίνει ἀνεράστως ἔχειν πρὸς αὐτό, de Gen. 111).

36. Didymus understands the everyday teaching of the tree of life to be the life imparted by preaching. For their own good, excommunicants are excluded from this preaching (de Gen. 111). V. the editors' (note 33 above) note 1 on sec. 111.

III. Unmasking Mimetic Violence: The Cross of Jesus Christ

Among the founding texts of Christianity, the Gospels in general, and the passion narratives in particular, represent the climax of the struggle described throughout the biblical tradition to unmask the structures of mimetic violence.[37] The mythic veil covering and justifying mimetic violence is a fabric woven of stories always told from the perspective of the perpetrators of violence. The narrative of the life and death of Jesus of Nazareth, however, is a definitive story, told not from the violent perpetrators' point of view, but from the perspective of an innocent victim. The story of Jesus is dangerous, because the dynamics of sin's progress are unmasked, and the underlying structures of mimetic violence are exposed for all to see.

A definitive revelation begins to occur in the high priest's decision to kill Jesus (Jn. 11.50), which is an unadorned, straightforward avowal of scapegoating. The text carefully notes that neither Caiaphas nor his listeners knows what they are saying or doing (Jn. 11.51); the pattern of mimetic violence is so deeply and culturally ingrained as to be unconscious. Two paths are now open: the murder of Jesus can be avenged, or it can be forgiven. The sentence that unmasks the unconscious persecutors lies at the heart of Luke's passion narrative: "Father, forgive them; they do not know what they are doing" (Πάτερ, ἄφες αὐτοῖς, οὐ γὰρ οἴδασιν τί ποιοῦσιν; *v. ap. crit.* Lk. 23.34).[38] By renouncing vengeance from His cross and choosing the path of forgiveness Jesus unmasks the primordial pattern of mimetic violence that has lain undetected within the human subconscious.

In the process of unmasking the embedded violence, the New Testament reports the murder of Jesus from the perspective of the victim. The cross of Jesus presents "the divine non-resistance to human evil" (*cf.* Mt. 5.39); God willingly endures human vengeance and renounces retaliation.[39] Although innocent, Jesus allows Himself to be cursed, abused, dri-

---

37. R. Girard, "Discussion" of "Generative Scapegoating," in R.G. Hamerton-Kelly, *Violent Origins: Walter Burkert, René Girard, and Jonathan Z. Smith on Ritual Killing and Cultural Formation* (Stanford 1987), p. 141. While the biblical tradition is primarily concerned with Israelite and Jewish religion and culture, the confrontation with mimetic violence is applicable to any religious and cultural setting.

38. Girard, *Le bouc* (note 5 above), pp. 169f., 166. Lk. 23.34, though missing from some important early witnesses, is well attested by writers closely linked with fourth-century monasticisim, *e.g.*, Origen, Epiphanius, Eusebius of Caesarea, and Gregory of Nyssa. *V. ad locc.* J. Allenbach *et al., BibPat,* vol. 3 (Paris 1980): *Origène;* vol. 4 (Paris 1987): *Eusèbe de Césarée, Cyrille de Jérusalem, Épiphane de Salamine;* and vol. 5 (Paris 1991): *Basile de Césarée, Grégoire de Nazianze, Grégoire de Nysse, Amphiloque d'Iconium.*

39. Hamerton-Kelly (note 6 above), p. 101.

ven out, and killed. The power of Jesus' non-violence is then vindicated by His resurrection (Rom. 1.4); so, too, is His unmasking of unconscious mimetic violence and His strategy of forgiveness (Acts 3.17–26). The Apostle describes this action of Jesus as a "new creation" (καινὴ κτίσις, 2Cor. 5.17; Gal. 6.15). The pattern of mimetic violence perpetrated by the guilty humanity of the first creation is now exposed as a lie (Rom. 5.12–19).

IV. The Desert Mimesis of *Agape:*
Taking on the Non-Violent Identity of Jesus

The letters of Paul present the death and resurrection of Jesus as an unmasking of human vengeance against God and as the disclosure of the remarkable fact that God does not fight back (Rom. 5.6–10). For Paul, this self-giving act of Jesus in dying for enemies is the essence of divine love (ἀγαπή) for humanity (*cf.* Gal. 2.19–21, esp. 2.20, ὑπὲρ ἐμοῦ; and 2Cor. 5.14, ὑπὲρ πάντων). This gratuitous display of divine generosity exposes the pretence of the rivalry between humanity and God.[40] Humanity now has the opportunity to see the true state of affairs in its own progress of sin, to recover its freedom by accepting responsibility for its own violence, and to adopt a new mimesis of *agape.*

Agape in its clear and radical claim to love one's enemies (Mt. 5.43–48; Rom. 13.8–10) is the direct counterpoint to mimetic rivalry. This *agape*, definitively revealed in the cross of Jesus, is what Paul holds out for imitation: "Be imitators of me, just as I am of Christ" (μιμηταί μου γίνεσθε, καθὼς κἀγὼ Χριστοῦ, 1Cor. 11.1; *cf.* 4.16). The context makes clear that the Apostle is urging imitation of the crucified Jesus in His act of self-giving love, not that of moral examples drawn from His life (1Cor. 1.17–25, 2.2).[41] In dramatic and stark form, the cross uncovers the roots of the human progress of sin and points the way to overcome this sin.

A disciple of Jesus is one who accepts in faith that God is Creator, not a rival. The process of divine self-emptying that culminates in the cross (Phil. 2.8) discloses the model for human self-emptying. This is a process that includes the possibility that the disciple, like Jesus, can become a scapegoat (περικάθαρμα) to the world of mimetic rivalry and violence (1Cor. 4.13). Collision with violence and the refusal to retaliate are simply facts of life in the disciple's long journey into life in Jesus, which begins in baptism (Rom. 6.1–11).

40. *Ib.*, p. 173.
41. *Ib.*, p. 176.

Already at the close of the first Christian century, the life of discipleship was understood as a conscious mimesis of the crucified Jesus, and this perception steadily intensified (*e.g.,* Ig., *Eph.* 3.1; *Rom.* 5.1–3; Eus., *H. E.* 5.1.41). By the fourth century, the conscious mimesis of *agape* becomes, in fact, the distinctive feature of early Christian monasticism. The desert disciple's way of life is a positive mimesis, constantly prompting a studied attention to the dynamics of violence and a search for ways to reverse humanity's slide into sin so that the disciple may live in tranquil love. Discipleship in the desert is a conscious attempt to take on the non-violent identity of Jesus; this conscious motive is profoundly biblical.

The world of desert monasticism was "a culture steeped in Scripture."[42] In formulating his own approach to meditative contemplation, which he calls "ardent prayer" (ἔμπυρος προσευχή), the desert disciple Evagrius (*c.* 345–99) considered penetration into the meaning of Scripture to be the first and foundational phase of the contemplative life (*Prak.* 84).[43] Clearly, meditation on the Scripture was a primary conduit for the desert mimesis of *agape.*

The other primary conduit for the desert mimesis was the living word of an *abba* or *amma,* a man or woman who had not only experience of desert life, but more importantly, a reputation for holiness. A new disciple, or even one who had been in the desert a long time, would approach the *abba* or *amma* and ask for a word (ῥῆμα) to help him on the way to salvation.[44] The word was always tailored to the circumstances of the person asking; it tended to be short and pithy, easily memorized for further thought and reflection. The words have deep implicit and explicit scriptural resonance; in fact, these occasional words gradually became indistinguishable from Scripture in terms of the authority they carried in shaping the desert mimesis. The result was a kind of double authority of word and Scripture for the desert disciples.[45]

From the fusion of scriptural meditation and words there emerged in the transmission of desert mimesis "a 'pedagogy of spiritual direction'"

---

42. D. Burton-Christie, *The Word in the Desert: Scripture and the Quest for Holiness in Early Christian Monasticism* (New York/Oxford 1993), p. vii.

43. A. and C. Guillaumont, *Évagre le Pontique, Traité pratique ou le moine,* vol. 2 (Paris 1971): *Édition critique du texte grec . . . traduction, commentaire et tables* = *SC,* vol. 171. V. Evagrius Ponticus, *The Praktikos and Chapters on Prayer,* trans. J.E. Bamberger (Kalamazoo, Mich. 1981), pp. lxxxviiif. For contemplation as ἔμπυρος προσευχή v. *De or.* 111, *PG,* vol. 79, col. 1192C. This work, published in *PG* among the works of Nilus of Ancyra, seems to be Evagrius'. V. Quasten, vol. 3, p. 174.

44. Burton-Christie (note 42 above), p. 77 and note 6, p. 99.

45. *Ib.,* p. 110.

that can be distinguished from "a pedagogy of a rule" characteristic of the larger, cenobitic communities.[46] The content and motive of this spiritual direction and of these rules was the mimesis of *agape;* it can fairly be called a new *paideia,* "an altogether original method of spiritual education,"[47] a fact clearly recognized by those trained in classical *paideia* (*Ap. pat.,* Arsenius 5f).

The new *paideia* practiced and propagated by the desert disciples embraces two moments of biblical revelation: a careful analysis and unmasking of the progress of humanity's primordial sin and the possibility of a systematic mimesis of *agape* disclosed in the cross of Jesus. Both Origen and Didymus describe the first moment: their analysis of Genesis 3 shows how desire corrupts itself in a downward spiral of violence driven by pride, envy, and concupiscence, resulting, finally, in a sin-filled state of affairs. The sayings of the desert disciples furnish a clear outline of the second moment: the possibility of a systematic mimesis of *agape,* whose purpose is a conscious attempt to confront and halt the primordial slide into accepted patterns of violence and then to reverse humanity's slide by holding out a way to imitate Jesus' own path back to God.

In pursuing a mimesis of *agape,* the desert disciples first had to face pride (ὑπερηφανία/*superbia*), which both Origen and Didymus identified as the cause of all sin. Pride induces a disciple to deny his contingency and to consider the self, not God, the cause of virtue (Evag., *Prak.* 14). The gospel imperative that unmasks pride is humility (ταπεινοφροσύνη). Humility is thinking of others as superior (ὑπερέχοντας) to oneself, and putting the needs and interests of others before one's own (Phil. 2.3f.). Humility is explicitly identified with the mind of Christ and particularly with the crucified Jesus in His act of self-giving love (Phil. 2.5–8). Humility is key to the mimesis of *agape,* because it is, first and foremost, a mimesis of the crucified Jesus, not the mimesis of moral examples from Jesus' life. A disciple should be crucified with Christ, dying to self, arms outstretched, calling out to God.[48] Humility is, thus, the foundation of the desert mime-

---

46. *Ib.,* p. 77.

47. J.-C. Guy, "Educational Innovation in the Desert Fathers," *ECR* 6 (1974), p. 45.

48. N143; F. Nau, "Histoire des solitaires Égyptiens [*Suite* (1); ms. Coislin 126, fol. 189 sqq.] ῞Οτι δεῖ τὴν ἡσυχίαν καὶ τὴν κατάνυξιν μεταδιώκειν," *ROC* 13 (1908), p. 49. I cite the anonymous sayings of the desert fathers according to the numbers assigned to them by F. Nau in his *editio princeps* of those preserved in Paris, Bibl. Nat., Coislinianus 126 (N), foll. 158ff.; *v. ROC* 12–14 (1907–09); and 17 (1912), and *cf.* W. Bousset, *APOPHTHEGMATA: Studien zur Geschichte des ältesten Mönchtums* (Tübingen 1923), pp. 107–10. Some of these anonymous apophthegmata and the entire alphabetical collection originally published by J. Cotelier (*Ecclesiae graecae monumenta,* vol. 1 [Paris 1677]; rpt. *PG,* vol. 65) are available in J.-C. Guy *Les Apophtegmes des Pères* (Paris 1993) = *SC,* vol. 387. For anonymous apophthegms

sis of *agape*, as essential for a desert disciple as the air one breathes (*Ap. pat.*, Poemen 49 and Theodora 6). The mimesis of Christ's humility can be captured in a simple phrase to live "by the cross" (ἐν σταυρῷ, *Ap. pat.*, John Colobos 34).

In the movement from pride to humility, the progress of sin is reversed. The mimesis of humility is a reversal of pride, for it entails the radical acceptance of contingency and so a willingness to curb overreaching desire. Human desire is not denied or repressed; rather, the propensity to overreaching is curbed, and desire is re-channeled in the direction of a generous and open-hearted mimesis. In fact, the energies of human desire, called in the desert the "passions" (πάθη), are not devalued; they remain essential to human life.[49] What the disciples notice is the way these indispensable energies easily degenerate into hostility toward others, toward oneself, and toward God, in whose image humanity is made (Gen. 1.26). Even a disciple well advanced can never lower his guard.[50]

The confrontation with mimetic rivalry occurs on two major fronts: in inter-personal relationships and within the individual wrestling with his own contradictory impulses, compulsions, and feelings—the passions. In the arena of inter-personal relationships, the most serious obstacle to the mimesis of *agape* is anger (ὀργή). According to Evagrius, anger is a fierce cauldron of rivalry and violence, "a boiling and stirring up of wrath against one who has given injury or is thought to have done so" (θυμοῦ γὰρ λέγεται ζέσις καὶ κίνησις κατὰ τοῦ ἠδικηκότος ἢ τοῦ δοκοῦντος ἠδικηκέναι, *Prak.* 11).[51] So serious is anger, says Evagrius, that it can lead to physical exhaustion, malnutrition, and hallucinations. The strategy against it is biblical: "The sun must not set on your anger" (ὁ ἥλιος μὴ ἐπιδυέτω ἐπὶ [τῷ] παροργισμῷ ὑμῶν, Eph. 4.26). This command is woven into words that acknowledge the prevalence of anger as well as the need to confront it daily (Ath., *Ant.* 55. 4f.).[52] The battle is clearly joined by a disciple who resists retaliation. At a council of desert disciples, Abba Moses, who was black, was abused with racial epithets by some of the others. Asked if he became angry at such treatment, he said, "I was upset, but I said

---

(*i.e.*, N sayings) that are not found in Guy's edition I provide reference to the relevant volume of the *ROC*.

49. In the desert literature, Evagrius is the great "anatomist of the passions"; his analysis embraced both their "wholesome operations" and their "disordered tendencies." V. Bamberger (note 43 above), pp. lxxxi–lxxxvii, esp. p. lxxxii.

50. N203 (note 48 above).

51. The translation follows Bamberger (note 43 above).

52. *Cf. Ap. pat.*, Poemen 177.

nothing" (ἐταράχθην, ἀλλ᾽ οὐκ ἐλάλησα, *Ap. pat.*, Moses 3).[53] Beyond silence, the disciple is called to non-violence: doing good to unmask evil (*Ap. pat.*, Poemen 177).

The doing of good, the mimesis of *agape*, itself was a source of mimetic tension among the desert disciples. Sometimes, the tension was between cenobites and anchorites as to whose life was more rigorous and faithful; sometimes the conflict represented tension between the first generation of largely illiterate Coptic monks and better-educated, Greek-speaking new arrivals.[54] In these instances, the disciples appear envious of the mimesis of Christ and compare their own relationship with Jesus favorably or unfavorably to that of others. This particular form of mimetic violence was never effectively unmasked.

The confrontation with mimetic violence was often an intense personal and interior struggle. Solitude did not protect a disciple from interior conflicts; in fact, in the desert, the struggle with personal passions often seemed intensified. This was particularly true in the battle against concupiscence (ἐπιθυμία) and its manifestation in erotic desire. For the desert disciples, the lack occasioned by erotic desire was focused, first of all, on food. The desert world lived on the edge of starvation.[55] The desperate circumstances characteristic of such an environment—Evagrius mentions fear of old age, inability to work to feed oneself, the debilitation of malnutrition, and the shame of having to rely on others for life's essentials (*Prak.* 9)—intensified internal conflicts. Unrelenting labor was necessary to ensure basic provisions for oneself and perhaps a tiny surplus that could be shared with visitors. The disciples were well aware that the primordial corruption of human desire was occasioned by an overreaching desire for food (Gen. 3.6). Fasting in the face of such a lack (*eros*) provided a concrete way of exposing and undoing the primordial sin.[56] In addition, the apparent preference for fasting and keeping vigil for forty-day periods suggests a mimesis of Jesus and His confrontation with, and unmasking of, the devil (Mk. 1.12f.; Mt. 4.1–11; Lk. 4.1–13).[57]

Erotic desire was also, of course, clearly present in sexual temptations. Often, the interior struggle with sexual passion was personified as a strug-

53. This saying also suggests a certain pattern of mimetic violence; the violence toward Moses is justified as an attempt "to test him" (θέλοντες αὐτὸν οἱ πατέρες δοκιμάσαι).

54. N229; F. Nau, "Histoire des solitaires Égyptiens [*Suite* (1); ms. Coislin 126, fol. 213 sqq.], (f. 213rᵇ) Περὶ διακρίσεως," *ROC* 14 (1909), p. 361. *Cf. Ap. pat.*, Arsenius 5; and Evagrius 7.

55. P. Brown, *The Body and Society: Men, Women and Sexual Renunciation in Early Christianity* (New York 1988), p. 218.

56. N145, 152 (note 48 above).

57. *Ap. pat.*, Sarmatas 2 and Phocas 1f.; N173 (note 48 above).

gle with the demon of impurity (ὁ τῆς πορνείας δαίμων, Evag., *Prak.* 8; *cf.* *Ap. pat.*, Sara 1). This personification made explicit the nature of the conflict occurring within the disciple, that between a mimesis of natural sexual or erotic desire and a mimesis of continence. Sexual desire in its ordinary form was considered to have been corrupted into domination and exploitation as a result of Adam and Eve's sin (Gen. 3.16). Continence was a way of unmasking sexual concupiscence and overcoming its inherent violence of domination and exploitation.

Evagrius notes that the demon of impurity attacks more fiercely those practicing continence (*Prak.* 8). In the progress of sin, a prohibition, even one self-imposed, usually inflames desire. The disciples realized that sexual desire required vigilance and equanimity.[58] The same was true of sexual lapses; what they required was forgiveness. In the intense and exalted atmosphere of the desert communities, a serious lapse in the mimesis of *agape,* usually a sexual lapse, was treated as a violation of a prohibition, for which the penalty was expulsion from the community. This kind of excommunication appears as the most dramatic form of scapegoating in early Christian monasticism. Patterns of scapegoating clearly appeared among the desert disciples, as did the strategies for unmasking them and reversing their violent effects. A poignant example comes from the black disciple, Abba Moses: Ἀδελφός ποτε ἐσφάλη εἰς Σκῆτιν. Καὶ γενομένου συνεδρίου, ἀπέστειλαν πρὸς τὸν ἀββᾶ Μωϋσῆν. Ὁ δὲ οὐκ ἠθέλησεν ἐλθεῖν. Ἀπέστειλεν οὖν πρὸς αὐτὸν ὁ πρεσβύτερος λέγων· Ἐλθέ, ὅτι ὁ λαός σε περιμένει. Ὁ δὲ ἀναστὰς ἦλθεν καὶ λαβὼν σπυρίδα τετρημένην ἐγέμισεν ψάμμου καὶ ἐβάστασεν. Οἱ δὲ ἐξελθόντες εἰς ἀπάντησιν αὐτοῦ λέγουσιν αὐτῷ· Τί ἐστι τοῦτο, πάτερ; Καὶ εἶπεν ὁ γέρων· Αἱ ἁμαρτίαι μου εἰσὶν ὀπίσω μου καταρρέουσαι καὶ οὐ βλέπω αὐτάς, καὶ ἦλθον ἐγὼ σήμερον ἀλλότρια ἁμαρτήματα κρῖναι. Οἱ δὲ ἀκούσαντες οὐδὲν ἐλάλησαν τῷ ἀδελφῷ, ἀλλὰ συνεχώρησαν αὐτῷ (*Ap. pat.*, Moses 2; "A brother at Scetis committed a fault. A council was called to which Abba Moses was invited, but he refused to go to it. Then the priest sent someone to say to him, 'Come, for everyone is waiting for you.' So he got up and went. He took a leaking basket, filled it with sand and lifted it up. The others came out to meet him and said to him, 'What is this, Father?' The old man said to them, 'My sins run out behind me, and I do not see them, and today I am coming to judge the errors of another.' When they heard that, they said no more to the brother but forgave him").[59] The scapegoating mechanism was in

58. *E.g.,* N164f. (note 48 above); *Ap. pat.*, Sara 1.

59. The translation follows, with slight revision, *The Sayings of the Desert Fathers: The Alphabetical Collection,* trans. B. Ward, rev. ed. (Kalamazoo, Mich. 1984), pp. 138f.

place: the victim had been designated; the judgment was in the hands of the crowd, and unanimity was desired and sought. One lone voice dissented: Abba Moses engaged in a parabolic gesture, reminiscent of the Hebrew prophets (*e.g.*, Is. 20.1–6; Jer. 13.1–11). He interpreted his gesture with a word that gave the victim a voice and thus unmasked the scapegoating mechanism. Moses refused to judge but rather accepted judgment on himself. In this instance, once exposed, the mechanism lost its power and yielded to a positive movement toward forgiveness.

In desert mimesis, this movement toward forgiveness is called compunction (πένθος), a deep sorrow for sin, often accompanied by tears. Compunction involves "a 'double movement' of the heart": the disciple accepts both judgment and mercy at the same time.[60] It is not just accepting the fact of one's sinfulness; it is also an active appeal to God's mercy (*Ap. pat.*, Poemen 122). Compunction reverses the double transference of guilt involved in the scapegoating mechanism. In the acceptance of judgment, the disciple undercuts the root of mimetic rivalry by accepting responsibility for his own sin; in the acceptance of God's mercy, the disciple's contagion is cleansed, and once cleansed, he is no longer an acceptable scapegoat. The disciples are then free to reverse the gesture of exclusion and to reconcile the lapsed disciple to the rest of the community.

The progress of sin from its first manifestation in the overreaching desire of human pride, through the corruption of desire into envy and concupiscence, and finally into scapegoating and expulsion, is definitively reversed in this desert mimesis of forgiveness and reconciliation. In desert mimesis, the definitive reversal of sin results in an attitude of hospitality (ξενοδοχία) that constitutes a foretaste of Paradise regained. The desert becomes a place of hospitality (ξενία), the same word used for a desert monk's cell (Pal., *Hist. Laus.* 47). From the same root comes also the word solitude (ξενιτεία); in the desert mimesis, the fruit of solitude is hospitality. Antony was a great example of this attitude. He constantly attracted others and received strangers with openness and welcome. He possessed a soul purged of mimetic rivalry, a stable character, a pure heart; even in a crowd, he was immediately recognized "as someone whose heart had achieved total transparency to others" (Ath., *Ant.* 67).[61]

The progress of the mimesis of *agape*—from the first attempts at humility to reverse pride's overreaching desire, through wrestling with envious violence by unmasking anger and renouncing retaliation, confronting the eros of concupiscence with strategies of fasting and continence, un-

---

60. Burton-Christie (note 42 above), p. 185.
61. Brown (note 55 above), p. 226.

masking the scapegoating mechanism by compunction and forgiveness, and reversing the violence of exclusion by reconciliation and hospitality— is the way the desert disciples consciously took on the non-violent identity of the crucified Jesus. This great effort of mimesis was to result in what Abba Evagrius called ἀπάθεια, a stable state of deep calm, which would arise from a "full and harmonious integration," not a denial or repression, of all forms of human desire, *i.e.,* all the passions, under the guidance of *agape* (*Prak.* 78).[62] *Apatheia* was conceived in obedience to the crucified Jesus, nourished by humility, and cultivated by compunction (*Prak.* 57). *Apatheia* represented a "decisive turning point" in the journey of a disciple.[63] Having renounced violence in all its forms, calm and at peace, one's life was now centered on a mimesis of *agape:* contemplation, hospitality to others, and living into the life of God (*Prak., prol.* 8 and sec. 79).

By gradually purifying all levels of motivation that prompted the initial *anachoresis,* the mimesis of *agape* could, and sometimes did, flower into genuine *apatheia* (*Prak.* 81). Attaining this new way of life was, in itself, sufficient motive and reward enough for all the effort involved. Some disciples even accepted violent death rather than abandon their desert of solitude and hospitality; this was simply a consequence of their mimesis of the crucified Jesus (*Ap. pat.,* Moses 10). As far as they could see, the desert mimesis was the only non-violent alternative for a world otherwise permanently submerged in violence and death. In the face of endless violence and death, these desert disciples consciously chose a new way of *agape* and life.

---

62. Bamberger (note 43 above), p. lxxxiv.
63. *Ib.,* p. lxxxvii.

TEN

Ritual and Conversion

The Case of Augustine

————————— ❧ —————————

Thomas M. Finn

ISTA CONTROVERSIA *in corde meo non nisi de me ipso adversus me ipsum. . . . ecce audio vocem de vicina domo cum cantu dicentis et crebro repetentis, quasi pueri an puellae, nescio: 'tolle lege, tolle lege'. . . . nihil aliud interpretans divinitus mihi iuberi nisi ut aperirem codicem et legerem quod primum caput invenissem. . . . itaque concitus redii in eum locum ubi sedebat Alypius: ibi enim posueram codicem apostoli. . . . arripui, aperui, et legi in silentio capitulum quo primum coniecti sunt oculi mei: 'non in comessationibus et ebrietatibus, non in cubilibus et impudicitiis, non in contentione et aemulatione, sed induite dominum Iesum Christum et carnis providentiam ne feceritis in concupiscentiis.' nec ultra volui legere nec opus erat. statim quippe cum fine huiusce sententiae quasi luce securitatis infusa cordi meo omnes dubitationis tenebrae diffugerunt.*[1]

The year was 386; the author, Augustine of Hippo; the passage, perhaps, the most celebrated conversion account in the literature of antiquity. The plethora of manuscripts of Augustine's *Confessions* testifies to the fact that Augustine's conversion burned into the medieval imagination and subsequently left its deep mark on western thought about conversion.[2] In fact,

1. Aug., *Conf.* 8.11.27 and 12.29. The text follows J.J. O'Donnell, *Augustine, Confessions,* vol. 1 (Oxford 1992): *Introduction and Text* and, with slight modification, the translation of H. Chadwick, *Saint Augustine, Confessions* (Oxford 1991). O'Donnell offers commentary in voll. 2f.

2. O'Donnell (*ib.,* vol. 1, note 107, p. lvi) gives the present count at 333. L. Verheijen sus-

students of conversion link Augustine in the garden at Milan, Paul of Tarsus on the road to Damascus, Luther in his Augustinian monastery, and John Wesley in the Aldersgate meeting at London as the quintessential converts.

Although the idea of conversion antedates modernity by twenty-five hundred years—the ancient Hebrews discovered and named it—William James and his fellow psychologists a hundred years ago were the first to attempt a systematic definition.[3] In the aftermath of America's second Great Awakening, James devoted two of his Gifford Lectures of 1902 (later published as *The Varieties of Religious Experience*) to conversion. This he defined as the process "gradual or sudden, by which a self hitherto divided, and consciously wrong, inferior and unhappy, becomes unified and consciously right, superior and happy, in consequence of its firmer hold upon religious realities."[4] To be sure, James and his heirs acknowledged that conversion entailed a gradual process. Nonetheless, the sudden change at a key moment commanded most of subsequent attention. This was true of Arthur Darby Nock's classic study of conversion in Greco-Roman antiquity.[5] Nock concluded that the ancients did not normally cross over familiar religious boundaries into new ones but conceded that they might readily seek and accept forms of worship as supplements. He called this phenomenon "adhesion," not conversion, because it involved no crisis, no new set of convictions, and no self-surrender, all essential criteria for James. The exceptions, he noted, were Judaism and Christianity, both "prophetic" religions that demanded a "deliberate turning from indifference or from an earlier form of piety to another, a turning . . . a consciousness that a great change is involved, that the old way was wrong and the new is right."[6] The underlying assumption from which he and James worked was that a religion worthy of the name requires intense experience of the holy that shapes one's inner life and values.

The scholarly study of conversion stayed pretty much as James and Nock left it until the 1950s, which saw the resurgence of born-again evangelical Christianity, the spread of the charismatic movement, and the ar-

---

pects that about another 100 remain uncatalogued; *v.* p. lx of *Sancti Augustini Confessionum libri XIII* (Turnhout 1981) = *CChr.SL,* vol. 27.

3. For a discussion of the term "conversion" in antiquity *v.* P. Aubin, *Le problème de la 'conversion': Étude sur un terme commun à l'hellénisme et au christianisme des trois premiers siècles* (Paris 1963).

4. W. James, *The Varieties of Religious Experience* (New York 1902), p. 189.

5. A.D. Nock, *Conversion: The Old and the New in Religion from Alexander the Great to Augustine of Hippo* (Oxford 1933).

6. *Ib.,* p. 7.

rival of the new religious movements; interest quickened especially among social scientists.[7] Although the current research is at once diverse and daunting, a serviceable model of conversion has emerged with the following concerns: (1) the convert's social, cultural, and religious worlds; (2) an identity crisis; (3) an active search for meaning and purpose in life; (4) an encounter with a new religious reality that engages the convert's emotional, intellectual, and cognitive needs; (5) a continual interaction with the community that embodies this new religious reality; (6) a clear-cut choice between the previous way of living and a new way that yields commitment; and, finally, (7) gradual transformation, resulting in a reorientation of attitudes and values mirrored in conduct.[8]

The fact is that contemporary research, although it assumes James' and Nock's conclusions about the nature of religion, has shifted their focus. While James and Nock emphasized the individual, the psychological, and the sudden, this research regards conversion as a developing and communal experience. The precise moment on which conversion turns, as if on an axis, may be sudden and fraught with crisis, but the process that leads up to and away from the axial moment is gradual and complex, involving extended interaction with the community that embodies the new religious realities. Indeed, a close scrutiny reveals that Augustine's conversion exemplifies just such a gradual and interactive process. At its heart, moreover, was the extended and richly articulated ritual process of conversion known as the catechumenate.[9]

7. For analysis and bibliography of contemporary research *v.* L. Rambo, "Current Research on Religious Conversion," *RelStR* 8 (1982), pp. 146–59; and L.D. Shinn, "Who Gets to Define Religion: The Conversion/Brainwashing Controversy," *ib.* 19 (1993), pp. 195–207. Both studies review the periodical literature. *V.* also W. Conn, *Christian Conversion: A Developmental Interpretation of Autonomy and Surrender* (New York/Mahwah, N.J. 1986); A.F. Segal, *Paul the Convert: The Apostolate and Apostasy of Saul the Pharisee* (New Haven, Conn. 1990); E.V. Gallagher, *Expectation and Experience: Explaining Religious Conversion* (Atlanta 1990), esp. pp. 1–10, 39–55; L. Rambo, *Understanding Religious Conversion* (New Haven, Conn. 1993); and C.D. Batson, P. Schoenrade, W.L. Ventis, *Religion and the Individual: A Social-Psychological Perspective* (New York/Oxford 1993).

8. The enumeration is Rambo's, *Understanding* (note 7 above), pp. 165–76, but *v.* also Shinn, (note 7 above), pp. 204f.

9. For its origins and development through the fifth century, *v.* the seminal study of North Africa and Augustine by B. Busch, "*De initiatione christiana secundum sanctum Augustinum,*" *EL.A* 52 (1938), pp. 159–78; and *id., "De modo quo S. Augustinus descripserit initiationem christianam,*" *ib.*, pp. 385–483. *V.* also, T.M. Finn, *Early Christian Baptism and the Catechumenate: Italy, North Africa, and Egypt* (Collegeville, Minn. 1992), pp. 54–76 (Zeno of Verona, Ambrose), pp. 115–40 (Tertullian, Cyprian), and pp. 147–71 (Augustine); and my study of the Lenten catechumenate in later fourth-century North Africa, "It Happened One Saturday Night: Ritual and Conversion in Augustine's North Africa," *JAAR* 58 (1990), pp. 589–616.

As an institution to prepare potential converts for baptism and full Christian life, the catechumenate first appeared in the late second century and flourished until the seventh, when infant baptism became the normal means of entering the church. Although far from uniform in the early Church, it was a process deeply embedded in rituals that demanded interaction between community and catechumen, the goal of which was the gradual transformation of both candidate and community.[10] Perhaps the lesson for contemporary researchers is that conversion is a deeply ritual process. Hence, Augustine's sudden and dramatic conversion, which has become paradigmatic of genuine conversion, is better understood as a ritual drama. For Augustine the rites of the catechumenate spanned some thirty-three years and involved constant interaction with members of the community for whom these rites were central.

Ritual and Journey: The Biography of a Catechumen and Convert

The garden experience is surely the critical moment in Augustine's turning toward Christ. Indeed, immediately after telling his mother what had happened, he spoke of the event as his conversion (*Convertisti enim me ad te*, 8.12.30) and in so doing chartered the manifold attempts to see the garden experience as the paradigm of conversion. But the life story that shines through the first nine books of the *Confessions* provides a corrective: the garden was a decisive moment, a turning point, in a long ritual journey that began in Augustine's infancy.

Augustine's mother, Monica, was a Catholic Christian and his father, Patricius, a pagan. Patricius became a catechumen a year before his son went to study in Carthage (2.3.6) and received baptism on his deathbed. As Augustine repeatedly insists, he grew up in a Christian home and attended to his religion. In infancy he was inscribed as a catechumen, a rite that involved exorcism, the imposition of hands, the sign of the cross, and the ingestion of salt. He tells us that he begged for baptism as a boy when gravely ill (1.11.17).[11] Augustine considered himself a believer, regularly attended church (*e.g.*, 3.3.5), prayed, and even missed the name of Christ—a name which, he says, he had drunk in with his mother's milk—in his rhetoric

10. Particularly insightful in the matter of community transformation is the work of V. Turner, *The Ritual Process: Structure and Anti-structure* (Chicago 1969), esp. his discussion of liminality and *communitas*, pp. 94–165.

11. *et signabar iam signo crucis eius, et condiebar eius sale iam inde ab utero matris meae.* For a description of the rite *v.* Aug., *Cat. rud.* 27.50. He composed this work for the preliminary instruction of those considering Christianity. The rite marked their determination to proceed.

books. Ever after, he says, "any book which lacked this name . . . could not entirely grip me" (*quidquid sine hoc nomine fuisset . . . non me totum rapiebat*, 3.4.8).

Disaffection struck during student days at Carthage, but not at first. In spite of the sexual and cultural provocation of the city, he continued to attend the instructional part of the eucharistic liturgy, which was all that was permitted to him as a catechumen; indeed, it was at the Mass of the Catechumens that he appears to have discovered and fallen in love with the young woman with whom he lived for the better part of fifteen years (3.4.8).[12] To be sure, his Old Latin version of the Bible with its translationese could not satisfy his increasingly sophisticated literary tastes (*sed visa est mihi indigna quam tullianae dignitati compararem*, 3.5.9). And the Manichees, whom he had just begun to encounter, had finely bound and decorated liturgical books as well as fascinating truths educed from their texts (3.6.10).[13] Nonetheless, as he began to slip his Catholic moorings, he discovered the study of philosophy while reading Cicero's *Hortensius: Ille . . . liber . . . ad te ipsum, domine, mutavit preces meas, et vota ac desideria mea fecit alia. . . . et surgere coeperam ut ad te redirem* (3.4.7; "The book . . . altered my prayers, Lord, to be towards you yourself. It gave me different values and priorities. . . . I began to rise up to return to you"). As he was turning away, he was turning toward.

Given the deeply cultic nature of North African religion,[14] and the way Augustine encodes his change, the "altered" prayers to which he gave new intention and direction seem to have been those of the Catholic liturgy, but he leaves no doubt that he was also associating with the Manichaeans and attending their liturgy, where Christ the teacher was accorded much importance.[15] By the time he returned to Thagaste to teach, he was a Manichee hearer and, much to his mother's horror, no longer a Catholic

12. Augustine's term, *solemnitas,* is already a technical term for the celebration of the Mass. He distinguishes the Eucharist or Mass of the Faithful from the Mass of the Catechumens in *Ser.* 49.8. *V.* also *Ep.* 126.5, where the catechumens are dismissed with the response *Deo gratias* when the lection is finished. Thus, they were hearers (*auditores*) of the Scriptures and homiletic commentary.

13. Augustine calls them *phantasmata splendida. Cf.* Chadwick (note 1 above), notes 15f., pp. 40f. For a recent study of Augustine as a Catholic and a Manichee *v.* L.C. Ferrari, "Young Augustine: Both Catholic and Manichee," *AugustinStud* 26 (1995), pp. 109–28.

14. O'Donnell (note 1 above) observes correctly (p. xxviii): "For Augustine, and for late-antique men and women generally, religion is cult—or, to use the word we use when we approve of a particular cult, religion is liturgy." The cults gave their devotees an experience of the divine and a sense of regeneration that begets hope and ardor, a sense that accounts for their wide appeal.

15. On Manichaean Christology *v.* O'Donnell (note 1 above) on 3.4.8: *quod nomen Christi non erat ibi. Cf.* Ferrari (note 13 above), p. 116.

catechumen. Monica refused to allow him to live at home (3.11.19).[16] Although he was still a Manichee when he went to Rome some years later (383), where, with the help of some co-religionists, he won the chair of rhetoric in Milan (5.13.23), disillusion about the sect had gradually set in, and he found himself adrift and a skeptic, and not, as some think, a convert from Manichaean cult to Christian cult (5.14.24–25).[17]

Enter Ambrose, bishop of Milan (374–97). While Augustine enthusiastically listened to Ambrose preaching to the people, he conceded, "I was led to him by you, unaware that through him, in full awareness, I might be led to you" (*ad eum . . . ducebar abs te nesciens, ut per eum ad te sciens ducerer,* 5.13.23). Augustine resumed old ways and attended the Mass of the Catechumens, though with no desire other than to enjoy the charm of Ambrose's rhetoric. "Nevertheless," he notes, "together with the words which I was enjoying, the subject matter . . . came to make an entry into my mind" (*veniebant in animum meum simul cum verbis quae diligebam res etiam,* 5.14.24). Therefore, he decided "for the time being to be a catechumen in the Catholic Church" (*Statui ergo tamdiu esse catechumenus in catholica ecclesia, mihi a parentibus commendata, donec aliquid certi eluceret quo cursum dirigerem,* 5.14.25).[18] He frequently came to hear Ambrose, who often saw him with his mother in church (6.2.2).

The rest of the events leading to Augustine's conversion happened within the context of the resumed catechumenate. "Every Lord's day" he says, "I heard [Ambrose] 'rightly preaching the word of truth' [2Tim. 2.15] among the people" (*Eum quidem in populo verbum veritatis recte tractantem omni die dominico audiebam,* 6.3.4). Although with spasms of uncertainty, he gradually came to see his natal religion from a more sophisticated perspective: "I was being turned around. And I was glad, my God, that your one Church, the body of your only Son in which on me as an infant Christ's name was put, did not hold infantile follies" (*convertebar, et gaudebam, deus meus, quod ecclesia unica, corpus unici tui, in qua mihi nomen Christi infanti est inditum, non saperet infantiles nugas,* 6.4.5).

---

16. Up to this point Augustine had been a Catholic "hearer." His decision to become a Manichaean hearer, his mother's reaction, and that of the bishop suggest a formal break with the Church, but *cf.* Ferrari (note 13 above), pp. 109–13. For the obligations of a Manichaean hearer, *v.* P. Brown, *Augustine of Hippo: A Biography* (London, *etc.* 1967), pp. 40–60, esp. pp. 48–55; C. Starnes, *Augustine's Conversion: A Guide to the Argument of Confessions I–IX* (Waterloo, Ont. 1990), pp. 89–112; and J.J. O'Meara, *The Young Augustine: An Introduction to the Confessions of St. Augustine* (London/New York 1980), pp. 61–91, esp. 78f.

17. On this point, *v.* R.J. O'Connell, *St. Augustine's Confessions: The Odyssey of Soul* (Cambridge, Mass. 1969), p. 14.

18. Ferrari (note 13 above) translates (p. 111) *esse* "remain" as does Starnes (p. 132; note 16 above).

Still racked by "insatiable sexual desire" (*insatiabilis concupiscentiae*, 6.12.22) Augustine, urged on by his mother, arranged a marriage and sent back to Africa the mother of his son: "The woman with whom I habitually slept was torn away from my side because she was a hindrance to my marriage. My heart which was deeply attached was cut and wounded, and left a trail of blood" (*avulsa a latere meo tamquam impedimento coniugii cum qua cubare solitus eram, cor, ubi adhaerebat, concisum et vulneratum mihi erat et trahebat sanguinem*, 6.15.25).[19] Nevertheless, since the bride-to-be was under age (6.12.23), he found another consort for the interim; he was convinced that he could not lead a celibate life (*caelibem vitam nullo modo posse degere*, 6.12.22). Racked also by the problem of evil in a world made by a good God, his legacy from the Manichees, he was weighted down with anxieties and afraid that he would die before finding the truth. Yet he remained a catechumen: "there was a firm place in my heart for the faith, within the Catholic Church, in your Christ. . . . This faith was still unformed and hesitant . . . yet my mind did not abandon it, but daily drank in more and more" (*stabiliter . . . haerebat in corde meo in catholica ecclesia fides Christi tui . . . adhuc informis et . . . fluitans, sed tamen non eam relinquebat animus, immo in dies magis magisque inbibebat*, 7.5.7). The primary source of resolve proved to be the homilies of Ambrose, who handled the Scriptures with allegorical insight and a rich admixture of Neoplatonism. Already disposed to platonic immaterialism, Augustine encountered the works of Plotinus and his disciple and editor, Porphyry. Though they offered an unacceptable polytheism, he found in them healing and admonition: *Et inde admonitus redire ad memet ipsum . . . intravi et vidi qualicumque oculo animae meae supra eundem oculum animae meae, supra mentem meam, lucem incommutabilem. . . . nec ita erat supra mentem meam, sicut oleum super aquam nec sicut caelum super terram, sed superior, quia ipsa fecit me, et ego inferior, quia factus ab ea. . . . et cum te primum cognovi, tu adsumpsisti me ut viderem esse quod viderem, et nondum me esse qui viderem* (7.10.16).[20] In short, he experienced a mystical union with God and was astonished to find that he "already loved" Him, "not a phantom

---

19. If a couple (or one of them) were slave, legal marriage (*iustum matrimonium*) was prohibited, but not their living together (*contuburnium*, literally = dwelling together in a tent). *V.* S.B. Pomeroy, *Goddesses, Whores, Wives and Slaves: Women in Classical Antiquity* (New York 1975), pp. 190–204; and J.E. Grubbs, "'Pagan' and 'Christian' Marriage: The State of the Question," *JEarlyChrSt* 2 (1994), pp. 361–412, esp. 361–82. The Church's position on the issue was defined in canon 17 issued by the Council of Toledo in 400. *V.* O'Donnell (note 1 above), intro. note on 6.15.25.

20. For discussion of Augustine and conversion to philosophy *v.* both O'Connell, (note 17 above), esp. pp. 13–21; and O'Donnell (note 1 above), vol. 1, pp. xxiii–xli, esp. note 53, p. xxxvi.

surrogate" (*iam te amabam, non pro te phantasma*, 7.17.23). From that point on Augustine was certain to whom he should attach himself; nonetheless, he could not do so, nor was he able to hang on to his mystical experience of Being, but was dragged down by physicality and a sense of the contingency of his being (7.17.23).[21] Hungry now for more mystical experience and the stable possession of it, Augustine dove into the New Testament, especially the epistles of St. Paul. He writes, I "found that all the truth I had read in the Platonists was stated here together with the commendation of your grace" (*inveni, quidquid illac verum legeram, hac cum commendatione gratiae tuae dici*). In the Neoplatonists he could not find the face of a human God, the "coeternal Son" (*quem genuisti coaeternum*, 7.21.27).

Augustine had made his tortuous journey along the ritual paths of the church of his birth, rituals, which, as he said of the rite of inscription, stamped their mark on him (1.11.17). The last leg of the journey now began, not to find more certainty—that he had—but "to be more stable in [God]" (*nec certior de te sed stabilior in te esse cupiebam*, 8.1.1). To that end he would now learn about the lives of people who had achieved the stability and continence for which he yearned. An aged priest, Simplicianus, who had baptized Bishop Ambrose, recounted the awesome moment when, in preparation for baptism some thirty years before, Marius Victorinus, the celebrated Neoplatonist teacher and African rhetor, whose statue stood in the forum of Trajan, had professed his faith before a dark and hushed church (8.2.3–5). This stimulated Augustine's ardor "to follow his example" (*exarsi ad imitandum*, 8.5.10). Next, a fellow African, Ponticianus, a high official in imperial service, chanced to tell the hesitant Augustine about the ascetic lives of the monks and nuns of the Egyptian desert, particularly of Antony (d. 356), the pioneer of desert monasticism, whose published life had become an instant success in Rome earlier in the century. Indeed, Augustine learned from Ponticianus that their reading of the *Life of Antony* had been instrumental in the recent conversion of two fellow imperial officials, who summarily departed court for a life of ascetic retreat (8.6.14–15).[22] Augustine reported that he was both attracted and appalled. After ten years or more in the search, he had seen ordinary, uneducated people storm and capture heaven with decision, but not himself, a man of high culture. "The tumult of my heart," he wrote "took me out into the garden where no one could interfere with the burning

21. V. O'Donnell (note 1 above) on 7.17.23.

22. One of them had an experience much like Augustine's: a garden, reading a book (the *Life of Antony*), and an inner conversion that helped rid his mind of the world.

struggle with myself in which I was engaged, until the matter could be settled. . . . My madness with myself was part of the process of recovering health, and in the agony of death I was coming to life" (*illuc me abstulerat tumultus pectoris, ubi nemo impediret ardentem litem quam mecum aggressus eram, donec exiret . . . : sed tantum insaniebam salubriter et moriebar vitaliter*, 8.8.19). Then followed the scene reported at the opening of this study.

Yet there was more. With his mother and his friend Alypius, Augustine withdrew to a friend's country estate at Cassiciacum (9.4.8). He determined to resign his chair of rhetoric; wrote Ambrose, asking advice about which books of the Bible to read; then returned to Milan. Together with Alypius and his son Adeodatus, now fifteen, he gave in his name as a candidate for baptism (9.5.13–6.14).

The trio were accepted, and they joined the ranks of the candidates for baptism. Ambrose baptized them in the Milanese cathedral on Easter, 387. Augustine says about the experience only that he wept during the chant: "The sounds flowed into my ears and the truth was distilled into my heart. This caused the feelings of devotion to overflow" (*voces illae influebant auribus meis, et eliquabatur veritas in cor meum, et exaestuabat inde affectus pietatis*, 9.6.14). The rest of his life's journey followed the by-then traditional ritual paths to ordination as a priest (390/91), to consecration as a bishop (395/96), and then to the countless ritual celebrations as chief liturgist of Hippo, until his death in 430.

Catechumenate and Initiation at Milan

The only first-hand record of the Milanese baptismal ritual comes from Ambrose himself, whose *On the Sacraments* (*De sacramentis*) dates from about the time of Augustine's baptism.[23] With a reticence customary for the ancients—one did not divulge the intimate ritual details (*cultus*) to outsiders—Ambrose does not provide a full picture of what Augustine

23. V. B. Botte, *Ambroise de Milan, Des sacrements, Des mystères, L'explication du symbole* (Paris 1961) = SC, vol. 25bis. *Sacr.* is considered a stenographic record, and *Myst.*, an edited version, of Ambrose's homilies to the newly baptized delivered successively from Tuesday of Easter Week. V. E. Yarnold, "The ceremonies of Initiation in the *De Sacramentis* and the *De Mysteriis* of S. Ambrose," pp. 453–63 of *StPatr* 10 (1970) = TU, vol. 107; O.T. Wheeler, *Baptism According to St. Ambrose* (Woodstock, Md. 1958); and T.M. Finn, *Early Christian Baptism* (note 9 above), pp. 57–76. For a discussion of the catechumenate and baptism in Milan and Hippo *v.* Busch (note 9 above) "*De initiatione*"; Finn, *Early Christian Baptism*, pp. 154–58, 160, 164; *id.*, "It Happened" (note 9 above); pp. 22–26 of S. Poque, *Augustin d'Hippone: sermons pour la Pâque* (Paris 1966) = SC, vol. 116; and W. Harmless, *Augustine and the Catechumenate* (Collegeville, Minn. 1995), pp. 98–105.

would have experienced as he neared and entered the baptismal font.[24] But
his homily on the Milanese baptismal creed and his homilies on the baptismal rites (*De sacramentis* and *De mysteriis*) allow one to reconstruct
with reasonable certainty the rites in which Augustine participated.

The first rite, when Augustine, Alypius, and Adeodatus gave in their
names, was enrollment (*Conf.* 9.6.14).[25] It took place on the Monday after
the Feast of Epiphany, which commemorated the baptism of Christ, his
first public appearance (*epiphaneia*).[26] Recalling Jesus' healing the blind
man in John 9.1–7, the rite involved smearing mud on the eyes to signify
the spiritual illumination to come in the weeks before Easter (*Sacr.* 3.11f.).[27]
Placing the rite in the context of the *Confessions*, we can reasonably speculate that it reminded Augustine of his experience in the garden at Milan.

In any case, from that point on, they were called *competentes*, a term
which underscored that they were a community seeking baptism together.[28] Daily instruction and frequent exorcism comprised the principal
work for the next weeks. The former was imparted twice daily (at 9:00
A.M. and 3:00 P.M.); Ambrose's homilies on Abraham probably give a good
idea of its content.[29] The exorcisms were what Ambrose calls the "mysteries
of the scrutinies."[30] Three in number, they were celebrated in vigils on the
third, fourth, and fifth Saturdays of Lent. In North Africa, from which the
only detailed description comes, the competents stood fasting and naked

24. For Augustine's reticence *v. Enn. in Ps.* 103.14: although the rites are visible, their
meaning is hidden. The purpose of pre- and post-baptismal instruction, reserved for the
competentes and the faithful, was to make clear what the rites accomplish and how.

25. Augustine's phrase, *nomen dare,* is the technical term for the rite of inscription. *Cf.
Ser.* 132.1: *Ecce Pascha est, da nomen ad Baptismum, PL,* vol. 38, col. 735.

26. Although Augustine's extant Epiphany sermons (199–204) and Prudentius' hymn for
Epiphany (*Cath.* 12) cite the visit of the Magi at Bethlehem as the first public appearance,
from the late second century the feast commemorated primarily Christ's baptism as his first
full and formal *epiphaneia. V.* my *Early Christian Baptism and the Catechumenate: West and
East Syria* (Collegeville, Minn. 1992), pp. 61f., 111–14, and 170; and T.J. Talley, *The Origins of
the Liturgical Year* (New York 1986), pp. 117–29.

27. *V.* also Aug., *Ser.* 132.1 and 216.1: as catechumens they hear the word and thus are
called *audientes.* Now as *competentes,* those who together seek baptism in order to dwell in
God's house, they are gradually initiated by rite and instruction.

28. *V.* Aug., *Ser.* 216.1: *Quid enim aliud sunt Competentes, quam simul petentes? PL,* 38, col.
1077.

29. The first book of *De Abraham,* which deals with the story of Abraham in Gen. 12–25,
is thought to have its origin in several homilies directed to catechumens, most likely those
chosen for baptism. The second book seems to have been addressed to the baptized.

30. Ambrose (*Expl. sym.* 1) is the first to use the term: *Celebrata hactenus mysteria scruta-
minum.* He describes it as a physical examination to determine whether there remained in
the candidate any physical signs of evil and indicates that it was an exorcism of body and
spirit. *V.* A. Dondeyne, "La discipline des scrutins dans l'Église latine avant Charlemagne,"
RHE 28 (1932), pp. 5–33, esp. pp. 26–30.

in the shadowy church before the congregation.[31] Enveloped by liturgical chants, each was subjected to an extended exorcism and a physical examination.

On Palm Sunday in a rite called *traditio symboli*, Ambrose confided the creed to the competents orally, article-by-article, with a brief explanation of each article.[32] During the week, sponsors and family coached the competent in its memorization, recitation, and where possible, its meaning. Again one may reasonably speculate that Augustine, Alypius, and Adeodatus had many a discussion about the creed they were internalizing.

The baptismal rites were celebrated early Easter morning at the end of the Holy Saturday vigil. They were preceded by the *redditio symboli*, during which each competent stood on a raised platform before the bishop and recited the creed.[33] Augustine discloses the drama of the profession in his account of the conversion of the noted philosopher-convert Marius Victorinus some thirty years before in Rome: *Denique ut ventum est ad horam profitendae fidei, quae verbis certis conceptis retentisque memoriter de loco eminentiore in conspectu populi fidelis Romae reddi solet ab eis qui accessuri sunt ad gratiam tuam . . . ubi ascendit ut redderet, omnes sibimet invicem, quisque ut eum noverat, instrepuerunt nomen eius strepitu gratulationis (quis autem ibi non eum noverat?) et sonuit presso sonitu per ora cunctorum conlaetantium, 'Victorinus, Victorinus.' cito sonuerunt exultatione, quia videbant eum, et cito siluerunt intentione, ut audirent eum. pronuntiavit ille fidem veracem praeclara fiducia, et volebant eum omnes rapere intro in cor suum. et rapiebant amando et gaudendo: hae rapientium manus erant* (8.2.5).

Baptism proper followed immediately. The rites began just outside the baptistery with the "opening" (*apertio*), recalling the incident in which Christ cured the deaf mute by putting his fingers into his ears and touching his tongue with saliva (Mk 7.33–35).[34] Ambrose touched the ears and nostrils of the baptizands as if to open the blocked channels to faith and piety (*Sacr.* 1.2). An anointing of the entire body with olive oil followed to ready the competent for an Olympic struggle with the Devil in baptism it-

---

31. The only full description is that of Quodvultdeus, *De symbolo* 1.1.4–19, which was delivered the morning following the scrutiny on the occasion of the *traditio symboli*. V. T.M. Finn, "It Happened" (note 9 above), pp. 601–3.

32. Aug. *Ser.* 212, 213, 214 and Ambr. *Exp. fid.* are homilies devoted to conveying the creed to *competentes*.

33. V. Aug., *Ser.* 215 for a homily on the occasion of the rite of the profession of faith. *Cf.* Ambr., *Exp. fid.*

34. V. Ambr., *Sacr.* 1.2: *Ergo quid egimus sabbato? Nempe apertionem: quae mysteria celebrata sunt apertionis quando tibi aures tetigit sacerdos et nares.*

self (1.4). Facing west, the competents then renounced the Devil and his works. Facing east, they then announced their allegiance to Christ.[35] Then, they entered the baptistery and saw the font and the bishop exorcising and consecrating the baptismal waters. He prayed, traced a sign of the cross on the waters, and plunged his shepherd's staff into them. In explaining the symbolism of the font, Ambrose evoked (1.11–23) renowned biblical types: Naaman the Syrian, whom Elisha sent to wash in the Jordan seven times to cure his leprosy (2 Kgs. 4.42–5.14); Jesus, whom John baptized in the Jordan (Mt. 3.13–17); Israel's Exodus through the Red Sea (Ex. 14.9–15.21); and the Flood (Gen. 7–9). The healing, regeneration, and salvation for which Augustine, Adeodatus, and Alypius yearned were at hand.

Their garments stripped off, the competents entered the font. They were asked three creedal questions: whether they believed in God the Father, in Christ the Son of God, and in the Holy Spirit, the Church, and the resurrection. With each response *Credo*, ("I believe") the competent was immersed. The triple immersion symbolized Christ's death and three-day burial in the tomb. Their emersion from the water symbolized his resurrection and made their own a ready expectation (*Sacr.* 2.17, 20).[36]

As the newly baptized emerged from the font, chrism was poured on their heads, and, in a rite that Ambrose considered unique to Milan, the bishop washed the feet of the newly baptized, thus recalling the account of Jesus washing the feet of the disciples at the Last Supper (Jn. 13.2–11), an account read at that point (*Sacr.* 3.4–7).[37] In fresh white garments, symbolizing their baptismal transformation, the newly baptized came before the bishop for the final rite; on their foreheads he made the sign of the cross with chrism. This signified for Ambrose the seven-fold gift of the Holy Spirit and the maturing of the gifts of baptism (3.8–10).

Once baptized, the neophytes received a liturgical embrace, the kiss of peace, to welcome the new born into the Christian family.[38] They then

---

35. After the baptizands renounced Satan and his works, they pledged their faith to Christ. The pledge might have been simple as in Antioch (συντάσσομαί σοι, Χριστέ), or it might have been a creedal profession. *V.* p. 145 of A. Wenger, *Jean Chrysostome, Huit catéchèses baptismales inédites* (Paris 1957) = *SC*, vol. 50; and T.M. Finn, *The Liturgy of Baptism in the Baptismal Instructions of St. John Chrysostom* (Washington 1967), pp. 104–10.

36. Ambrose calls the baptismal font a tomb and implies that it is a womb as well. For this long-standing symbolism *v.* W.M. Bedard, *The Symbolism of the Baptismal Font in Early Christian Thought* (Washington 1951), pp. 4–36.

37. On the symbolism of the chrism *v.* E. Yarnold, *The Awe-Inspiring Rites of Initiation: Baptismal Homilies of the Fourth Century* (Slough, U.K. 1972), pp. 22f.

38. *V. Sacr.* 3.2f., where Ambrose recites for the newly baptized the words of Ps. 2.7 applied to Christ in Acts 13.33: *Filius meus es tu, ego hodie genui te.* The participative union created by baptism allows him to see here an address also to the newly baptized: as Christ was

processed into the church to celebrate their first Eucharist, during which they were given milk mixed with honey, a rite that recalled the Israelites' entry into the Promised Land.[39]

For the rest of Easter Week, the newly baptized attended the Eucharist in their white robes.[40] Commenting on the twenty-second Psalm, which the newly baptized chanted on their way to their first Eucharist, Ambrose observed, "See how fittingly [this passage] applies to the heavenly sacraments: 'The Lord feeds me. . . . He has set me in a place of pasture; he has brought me to the water of refreshment; he has converted my soul.'" (*Vide quemadmodum aptus sit caelestibus sacramentis.* Dominus pascit me . . . in loco pascuae ibi me conlocauit. Super aquam refectionis educauit me, animam meam conuertit, 5.13).[41]

These rites constituted the climax of Augustine's journey through his complex social, cultural, and religious world. In this journey he (1) faced an extended identity crisis; (2) launched an intensely active search for new identity, meaning and purpose; (3) encountered anew in Ambrose's Milan the religious reality of Catholic Christianity that engaged his emotional, intellectual, and cognitive needs; (4) undertook the continual interaction with Ambrose and his community that led to his becoming a competent and eventually one of the faithful; (5) made a definitive choice between his previous way of thought and a life characterized by overwhelming sexual appetite on the one hand and ascetic Christianity on the other; and (6) underwent a remarkable transformation that resulted in strikingly new attitudes and values mirrored in his matching conduct and way of life. These are the very elements contemporary researchers would recognize as an authentic conversion.[42]

---

declared Son, so too they have become sons and daughters. Indeed, Ambrose indicates that the *competentes* have been given the Lord's Prayer, which he explains to them petition by petition (*Sacr.* 4.29 and 5.18–29). The *traditio orationis dominici* was also part of the baptismal liturgy in Augustine's North Africa and was celebrated a week after the *competentes* were given the creed (*Ser.* 113.8). Augustine's older contemporary, John Chrysostom remarks (*in Mt.* 19.5) that the Lord's prayer is particularly the property of the baptized: before baptism God was not properly speaking their Father, but now, as adopted children, they can address Him with the boldness of members of the family. *V.* Finn, *The Liturgy of Baptism* (note 35 above).

39. The rite appeared first in Rome toward the end of the second century. *V.* Hippol., *Trad. apost.* 21, where it signifies the baptismal return to the Promised Land. Ambrose looks to the Song of Songs for its significance as a symbol of Paradise (*Sacr.* 5.15–17).

40. According to Ambrose (*Sacr.* 4.5–7), the robes were the sign of baptismal regeneration and reflected the inner splendor of grace in the newly baptized. For the Pythagorean and Egyptian origin of white linen as a symbol of immortality, *v.* J. Quasten, "A Pythagorean Idea in Jerome," *AJP* 63 (1942), pp. 207–15.

41. My translation.

42. *V.* note 7 above, esp. Rambo, *Understanding,* pp. 165–70.

Conclusion

To be sure, taken as a whole, the *Confessions* is Augustine's intellectual autobiography, tracing the development of his thinking on matters of religion and philosophy from when he first achieved the use of reason to 397. Nevertheless, it also documents far more than the conversion of his mind. The central decision he faced was not whether to believe but whether to present himself for initiation, which he decided to do in the summer of 386. Well before that, as we have seen, his mind was made up about the content of Catholic belief. No, the problem was to become, to enter. I have attempted to show that the *Confessions* documents Augustine's conversion through the ancient ritual process known as the catechumenate. Although it is not customary to read the *Confessions* as the account of a ritual or liturgical journey, it is clear that Augustine's conversion was neither sudden nor limited to the garden in Milan. Rather it was a process that began with his inscription in the catechumenate as an infant in November 354 and ended when he laid aside his white baptismal garment on the Sunday after Easter, April 25, 387: a thirty-three year journey from first-born to new-born.[43] To be sure, his journey was not the journey of every ancient convert, but the ritual process that assured Augustine's conversion, *mutatis mutandis,* attended the conversion of everyone, at least every documented case, who became a Christian in late antiquity. The case of Augustine establishes with clarity that *conversio* goes beyond the turning of one's mind to the turning of one's self, for which, at least in antiquity, ritual was indispensable. The ritual process was the normal means in the religions of antiquity to form and to reform the self in a community whose ideal was transformation.

43. Although in the *Confessions* Augustine speaks of his experience in the garden at Milan as his *conversio* (8.12.30), in his baptismal homilies the word has a distinctly liturgical reference and points to the pre-baptismal and baptismal rites that stabilized conversion by enacting it. The pivotal rites were the scrutiny, the renunciation of Satan, and the profession of faith, which accomplished the inner turning away (*aversio*) from sin and the turning to Christ (*conversio*) constitutive of Augustine's experience in the garden. V. T.M. Finn, "It Happened" (note 9 above), pp. 598, 606–8; and O'Donnell (note 1 above), pp. xxvii–xxx.

ELEVEN

De Raptu Proserpinae in the Church Fathers

The *Sacrum Mysterium* of Marriage

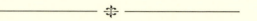

Cynthia White

FOR OUR KNOWLEDGE of the Eleusinian mysteries we are largely dependent upon the reports of early Christian authors. Though these are often tendentious, sometimes inaccurate, and even contradictory in details, they do confirm the close connection between the *Homeric Hymn to Demeter* and the Eleusinian ritual: it is likely that the myth of the rape of Persephone was ritually re-enacted at Eleusis. The reports of the Church Fathers indicate that certain notions—abduction and separation, descent into death (*i.e.*, marriage), and a mystical union as an act of reconciliation—were central to the rites. In this paper I purpose to examine selected passages from classical and later Latin epithalamia in the light of patristic descriptions of the Eleusinian mysteries. This comparison will suggest that the rites of the pagan *mystai* parallel the *topoi* in the literary epithalamia that detail the transition from maiden- to womanhood through marriage. Further, I shall argue that the condemnation of the secret rituals of the Eleusinia by the Church Fathers may have supported, as did much apologetic literature, a new Christian ideal of marriage—a union with the divine that promised immortality. The first epithalamium presenting marriage as a union with the divine—like the transcendent union possibly enacted in the final initiation ritual at Eleusis—is the Christian epithalamium of Paulinus of Nola (*C.* 25). In turn, Paulinus' epithalamim was a model for subsequent nuptial literature explicating and advocating the fourth-century ideal of the mystic marriage between Christ and his virgin brides.

Already from a time roughly contemporaneous with the *Homeric Hymn to Demeter*, the South Italian colonies of the Locri Epizephyri, along with many cult sites in Sicily, sustained a singularly intense devotion to Persephone, as the chthonic goddess of nuptials and death.[1] Marriage, like any initiation ritual, was an encounter with death, through which death could be overcome.[2] A maiden had to die, *i.e.*, suffer a symbolic death at her marriage—a death to (by separation from) her former life in family and community, as well as to her maiden state. In marriage, however, she could overcome death through childbirth. With her shared nuptial and funerary associations, Persephone represents the death of maiden and birth to wife and mother through marriage. An early fifth-century collection of *pinakes*, a series of small clay votive offerings to Persephone, attests to this initiation. The *Locri pinakes*[3] depict scenes of her abduction by Hades, her marriage, and her sovereignty in the underworld. When Persephone is relegated to the underworld through the institution of marriage, she becomes sovereign over death and regeneration as well. Persephone, the maiden, becomes, through marriage, the goddess of death, who, even if her own marriage is sterile, bestows the natural cycle of fertility, regeneration, and death upon those above. Thus the consequence of her marriage, and of all human and divine marriage, is immortality through procreation, which has as its visible manifestation the annual death and regeneration of vegetation.

1. The maiden Proserpina becomes, through marriage, goddess of death, yet regenerative; *v.* G. Zuntz, *Persephone: Three Essays on Religion and Thought in Magna Graecia* (Oxford 1971), p. 165. For this peculiarly Locrian version of the myth *v.* C. Sourvinou-Inwood, '*Reading*' *Greek Culture: Texts and Images, Rituals and Myths* (Oxford 1991), ch. 3: "Persephone and Aphrodite at Locri: A Model for Personality Definitions in Greek Religion," pp. 147–88; P. Zancani Montuoro, "Il rapitore di Kore nel mito locrese," *RAAN* 29 (1954) 79–86.

2. W. Burkert, *Homo Necans: Interpretationen altgriechischer Opferriten und Mythen* (Berlin/New York 1972), pp. 325f. *Cf.* Cic., *Leg.* 2.14.36: *initiaque, ut appellantur, ita re vera principia vitae cognovimus, neque solum cum laetitia vivendi rationem accepimus, sed etiam cum spe meliore moriendi* (G. de Plinval, *Cicéron, Traité des lois* [Paris 1959]); Arist. Or. 22.10: ἀλλὰ μὴν τό γε κέρδος τῆς πανηγύρεως οὐχ ὅσον ἡ παροῦσα εὐθυμία οὐδ᾽ αἱ τῶν ἐκ τοῦ πρότερον χρόνου δυσκολιῶν λύσεις καὶ ἀπαλλαγαί, ἀλλὰ καὶ περὶ τῆς τελευτῆς ἡδίους ἔχειν τὰς ἐλπίδας ὡς ἄμεινον διάξοντας, καὶ οὐκ ἐν σκότῳ τε καὶ βορβόρῳ κεισομένους, ἃ δὴ τοὺς ἀμυήτους ἀναμένειν; A. Humbel, *Ailios Aristeides, Klage über Eleusis (Oratio 22): Lesetext, Übersetzung und Kommentar* (Vienna 1994).

3. On the *pinakes v.* H. Prückner, *Die lokrischen Tonreliefs: Beitrag zur Kultgeschichte von Lokroi Epizephyrioi* (Mainz 1968), pp. 68–74; C. Sourvinou-Inwood, "The Young Abductor of the Locrian Pinakes," *BICS* 20 (1973), pp. 12–21; *id.*, "A Series of Erotic Pursuits: Images and Meanings," *JHS* 107 (1987), pp. 139f.; P. Zancani Montuoro,"Note sui soggetti e sulla tecnica delle tabelle di Locri," *ASMG* 9 (1954) 1:71–106; *id.*, "Il tempio di Persefone a Locri," *RAL*, 8th ser., 14 (1959), pp. 225–32.

These themes of the wedding story of Persephone—abduction and sep-aration, descent into death (*i.e.,* marriage), and reconciliation and procre-ation—are familiar from the *Homeric Hymn to Demeter* and the cult of Persephone among the Locri Epizephyri. This sequence informing the myth and the cult gives rise to the *topoi* of the nuptial literature. The first *topos,* that of the separation of the bride from her mother, is already estab-lished in the epithalamic fragments of Sappho.[4] Indeed, it was a major theme as far back as the wedding songs of the Mesopotamian Inanna and Dumuzi, models that influenced the Greek songs.[5] There are many exam-ples in tragedy, but this fragment from Sophocles perhaps best expresses the experience of the young bride: νῦν δ' οὐδέν εἰμι χωρίς. ἀλλὰ πολλάκις / ἔβλεψα ταύτῃ τὴν γυναικείαν φύσιν, / ὡς οὐδέν ἐσμεν. αἳ νέαι μὲν ἐν πατρὸς / ἥδιστον, οἶμαι, ζῶμεν ἀνθρώπων βίον· / τερπνῶς γὰρ ἀεὶ παῖδας ἀνοία τρέφει. / ὅταν δ' ἐς ἥβην ἐξικώμεθ' ἔμφρονες, / ὠθούμεθ' ἔξω καὶ διεμπολώμεθα / θεῶν πατρῴων τῶν τε φυσάντων ἄπο, / αἱ μὲν ξένους πρὸς ἄνδρας, αἱ δὲ βαρβάρους, / αἱ δ' εἰς ἀγηθῆ δώμαθ', αἱ δ' ἐπίρροθα. / καὶ ταῦτ', ἐπειδὰν εὐφρόνη ζεύξῃ μία, / χρεὼν ἐπαινεῖν καὶ δοκεῖν καλῶς ἔχειν (Now, apart [*sc.* from my family], I am nothing. Often have I seen women's nature this way, how we are nothing! We young women, in our father's home, live, I think, the sweetest existence known to mortals, be-cause innocence always nurtures children with joy. But when we reach pu-berty and can understand, we are thrust out and sold away from our an-cestral gods and from those who gave us birth, some to strangers, others to foreigners, some to joyless, others to hostile, houses. All this, once a single night has yoked us [*sc.* to a husband], we are forced to praise and hold as right).[6]

The twin themes of ἔρος and θάνατος, love and death, marriage and separation, are also intertwined in several nuptial Hellenistic epigrams. In her epigram for a new bride, Erinna laments that Baukis' father-in-law lit her funeral pyre with the same torches that were burning when they sang the marriage song. Hymenaeus, the god of marriage changed the wedding

4. Fragg. 104a, 105a, E. Lobel and D. Page, *Poetarum lesbiorum fragmenta* (Oxford 1955); *Cf.* Theoc., *Id.* 18.12–14; Cat., 61.56–60, 79–81; 62.20–25. Statius also plays on this *topos* (*Silv.* 2.137–39), though the bride is marrying for the second time.

5. D. Wolkstein and S.N. Kramer, *Inanna: Queen of Heaven and Earth: Her Stories and Hymns from Sumer* (New York 1983), p. 35: "The shepherd went to the royal house with cream. / Dumuzi went to the royal house with milk. / Before the door, he called out: / 'Open the house, My Lady, open the house!' / Inanna ran to Ningal, the mother who bore her."

6. F583, *Tereus;* S. Radt, *TrGF* (Göttingen 1977). For the theme in Greek tragedy, *v.* R. Seaford, "The Tragic Wedding," *JHS* 107 (1987), pp. 106–30; and R. Rehm, *Marriage to Death: The Conflation of Wedding and Funeral Rituals in Greek Tragedy* (Princeton 1994). Unless otherwise indicated, all translations are my own.

hymn into a funeral dirge: τὰν παῖδ' Ὑμέναιος ἐφ' αἷς ἀείδετο πεύκαις / τᾶσδ' ἐπὶ καδεστὰς ἔφλεγε πυρκαϊᾶς, / καὶ σὺ μέν, ὦ Ὑμέναιε, γάμων μολπαῖον ἀοιδάν / ἐς θρήνων γοερὸν φθέγμα μεθαρμόσαο (*AP* 7.712.5–8).[7] In the following epigram of Leonidas of Tarentum we find a similar theme presenting the dead woman as the bride of Hades.[8] In an image reminiscent of the myth of Persephone, Hades, the envious god, is said to carry off the maiden: Παρθενικὴν νεάοιδον ἐν ὑμνοπόλοισι μέλισσαν /Ἤριυναν Μουσέων ἄνθεα δρεπτομένην / Ἅιδας εἰς ὑμέναιον ἀνάρπασεν (*AP* 7.13.1–3; While Erinna, a maiden and new singer among the poets, was gathering, like a bee, the flowers of the Muses, Hades carried her off to marry her).[9]

The second element of the nuptial initiation—descent into death (*i.e.,* marriage)—is likewise well attested in classical nuptial texts. After Theocritus has lamented the separation of Helen from her girlhood friends and her mother, he offers the jubilant conclusion: ὦ καλά, ὦ χαρίεσσα κόρα, τὺ μὲν οἰκέτις ἤδη (*Id.* 18.38; O lovely, graceful maiden, now you are a housewife).[10] Catullus 61 celebrates the marriage of Vibia Arunculeia and Manlius Torquatus in three distinct locations that parallel the marriage initiation of Persephone and the re-enactment of her abduction and marriage during the Eleusinia: outside the bride's house (abduction and separation), along the road to the home of the groom (death, *i.e.,* marriage), and in the groom's house (reconciliation and procreation). The moment of the arrival at the home of the groom marks the final separation, the marriage: *en tibi domus ut potens / et beata viri tui, / quae tibi sine serviat* (*C.* 61.149–51; Here is the powerful and bountiful home of your husband, which you must allow to serve you).[11]

The third element of the initiation, reconciliation and procreation, informs the rhetorical prayer for progeny, the conclusion of almost all extant Greek and Roman marriage poems. In the epithalamium of Theocritus the couple is wished fair children, love, and prosperity: Λατὼ μὲν δοίη,

7. = Erinna, 2, ll. 1793–96 in A.S.F. Gow and D.L. Page, *The Greek Anthology: Hellenistic Epigrams*, vol. 1 (Cambridge 1965): *Introduction, Text, and Indexes of Sources and Epigrammatists.*

8. H.J. Rose, "The Bride of Hades," *CP* 20 (1925), pp. 238–42.

9. = Leonidas of Tarentum, 98, ll. 2563–65 in Gow and Page (note 7 above). Aus., *Epigr.* 53 is a version for young men: *Laeta bis octono tibi iam sub consule pubes / cingebat teneras, Glaucia adulte, genas. / et iam desieras puer anne puella videri, / cum properata dies abstulit omne decus. / sed neque functorum socius miscebere vulgo / nec metues Stygios flebilis umbra lacus, / verum aut Persephonae Cinyreius ibis Adonis / aut Iovis Elysii tu Catamitus eris;* R.P.H. Green, *The Works of Ausonius edited with Introduction and Commentary* (Oxford 1991).

10. A.S.F. Gow, *Theocritus*, 2nd ed., vol. 1 (Cambridge, *etc.* 1952): *Introduction, Text, and Translation.*

11. C.J. Fordyce, *Catullus* (Oxford 1961).

Λατὼ κουροτρόφος, ὕμμιν / εὐτεκνίαν, Κύπρις δέ, Θεὰ Κύπρις, ἴσον
ἔρασθαι / ἀλλάλων, Ζεὺς δέ, Κρονίδας Ζεύς, ἄφθιτον ὄλβον (*Id.* 18.50–52;
May Leto, nurturing Leto, give you lovely children, and Cypris, Goddess
Cypris, mutual love, and Zeus, Zeus son of Cronos, enduring happiness).
In Catullus the prayer for progeny is an invitation to unfettered enjoyment
of amorous pleasures: *ludite ut lubet* (*C.* 61. 204). "And in a short time, produce children. So ancient a name must not be childless, but be ever 'in-
bred from the same source'" (*et breui / liberos date. non decet / tam uetus
sine liberis / nomen esse, sed indidem / semper ingenerari, C.* 61.204–208).[12]

The Myth in the Church Fathers

The nuptial ideas embodied in the myth of Demeter and Persephone,
the cult of Persephone among the Locri Epizephyri, and the literature of
the classical epithalamic texts have as their ritual component the rites of
Demeter and Persephone at Eleusis. From the references in the Church Fathers to these rites, we can reconstruct the same tripartite nuptial initiation. The Fathers refer to the Eleusinian mystery rites in order to charge
pagans with moral degeneracy. Their accounts of what happened at Eleusis concentrate on two main points of discussion: (1) that the rituals constituted a mystery drama re-enacting the myth of the abduction of Persephone, Demeter's wandering, and their reunion; (2) that, in an allegory of
the agricultural cycle, the rituals celebrated an illicit union, perhaps a mystical marriage, that culminated in a mysterious revelation, either the birth
of a child or the exposition of a fresh ear of cut wheat.[13]

The mysteries took place once a year during the month of Boedromion
(our late September/early October). Initiates came from all over the greco-
roman world. The primary deities involved were Demeter, Kore/Perse-
phone, and Hades, god of the lower world. Iacchos is also associated with
the cult; he may have been the personification of the shouting and enthusiasm that characterized the procession from Athens to Eleusis. There were
public rites and secret rites. According to the Fathers, the public rites—the
bearing of the hiera from Athens to Eleusis, the sacrifice of pigs, the parade
with the accompanying shouts to Iacchus, and the brandishing of torches

12. *V.* Fordyce's (*ib.*) on 61.208.
13. *V.* G.E. Mylonas, *Eleusis and the Eleusinian Mysteries* (London 1961), p. 228. Mylonas
has argued that some ceremonies and ritual proclamations attributed to the rites of Eleusis
by the early Christian authors were actually Orphic rites, that from the basic Orphic doctrine—that Zagreus, or Sabazius, is the son of Zeus and Persephone—sprang the Christian
charges that the rites involved a sexual union, *i.e.*, a sacred marriage, and the birth of a child
or the revelation of a stalk of wheat.

outside the hall of initiation—re-enacted the rape of Persephone and the wandering of Demeter.

On the first day of the festival, Boedromion 19, those wishing to be initiated gathered with priests and priestesses carrying the sacred cult objects and the statue of Iacchos for the fourteen-mile procession from Athens to Eleusis. Just as Demeter came to Eleusis in search of her daughter, the initiates walked the road to Eleusis in search of enlightenment. The procession crossed the river Kephisos in Athens, and on the bridge the participants exchanged jests with a woman or a man dressed as a woman. This crude bantering at the bridge recalled Iambe who, in the *Homeric Hymn to Demeter*, was able to make Demeter laugh with her jokes and obscene gestures: ἀλλ᾽ ἀγέλαστος ἄπαστος ἐδητύος ἠδὲ ποτῆτος / ἧστο πόθῳ μινύθουσα βαθυζώνοιο θυγατρός, / πρίν γ᾽ ὅτε δὴ χλεύης μιν Ἰάμβη κέδν᾽ εἰδυῖα / πολλὰ παρὰ σκώπτουσ᾽ ἐτρέψατο πότνιαν ἁγνὴν / μειδῆσαι γελάσαι τε καὶ ἵλαον σχεῖν θυμόν (200–204; "Unsmiling, tasting neither food nor drink, she sat wasting with desire for her deep-girt daughter, until knowing Iambe jested with her and mocking with many a joke moved the holy goddess to smile and laugh and keep a gracious heart").[14]

After the jesting at the bridge the initiates drank the cyceon and shouted the rhythmic cry Ἴακχ᾽ ὦ Ἴακχε.[15] By the time the procession arrived at Eleusis the sun was setting; they lit torches and began the search for Persephone. After some wandering, the *mystai* arrived at the telesterion, the hall of initiation, and put out the torches, so that it became like a dark entry into the underworld. The *mystai* entered the sanctuary with Iacchos, personified as the statue of a child.[16] The hierophant completed the initiation in the telesterion and then went into the anaktoron, the small room off the telesterion to which only he had access.

---

14. N.J. Richardson, *The Homeric Hymn to Demeter* (Oxford 1974). The translation follows H.P. Foley, *The Homeric Hymn to Demeter* (Princeton, N.J. 1994). *Cf.* Apollod., *Bibl.* 1.30.

15. Aristoph., *Frogs* 341; V. Coulon, *Aristophane*, vol. 4 (Paris 1928): *Les thesmophories, Les grenouilles*. For Iacchos as a divinity identified with Dionysus, *v.* Foley (note 14 above), note 33, p. 232; Richardson (note 14 above), p. 27.

16. The *Homeric Hymn to Demeter* tells (238–55) how Ceres, wishing to confer immortality on Demophon, held him in the fire in order to purify him; the process was inadvertently interrupted by the boy's mother. The only child accompanying the *mystai* was a young boy, who must have represented not only the counterpart of the Demophon of the myth but also the young boy in the Athenian wedding celebration/initiation. *V.* Burkert (note 2 above), pp. 309f.; Richardson (note 14 above), pp. 231–34; Plut., *Prov.* 16: Ἀθήνησι . . . ἐν τοῖς γάμοις ἔθος ἦν ἀμφιθαλῆ παῖδα . . . λίκνον ἄρτων πλήρη περιφέροντα λέγειν, Ἔφυγον κακὸν, εὗρον ἄμεινον; E.L. von Leutsch and F.G. Schneidewin *Corpus paroemiographorum graecorum*, vol. 1 (Göttingen 1839; rpt. Hildesheim 1958): *Zenobius, Diogenianus, Plutarchus, Gregorius Cyprius cum Appendice Proverbiorum.*

It is generally agreed among the Fathers who describe the Eleusinia that, up to the point when the hierophant withdrew into the closed sanctuary, the rites re-enacted the story of Demeter and Persephone. According to Clement of Alexandria, "Demeter and Persephone have become the subject of a mystery drama, and Eleusis commemorates with torches the rape of the one and the sorrow and wandering of the other" (Δηὼ [= Demeter] δὲ καὶ Κόρη δρᾶμα ἤδη ἐγενέσθην μυστικόν, καὶ τὴν πλάνην καὶ τὴν ἁρπαγὴν καὶ τὸ πένθος αὐταῖν Ἐλευσὶς δᾳδουχεῖ, *Protr.* 2.12.2).[17] "This is the same myth women celebrate at various times in the city, when in different ways they dramatize the rape of Persephone" (ταύτην τὴν μυθολογίαν αἱ γυναῖκες ποικίλως κατὰ πόλιν ἑορτάζουσι ... πολυτρόπως τὴν Φερεφάττης ἐκτραγῳδοῦσαι ἁρπαγήν, *Protr.* 2.17.1). In addition, Arnobius supplies the details that, in the course of seeking her daughter, Demeter came to Attica, introduced wheat, and laughed at Baubo's crude jests: *Eleusinia illa mysteria et sacrorum reconditi ritus cuius memoriam continent? nonne illius erroris quo in filiae conquisitione Ceres, fessa oras ut uenit ad Atticas, triticeas attulit fruges, Nebridarum familiam pellicula cohonestauit hinnulae et illud spectaculum maximum Baubonis in inguinibus risit* (*Adv. nat.* 5.39; What do those Eleusinian mysteries and the secret rites memorialize? Are they not the memorial of that famous wandering during which Ceres, worn out in the search for her daughter, arrived in the territory of Attica, introduced the cultivation of wheat, honored her retinue of nebris-wearers with the fawn skin, and laughed at that impressive display of Baubo's genitals)?[18] Lactantius gives a vivid account of the darkness and torches and reveling that must have been a part of the re-enactment of the search for Persephone: *his etiam Cereris simile mysterium est, in quo facibus accensis per noctem Proserpina inquiritur et ea inventa ritus omnis gratulatione ac taedarum iactatione finitur* (*D. inst. ep.* 18[23].7; Similar to these [*sc.* the rites of Isis] is the mystery cult of Ceres during which people seek out Persephone at night with lit torches and, when they have found her, conclude the whole ceremony amidst rejoicing and the brandishing of torches).[19]

17. O. Stählin, *Clemens Alexandrinus*, vol. 1 (Leipzig 1905): *Protrepticus und Paedagogus* = *GCS*, vol. 12.

18. A. Reifferscheid, *Arnobii Adversus nationes libri VII* (Vienna 1875) = *CSEL*, vol. 4.

19. *Cf.* Lact., *D. inst.*, 1.21.24: *sacra uero Cereris Eleusinae non sunt his dissimilia. nam sicut ibi Osiris puer planctu matris inquiritur, ita hic ad incestum patrui matrimonium rapta Proserpina: quam quia facibus ex Aetnae uertice accensis quaesisse in Sicilia Ceres dicitur, idcirco sacra eius ardentium taedarum iactatione celebrantur;* S. Brandt and G. Laubmann, *L. Caeli Firmiani Lactanti Opera omnia*, vol. 1 (Vienna 1890): *Diuinae institutiones et Epitome diuinarum institutionum* = *CSEL*, vol. 19.

Mystic Marriage and Child

In the enclosed sanctuary of the anaktoron, the hierophant performed the main ritual that left the initiates in awe. The climax in the mysteries occurred when the hierophant stood in front of the initiates and, in the midst of radiant light, exhibited the hiera to them.[20] The nature of these sacred objects is still a topic of debate, but, according to the patristic accounts, the *mystai* were transported at the sight by experiencing a mystic union with the divine that left them serenely reconciled to death.

Some Fathers claim that the revelation by the hierophant was the announcement of the birth of a divine child, that, in fact, a sacred marriage symbolizing the union with the divine was consummated in the anaktoron. Hippolytus (*Ref.* 5.8.40) reports the sacred Eleusinian formula, "ἱερὸν ἔτεκε πότνια κοῦρον βριμὼ βριμόν", τουτέστιν ἰσχυρὰ ἰσχυρόν (Holy Brimo has born a sacred child, Brimos, the mighty gave birth to the mighty).[21] Since Clement attributes the title Brimo to Demeter, the birth of a child has been associated with the Eleusinian mysteries,[22] and it has been assumed that the hiera would have included some representation of that child.

It is true that Clement (*Protr.* 2.15f.) and, after him, Arnobius (*Adv. nat.* 5.20f.) placed their accounts of the mystic marriage and birth of a child in discussions of the Sabazian Mysteries.[23] Yet they implied that marriage and birth figured also among the rites of Eleusis. Clement charged that the sacred marriage was the illicit union of Demeter with her son Zeus and with his daughter by that union, Persephone: "The mysteries of Demeter [celebrate] the sexual advances of Zeus toward his mother, Demeter, and her anger" (Δηοῦς δὲ μυστήρια ... Διὸς πρὸς μητέρα Δήμητρα ἀφροδίσιοι συμπλοκαὶ καὶ μῆνις ... τῆς Δηοῦς, *Protr.* 2.15.1). Arnobius recounted that Jupiter conceived an illicit passion for Ceres, whom the Phrygians believed to be his mother. Having contrived a clever plan that would permit him to defile his mother without her suspecting it, he changed himself into a bull

---

20. Tertullian claims (*Valent.* 1.3) that the sacred symbol shown to the initiates was a phallos: *Ceterum tota in adytis diuinitas, tota suspiria epoptarum, totum signaculum linguae simulacrum membri uirilis reuelatur;* A. Kroymann, Q. S. Fl. *Tertulliani Aduersus ualentinianos liber* = #16 in *Quinti Septimi Florentis Tertulliani Opera*, vol. 2 (Turnhout 1954): *Opera montanistica* = CChr.SL, vol. 2.

21. P. Wendland, *Hippolytus Werke*, vol. 3 (Leipzig 1916): *Refutatio omnium haeresium* = GCS, vol. 26. Hippolytus himself denies the possibility of a sexual union, for he claims that the hierophant was rendered impotent by drinking hemlock. V. J. Harrison, *Prolegomena to the Study of Greek Religion*, 3rd ed. (Cambridge 1922; rpt. New York 1975), p. 549.

22. *Protr.* 2.15.1: μῆνις ... τῆς Δηοῦς, ἧς δὴ χάριν Βριμὼ προσαγορευθῆναι λέγεται.

23. The Sabazian mysteries were Phrygian orgiastic rites.

and rushed madly upon her. After this union, Ceres bore a beautiful daughter named Proserpina.[24] When Jupiter had seen the beautiful maiden, he changed into a dragon and then consorted also with her. As a result, Proserpina conceived and gave birth to a bull, the memorial of her seduction by Jupiter (*Iouialis monumenta pellaciae*). Both Clement and Arnobius sum up this tale with the trimeter: "The bull begat a dragon and the dragon a bull" (ταῦρος δράκοντος καὶ πατὴρ ταύρου δράκων, *Protr.*, 2.16.3; *taurus draconem genuit et taurum draco, Adv. nat.* 5.21).

In this attribution to the mysteries of Demeter of rites known also from the Orphic mysteries of Sabazios and the Great Mother, Clement and Arnobius were followed by Jane Harrison. Harrison argued that both the sacred marriage between the chief priestess of Demeter and the hierophant and the birth of a child formed part of the Eleusinian mysteries; that the child, Dionysus (= Iacchus at Eleusis), was a symbol of fertility and fruits of the earth; and that Eleusis was a harvest festival including rites of purification preceded by Orphic/Dionysiac rites of fasting. For the sacred marriage and birth of a child she cites the testimony of Asterius, bishop of Apamea in the late fourth century, who claimed that in the ceremonies at Eleusis there was a holy union of the hierophant and the priestess.[25]

The presence of a child is certainly a feature of the cult of Persephone among the Locri Epizephyri. This suggests that Harrison was correct in attributing a sacred marriage and birth to the ritual of Persephone at Eleusis. On the Locrian pinakes Persephone is depicted opening a basket to find, with delighted surprise, the child Adonis. There are several accounts of the love between Persephone and Adonis in the writings of the Fathers, and, according to Apollodorus, Zeus settled an argument between Persephone and Venus about the child: Adonis, because of his beauty, was se-

24. Other Christian authors mention that Proserpina is the daughter of Jupiter, *e.g.* Or., *C. Cels.* 1.25: καὶ οὐ λέγω ὅτι τῷ Διὶ εὐθέως συνεξακούεται ὁ Κρόνου καὶ Ῥέας υἱὸς καὶ Ἥρας ἀνὴρ καὶ Ποσειδῶνος ἀδελφὸς καὶ Ἀθηνᾶς καὶ Ἀρτέμιδος πατὴρ καὶ ὁ τῇ θυγατρὶ Περσεφόνῃ μιγείς; M. Borret, *Origène, Contre Celse*, vol. 1 (Paris 1967): bkk. 1–2 = *SC*, vol. 132. *Cf.* Lact., *D. inst. ep.* 9.1: *Ceres unde Proserpinam nisi de strupro genuit?*

25. Harrison (note 21 above), p. 550. Tertullian also implies a sexual union (*Ad nat.* 2.7.15): *Cur rapitur sacerdos Cereris, si <nihil> tale Ceres passa est*; J.G.P. Borleffs, *Q. S. Fl. Tertulliani Ad nationes libri II* = #2 in *Quinti Septimi Florentis Tertulliani Opera*, vol. 1 (Turnhout 1954): *Opera catholica* = *CChr.SL*, vol. 1. For the descent and sacred marriage, *v.* Asterius, who asks *Hom.* 10 (*in ss. martt.*): Οὐκ ἐκεῖ τὸ καταβάσιον τὸ σκοτεινόν, καὶ αἱ σεμναὶ τοῦ ἱεροφάντου πρὸς τὴν ἱέρειαν συντυχίαι, μόνου πρὸς μόνην, *PG*, vol. 40, col. 324B. Mylonas (note 13 above) argues (p. 314) that no *katabasion* has been found in the area of the telesterion, and that these rites more probably refer to Phrygian mysteries. But *cf.* Harrison (note 1. p. 536), who quotes Aristotle (*Ath.* 3.5) as corroborating the existence of a marriage chamber in Athens; P. Foucart, *Les mystères d'Eleusis* (Paris 1914; rpt. New York 1975), pp. 475–87.

creted away in a chest by Venus. To keep him away from the gods, she left him with Persephone. When Persephone saw him, she refused to return him. The matter was brought to Jupiter for arbitration, and he ordered Adonis to spend one-third of the year with Persephone, one-third with Venus, and to keep one-third for himself. Adonis joined his portion with that of Venus and spent two-thirds of the year with her.[26]

Sheaf of Wheat

Augustine reports that Varro interpreted the myth of Persephone and the ritual at Eleusis as symbolic of the annual vegetative cycle: Proserpina is the symbol of fertility whom Hades kidnapped. Her name, *proserpere*, means "to sprout forth." Her abduction is publicly mourned, and her return to earth publicly celebrated in the form of a religious rite. During her absence, the earth grieved with Ceres and so was barren; at her return, it became fecund. The Eleusinian Mysteries celebrate the introduction of crops: *Dicit deinde multa in mysteriis eius tradi, quae nisi ad frugum inuentionem non pertineant* (*Civ. dei* 7.20; [Varro] says next that many things are handed down concerning her mysteries, which refer only to the invention of agriculture).[27] From this it is easy to imagine that the hiera symbolically represented this agricultural cycle.

Harrison argues that the birth of a child and the revelation of a sheaf of wheat were two aspects, one anthropormorphic, the other symbolic, of a resurrection. Citing the text of Hippolytus, she argues that the Eleusinian initiations included an exposition of this marvelous mystery—an ear of grain reaped in silence and the birth of a sacred child, both elements of Dionysiac mysteries:[28] τὸ μέγα καὶ θαυμαστὸν καὶ τελειότατον ἐποπτικὸν ἐκεῖ μυστήριον ἐν σιωπῇ, τεθερισμένον στάχυν. . . . αὐτος ὁ ἱεροφάντης

26. For depictions of the contest in vase paintings, *v.* A.D. Trendall and A. Cambitoglou, *The Red-Figured Vases of Apulia*, vol. 2 (Oxford 1982): Late Apulian, plate 174.2, p. 489, and plate 175.1, p. 490. Literary references to Persephone's love for Adonis and her rivalry with Venus are numerous: *v.* Apollod., *Bibl.* 3.184f.; Just. Mar., *Apol.* sec. 1.25. Arn. (*Adv. nat.* 4.27) writes that female, as well as male, divinities engage in love affairs: *nonne uestris cautum est litteris . . . arsisse . . . Proserpinam in Adonem.* The apologist, Aristides, relates (*Apol.* sec. 11) that Aphrodite descended to Hades to ransom Adonis from Persephone. According to Ausonius (*Cup.* 57f.), Proserpina, distraught at his love for Venus, once beat Adonis: *cruciaverat illic / spreta olim memorem Veneris Proserpina Adonin.*

27. *V. Sancti Aurelii Augustini De ciuitate dei* (Turnhout 1955) = *CChr.SL,* vol. 47: bkk. 1–10, based on B. Dombart and A. Kalb, *Sancti Aurelii Augustini episcopi De ciuitate dei,* 4th ed. (Leipzig 1928). This interpretation is well attested in classical authors, *v.* A. Avagianou, *Sacred Marriage in the Rituals of Greek Religion* (New York 1991), note 306, p. 113.

28. Harrison (note 21 above), pp. 548f.

... βοᾷ καὶ κέκραγε λέγων· "ἱερὸν ἔτεκε πότνια κοῦρον βριμὼ βριμόν", τουτέστιν ἰσχυρὰ ἰσχυρόν (*Ref.* 5.8.39f.; the great and complete epoptic mystery, grain reaped in silence. . . . Holy Brimo has born a sacred child, Brimos, that is, the mighty gave birth to the mighty).

The only thing we can conclude with certainty from the patristic accounts of these secret rites is that there was a sacred dramatization of the myth of Demeter and Persephone, in which initiates shared the experiences of distress, suffering, and exultation that attended the loss of Persephone and her reunion with Demeter. The details, however, remain obscure. This drama symbolized the vegetative cycle—life, death, and life again—that gave initiates hope for happiness in Hades. Whether there was also an enactment of a sacred marriage and/or a sacred birth, or even a revelation of a blade of wheat remains undetermined. Yet it seems probable that the myth of Persephone as told in the *Homeric Hymn to Demeter* and the initiation at Eleusis share a parallel tripartite structure: the procession representing the abduction and separation of Persephone from her mother, the descent into darkness by the hierophant and, perhaps, the priestess of Demeter representing the marriage or encounter with death, and the revelation of the child and/or ear of wheat representing the procreative union with the divine or reconciliation.

The Initiation of Marriage in Later Latin Epithalamia

In the later Latin literary epithalamia, we can identify a parallel tripartite cycle of initiation. The nuptial poetry of Statius, Claudian, and Paulinus of Nola includes the very features of the mystery initiation we have isolated in the drama re-enacted at Eleusis and in the classical epithalamia of Sappho, Theocritus, and Catullus: separation or abduction, descent into death (*i.e.,* marriage), and reconciliation and procreation. A maiden suffers a symbolic death at her separation from her parents, family, and community, and then through her marriage becomes regenerative and overcomes death through childbirth.

In Statius' *Epithalamion in Stellam et Violentillam* (*Silv.* 1.2) the bride is resistant to marriage. She has her eyes cast down and blushes in modesty (*nuptam . . . / lumine demissam et dulci probitate rubentem, Silv.* 1.2.11f.).[29] She must be persuaded to submit to the yoke of marriage by Venus, who

---

29. A. Marastoni, *P. Papini Stati Silvae,* 2nd ed. (Leipzig 1970). Marastoni prints *lumine* rather than *lumina,* the reading preferred by F. Vollmer (*P. Papinii Statii Silvarum libri* [Leipzig 1898]); J.S. Phillimore (*P. Papini Stati Silvae,* 2nd ed. [Oxford 1917]); H. Frère (*Stace, Silves,* vol. 1 [Paris 1944]: bkk. 1–3).

reminds her that youth will pass: *quonam hic usque sopor vacuique modes-tia lecti, / . . . numquamne virili / summittere iugo? veniet iam tristior aetas* (*Silv.* 1.2.162, 164f.; How long will you persist in this indifference? How long will you modestly lie on this empty bed? Will you never submit to be yoked to a husband? A sadder age will come yet). After praising the beauty and noble birth of the groom, Stella, Venus concludes by commanding Violentilla to yield to marriage as do the animals and the realms of the physical universe: *ergo age, iunge toros atque otia deme iuventae. / quas ego non gentes, quae non face corda iugali? / alituum pecudumque mihi durique fer-arum / non renuere greges; ipsum in conubia terrae / aethera, cum pluviis rarescunt nubila, solvo* (*Silv.* 1.2.182–86; Come now share a marriage bed and do away with youthful dallyings. What peoples, what hearts have I not joined with my marriage torch? No flocks of birds, no herds of cattle, no beasts have ever opposed me; I melt the air itself into a union with the earth, when clouds empty themselves of rain).

Like Violentilla, Maria, the bride of Claudian's *Epithalamium dictum Honorio Augusto et Mariae* (*C.* 10), must be persuaded by Venus to marry. Unaware that her marriage is being arranged, she engages in edifying conversation with her mother and studies the traditional tales of maidenly virtue: *illa autem secura tori taedasque parari / nescia diuinae fruitur sermone parentis / maternosque bibit mores exemplaque discit / prisca pudiciti-ae* (*C.* 10.229–32).[30] Maria, learned in both Greek and Latin authors, studies Homer, Orpheus, and Sappho (*C.* 10.232–35). As Venus orders Statius' Violentilla to marry Stella, so she orders Claudian's Maria to marry Honorius and share the empire with him: *o digno nectenda uiro tantique per orbem / consors imperii* (*C.* 10.276f.; Thou who art to be bound to a worthy husband, to be co-ruler of this great empire throughout the whole world)!

Claudian plays upon the theme of resistance more explicitly in the last of the series of bawdy Fescennine verses that precede his epithalamium. Honorius is urged to consummate the marriage, though the bride is trembling with modesty, and her veil shows traces of her tears: *iam nuptae tre-pidat sollicitus pudor, / iam produnt lacrimas flammea simplices* (*C.* 14.3f.; Now that anxious modesty overwhelms the bride; now her red veil betrays her simple tears). He must insist despite the bride's resistance: *ne cessa, iu-uenis, comminus adgredi, / inpacata licet saeuiat unguibus* (*C.* 14.5f.; Don't hesitate to approach her, youth, even if she attack you with her nails!).

In his epithalamium for Julian and Titia, Paulinus rejects the *topos* of abduction and separation and extolls, instead, the equality of the Christian

---

30. J.B. Hall, *Claudii Claudiani Carmina* (Leipzig 1985).

marriage. In a Christian marriage, according to Paulinus, harmonious souls are joined; a woman is equal to her husband, who is her vertex, as Christ is his (1Cor. 11.3). The slavery of woman to man that was the consequence of Eve's sin (Gen. 3.16) has been abolished; like Sarah, the bride will be equal to her husband: *inque uicem mulier, sancto sit ut aequa marito, / mente humili Christum in coniuge suscipiat, / crescat ut in sanctum texta conpagine corpus, / ut sit ei uertex uir, cui Christus apex. / tali coniugio cessauit seruitus Euae, / aequauitque pium libera Sara uirum* (*C.* 25.145–50; And in turn, let the woman with humble heart receive Christ in her spouse so that she may be equal to her holy husband; let her grow engrafted into the holy body so that her husband may be her head, just as Christ is his. In such a marriage Eve's slavery has come to an end, and Sarah is free and equal to her pious husband).[31] There is neither male nor female in Christ, but the same body and one faith (179f.).[32]

For Statius and Claudian, the marriages of their honorands are a cause for all of Rome to rejoice (*Silv.* 1.2.232) for soldiers to put down their weapons and scatter flowers (*C.* 10.295–98), for houses to be decorated with festal pomp (*Silv.* 1.2.230). We are to imagine that the bride, once she has been persuaded by Venus to marry, assumes the role of matron with all its attendant honors. Thus the marriage (*i.e.*, death) becomes a reconciliation, a procreative union of the couple publicly celebrated and recognized.

The wedding song of Persephone and Hades at the end of book 2 of Claudian's *De raptu Proserpinae*, though not a proper rhetorical epithalamium, effectively combines the elements of mystery ritual and literary epithalamium. As she is carried off by Hades to her death (*i.e.*, marriage = initiation), Persephone laments her loss of maidenhood and the light of day: *o fortunatas alii quascumque tulere / raptores! saltem communi sole fruuntur. / sed mihi uirginitas pariter caelumque negatur, / eripitur cum luce pudor, terrisque relictis / seruitum Stygio ducor captiua tyranno* (2.260–64; How lucky are those seized by other raptors! At least they enjoy the sunlight given to all. But I am deprived not only of my virginity but even of the sky above; maidenhood is snatched from me along with the light of day, and, leaving earth behind, I am led captive to serve the Stygian tyrant).[33] Hades consoles her and begs her to accustom herself to her new

---

31. W. Hartel, *Sancti Pontii Meropii Paulini Nolani Carmina* (Vienna 1894) = *CSEL*, vol. 30.

32. *Cf.* Tert., *Ux.* 2.8.7: *Ambo fratres, ambo conserui; nulla spiritus carnisue discretio*; A. Kroymann, *Q. S. Fl. Tertulliani Ad uxorem libri II* = #12 in *Quinti Septimi Florentis Tertulliani Opera*, vol. 1 (note 25 above).

33. *Cf.* C. Gruzelier, *Claudian, De Raptu Proserpinae* (Oxford 1993), notes *ad locc.*, esp. on 2.361–72.

state in an act of reconciliation/mystical union that promises greater things. She will possess the tree of life and its harvest: *[Pluto] placida maestum solatur uoce dolorem: / 'desine funestis animum, Proserpina, curis / et uano uexare metu. maiora dabuntur / sceptra . . . / . . . lumenque uidebis / purius Elysiumque magis mirabere solem / cultoresque pios; . . . / est etiam lucis arbor praediues opacis / fulgentes uiridi ramos curuata metallo: / haec tibi sacra datur fortunatumque tenebis / autumnum et fuluis semper ditabere pomis'* (2.276–79, 283–85, 290–93; Pluto eased her pangs of sorrow with a gentle voice: Cease vexing your heart with thoughts of death and pointless fear, Proserpina. Greater sceptres will be yours. . . . You will see a purer light: henceforth at the sun of Elysium and its pious inhabitants will you marvel. . . . There in the shadowy groves is a most bounteous tree whose gleaming branches bend under the weight of verdent gold: This will be dedicated to you. You will be mistress of autumn's bounty and ever enriched with golden fruit). As matron of the Underworld Persephone will have the power to bestow immortality through regeneration to all living things; thus her initiation is complete: '. . . *cuncta tuis pariter cedent animalia regnis / . . . omnia mors aequat—; tu damnatura nocentes, / tu requiem latura piis . . . / sit fatum quodcumque uoles'* (2.297, 302f., 306; All living things alike will yield to you. . . . Death equalizes all things—you will condemn the sinners and give rest to the pious. . . . Let whatever you wish be fated). The closing of the book and of the epithalamium-like passage echoes the nuptial initiation in its stock conclusion, a prayer for progeny, the hope for immortality through the birth of children (2.367–72): '*nostra potens Iuno tuque o germane Tonantis / et gener, unanimi consortia discite somni / mutuaque alternis innectite uota lacertis. / iam felix oritur proles; iam laeta futuros / expectat Natura deos. noua numina rebus / addite et optatos Cereri proferte nepotes*' (Our powerful Juno (*i.e.*, Persephone), and you, brother and son-in-law of the Thunderer (*i.e.*, Hades), learn the union of a like-minded sleep and bind your shared wishes in each other's embrace. Soon a healthy child will be born; now joyful Nature awaits new gods. Give new divinities to the world, and present to Ceres the grandchildren she longs for).

The hope for immortality, the third element in the mystery drama, is implicit in the rhetorical prayer for progeny concluding Statius' epithalamium. While the prayer is commonplace in epithalamia,[34] Statius offers a beguiling twist: he asks that Violentilla give birth to sons, but that the birth

---

34. V. Men. Rh., 411: εἶτα εὐχὴν ἐπιθήσεις τοῖς εἰρημένοις, αὐτὸς αἰτῶν αὐτοῖς παρὰ τῶν κρειττόνων . . . παίδων γενέσεις; D.A. Russell and N.G. Wilson, *Menander Rhetor* (Oxford 1981).

neither mar her beauty nor steal her youthfulness. Ever young, then, Violentilla will participate in the natural procreative cycle that likewise ensures her immortality: *sic damna decoris / nulla tibi; longe viridis sic flore
iuventae / perdurent vultus, tardeque haec forma senescat* (*Silv.* 1.2.275–77;
May you suffer no loss of beauty; long may your face have the flower of
budding youth, and may this loveliness be slow to fade).

Paulinus offers a new variation of the prayer for progeny. His excursus
upon Mary "who gave birth to God with her virginity intact" (*quae genuit
salua uirginitate deum, C.* 25.154) reveals his adherence to the ascetic movement of his day and shows that he is well acquainted with a persistent
nuptial literary motif—the perpetual youthfulness of the bride. His description of Mary further develops that literary motif which was present
already in the myth of Persephone, and which was introduced by Statius
into the genre of marriage poetry. For Persephone was the source of regenerative fertility in all of nature, although she did not age through childbirth, and Violentilla, although she gave birth in Statius' epithalamium,
did not lose her youth or beauty.

The story of Persephone's abduction, marriage, and subsequent reunion with her mother interweaves notions of marriage and mystery initiation ritual that are manifest in the annual agricultural cycle of death and
regeneration. Her marriage through death is a mystical marriage that establishes her as genetrix of immortality, that is, the perpetual agricultural
cycle of yearly death and rebirth.[35] The sort of Christian marriage advocat-
ed by Paulinus has a like premise: man and woman enter into a holy union
that, while sterile, ensures their place among the angels in heaven.[36] The
mystic marriage to Christ, outside the bonds of mortal union altogether,
is, like the virgin birth, an amalgamation of themes from the mystery initiation ritual and the parallel *topoi* of nuptial poetry.[37]

35. The rape is, in fact, a marriage; *v.* W. Blake Tyrell and F.S. Brown, *Athenian Myths and
Institutions* (New York/Oxford 1991), p. 112; M.R. Lefkowitz, "Seduction and Rape in Greek
Myth," in *Consent and Coercion to Sex and Marriage in Ancient and Medieval Societies,* ed.
A.E. Laiou (Washington 1993), pp. 17–37; F. Zeitlin, "Configurations of Rape in Greek Myth,"
in *Rape,* ed. S. Tomaselli and R. Porter (Oxford 1986), p. 125.

36. *E.g.* Tert., *Ux..* 2.8.6: *Vnde <uero> sufficiamus ad enarrandam felicitatem eius matri-
monii, quod ecclesia conciliat et confirmat oblatio et obsignat benedictio, angeli renuntiant, pater rato habet?*

37. *V., e.g.,* Chrys., *Virg.* 49.1: Διὰ τί γὰρ οὐχ οὕτως εἶπεν· Ἐὰν γὰρ καὶ γήμη ἡ παρθένος,
οὐχ ἥμαρτε, τῶν δὲ ἀπὸ τῆς παρθενίας ἑαυτὴν ἀπεστέρησε στεφάνων, τῶν μεγάλων καὶ ἀπορ-
ρήτων δωρεῶν; Διὰ τί μὴ διηγήσατο τὰ μετὰ τὴν ἀθανασίαν αὐταῖς ἀποκείμενα καλά, πῶς εἰς
ἀπάντησιν τὰς λαμπάδας λαβοῦσαι μετὰ δόξης πολλῆς καὶ παρρησίας συνεισέρχονται εἰς τὸν
νυμφῶνα τῷ βασιλεῖ; Πῶς μάλιστα πάντων πλησίον ἐκείνου τοῦ θρόνου καὶ τῶν παστάδων
λάμπουσι τῶν βασιλικῶν; H. Musurillo and B. Grillet, *Jean Chrysostome, La virginité* (Paris
1966) = *SC,* vol. 125.

In the epithalamia of Statius and Claudian and in the epithalamium-like passage of *De raptu Proserpinae* we can trace *topoi* parallel to the mystery initiation rites of the Eleusinia. But in Paulinus' epithalamium (*C.* 25), the first extant Christian epithalamium, the *topoi* of epithalamia have been transformed into mystic hymenaeal rites that culminate in a Christian immortality. Here the virtues of a chaste marriage are extolled: *sitis ut aeterni corporis una caro. / hic uos nectat amor, quo stringit eclesia Christum / quoque uicissim illam Christus amore fouet* (*C.* 25.196–98; May you be one flesh of the eternal body. Let this love bind you, by which the Church is bound to Christ, and with which, in turn, Christ cherishes her). Paulinus likewise changes the conventional conclusion of an epithalamium, the prayer for progeny, to a prayer for virginity or, if there are to be children, a prayer for children who will be virgins consecrated to God: *perque manus castas corda pudica iuua, / ut sit in ambobus concordia uirginitatis / aut sint ambo sacris semina uirginibus. / uotorum prior hic gradus est, ut nescia carnis / membra gerant; quod si corpore congruerint, / casta sacerdotale genus uentura propago, /. . . sit* (*C.* 25.232–36; With chaste hands aid modest hearts, so that they may both agree upon a harmonious virginity, or they may both be seeds for sacred virgins. My first and principal wish is that they keep their limbs ignorant of carnal intercourse; but if they do unite in the flesh, may there be born chaste children, a priestly line). In the epithalamium of Paulinus marriage is an initiation into a mystic union that is antithetical to, and an inversion of, the pagan concept of marriage as death and rebirth through procreation (*C.* 25.181–87). He begins his description of his ideal Christian marriage by disclaiming its regenerative and procreative, and by emphasizing its mystical and sacred, nature.

The unexpected collocation of death with marriage found in the nuptial literature was, as we have seen, constitutive of the myth (*Homeric Hymn to Demeter*), cult (at Locri Epizephyri), and ritual (at Eleusis) of Persephone. Thus, we conclude that the ancients considered marriage a sacred initiation. Examination of the tripartite structure of the classical and later Latin epithalamia has corroborated this conclusion. The vituperative patristic accounts of the sexual union at Eleusis may give voice to an ascetic Christian ideal of marriage. By attacking the procreative aspect of the initiation at Eleusis, the Fathers showed their preference for the sort of mystic union leading to a non-regenerative immortality that we find in the epithalamium of Paulinus of Nola. Viewed as an initiation rite of death and rebirth, the ascetic Christian union celebrated by Paulinus reveals fundamental similarities of structure and purpose to the mysteries of Demeter celebrated at Eleusis, the ancient Greek paradigm for marriage.

IV. AUGUSTINE

TWELVE

The Immaterial and the Material
in Augustine's Thought

John J. O'Meara

O NE CAN CONSIDER Saint Augustine as the first modern man, or at any rate a bridge-maker between the world of antiquity and the western world of today. Since he was a very well-known bishop, his extensive correspondence was read by high and low with avidity throughout the sphere of Latin influence; his sermons reached a far wider, and more appreciative, audience than his sometimes restless listeners in Hippo. Above all, the fame of his conversion as described in his *Confessions* and the great works that issued from his controversies with the Manichees, Donatists, and especially the Pelagians ensured that the Christian Church in the West, finding its way toward a theological and philosophical system adequate to its actual dominating role in the Roman Empire, spoke henceforth often with the mind of Augustine.

Augustine was a complex, even an ambivalent, man. One stream of mysticism in the West finds its Christian origin in him. André Mandouze has spent his life studying the mysticism of Augustine, with ever-new results.[1] Paul Henry wrote an evocative book, *La vision d'Ostie*, in which he expounded the ecstasy experienced, Augustine says, by his mother and himself at Ostia, just before she died.[2] The vision at Ostia is, as Henry demonstrated, inspired by the *Enneads* of Plotinus, in particular 1.6, "On Beauty" (ΠΕΡΙ ΤΟΥ ΚΑΛΟΥ).[3] The philosophy of Plotinus is essentially

1. "Où en est la question de la mystique augustinienne," *Augustinus Magister,* vol. 3 (Paris 1954), pp. 103–63; *Saint Augustin: L'aventure de la raison et de la grâce* (Paris 1968).

2. *La vision d'Ostie: Sa place dans la vie et l'oeuvre de saint Augustin* (Paris 1938).

3. Quotations of Plotinus and of Porphyry's *Vita Plotini* follow P. Henry and H.-R. Schwyzer, *Plotini Opera*, vol. 1 (Oxford 1964): *Porphyrii Vita Plotini, Enneades I–III.*

immaterialistic. His disciple, Porphyry, who for the most part transmitted to us Plotinus' teaching, summed this up succinctly in a phrase rendered by Augustine as: *omne corpus fugiendum* (*Civ. Dei* 10.29.89; one should avoid every kind of body).[4] Augustine, who says that throughout all his life he had been unable to conceive of a spiritual, immaterial deity until he read the Neoplatonists, was, one might say, infatuated by their teaching, at least for a period. Even when he later controverted them, he often spoke in a friendly way about them and used their speculations where he felt that he could. Immaterialism had appeal for him right to the end.

But there was another side to Augustine: a strong loyalty to, and indeed, deep preoccupation with, the body. For him the body was exalted by Christ in the Incarnation. It would be glorified in heaven. In attempting to account for a material or sensible body in an immaterial heaven, he distinguished between sensibles that were corruptible (our bodies on earth) and sensibles that were not corruptible (our bodies in heaven). Not everyone would accept such a distinction. Here, then, I shall say something of the immaterial and material, of the spiritual and corporeal, in Augustine's thought. In practice I shall be speaking of Augustine's initial enthusiasm for the immaterialist philosophy of the Neoplatonists and his later fundamental rejection of it.

Somewhat more than one hundred years ago, Gaston Boissier and Adolf von Harnack came to the conclusion that Augustine, in writing his *Confessions* in 396, misrepresented his conversion in 386 which, according to them, judging from his writings at the time of his conversion, was to Neoplatonism, not to Catholicism.[5] Louis Gourdon in 1900 went further and declared that Augustine was not entirely converted to Catholicism until 400, four years after he had become a bishop.[6]

This was not so improbable then as it might appear now. Synesius of Cyrene, for example, who was nearly a contemporary of Augustine and lived in North Africa too, was elected bishop by his countrymen for material services rendered, but he continued to hold views influenced by Neoplatonism: he accepted the pre-existence of the soul and the eternity of the

---

4. Unless stated otherwise, translations are by the author. In this section of *Civ. dei* (10.29.62) this statement is quoted as from a work of Porphyry's that Augustine describes as *de regressu animae*. Quotations of *Civ. dei*, indicated by book, chapter, and line numbers, follow *Sancti Aurelii Augustini De ciuitate dei* (Turnhout 1955) = CChr.SL, voll. 47: *Libri I–X* and 48: *Libri XI–XXII*. This is based on B. Dombart and A. Kalb, *Sancti Aurelii Augustini episcopi De ciuitate dei, libri I–XXII*, 4th ed. (Leipzig 1928–29).

5. G. Boissier, "La Conversion de Saint Augustin," *RDM* 85 (1888), pp. 43–69; A. von Harnack, *Augustin's Confessionen: ein Vortrag*, 2nd ed. (Giessen 1895), pp. 16f.

6. *Essai sur la conversion de saint Augustin* (Paris 1900).

world and took the resurrection of the body to be merely allegorical. Synesius may not have been baptized when he was elected, but in any case, even while a professed Christian, he remained in his heart a Neoplatonist.[7] What Synesius did was not, of course, necessarily done by Augustine, even if the latter was not far removed in time and region. But neither should we assume that to Augustine none of this was a possibility. Augustine could have been a bishop, using material notions for a carnal people while being an out and out Neoplatonic immaterialist.

One of the most thorough examinations of Augustine's espousal of Neoplatonism was made by Prosper Alfaric in his *L'évolution intellectuelle de saint Augustin*. He concludes that Augustine accepted the Christian tradition but considered it only as a popular adaptation of Platonic wisdom. It was not until much later that he came to submit reason to faith.[8] There have been, however, many other books written since Boissier, von Harnack, and Alfaric arguing, on the whole successfully, that Augustine was sincerely converted to Christianity, even if he also hoped for a time that Neoplatonism would afford rational explanations for his Christian beliefs.[9] The depth of Augustine's enthusiasm for the immaterialist doctrine of the Neoplatonists before his conversion was fully appreciated and underlined in these books. Courcelle, for example, suggested that there was something approaching a Christian-Neoplatonist circle in Milan, including Mallius Theodorus, Ambrose, and Ambrose's mentor but also aged successor, Simplicianus, with all of whom Augustine was directly in contact.[10] Moreover, Courcelle picked out a number of texts from the *Confessions* that he described as representing attempts, in the event unsuccessful, to achieve the kind of ecstasy described by Plotinus. Any one of these can be used to illustrate how much under the spell of Neoplatonism Augustine seems to have been at this juncture. Consider this passage from what is called the "vision of Ostia": *Cumque ad eum finem sermo perduceretur, ut carnalium sensuum delectatio quantalibet, in quantalibet luce corporea, prae illius vitae iucunditate, non comparatione sed ne commemora-*

---

7. For an excellent bibliographical guide, with comment, on Synesius of Cyrene *v.* T.P. Halton and R.D. Sider, "A Decade of Patristic Scholarship, 1970–1979," *ClW* 76 (1983), p. 318. On Synesius' insistent neo-Platonism *v.* especially, J. Vogt, "Philosophie und Bischofsamt: Der Neuplatoniker Synesios in der Entscheidung," *GB* 4 (1975), pp. 295–309.

8. Vol. 1 (Paris 1918): *Du Manichéisme au Néoplatonisme*, p. 399; *cf.* pp. viii, 515f., 527.

9. *E.g.* F. Wörter, *Die Geistesentwickelung des hl. Aurelius Augustinus bis zu seiner Taufe* (Paderborn 1892); J. Mausbach, *Die Ethik des heiligen Augustinus*, 2 voll., 2nd ed. (Freiburg im Breisgau 1929). *Cf.* p. 21 and notes of my *St. Augustine, Against the Academics* (Westminster, Md. 1950) = *ACW*, vol. 12.

10. *Recherches sur les Confessions de Saint Augustin* (Paris 1950), pp. 93–106, 153–56, 168–74.

*tione quidem digna videretur, erigentes nos ardentiore affectu in idipsum,
perambulavimus gradatim cuncta corporalia et ipsum caelum, unde sol et
luna et stellae lucent super terram. et adhuc ascendebamus interius cogitando
et loquendo et mirando opera tua. et venimus in mentes nostras et tran-
scendimus eas, ut attingeremus regionem ubertatis indeficientis ... et dum
loquimur et inhiamus illi, attingimus eam modice toto ictu cordis. et suspi-
ravimus et reliquimus ibi religatas primitias spiritus et remeavimus ad
strepitum oris nostri (9.10.24).*[11]

Ambrose had disabused Augustine of the whole campaign of the
Manichees against the Old Testament, when he insisted that the letter kills,
but the spirit gives life (*Conf.* 5.14.24). The Old Testament, with all its scandalous tales of the patriarchs and its from time to time patent incredibility
if interpreted strictly according to the letter, became acceptable if it were
taken allegorically. This raised a grievous burden from Augustine's mind
in relation to the religion inculcated by his mother. And the revelation of
Neoplatonism to him, whether in Christian or pagan circles in Milan, allowed him for the first time in his life to conceive of a spiritual deity and
seemed to promise much more: the three Neoplatonic hypostases, the Father, Word and Soul, had been plausibly paralleled with the Christian
Trinity. Neoplatonism went to his head: *ecce tibi libri quidam pleni ...
bonas res Arabicas ubi exhalarunt in nos, ubi illi flammulae instillarunt pre-
tiosissimi unguenti guttas paucissimas, incredibile Romaniane, incredibile et
ultra quam de me fortasse tu credis ... etiam mihi ipsi de me ipso incredibile
incendium conciliarunt. Quis me tunc honor, quae hominum pompa, quae
inanis famae cupiditas, quod denique huius mortalis uitae fomentum atque
retinaculum commouebat* (*C. ac.* 2.2.5; But lo! when certain books full to
the brim ... had wafted to us good things of Arabia, when they had let a
very few drops of most precious unguent fall upon a meagre flame, they
stirred up an incredible conflagration—incredible, Romanianus [the dedi-
catee of the treatise], incredible, and perhaps beyond even what you would
believe of me ... beyond even what I would believe of myself. What honour, what human pomp, what desire for empty fame, what consolations or
attractions of this mortal life could move me then)?[12] These words were
written not long after his reading of the Neoplatonist books, and after he
had renounced both a promising marriage and the prospect of the gover-
norship of a province at least, for which he had so long driven himself so

11. Throughout, the text of the *Confessions* follows J.J. O'Donnell, *Augustine, Confessions,*
vol. 1 (Oxford 1992): *Introduction and Text.*

12. Throughout the text of *C. ac.* follows W.M. Green, *Contra academicos* in *Sancti Aurelii
Augustini Contra academicos, De beata uita, De ordine, etc.* (Turnhout 1970) = *CChr.SL,* vol.
29, the translation my *St. Augustine, Against, etc.* (note 9 above).

feverishly. Later in the *Confessions* he censured in a frigid phrase his excess of enthusiasm for Neoplatonism at this time: *garriebam plane quasi peritus et, nisi in Christo, salvatore nostro, viam tuam quaererem, non peritus sed periturus essem* (*Conf.* 7.20.26; "I prated as if I were well skilled, but if I had not sought Your Way in Christ, our Saviour, I would have been killed, not skilled").[13] So much for Augustine's immaterialism.

Augustine reports that his conversion was worked, so to speak, as Anthony's had been, by a text of Scripture (*Conf.* 8.12.29). Anthony chanced to hear the text, "Go sell what you possess, and give to the poor, . . . and come, follow me" (Mt. 19.21), and had on the spot followed the injunction. For Augustine the text was "Not in reveling and drunkenness, not in debauchery and licentiousness, not in quarreling and jealousy. But put on the Lord Jesus Christ, and make no provision for the flesh, to gratify its desires" (*non in comessationibus et ebrietatibus, non in cubilibus et impudicitiis, non in contentione et aemulatione, sed induite dominum Iesum Christum et carnis providentiam ne feceritis in concupiscentiis,* Rom. 13.13f.). The corresponding positive injunctions here are: abandon the flesh and put on Christ. Of these the one pertaining to the flesh has tended to distract attention from the more crucial putting on Christ. It was the putting on of Christ that enabled him to put off the flesh. But the putting on of Christ had also a special significance for him.

In putting on—in accepting—Christ, Augustine was in one sense doing no more than following the logic, indeed yearning, of his whole life since he drank in the name of Christ with his mother's milk (*Conf.* 3.4.8). Of any new system of philosophy or religion that attracted his support, he asked if Christ's name was in it (*Conf.* 5.14.25). Thus the enthusiasm aroused in him at nineteen years of age by Cicero's *Hortensius,* an exhortation to philosophy, where Christ was not mentioned (*Conf.* 3.4.7), was diverted immediately to the professedly rational system of the Manichees, where Christ seemed to be held in honour. When he abandoned Manicheism finally in his early thirties, he was attracted by the sceptics of the New Academy, but he did not commit himself to them, because their philosophy was without the saving name of Christ. He, therefore, decided, he says, "to continue as a catechumen in the Catholic Church, commended to me by my parents" (*statui ergo tamdiu esse catechumenus in catholica ecclesia mihi a parentibus commendata, Conf.* 5.14.25).[14] When he had listened to the ser-

---

13. The translation follows, with modification, E.B. Pusey, *The Confessions of S. Augustine,* rev. ed. (Oxford 1843).

14. The translation follows J.K. Ryan, *The Confessions of St. Augustine* (Garden City, N.Y. 1960).

mons of Ambrose a little later, he absorbed more and more of the faith of
Christ so firmly fixed within his heart. When he came soon to read the
Neoplatonists, he was astonished how nearly their teaching approached
that of the prologue to the Gospel of St. John. But he complained again
that neither the birth of Christ, who claimed to be the Mediator between
God and man, nor his death was to be found there (*Conf.* 7.9.13f.). And in
Against the Academics, written between his conversion and baptism, he
speaks of his conversion as no more than like looking back from the end of
a journey to that religion that is implanted in us in our childhood and
bound up in the marrow of our bones: *ipsa ad se nescientem rapiebat* (*C.
ac.* 2.2.5; she . . . was drawing me unknowing to herself). The conclusion of
A.D. Nock is that Augustine's conversion rests in the last resort on the permanence of an early impression and of the religious atmosphere with
which his mother had invested his childhood, in which he drank in the
name of Christ with her milk.[15]

In the dialogues, written within a few months of his conversion, Augustine asserts that Christ is God, and Christ is man (*Ord.* 2.16). He may well
not have understood, given the state of the theology of the Incarnation at
the time, the theological accounts of the relations of the Father and the
Word, but he clearly accepted that the God-Word was flesh. He can speak
of his hopes that what Revelation teaches, Neoplatonism will explain: *Mihi
ergo certum est nusquam prorsus a Christi auctoritate discedere; non enim
reperio ualentiorem. Quod autem subtilissima ratione persequendum est—
ita enim iam sum affectus, ut quid sit uerum non credendo solum sed etiam
intellegendo apprehendere impatienter desiderem—apud Platonicos me interim, quod sacris nostris non repugnet, reperturum esse confido* (*C. ac.*
3.20.43; I, therefore, am resolved in nothing whatever to depart from the
authority of Christ—for I do not find a stronger. But as to that which is
sought out by subtle reasoning—for I am so disposed as to be impatient in
my desire to apprehend truth not only by faith but also by understanding—I feel sure at the moment that I shall find it with the Platonists, nor
will it be at variance with our sacred mysteries). Augustine supposes that
there was now at last a synthesis between reason and faith, that is between
Neoplatonism and Christianity, the one for the few, the other for all. Even
as late as 390, in *De vera religione* he says that "with the change of a few
words and statements" the Neoplatonists would have become Christians
(*paucis mutatis verbis atque sententiis Christiani fierent,* 4.7.23).[16]

15. *Conversion: The Old and the New in Religion from Alexander the Great to Augustine of
Hippo* (Oxford 1933), p. 266.

16. W.M. Green, *De vera religione liber unus, Sancti Aurelii Augustini Opera, sect. VI pars V*
(Vienna 1961) = *CSEL,* vol. 77.

But Porphyry, the reigning Neoplatonist of Augustine's time, was a problem. Augustine had read an attack of his on the notion of Christ's being God, in which he scoffed at the birth of God from a virgin and the crucifixion of God on a gibbet (*e.g. Civ. dei* 10.29; 19.23).[17] Augustine attributed Porphyry's blindness, as he saw it, to his pride and worship of demons (*e.g.* 10.26, 28). Hence his putting on of Christ and belief in the Incarnation was a conscious rejection of Porphyry and his slogan *omne corpus fugiendum*. We know that Porphyry intended his slogan to refer not only to the need for purification in this life, but also to what he regarded as the untenable Christian notion of a deity or a soul in heaven being joined to a body.[18] Augustine's *Retractations* (1.4.3) indicate that before his baptism he accepted the resurrection of bodies into heaven, if in a glorified state; they would not be corruptible. In *De quantitate animae*, written one year after his baptism, he writes, *Videbimus etiam naturae huius corporeae tantas conmutationes et vicissitudines ... ut ipsam etiam resurrectionem carnis, quae partim tardius, partim omnino non creditur, ita certam teneamus, ut certius nobis non sit solem, cum occiderit, oriturum* (33.76; we shall see also such great transformations and changes of our corporeal nature that we shall hold the very resurrection itself of the flesh, which some accept reluctantly, and others altogether reject, with such certainty, that it cannot be more certain to us than that when the sun sets, it will rise again).[19]

Augustine, then, from the time of his conversion appears deliberately to support against, or perhaps alongside of, the immaterialism of the Neoplatonists materialist claims of the body. This special espousal of the body by Augustine has had the most serious consequences for western theology: in sexuality, in the nature of the resurrection of bodies and in other important matters. One wonders why he so espoused the body? Was it, for example, his background in materialist Manicheism throughout his impressionable twenties? In later life some accused him of never having ceased to be a Manichee.[20] Or was his mother's religion that was the environment of the whole of his first thirty years, in which he could not even conceive the idea

17. *V.* my *Porphyry's Philosophy from Oracles in Augustine* (Paris 1959), pp. 150, 162.

18. *Ib.*, pp. 129–48.

19. W. Hörmann, *De quantitate animae, etc.* in *Sancti Aurelii Augustini Opera, sect. I pars IV* (Vienna 1986) = *CSEL*, vol. 89. *V.* M.R. Miles' discussion of Augustine's early teaching on the resurrection of the body in *Augustine on the Body* (Missoula, Mont. 1979), pp. 106–13. She argues that in this passage of *Quant. an.*, which she mistakenly cites as 23.76, "There is no continuity between our bodily experience and our anticipation of the resurrection of the body. . . . Augustine at this time does not see or describe any connection between our mortal bodies and resurrection bodies."

20. *E.g.*, Megalius of Calama; *C. litt. Petil.* 3.16.19; *C. Crescon.* 3.79.91–80.92.

of anything that was not material, responsible? Or was it simply the dominating and all-pervasive materialism of Rome and Roman thinking? Or
was there something within his own personality that elevated the flesh?

To illustrate how, in choosing to espouse the body in this way, Augustine departed, not only from Porphyry, but from the entire tradition of
platonizing Christianity, we may briefly introduce one of its exponents,
Joannes Scotus Eriugena (ninth century).[21] According to Eriugena, man
was created and placed in an Eden that was wholly spiritual. The sexual
differentiation between male and female was an anticipation of the consequence of sin as foreseen and so provided for by God. Man's body was
wholly spiritual. Augustine, on the other hand, held very firmly that Eden
was corporeal as well as spiritual, that man's body was animal, and that
sexual differentiation was intended by God from the beginning and was
not a consequence of sin. Even more, Adam and Eve could exercise their
sexuality and experience *libido*, but a *libido* that did not escape obedience
to reason: *libido non est bonus et rectus usus libidinis* (*Retrac.* 2.22.2; the
good and correct use of *libido* is not *libido*).[22] Sexuality had nothing to do
with the first sin of man; that was a sin of disobedience. The condign punishment for this in man, as he now is, is his inability to command *libido*.[23]

Eriugena, anxious to excuse Augustine from holding what he considered scandalous propositions, is happy to believe that Augustine did hold
that Eden was wholly spiritual. He is oppressed, however, by the overwhelming evidence of Augustine's views having been ordinarily otherwise
and supposes that Augustine, while holding views acceptable himself, was
but adapting his teaching to an audience capable of carnal thinking only.
And so also for the animality of man in Eden. "I do not cease to be
amazed," writes Eriugena, "why he calls that body animal" (*Mirari non
desino, cur illud corpus appellat animale, Div.* 4.14, 805B).[24]

---

21. For early Christian precedents for Eriugena's understanding of the origin of sexual
differentiation *v., e.g.,* Ath., *Exp. in Ps.* 50.7; Greg. Nys., *Op. hom.* 17; Ambr., *Exh. virg.* 6.36. *Cf.*
G. Madec, *Saint Ambroise et la philosophie* (Paris 1974), pp. 296–98; and P. Brown, *The Body
and Society: Men, Women and Sexual Renunciation in Early Christianity* (New York 1988), pp.
293–96.

22. A. Mutzenbecher, *Sancti Aurelii Augustini Retractationum libri II* (Turnhout 1984) =
CChr.SL, vol. 57. V. pp. 63–87 of my *The Creation of Man in St. Augustine's* De genesi ad litteram, *Saint Augustine and the Augustinian Tradition* (Villanova, Pa. 1980) = *The Saint Augustine Lecture 1977*; rpt. in *Understanding Augustine* (Dublin 1996), pp. 131–41; my *Eriugena*
(Oxford 1988), especially the analysis of *Div.* bkk. 4f. (pp. 121–54); and my *Studies in Augustine and Eriugena,* ed. T.P. Halton (Washington 1992), pp. 233–83.

23. *Cf.* Brown, *The Body and Society* (note 21 above), pp. 416–19.

24. H.J. Floss, *Joannis Scoti Opera quae supersunt omnia* (Paris 1853) = *PL*, vol. 122. Reference to *De divisione naturae* (*Periphyseon*) is by the book and chapter of the ancient work
and then by the number and letter of the column in the printed volume.

In relation to Augustine's belief in the resurrection of human bodies in a glorified condition, Eriugena is staggered: *dum talia in libris sanctorum Patrum lego, stupefactus haesito, maximoque horrore concussus titubo* (*Div.* 5.37, 986B; When I read of such things in the books of the Holy Fathers, I stagger, so to speak, amazed and horror struck). These Fathers, including Augustine, he says, by the power of contemplation have risen above the whole sensible world themselves. They must have been considering only carnal men who, if they were to be told that there was to be no body in heaven, could conclude only that there would be nothing. So it was, Eriugena thinks, that such great men taught that earthly bodies would be transformed into heavenly and spiritual bodies. Ambrose's teaching, however, according to Eriugena, was that the change was not from an earthly into a heavenly body, but a complete passing into pure spirit: man's body, soul, and mind would, according to Ambrose, be one spirit, one mind (*Div.* 5.37, 987B).

Augustine's teaching that Christ's resurrected, immortal body was subject to spatial limitations, as it had been on earth, also caused Eriugena great unease. Once again, rather than suppose that that most skillful enquirer into all things human and divine should have been in disagreement with Ambrose and Gregory, he can only conclude that Augustine was writing in a manner suited to the limited intelligence of his audience (*Div.* 5.37, 992A).

This topic of Augustine's opting for the inclusion also of the corporeal, even if incorruptible, in situations where Ambrose and Greek Fathers totally eschew any intrusion of the corporeal, could be pursued much further. But enough has been said to illustrate Augustine's departure, not only from the Greeks, to whom he is indebted in *de Genesi ad litteram*, but most significantly from Ambrose. In that departure Augustine not only blocked off Neoplatonism from becoming a dominant influence in the West but also put an emphasis on the human body that some consider to have been tragic in its consequences.

There is a connected matter on which Augustine preferred to follow emphases on the physical rather than traditional Christian refinements. That is in the use of the term *amor,* "love." He adverts to this on a number of occasions as, for example, in the *City of God* 14.7. Here Augustine notes that to signify the love of God and neighbor (*i.e.,* the Greek ἀγαπή, ἀγαπᾶν) his Latin version of the Scriptures more often employed *caritas, dilectio/diligere* than *amor/amare.* He implies that many believed this selection to have been determined by the carnal associations of the latter pair. The matter arises for discussion particularly in connection with St. John's

Gospel 21.15–17, where Christ asks Peter if he loves him. There Christ twice uses the term *diligo*. Peter replies using the term *amo*. On the third occasion Christ changes from *diligo* to *amo*, while Peter continues to use *amo*. Ambrose had expressed surprise that Christ, speaking of love, should on the third occasion, as a climax, have resort to the term *amo*. He concludes that, in this instance, *amo* is more suitable than *diligo* as indicating that Peter loved Christ with the ardor of his body as well as that of his soul: *Petrum opinor non solum animi sed etiam corporis sui circa dei cultum signare flagrantiam, in Lc.* 10.176).[25] Augustine, however, deduces from this dialogue that, even in sacred usage, *amor* with its strong connotations of passionate desire (*cf. amor inhians habere quod amatur, cupiditas est, Civ. dei* 14.7.41f.) is not restricted to a bad kind of love, nor is *diligere* reserved for a higher: *scripturas religionis nostrae, quarum auctoritatem ceteris omnibus litteris anteponimus, non aliud dicere amorem, aliud dilectionem uel caritatem, insinuandum fuit.*[26] In rejecting the distinction in terminology between physical and spiritual love, Augustine implies that the two may be inseparable.[27]

Love, mental and physical, is indeed the great motivation in Augustine's life. He is a man of intellect, it is true, but he is even more a man of will, a man of love. The poet in him wrought prose, rhetorical indeed, but instinct with the incantation of poetry: *Sero te amavi, pulchritudo tam antiqua et tam nova, sero te amavi! et ecce intus eras et ego foris, et ibi te quaerebam[.]* . . . *vocasti et clamasti et rupisti surditatem meam; coruscasti, splenduisti et fugasti caecitatem meam; fragrasti, et duxi spiritum et anhelo tibi; gustavi et esurio et sitio; tetigisti me, et exarsi in pacem tuam* (*Conf.* 10.27.38; "Too late loved I Thee, O Thou Beauty of ancient days, yet ever new! too late I loved Thee! And behold, Thou wert within, and I abroad, and there I searched for Thee; . . . Thou calledst, and shoutedst, and burstest my deafness. Thou flashedst, shonest, and scatteredst my blindness. Thou breathedst odours, and *I drew in breath* and *pant for Thee.* I tasted, and hunger and thirst. Thou touchedst me, and I burned for Thy peace").[28] How physical that famous passage is, how full of the five senses!

25. M. Adriaen, *Sancti Ambrosii mediolanensis Opera*, part 4: *Expositio evangelii secvndum Lvcam, etc.* (Turnhout 1957) = CChr.SL, vol. 14.

26. *Cf. Tract in Ioh.* 123.5.30f. on Jn. 21.15–17: *demonstratur unum atque idem esse amorem et dilectionem;* R. Willems, *Sancti Aurelii Augustini in Iohannis evangelium tractatus CXXIV* (Turnhout 1954) = CChr.SL, vol. 36. In the passages cited from *Exp. ev. sec. Luc.* and *Civ. dei* Ambrose and Augustine were both using texts of Jn. 21.15–17 in which the alternation of the verbs *amare* and *diligere* conformed to that found in the Vulgate; *cf.* M. Pontet, *L'exégèse de S. Augustin prédicateur* (Marseilles 1945), note 115, p. 224.

27. For a good discussion of this topic *v.* pp. 529–31 of *La Cité de Dieu, Livres XI–XIV*, intro. and notes by G. Bardy, trans. G. Combès (Paris 1959) = BAug, vol. 35.

28. The translation follows Pusey (note 13 above).

In the *Confessions* the soul is commonly regarded as immaterial. Here, however, as A. Solignac has pointed out, it is portrayed as having a head (10.7.11), eyes (7.10.16), a back, sides, and a belly (6.16.26). The heart has a mouth (6.3.3) and ears (1.5.5) and suffers the toils of labour (7.7.11), and it is our heart, not our mind, that is restless until it rests in God (*inquietum est cor nostrum donec requiescat in te*, 1.1.1).[29]

Nevertheless, in spite of his espousal of the material body, Augustine is ambivalent about love and about the body, which gives it physical expression. His attitude reminds one of Virgil, who, according to the *Confessions*, made a very deep impression on Augustine as a child (1.13.20f.), and whom, as a rhetor, he professionally interpreted right up to the time of his conversion. Virgil appears to have been by far the major literary influence upon him.

Virgil was drawn inescapably to the theme of love: the *Aeneid* is indeed the epic of Rome, but it is most remembered, as Augustine himself remembered it, for the story of the fatally lovesick Dido. The *Georgics* celebrate fecundity and have a remarkable passage in the third book (ll. 242–83) on the destructiveness of love as it affects animals, who are expressly depicted as models having the same experience as man. It ends with the haunting and tragic story of Orpheus, who brought destruction on Eurydice and himself through the madness of love. The *Eclogues* sing of many loves and end with: *omnia vincit Amor: et nos cedamus Amori* (10.69; Love conquers all: let us too yield to Love).[30]

But Virgil did not yield to Love. He had inherited through Lucretius from Greek literature a scarifying account of love, which he passed on most powerfully.[31] Witness Dido herself: for her, love is represented as an enemy, a wound, a plague, a disease, an evil, a poison; it is a slavery; it is blind, incurable, invincible.[32] Philosophy and the highly regarded state of matrimony, in which the mother played an important family role, were competing and, to an extent, successful rivals of love in the Graeco-Roman world. Virgil had his experiences, and does not conceal his fascination with the theme of love, but he lived his life, not as did his near contemporary Catullus, amidst the hazards of romantic love at Rome, but in a circle of poets and philosophers at Naples.[33]

So, too, Augustine loved the body, yet still was ready to consign it to

---

29. *V.* p. 227 of *Les Confessions, Livres I–VII*, intro. and notes by A. Solignac, trans. E. Tréhorel and G. Bouissou (Paris 1962) = *BAug*, vol. 13.

30. Quotations of Virgil follow R.A.B. Mynors, *P. Vergili Maronis Opera* (Oxford 1969).

31. For love in Greek literature, *v.* my *Studies* (note 22 above), p. 73; *cf.* Lucr., 4.1058–1191.

32. *V.* my *Studies* (note 22 above), pp. 81–84.

33. *Ib.*, pp. 72–81.

eternal punishment. He exaggerated the carnal excesses of his life up to the time of his conversion, even if he was a sensual man.[34] His attachment to the body was redirected and reinforced by his conscious acceptance of belief that in Christ God had taken into union with Himself a human body, such as that which Augustine had. As Christ's, so his body would be resurrected and become immortal: *Detrahatur mors novissima inimica, et erit mihi in aeternum caro mea amica* (*Ser.* 155.14.15; "Take away death, the last enemy, and my own flesh shall be my dear friend throughout eternity").[35]

Augustine, as Virgil, treated love as greatly tempting but destructive.[36] When, as a very mature bishop, he came to explain why Adam yielded to the temptation represented by the proffering of the apple to him by Eve, he explained that Adam was fully aware that in tasting the apple he would commit the greatest possible sin, the direct disobedience of an express injunction of the Almighty. Yet he took the apple through too much attachment to Eve: [*Adam*] *noluit eam contristare, quam credebat posse sine suo solacio contabescere, si ab eius alienaretur animo, et omnino illa interire discordia* (*de Gen. ad lit.* 11.42; Adam did not wish to sadden her. He was afraid that without his comfort, and estranged from his mind, she would pine away and, if they were at variance, even die).[37] Orpheus and Adam, unlike Aeneas, listened to the instinct to love rather than the dread command to obey. The result for Adam and all of us was a Fall into incalculable misery, and finally, for the majority, Hell.

If the saved will be possessed of their bodies, glorified, in heaven, so the damned also will possess their bodies, to be physically tormented in Hell. Augustine reports that some believe that the fire there affects only the soul while others believe that it affects the body too. He prefers to believe that the fire is intended expressly to affect the body only, while it is implied that pain is suffered by the soul also (*Civ. dei* 21.9, 23). The admission that there was a less material choice is, however, perhaps significant. He goes, nevertheless, to much trouble to show how it is not impossible for a material body to be subjected to fire for all eternity and never be destroyed. Augustine followed the age-old path trodden by Virgil, who had described a riv-

34. *V.* my *Young Augustine: The Growth of St. Augustine's Mind up to His Conversion* (London 1954; rpt. 1980), pp. 55f., 8f.

35. The translation follows P. Brown, *Augustine of Hippo: A Biography* (London, *etc.* 1967), p. 366.

36. *Cf.* Brown, *The Body and Society* (note 21 above), p. 426: "[Augustine] created a darkened humanism that linked the pre-Christian past to the Christian present in a common distrust of sexual pleasure."

37. J. Zycha, *Sancti Aureli Augustini De genesi ad litteram libri duodecim, etc.* (Vienna 1894) = *CSEL,* vol. 28.

er of eternal fire surrounding Tartarus and the brutal lashings and the groans of the damned that could be heard from within (*Aen.* 6.548–58). Virgil was using what for him was probably no more than a colourful and, for literary purposes, useful mythology. But by Augustine and his successors Hell was represented as no mere mythology, no just useful allegory, no "milk" to nourish only the weak (1Cor. 3.2). He elected for this emphasis on the body, and he especially has been followed in the West.

Similarly, in his bitter controversies with the Donatists and Pelagians, Augustine manifested a very pragmatic, non-philosophic and non-ascetic spirit. In the case of the Donatists he championed the cause of those who did not claim to be purists, and he even used force, if only in the end, to overcome these opponents. Against the Pelagians he championed the cause of those who relied wholly on God's grace since they accepted that they could merit nothing of themselves. The exercise of virtue did not attract that grace; the neglect of virtue did not repel it. Nevertheless, not to have been the object of God's unmerited grace in this life resulted in never-ending Hell.[38] The Incarnation put an end to the cycle of existences; there was no second chance. Peter Brown speaks of Augustine's writings against the Donatists and Pelagians as "a significant landmark in that process by which the Catholic church had come to embrace, and so to tolerate, the whole lay society of the Roman world, with . . . the depressing resilience of its pagan habits."[39]

In the pursuit of this practical aim Augustine was active and resourceful as the leading bishop in North Africa. From being one who had looked askance at miracles, he became promoter of the miracles wrought by the relics of the Protomartyr, St. Stephen (*Civ. dei* 22.8). He may have accommodated his real beliefs to the weak understanding of an audience; he may have used figures of speech that explained his saying the opposite of what he meant; he may well have had such a lively belief in Providence and grace that he felt assured that God would have His way, no matter what the

---

38. Miles (note 19 above) emphasizes (pp. 70–77) the anti-intellectual tone of Augustine's polemic against Pelagianism and the way in which he set out to mobilize popular opinion in favor of a Church that was no longer "a persecuted body" but "a major social and political grouping" (p. 71): "The later writings [*C. Iul. op. imp.*], while apparently focusing on sexuality actually use the issue as the testing ground for other issues: the power and the authority of the Church and the question of whether the Church will be the bastion of intellectual specialists or a layman's church" (pp. 76f).

39. *Augustine of Hippo* (note 35 above), p. 350. *Cf.* also *The Body and Society* (note 21 above), pp. 398–406, where Brown discusses Augustine's defense of marriage in *De bono coniugali* and his non-ascetic exegesis of Gen. 2f. as indicative of his concern to validate the structures of Roman secular society that guaranteed the unity and continuity of the Catholic Church.

preacher might say or leave unsaid. But all of these approaches, understandable, perhaps, in relation to being pragmatic in those times, do not commend him to us now as primarily an intellectual. Here we see Augustine the extreme pragmatist and materialist.[40]

One wonders if Eriugena's constructions on the pronouncements of Augustine that shocked him may not, after all, be correct: that while having more immaterial ideas himself he had decided that only material ideas could or would be grasped by the carnal audience he was aiming to attract and keep. Augustine could have cited the example of St. Paul who explains to the Corinthians (1Cor. 3.2f.), "I fed you with milk, not solid food; for you were not ready for it; and even yet you are not ready, for you are still of the flesh." Furthermore, in antiquity the idea was widespread that some philosophers, including Plato, had an esoteric and an exoteric teaching, each of which they dispensed to the audience considered appropriate.[41]

There is an instructive instance of this in Augustine's *Epistles*. In *Ep.* 92 to Italica in 408 he says in effect that in the after-life God cannot be seen by the eyes of the body (secc. 2f.), and in *Ep.* 147 to Pauline in 413 he repeats the same view (sec. 15.37). Again in 413 in *Ep.* 148 he writes to the bishop of Sicca to calm the anxieties of a third bishop, who had been upset by Augustine's view that in the after-life we would not see God with the eyes of the body. Augustine regrets causing anxiety to the bishop but repeats the same spiritualizing doctrine. He adverts, however, to the possibility that our bodies might be transformed so marvelously as to see God. In that case, such a vision will be added to the former interior vision of our souls, not substituted for it (secc. 17f.). But his final teaching on this matter is found in the *City of God* 22.29, dated between 425 and 427. There he states we shall see the incorporeal God through our bodies: *incorporeum Deum . . . per corpora contuebimur* (196f.). This is, he says, a possible, credible, and most easily understood view in that one will see God indirectly with the eyes of the body just as we see with our bodily eyes the life of those around us, which in itself is invisible, from the exterior and corporeal manifestations of that life. On the other hand, notwithstanding his pronouncements of 408 and 413 that the vision of God in the after-life is an interior vision of the soul, he now states that it is very difficult, if not im-

40. For Augustine's early denial that miracles had continued beyond the early history of the Church v. *Vera relig.* 25.47 and *Util. cred.* 16.34; cf. Miles (note 19 above), pp. 35–39, especially 38f.: "It is only in the context of Augustine's gradual development of thought concerning the role and value of sensation that we can understand his later preoccupation with miracles."

41. V. my *Studies* (note 22 above), pp. 6of.

possible, to demonstrate this by an example or from the testimony of the Scriptures. Augustine has here not abandoned a strictly immaterialist view of the question, but he now teaches as preferable a solution which, although it may not be materialistic, can be deceptively like one that is materialistic: after all, however qualified, the words *incorporeum Deum omnia regentem etiam per corpora contuebimur* (22.29.196f.) may appear to suggest to the simple a view that was materialistic.

In the last two books of the *Confessions* Augustine puts much emphasis not only on various possible and true understandings of Scripture, but stresses too a distinction between spiritual and carnal men (*Cf., e.g.,* 12.27.37–28.39). He himself would like, he says, to speak in such a way that all would gather the appropriate truth from his words (12.26.36, 31.42). He is particularly anxious that those who are wholly sense conscious should be accommodated, for there is danger that one of them may strive too hard and, like a young bird, stretching, may fall from the mother's nest and, a featherless little bird, be trampled by those that pass: *si . . . extra nutritorias cunas . . . se extenderit, heu! cadet miser et, domine deus, miserere, ne implumem pullum conculcent qui transeunt uiam* (12.27.37). This deeply compassionate note is not always present in Augustine—one remembers some of his pronouncements on predestination and on the damnation of all mankind and the material and on the eternal fire of Hell—but it is frequent and entails concession to the materially minded. Side by side with this, we have the subtle, intellectual, spiritual discussions of *de Genesi ad litteram* where anyone's believing that God made Adam from the dust is described as puerile (*quod enim manibus corporalibus deus de limo finxerit hominem nimium puerilis cogitatio est*, 6.12).

Augustine's departure from Porphyry at his conversion and his life as a bishop, engaged in the practical side of controversies and looking after his flock, tended to increase his preoccupation with the material. Few, if any—perhaps not even Plotinus, "who seemed ashamed of being in the body," (ἐῴκει μὲν αἰσχυνομένῳ ὅτι ἐν σώματι εἴη, *Plot.* ch. 1)—can live the life logical to immaterialism. On the whole, Augustine has left a very much reduced immaterialism to the West. It is in this sense that E. Gilson's declaration can best be understood: for all Augustine's debt to the Platonists and admiration for their teaching and ideals, he did more to arrest the influence of Platonism than to pass it on.[42]

42. *History of Christian Philosophy in the Middle Ages* (New York 1955), p. 67.

THIRTEEN

Augustine on *Fama*

The Case of Pinianus

—————————— ✢ ——————————

Louis J. Swift

A UGUSTINE'S handling of Pinianus' visit to the basilica at Hippo in 411 was inept and embarrassing for all concerned. When the congregation pressed Pinianus to accept priestly ordination and thereby become a permanent member of the Catholic community, the astonished visitor resisted, and a volatile situation quickly developed. In the course of the tumult, which involved some tense exchanges between Augustine and his parishioners, Pinianus quite unexpectedly offered to stay in Hippo with the proviso he could remain a layman. The congregation endorsed this idea on condition that if Pinianus ever chose to accept ordination, he would do so in their city. Pinianus agreed, and after some tense negotiations about the nature of his commitment, he signed an oath to remain in Hippo or to leave the city only with the conscious intention of returning.

This development created consternation in the mind of Pinianus' mother-in-law, Albina, who had accompanied him to Hippo but had not witnessed Pinianus' action. Neither she nor Augustine's fellow bishop, Alypius, who had witnessed events at the basilica, could believe that a vow taken under such duress was binding. Albina, in fact, intimated that Augustine's greed had prompted him to mastermind the whole affair in an effort to recruit a well-to-do parishioner.[1]

In the two letters that constitute our only source for this episode (*Epp.*

1. The sequence of events is outlined very well by A. Mandouze, *Saint Augustin: L'aventure de la raison et de la grâce* (Paris 1968), pp. 629–35. For background on the journeys of

125 and 126),[2] Augustine is clearly on the defensive as he attempts to explain what has taken place and to provide some justification for his own part in the whole business. He is obviously more than a little anxious to restore friendly relations with his wealthy and influential guests from Italy while at the same time holding Pinianus to his oath. Most of his attention in these letters focuses on the nature of *adiuratio;*[3] the ethics of oath-taking are discussed in some detail, and the binding nature of Pinianus' obligation is firmly reiterated. Behind these theological points, however, lie both an obvious unwillingness to sever ties with a wealthy patron and concern in Augustine's mind about *fama, avaritia,* and his pastoral responsibility. These latter elements lend a certain degree of urgency to the situation and make his efforts at explanation something more than a political maneuver or personal *apologia.*

In both letters Augustine insists that no private gain was intended by his actions, but he is quite aware that having a clear conscience about the matter is not sufficient. What occurred in the basilica has raised suspicions that he is exploiting his friendship with Pinianus for material ends, and Augustine senses a need for publicly establishing his motives, or, more precisely, his freedom from unworthy motives. The issue is clearly of great importance to the bishop: fully half of his letter to Alypius (*Ep.* 125) is devoted to the necessity of maintaining one's personal integrity in the public eye, and in the epistle to Albina he takes a rather extraordinary step in order to exonerate himself of any wrongdoing. Augustine closely associates *bona fama* with being an effective pastor, and he is obviously distressed that others ascribed his actions to *cupiditas pecuniae.*[4]

Pinianus, his wife Melania, and mother-in-law Albina, *v.* the recent study of V.A. Sirago, "Incontro di Agostino con Melania e Piniano," *L'umanesimo di Sant' Agostino: Atti del congresso internazionale, Bari, 28–30 ottobre 1986,* ed. M. Fabris (Bari 1988), pp. 629–48. For a very helpful analysis of the episode from a perspective different from that adopted here, consult G.A. Cecconi, "Un evergete mancato: Piniano a Ippona," *At.* 66 (1988), pp. 371–89. *V.* also M. Card. Rampolla del Tindaro, *Santa Melania Giuniore senatrice romana* (Rome 1905), pp. 205–10; C. Daux, "Un incident à la basilique d'Hippone en 411," *RQH,* 80, n.s. 36 (1906), pp. 31–73; and E. Clark, *The Life of Melania the Younger: Introduction, Translation and Commentary* (New York/Toronto 1984), pp. 110f.

2. All citations of the letters will follow A. Goldbacher, *S. Aureli Augustini hipponiensis episcopi Epistulae,* vol. 3 (Vienna 1904): *Epp.* 124–184A = *CSEL,* vol. 44. Unless otherwise indicated, all translations of Augustine's works are my own.

3. I have discussed this dimension of the episode in "Augustine on the Oath of Pinianus," *Congresso internazionale su S. Agostino nel XVI centenario della conversione, Roma, 15–20 settembre 1986: Atti,* vol. 1: *Cronaca del congresso, Sessioni generali, Sezione di studio I = Studia Ephemeridis "Augustinianum"* 24 (Rome 1987), pp. 371–79.

4. *Cf. Ep.* 125.2. Peter Brown makes this point succinctly in *Augustine of Hippo: A Biography* (London, *etc.* 1967), p. 205: "If he was to be effective, he had, at least, to be admired; he must concern himself with his reputation." Brown also deals (pp. 204–6) with the tensions this necessity created within Augustine.

Augustine's preoccupation with *fama* in this episode is neither out of character nor free of irony. He was, in fact, highly critical of the role that *gloria* played in Roman society and of the ways in which the pursuit of glory tended to vitiate much that was considered virtuous in the Roman scheme of values.[5] In fact, he argues that the Christian's approach to *gloria* is different from that of the pagans. For the latter, he contends, *gloria* is either a code word for conquest and bloodletting, *i.e.*, a form of the *libido dominandi,* or is the temporal reward accorded to pagan heroes, who are good men "according to their own standards" (*qui pro suo modo boni erant, Civ. dei* 5.12.154).[6] For the Christians, on the other hand, *gloria* has transcendent rather than temporal significance. Augustine makes this point most explicitly in the fifth book of the *City of God*, where he describes the apostles as not resting on the temporal glory of their own virtuous endeavor but of passing that glory on to God and thereby instilling in others a love for the source of all goodness. "For their master," he says, "had taught them not to be good for the sake of human glory. . . . But . . . lest they should take this in the wrong sense and . . . by concealing their goodness, should be of less help to others, he showed them what their aim ought to be in attracting attention: 'Let your works so shine before men that they may see your good deeds and glorify your father who is in heaven [Mt. 5.16]'" (*Namque ne propter humanam gloriam boni essent, docuerat eos magister illorum. . . . Sed rursus ne hoc peruerse intellegentes . . . minus . . . prodessent latendo, quod boni sunt, demonstrans quo fine innotescere deberent: Luceant, inquit, opera uestra coram hominibus, ut uideant bona facta uestra et glorificent patrem uestrum, qui in caelis est, Civ. dei* 5.14.31–40). Temporal *gloria*, then, is not meant to be an end but a means to an end, a way of leading others to a state in which God himself is "life and salvation and sustenance and richness and glory and honor and peace

---

5. The role of *gloria* in Roman affairs and Augustine's assessment of it is a much-discussed issue. Elsewhere, I have tried to describe the three different senses in which Augustine uses the term in *The City of God*. V. "Defining *Gloria* in Augustine's *City of God*," *Diakonia: Studies in Honor of Robert T. Meyer,* ed. T.P. Halton and J.P. Williman (Washington 1986), pp. 133–44. V. also the good discussions by A.F. von Müller, *Gloria Bona Fama Bonorum. Studien zur sittlichen Bedeutung des Ruhmes in der frühchristlichen und mittelalterlichen Welt* (Husum 1977), pp. 28–38; U. Knoche, "Der römische Ruhmesgedanke," in *Ph.* 89 (1934) 102–24.

6. For *libido dominandi v. Civ. dei* 1.30.30 and 3.14.51, 55, 57. Citations are by book, chapter, and line numbers to *Sancti Aurelii Augustini De ciuitate dei* (Turnhout 1955) = *CChr.SL,* voll. 47: *Libri I–X* and 48: *Libri XI–XXII*. This is based on B. Dombart and A. Kalb, *Sancti Aurelii Augustini episcopi De ciuitate dei, libri I–XXII,* 4th ed. (Leipzig 1928–29). I follow, with modification, W.M. Green's translation in *St. Augustine, The City of God against the Pagans,* vol. 2 (Cambridge, Mass./London 1963): bkk. 4–7.

and all good things (*et uita et salus et uictus et copia et gloria et honor et pax et omnia bona, Civ. dei* 22.30.30–32).[7] This functional understanding of *gloria* or *fama,* as we shall see, is highly relevant to Augustine's assessment of his own responsibility in the aftermath of Pinianus' oath.

In his letter to Alypius (*Ep.* 125), where he shares his concern about removing public suspicion about any *cupiditas pecuniae* on his part, Augustine indicates why he thinks that he should not be satisfied solely with having a clear conscience about his actions in the basilica. "If we are not irresponsible servants of God," he says, "if there still burns in us some of that little fire by which charity 'does not seek its own' [1Cor. 13.5], we ought to do our good works not only before God but also before men, lest, while drinking clear water in our own conscience we be convicted of acting in such a way with our careless feet that the Lord's sheep drink muddy water" (*Si enim serui dei non reprobi sumus, si aliquid uiget in nobis illius igniculi, quo caritas non quaerit, quae sua sunt, prouidere utique debemus bona non solum coram deo sed etiam coram hominibus, ne tranquillam aquam bibentes in nostra conscientia pedibus incautis agere conuincamur, ut oues dominicae turbidam bibant, Ep.* 125.2). This manner of expressing his pastoral responsibilities is quite revealing. The imagery of tranquil and muddy water is a reference to Ez. 34.18f.,[8] where the prophet talks about the differences between a responsible and an irresponsible shepherd, *i.e.,* between the one who makes sure that his flock has fresh pastures and clear streams and the shepherd who takes care of himself but leaves the sheep with trampled grazing land and dirty water.

Augustine's application of this text to the Pinianus affair becomes more explicable and more revealing when we consider two anti-Donatist works, *Sermones* 46 and 47, which provide a lengthy commentary on Ezekiel's words.[9] The bishop's remarks in these sermons provide a good gloss on what he was about when he sought to defend Pinianus' oath and at the

---

7. The reason for this dichotomy between typical Roman and Christian senses of *gloria,* Augustine claims, is that the perspectives of the Christian and the pagan heroes differ. The latter were dwellers in an earthly city and, as such, were concerned only about glory that would survive on the lips of others. The Christian's destiny is an eternal city "which is as far removed from Rome as heaven from earth, eternal life from temporal joys, solid glory from hollow praise" (*cum illa ciuitas, in qua nobis regnare promissum est, tantum ab hac distet, quantum distat caelum a terra, a temporali laetitia uita aeterna, ab inanibus laudibus solida gloria, Civ. dei* 5.17.36–39).

8. Goldbacher, the editor of the *Epp.* for the *CSEL,* mistakenly identifies this as an allusion to Jer. 2.18.

9. It should not be forgotten that at the time of the Pinianus affair Augustine was much embroiled in his dispute with the Donatists. Cecconi (note 1 above) sees this conflict as highly relevant to Augustine's actions. For the text of the *Sermones, v. PL,* vol. 38.

same time to maintain his own *fama* in the face of Albina's suspicions. In *Sermo* 46 Augustine argues that bishops and priests enjoy a twofold gift of being Christians and of being people in authority. By virtue of the latter they must be concerned about feeding their flock rather than themselves, and this responsibility goes beyond lending material assistance and providing spiritual encouragement. It involves the correction of wrongdoers, even at the risk of alienating others, and the responsibility to avoid giving bad example. Bad example, Augustine argues, is a form of killing the flock of the Lord (*Ser.* 46.3.7–4.9).

These concerns seem not to be far from the mind of Augustine as he deals with the prospect of Pinianus' renouncing his commitment. To both Alypius and Albina he insists not only that such action would be sinful but that any retreat from a strict interpretation of the oath would set a bad precedent and would seriously compromise Augustine's and Alypius' credibility within the community: "Let the promise be kept," he says, "and let the hearts of the weak (Augustine frequently speaks of the congregation as *infirmi*) be healed in order to avoid a situation in which those who are sympathetic to [Pinianus'] action be encouraged to imitate his perjury and those who are unsympathetic claim, quite rightfully, that none of us can be trusted, not only when we promise something but even when we swear to it" (*Fiat ergo, quod promissum est, et infirmorum corda sanentur, ne tanto exemplo, quibus hoc placuerit, ad imitandum periurium aedificentur, quibus autem displicet, iustissime dicant nulli nostrum credendum esse non solum promittenti aliquid sed etiam iuranti, Ep.* 126.14).

More to the point, however, are the bishop's two interpretations of Ezekiel's text in *Sermo* 47 (8.9f. and 9.11–14). Commenting on the prophet's remarks about the shepherd's partaking of the *bonam pascuam* and *bonam aquam* himself while leaving trampled pasture and dirty water for his flock, Augustine first sees in this text a lesson about the manner in which Christian truths should be transmitted from teacher to learner. If an instructor who has himself grasped the Christian message in tranquility and peace treats those under his tutelage in a caustic and hostile manner (*animo amaro, animo invido*, 8.10), he is like the shepherd who tramples the pasture land and befouls the streams.

Augustine tries very hard in his letters to Alypius and to Albina to avoid that kind of mistake. In both epistles he emphasizes the need to heal rather than to argue or make accusations (*sanandum* as opposed to *arguendum/accusandum, Epp.* 125.1f. and 126.1,9), and it is evident throughout both letters that he is trying to accommodate Albina's feelings while not accommodating her views. If he rejects her interpretation of Pinianus'

oath and of his own motives in the affair, he does so with considerable deference. Though Augustine had good political reasons for treading carefully in dealing with his wealthy and influential visitor, he also seems to have
considered this approach as part of his role as a Christian teacher.

The alternate interpretation Augustine gives to Ezekiel's text in *Sermo*
47 gets to the heart of the dilemma he faces in being concerned about his
own *fama* in the Pinianus affair (9.11–14). He suggests that there are some
virtuous individuals who believe that having a clear conscience about their
activities is always sufficient; they are oblivious of the fact that perfectly
innocent actions can sometimes lead to scandal. But since the virtuous
man's conscience is known to God alone, the outside observer can be led
astray by appearances if great care is not taken. "What good does it do,"
Augustine asks his congregation, "if you drink the pure water of a good
conscience, but [another person] drinks dirty water because of your negli-
gent conduct" (*quid prodest quia venter conscientiae tuae hausit aquam pu-
ram, et ille de tua negligenti conversatione bibit turbatam, Ser.* 47.9.11).

There is, as Augustine admits, good scriptural justification for being indifferent to the opinions of others. In Gal. 1.10, Paul proclaims that if he
wanted to please men, he would not be a servant of Christ, and to the people of Corinth he speaks quite specifically about "This our glory, the testimony of our conscience" (*Gloria nostra haec est, testimonium conscientiae
nostrae,* [2Cor. 1.12]). Indeed, in the gospels themselves Jesus warns his
hearers about "not parading their good deeds before men to attract attention" (*Cavete justitiam vestram facere coram hominibus . . . ut videamini ab
eis* [Mt. 6.1], *Ser.* 47.9.12f.).

As Augustine points out, rejoinders to such advice are easy to find in
the New Testament. In the same evangelical discourse in which Jesus talks
about not publicizing one's deeds, we also find an injunction about letting
"your works shine before men so that they may see your good deeds and
glorify your father in heaven" (*Luceant opera vestra coram hominibus, ut
videant bona facta vestra, et glorificent Patrem vestrum qui in coelis est,* [Mt.
5.16]), and Paul says to the Corinthians, "We are trying to do right not only
in the sight of God but also in the sight of men" (*Providemus enim bona,
non solum coram Deo, sed etiam coram hominibus,* [2Cor. 8.21]). He advises
his hearers to follow his example of pleasing all men in all things and to be
"without offense to Jews, Greeks and the Church of God" (*sine offensione
. . . Judaeis et Graecis, et Ecclesiae Dei* [1Cor. 10.32f.], *Ser.* 47.9.12f.).

In attempting to harmonize these conflicting texts, Augustine argues in
Sermo 47 that one must attend to the motives behind the action. The point
of doing good is to seek not our own *utilitas* but the *salus* of others so that

by following our lead they may become imitators of Christ (*Ser.* 47.9.12). In effect, the disparate scriptural injunctions cited above are addressed to different audiences. Those who are inclined to make human praise the end of good works are warned against doing virtuous acts in the sight of others. Those, however, whose *finis* is to have others glorify the Father in heaven are encouraged to make their deeds public (*Ser.* 47.9.13).

The principle of providing virtuous paradigms for others has its counterpart in concern over bad example. We should, Augustine contends, take care not only to live rightly and have a good conscience, but to avoid doing anything that could create suspicion in the minds of the *infirmi* "lest in eating the pure grass and drinking the pure water we trample the pasture of God, and the weak sheep eat what is trodden and drink what is polluted" (*ne forte puras herbas mandendo, et puras aquas bibendo conculcemus pascua Dei, et oves infirmae conculcatum manducent, et turbatum bibant, Ser.* 47.9.14).

The tension involved in providing public example while remaining indifferent to public acclaim is an issue of some moment for Augustine, and his treatment of the subject seems to vary from one context to another. In *Sermo* 149, for example, the problem seems to take care of itself. Here Augustine focuses on motives and insists that one must be *manifestus in opere* but *devotus in corde*. We should remember that human motives are perforce hidden from others, and we should have confidence that good example will have its effect provided that our own motives are pure. No one can tell whether another is seeking his own glory or that of God, "but people of good will who are prepared to follow the good action they see believe that it was done with good intention and they praise God whose precept and gift make such things possible" (*Sed tamen illi qui studio benevolo ad imitandum parati sunt, quod bonum fieri vident, etiam pio animo fieri credunt; et laudant Deum, cujus praecepto et dono talia fieri vident, Ser.* 149.12.13). In the last analysis, then, the whole issue of motives and appearances is in God's hands.

Elsewhere, however, Augustine is not so sanguine about focusing on integrity of motives while remaining relatively unconcerned about external appearances. In his treatise, "On the Blessing of Widowhood," he argues that those who lead good lives but care not what others think of their actions are both unwise and cruel because of the harmful effects they have on others. "Therefore," Augustine suggests, "the one who guards his life against accusations of crime and sin does himself a service; the one who guards his reputation exercises mercy toward others as well. Our lives affect ourselves; our reputations influence others" (*proinde quisquis a cri-*

minibus flagitiorum atque facinorum uitam suam custodit, sibi bene facit; quisquis autem etiam famam, et in alios misericors est. nobis enim necessaria est uita nostra, aliis fama nostra).[10] The bishop again cites numerous texts to show that Paul was not at all disinterested in his reputation as a means of leading others to God. "Of the two things," Augustine argues, "that is, a good life and a good reputation, or, to put it more simply, virtue and praise, Paul very wisely maintained the one for its own sake, and he very mercifully looked after the second for the sake of others" (*Sed illorum duorum, id est bonae uitae et bonae famae uel, quod breuius dicitur, uirtutis et laudis, unum propter se ipsum sapientissime retinebat, alterum propter alios misericordissime prouidebat, Bono uid.* 22.27).[11] The solace of a good conscience is intended for those times that necessarily come in the lives of good men when they cannot avoid the suspicions of others no matter how hard they try. With an allusion to Mt. 5.11f. Augustine declares that one is consoled or even thankful that a great treasure is laid up in heaven for those who live justly.

Before considering Augustine's efforts to defend himself against charges of greed, we should consider the kind of threat *avaritia* posed to his *fama,* and why he makes a special effort to remove any suspicions on this score. From Augustine's perspective one could scarcely imagine a vice more inimical to the pastoral role than avarice. This point is most clearly demonstrated in a well-known passage of the *de Genesi ad litteram,* which was composed around the time of Pinianus' visit to Hippo. Here Augustine defines avarice as the vice by which one "desires something more than he should for the sake of his own promotion and out of love for his own concerns" (*quisque adpetit aliquid amplius quam oportet propter excellentiam suam et quendam propriae rei amorem*). Avarice is, in fact, identified with *superbia,* and by its very nature it destroys the notion of communal responsibility essential to the Christian life. It contrasts with *caritas* inasmuch as it promotes one's private good instead of the good of the whole; it contributes to the destruction of community rather than to the building up of community; it rules in the interest of those governing rather than the governed. It is, in effect, the foundation of all the other vices (*de Gen. ad lit.* 11.15).[12] On many counts, then, *avaritia* is the very antithesis of pub-

---

10. J. Zycha, *Sancti Aureli Augustini De fide et symbolo . . . De bono uiduitatis, etc.* (Vienna 1900) = *CSEL*, vol. 41. I prefer the *aliis fama nostra* of *PL* (vol. 40) to Zycha's inconsistent *uestra.*

11. V. von Müller (note 5 above), pp. 69f.

12. J. Zycha, *Sancti Aureli Augustini, de Genesi ad litteram libri duodecim, etc.* (Vienna 1894) = *CSEL*, vol. 28. *Cf. in Ioh. Ep. ad Parth. Tract.* 8.6 and for bibliography on this theme, *v.* Swift (note 5 above), notes 17f., p. 137.

lic responsibility, and if the suspicions of avarice leveled at Augustine were made to stand, they would clearly have some negative effect on his pastoral effectiveness.

It is no mystery, then, why both *avaritia* and *fama* loom rather large in the bishop's letters to Alypius and Albina. Augustine is in a position where a good conscience will not suffice, and where it is exceedingly difficult to establish his own motives. Because issues of this kind are internal and ultimately not susceptible to demonstration, he has recourse in his letter to Albina to taking an oath himself about the integrity of his intentions in allowing Pinianus solemnly to commit himself to remain in Hippo.

The personal dynamics of this action and the irony involved in it are heightened by Augustine's convictions about oaths and oath taking. There are many dimensions to the act of *adjuratio*, but it is sufficient in the present context to point out that for Augustine oath taking is a legitimate, but problematic act.[13] The danger of perjury is always present, especially when one has a habit of swearing, and false oaths are in all circumstances a grievous wrong (*Ser.* 308.3.2).[14] The need for oaths in human affairs springs, in fact, from human incredulity and the inability of any person to see into the hearts of others.[15] Whatever be the cause, oaths involve the most serious obligation, and it is for this reason, among others, that Augustine is quite intransigent about Pinianus' commitment to the community at Hippo, however stressful or volatile the circumstances in the basilica might have been.

And given Augustine's views about the relationship between *fama* and pastoral responsibilities, it is scarcely surprising that in his letter to Alypius he stresses compliance with the oath: *Nam ut omittam, quod mecum nosti, quam sit tremendum de periurio diuinum iudicium, illud certe scio, nulli nos deinceps suscensere debere, qui nobis iurantibus non crediderit, si talis uiri periurium non modo aequo animo ferendum uerum etiam defendendum*

13. For a good general study of Augustine's views on oaths in the context of the early Christian traditions *v.* the excellent study of M. Calamari, "Richerche sul giuramento nel diritto canonico," *RSDI* 11 (1938), pp. 127–83 (esp. 161–68) and my discussion (note 3 above) of Augustine's ideas on the subject.

14. *V.* Calamari's (note 13 above) clear discussion (p. 166) of this point.

15. *Ser.* 308.3.3: *Si ab alio provocatus fueris, ab ipsius malo erit quod juras, non a tuo. Et hoc est prope a malo communi generis humani, quoniam corda nostra videre non possumus. Nam si corda nostra videremus, cui juraremus? Quando a nobis exigeretur juratio, quando videretur oculis proximi ipsa cogitatio? Cf. Mend.* 15.28 and 18.37 and *de Ser. dom.* 1.17.51: *Quapropter qui intellegit non in bonis sed in necessariis iurationem habendam, refrenet se quantum potest, ut non ea utatur nisi necessitate, cum uidet pigros esse homines ad credendum quod eis utile est credere, nisi iuratione firmentur;* A. Mutzenbecher, *Sancti Aurelii Augustini de Sermone domini in monte* (Turnhout 1967) = *CChr.SL*, vol. 35.

putabimus (*Ep.* 125.4; To pass over what you and I both know, namely, how fearful is God's judgment on perjury, I am sure of one thing: we ought not to be incensed at anyone who does not believe us when we take an oath if we think that perjury by a man like this should not only be condoned but even defended).

This passive anxiety about the loss of *fama* takes an active turn in Augustine's letter to Albina, where his own claims of innocence are matched by Albina's incredulity. The situation here seems to match almost perfectly the circumstances in which Augustine agrees that oaths are required. When it is impossible to prove one's motives, *quid . . . restat nisi Deum testari* (*Ep.* 126.8). If the bishop is to establish his credibility with Albina and maintain his effectiveness with his congregation he has both to defend the legitimacy of the oath and to affirm the purity of his own intentions. We have a classic instance of the point he made in *Sermo* 180: *Quantum ad me pertinet, juro; sed quantum mihi videtur, magna necessitate compulsus* (9.10).[16]

Thus Augustine's preoccupation with securing his own *fama* in this episode appears to be something more than a brief excursion into vanity or a stratagem for retaining a potential donor. Obviously, he had personal motives for wanting to cut a good figure with Albina, and he was undoubtedly anxious to extricate himself as much as possible from an embarrassing situation he had bungled badly from the start. Nor was he about to discourage generosity on Pinianus' part. Nonetheless, there is more involved in the episode. If the issue of his *fama* seems a bit overdrawn to the modern reader, Augustine takes it seriously, and he appears to be motivated, at least in part, by a concern for his pastoral role within the community at Hippo.

16. *Cf.* Calamari (note 13 above), pp. 163f.

V. TRANSMISSION OF

TEXTS AND LEARNING

FOURTEEN

Evidence for Deliberate Scribal Revision in Chrysostom's *Homilies on the Acts of the Apostles*

‡

Francis T. Gignac, S.J.

T IS BOTH AN HONOR AND A PLEASURE for me to dedicate this article to Professor Thomas Halton. His outstanding competence in patristic studies has long been an inspiration to me, and my forthcoming critical edition of St. John Chrysostom's *Homilies on the Acts of the Apostles* has profited immensely from his interest and kind services.

Chrysostom's fifty-five homilies on Acts, delivered in Constantinople during the Easter season of A.D. 400, the third year of his residence there (*Hom.* 44.4), constitute a valuable commentary on the entire book of Acts, the only one extant from the first ten centuries. They are also significant for textual studies of the New Testament. The entire text of Acts, except for a very few verses and half-verses, can be reconstructed from these homilies. Not surprisingly, the text is basically that of the Antiochene-Constantinopolitan type that developed into the *textus receptus;*[1] but there are 271 readings that correspond to the Alexandrian and 89 to the Western text types.[2]

1. This term first appears in the preface to Bonaventure and Abraham Elzevir's second edition of the Greek New Testament, Τῆς καινῆς διαθήκης ἄπαντα, *Novi Testamenti libri omnes, etc.* (Leiden 1633). It denotes the text found in most late uncial and minuscule manuscripts, which Erasmus had printed in the *editio princeps* of the Greek New Testament (1516), and which had become the basis of all subsequent early editions. Characterized by conflations and stylistic improvements, the *textus receptus* originated in the late third century around Antioch and soon permeated the Byzantine world.

2. V. F.T. Gignac, "The Text of Acts in Chrysostom's Homilies," *Tr.* 26 (1970), pp. 308–15. The Alexandrian text type, reflected in papyri from Egypt and in Coptic versions as well as in the best fourth-century codices, is a neutral text (*i.e.,* one that has not been affected by major grammatical and stylistic revisions) characterized by brevity. The so-called Western text, found primarily in *Codex Bezae*, Old Latin versions, and quotations of western Church Fathers, is characterized by interpolations. The term "Western" is a nineteenth-century misnomer, for the principal witness was written in North Africa or Egypt, perhaps in the second century.

I inherited this critical edition from a highly esteemed teacher of mine, the Rev. Dr. Edgar R. Smothers, S.J. Smothers was, in turn, building upon the work of Sharon Lea Finch. In his doctoral dissertation, Finch had shown that the manuscripts of these homilies fall into three distinct families.[3] In his own dissertation, Smothers established that these families represent an original, very rough, unrevised recension apparently constructed from notes taken by a stenographer at the time of delivery; a posthumous systematic revision in which a later editor or editors smoothed out the style; and a composite text produced by copyists who mixed readings of the two traditions.[4] He pointed out many inconcinnities and contradictions between the rough and smooth recensions and thereby excluded the possibility that these two recensions might reflect a genuinely bicephalous tradition.[5] Furthermore, he amply demonstrated from the starkly contrasting recensions that no plausible case can be made for a mixed text. Yet all the printed editions of the Greek text of these homilies provide a mixed text with a preference for the smooth recension.

The *editio princeps* of these homilies was produced by Hieronymus Commelin in 1603 from manuscripts of the Palatine Library and libraries of Bavaria, Augsburg, and Pistoia.[6] His text is mixed, closely following Palatine 11, a late fourteenth-century codex now at the Vatican.[7]

The magnificent 1613 edition by Henry Savile, of which 1000 copies were printed,[8] was supposedly based on three sources: an eleventh-century manuscript in the collection of New College, Oxford,[9] a thirteenth-century codex lent by J.A. de Thou,[10] and Commelin's edition. In his preface

3. S.L. Finch, "Codex Michiganensis and the Text of St. John Chrysostom's Homilies on the Acts of the Apostles" (Ph.D. diss., The University of Michigan 1932).

4. E.R. Smothers, "The Twofold Tradition of St. John Chrysostom's Homilies on Acts" (Ph.D. diss., The University of Michigan 1936).

5. F.G. Conybeare suggested (pp. 375f.) that Chrysostom "delivered the homilies twice over" and that the different recensions "rest upon the shorthand notes of two different deliveries"; *v.* "The Commentary of Ephrem on Acts," in *The Text of Acts,* ed. J.H. Ropes = *The Beginnings of Christianity, Part I: The Acts of the Apostles,* ed. F.J. Foakes Jackson and K. Lake, vol. 3 (London 1926).

6. *Sancti patris Joannis Chrysostomi . . . Expositio perpetua in nouum Iesv Christi testamentum,* 4 voll. The *Homilies on the Acts of the Apostles* (*Sancti patris Joannis Chrysostomi . . . Expositio perpetua in acta apostolorum*) appear on pp. 445–858 of vol. 2 (Heidelberg 1603).

7. *V.* H. Stevenson, *Codices manuscripti palatini graeci bibliothecae vaticanae* (Rome 1885).

8. Τοῦ ἐν ἁγίοις πατρὸς ἡμῶν Ἰωάννου . . . τοῦ Χρυσοστόμου τῶν εὑρισκομένων τόμος τέταρτος (Eton 1612), pp. 607–919.

9. The New College manuscript is a two-volume codex, *Collegii Novi* 75 and 76, the first containing *Homilies* 1–27 and the second, *Homilies* 28–55. *V.* H. Coxe, *Catalogus codicum mss. qui in collegiis aulisque oxoniensibus hodie adservantur,* vol. 1 (Oxford 1852; rpt. from the annotated copy in the Bodleian Library under the title *Catalogue of the Manuscripts in the Oxford Colleges* [Wakefield 1972]).

10. Paris, Bibl. Nat., gr. 727. *Cf.* the note to p. 1, vol. 9, of the edition of Chrysostom's works cited in note 15 below.

Savile recognizes that these sources reflect two ancient recensions.[11] But his printer's copy, preserved in the Bodleian Library, consists primarily of printed pages of Commelin with occasional revisions from the two manuscripts at his disposal.[12]

Subsequent editions, including those by Charles Morel,[13] Bernard de Montfaucon,[14] and the Benedictine revision of 1839 by Theobald Fix,[15] were basically reprints of Commelin's text. Although Fix acknowledged Savile's hypothesis of two ancient recensions of the homilies, and he himself preferred the smoother,[16] he was constrained to reproduce Montfaucon's edition in the main.[17]

The nineteenth-century English version of the homilies by Henry Browne, on the other hand, is in principle based on manuscripts of the rough recension alone; Browne's introduction, in Part II of his translation,[18] is a sound exposition of his reasons for his choice, although his extensive reordering of passages detracts from the usefulness of his translation.[19] Browne never published a Greek text of these homilies, and all the

11. *Duas iam inde ab antiquis temporibus* . . . ἐκδόσεις; Savile (note 8 above).

12. #2773 in F. Madan and H.H.E. Crasten, *A Summary Catalogue of Western Manuscripts in the Bodleian Library at Oxford,* vol. 2, pt. 1 (Oxford 1922): Nos. 1-3490.

13. *Sancti Ioannis Chrysostomi* . . . *Explanationes in novvm testamentum in sex tomos distributae, editio nunc primum in Gallia graece et latine elaborata* . . . *ex collatione variarum editionum et recensione R.P. Frontonis Ducaei* . . . *recognita, suppleta et ad exemplar authenticum anglicanae editionis correcta et emendata* = voll. 7–12 of *Sancti patris nostri Ioannis Chrysostomi* . . . *Opera omnia in duodecim tomos distributa graece et latine coniunctim edita.* The frontispiece of volume 1 lists only Fronto Ducaeus as editor. The *Homilies on the Acts of the Apostles* (*Sancti patris nostri Ioannis Chrysostomi* . . . *Commentarium in acta apostolorum*) appear on pp. 1–481 of vol. 3 of the *Explanationes in novvm testamentum* = vol. 9 (Paris 1636) of the *Opera omnia.*

14. B. De Montfaucon, *Joannis Chrysostomi* . . . *Opera omnia,* vol. 9 (Paris 1731), pp. 1–416.

15. *Sancti patris nostri Joannis Chrysostomi* . . . *Opera omnia quae extant, opera et studio D. Bernardi de Montfaucon, editio Parisina altera, emendata et aucta,* 13 voll. The *Homilies on the Acts of the Apostles* are in vol. 9 (Paris 1837), pp. 1–454. V. Fix's discussion of these *Homilies* in vol. 13, "Epilogue," pp. vif. *PG,* voll. 47–64 represents, in the main, a reprint of this edition. The *PG,* however, omits some of the footnotes and Fix's discussion of the *Homilies. Cf.* Quasten, vol. 3, p. 430.

16. *Sancti patris nostri Joannis Chrysostomi* . . . *Opera omnia* (note 15 above), vol. 9, note c, p. 62.

17. *Ib.,* vol. 13, "Epilogue," pp. vif.

18. H. Browne, *Saint Chrysostom, Homilies on the Acts of the Apostles and the Epistle to the Romans,* vol. 1 (Oxford 1851): Hom. I–XXVIII = *The Oxford Library of the Fathers,* vol. 33; vol. 2 (Oxford 1852) : Hom. XXIX–LV = *The Oxford Library of the Fathers,* vol. 35. This version is a revision of a translation originally made from Savile's text (note 8 above) by J. Walker and J. Sheppard (vol. 1, p. vii). It may conveniently be found in *NPNF,* vol. 11, ser.1 (New York 1899; rpt. Grand Rapids, Mich. 1989).

19. Browne believed that these homilies were reconstructed from notes taken during the delivery. To justify these transpositions he assumed that (1) the reporter frequently failed to note the text of Scripture upon which Chrysostom was commenting, and (2) the reporter's notes were often transcribed from tablets in the wrong order; *v. Saint Chrysostom,* vol. 2 (note 18 above), pp. xif.

printed editions contain such a large number of smooth readings that it would be impossible to correct any one of them to the rough form without inconsistency.

Smothers's dissertation and his subsequent studies[20] fully confirmed Browne's thesis and supplemented his argument, leading to the conclusions that the rough text alone is primitive, that the smooth recension is a posthumous deliberate revision from first to last, and that a sound edition of these homilies should be established from manuscripts of the rough recension exclusively. For this reason Smothers made a complete transcript of *Codex michiganensis* 14, a manuscript unknown to the older editors and containing a complete and consistent text of the rough recension, as a basis for collations with other manuscripts of the same family. Later, he examined fifty-two other manuscripts of these homilies, most of which exhibited the smooth text or a mixed recension. He isolated twelve manuscripts that reflected the text of the rough recension.

Ill health precluded the completion of a critical edition by Smothers and, *pietatis causa*, I assumed responsibility for it. I produced studies on important individual manuscripts,[21] collated the twelve manuscripts of the rough recension, established the text, and am preparing a critical apparatus with variants from the rough recension as well as a special apparatus illustrating the history of the text type of Acts. In the course of comparing the readings of the rough recension with those of the printed editions, I found evidence at every turn for deliberate scribal revision of the primitive text of these homilies. In this brief article, I can only give examples of several of the main types of revisions. At the beginning of each section, I first identify the chapter, verse, and narrative context of the passage of Acts on which Chrysostom is commenting. Then in the left column, I give the rough recension of the passage under discussion and a translation. In the right column, I present the smooth recension, with the main variants underlined for clarity, and a translation.

1. Sometimes the editor seems to have missed Chrysostom's allusions to biblical texts. An example of this occurs at the beginning of *Hom.* 4.1 (col. 41.48–col. 42.45),[22] where Chrysostom is commenting on Acts 2.1, the first Pentecost, and quoting passages from Jn. 4.35 and Mt. 9.37 // Lk. 10.2:

20. Summarized in "Toward a Critical Text of the Homilies on Acts of St. John Chrysostom," pp. 53–57 of *StPatr* 1 = *TU* 63 (1957).

21. "Messina, Biblioteca Universitaria, Cod. gr. 71 and the Rough Recension of Chrysostom's Homilies on Acts," pp. 30–37 of *StPatr* 12 = *TU* 115 (1975); "Codex Monacensis Gr. 147 and the Text of Chrysostom's *Homilies on Acts*," in *Diakonia: Studies in Honor of Robert T. Meyer*, ed. T.P. Halton and J.P. Williman (Washington 1986), pp. 14–21.

22. I shall cite the *Homilies on the Acts of the Apostles* according to the Fix-Benedictine edition (note 15 above) as reprinted in *PG*, vol. 60. Column numbers are followed by line

Rough Recension	Smooth Recension
Εἶδες τὸν τύπον; Τίς ἐστιν αὕτη ἡ Πεντηκοστή; Ὅτε τὸ δρέπανον ἐπιβάλλειν ἔδει τῷ ἀμητῷ· ὅτε τοὺς καρποὺς συνάγειν ἐχρῆν.	Τίς ἐστιν αὕτη ἡ Πεντηκοστή; Ὅτε τὸ δρέπανον ἐπιβάλλειν ἔδει τῷ ἀμητῷ· ὅτε τοὺς καρποὺς συνάγειν ἐχρῆν. Εἶδες τὸν τύπον; Βλέπε πάλιν τὴν ἀλήθειαν.
Βλέπε πάλιν τὴν ἀλήθειαν.	
. . .	. . .
Ἄκουε γὰρ τοῦ Χριστοῦ λέγοντος· Ἐπάρατε τοὺς ὀφθαλμοὺς ὑμῶν, καὶ θεάσασθε τὰς χώρας, ὅτι λευκαί εἰσι πρὸς θερισμὸν ἤδη· καὶ πάλιν· Ὁ θερισμὸς πολύς, οἱ δὲ ἐργάται ὀλίγοι. Τὴν δὲ ἀπαρχὴν λαβὼν αὐτὸς ἀνήγαγεν, αὐτὸς ἐπέβαλε τὸ δρέπανον πρότερος.	Ἄκουε γὰρ τοῦ Χριστοῦ λέγοντος· Ἐπάρατε τοὺς ὀφθαλμοὺς ὑμῶν, καὶ θεάσασθε τὰς χώρας, ὅτι λευκαί εἰσι πρὸς θερισμὸν ἤδη· καὶ πάλιν· Ὁ μὲν θερισμὸς πολύς, οἱ δὲ ἐργάται ὀλίγοι. Ὥστε αὐτὸς ἐπέβαλε τὸ δρέπανον πρότερος. Αὐτὸς γὰρ ἀνήγαγεν εἰς οὐρανοὺς ἀπαρχήν, τὸ ἡμῶν προσλαβών. Διὰ τοῦτο καὶ θερισμὸν τὸ τοιοῦτον καλεῖ.
Διὰ τοῦτο καὶ σπόρον καλεῖ.	
(Do you see the type? What is this Pentecost? When it was time to put the sickle to the harvest, when it was time to gather in the crops.	(What is this Pentecost? When it was time to put the sickle to the harvest, when it was time to gather in the crops.
	Do you see the type?
Look again at the fulfillment.	Look again at the fulfillment.
. . .	. . .
For hear Christ saying, "Raise your eyes, and see the fields ripe for the harvest." And again, "The harvest is abundant, but the laborers are few."	For hear Christ saying, "Raise your eyes, and see the fields ripe for the harvest." And again, "The harvest is abundant, but the laborers are few." So he put in the sickle first.
	For, adopting our nature,
But he took the firstfruits and raised them up, and put in the sickle first. Therefore, he even calls it [the Word] the seed.)[23]	he raised the firstfruits up to heaven. Therefore, he calls this the harvest.)

---

numbers reckoned according to the method used by the *TLG* in marking their electronic version of this text: one counts from the top of the column all lines containing words, including titles and textual notes. There is an average of 62 lines to a column.

23. This and all the following translations are mine.

This passage reflects the many kinds of variations observable between the two recensions of these homilies. But the main issue here is the final phrase. Chrysostom concentrates on Christ's leadership of the apostles: He is the first to harvest the crop, the one who makes the offering of first-fruits (ἀπαρχὴν . . . αὐτὸς ἀνήγαγεν, αὐτὸς ἐπέβαλε τὸ δρέπανον πρότερος); in fact, he is even the seed. The editor fails to understand this emphasis on Christ's priority and misses the point of Chrysostom's allusion to the parable of the sower and his reference to the role of the Word of God as the seed that produces the harvest. Instead, he focuses on the resurrection of the humanity joined to the person of Christ (Αὐτὸς γὰρ ἀνήγαγεν εἰς οὐρανοὺς ἀπαρχήν, τὸ ἡμῶν προσλαβών. Διὰ τοῦτο καὶ θερισμὸν τὸ τοιοῦτον καλεῖ).

Conversely, a subtle allusion to a biblical text by Chrysostom is sometimes made explicit by the editor of the smooth tradition. This happens in *Hom.* 16.2 (col. 130.34–36):

Rough Recension	Smooth Recension
Ὅρα τὰ αὐτὰ ῥήματα ἃ πρὸς τὸν Χριστὸν ἔλεγον· Τίς σε κατέστησεν ἄρχοντα καὶ δικαστὴν ἐφ' ἡμῶν;	Ἀπὸ τῆς αὐτῆς γνώμης τὰ αὐτὰ καὶ πρὸς τὸν Χριστὸν φαίνονται λέγοντες· Οὐκ ἔχομεν βασιλέα, εἰ μὴ Καίσαρα.
(See the same words that they said to Christ, "Who made you a ruler and judge over us?")	(With the same intent they appear to have said the same things against Christ, "We have no king but Caesar.")

The editor of the smooth tradition is not content here with an obvious allusion to the reply of the Jews when Pilate asked them, "Shall I crucify your king (Τὸν βασιλέα ὑμῶν σταυρώσω, Jn. 19.15)?" Dropping the Hebrew's question to Moses (Ex. 2.14), he quotes in its place the New Testament text with a more polished formula of introduction.

2. The scribes also tended to remove apparent illogicalities in the text of these homilies. Thus, *Hom.* 44.2 (col. 310.8f.) refers to Acts 20.22–25, where Paul at Miletus tells the presbyters of the church of Ephesus that he is going to Jerusalem to accept whatever comes, and that they will never see his face again (*v.* esp. 20.25: Καὶ νῦν ἰδοὺ ἐγὼ οἶδα ὅτι οὐκέτι ὄψεσθε τὸ πρόσωπόν μου ὑμεῖς πάντες ἐν οἷς διῆλθον κηρύσσων τὴν βασιλείαν). Chrysostom comments that Paul offered them a twofold consolation:

Rough Recension	Smooth Recension
Διπλῆ ἡ παραμυθία,	Διπλῆ ἡ <u>λύπη</u>·
ὅτι τὸ πρόσωπόν μου	τό τε, <u>Τὸ</u> πρόσωπον αὐτοῦ
οὐκ ὄψεσθε·	οὐκ ἔτι ὄψεσθαι,
τοῦτ' ἔστιν, τῇ γὰρ διανοίᾳ	
μεθ' ὑμῶν εἰμι·	
καὶ τὸ μὴ αὐτοὺς μόνους.	καὶ τὸ, <u>Αὐτοὺς</u> πάντας.
(The consolation is twofold,	(The <u>sorrow</u> is twofold: both the
that you will not see my face	"not seeing his face any longer"
again: that is, I am with you	
in thought and that it was	and the
not they alone.)	"<u>all of them.</u>")

The editor of the smooth recension realized that Paul's permanent absence
could hardly be much of a consolation to the elders of Ephesus and missed
Chrysostom's point that Paul's meaning was that, although absent in person, he would be with them in spirit, and that they were not the only ones
who would be bereft of his presence. Therefore, he changed παραμυθία
(consolation) to λύπη (sorrow) and added πάντας (all) to emphasize the
extent of the sorrow.

3. There are many instances in which the scribes seem to have misunderstood either the circumstances of events in the Acts of the Apostles or
the texts to which Chrysostom was referring. An example of the former is
found in the recapitulation of *Hom.* 52.3 (col. 362.44–49), in an excerpt
constituting a comment on Acts 26.2–4, the beginning of Paul's speech before King Agrippa and the governor Festus:

Rough Recension	Smooth Recension
Καὶ ὅτε ὅλος ὁ δῆμος παρῆν, τότε	Καὶ ὅτε ὅλος ὁ δῆμος παρῆν, τότε
καλεῖ αὐτῶν τὴν μαρτυρίαν,	καλεῖ αὐτῶν τὴν μαρτυρίαν.
οὐκ ἐπὶ τοῦ δικαστηρίου, ἀλλ'	Οὐκ ἐπὶ τοῦ δικαστηρίου <u>δὲ</u>
ἐπὶ τοῦ Λυσίου. Καὶ	<u>τοῦ Λυσίου τοῦτο ποιεῖ</u>
πάλιν ἐνταῦθα, ὅτε πλείους παρῆσαν·	<u>μόνον, ἀλλὰ καὶ</u> ἐπὶ τοῦ <u>Φήστου</u>· καὶ
ἐκεῖ δὲ οὐ πολλῆς ἀπολογίας ἔδει, τῶν	πάλιν ἐνταῦθα, ὅτε πλείους παρῆσαν·
γραμμάτων τοῦ Λυσίου ἀφιέντων αὐτόν.	ἐκεῖ δὲ οὐ πολλῆς ἀπολογίας ἔδει, τῶν
(And when all the people were	γραμμάτων τοῦ Λυσίου ἀφιέντων αὐτόν.
present, he challenged their	(And when all the people were
testimony, not	present, he challenged their
before the tribunal,	testimony. <u>He did this not only</u>
but before Lysias.	<u>before the tribunal</u>
	<u>of Lysias</u>, but <u>also</u> before <u>Festus.</u>

And again here, when more were
present; there, however, not much
testimony was needed since
Lysias' letter acquitted him.)

And again here, when more were
present; there, however, not much
testimony was needed since
Lysias' letter acquitted him.)

Misunderstanding the circumstances of the events recounted in Acts, the smooth recension says that Paul challenged the testimony of the Jewish leaders when the populace (ὁ δῆμος) was present: not only before the tribunal of Lysias, but also before Festus. This is to miss the distinction drawn between the circumstances of the apology before Festus (Acts 25.8–12) and this apology before Agrippa and Festus, on the one hand, and those of the apology delivered before Lysias (Acts 22.1–21), on the other. Paul had challenged the testimony of the Jewish leaders in a speech to the people delivered in the presence of Lysias (*cf.* Acts 21.37 and 23.26), who as a cohort commander had no tribunal. Both the apology before Festus and that before Agrippa and Festus took place before a tribunal to which the populace was not admitted.

In *Hom.* 33.3 (col. 242.44–50) we find an example of a scribe misunderstanding a text to which Chrysostom was referring. Here he cites Acts 15.28 (ἔδοξεν γὰρ τῷ πνεύματι τῷ ἁγίῳ καὶ ἡμῖν μηδὲν πλέον ἐπιτίθεσθαι ὑμῖν βάρος πλὴν τούτων τῶν ἐπάναγκες), part of the letter containing the decree of the apostolic council of Jerusalem:

Rough Recension	Smooth Recension
Δείκνυσιν πῶς ἀξιόπιστοί εἰσιν· οὐκ	Δείκνυσι πῶς ἀξιόπιστοί εἰσιν· οὐκ
ἐξισοῦντες ἑαυτούς, οὐχ οὕτω	ἐξισοῦντες ἑαυτούς, φησίν· οὐχ οὕτω
μαίνονται, ἀλλὰ διὰ τί τοῦτο τίθησιν;	μαίνονται. Διά τοι τοῦτο καὶ τὸ
	Ἀνθρώποις παραδεδωκόσι τὰς ψυχὰς
	αὐτῶν ὑπὲρ τοῦ ὀνόματος τοῦ Κυρίου
Διὰ τί προσέθηκαν·	ἡμῶν Ἰησοῦ Χριστοῦ, προσέθηκε· καὶ
Ἔδοξε τῷ ἁγίῳ	τίνος ἕνεκεν εἶπεν, Ἔδοξε τῷ ἁγίῳ
Πνεύματι καὶ ἡμῖν; Καίτοι ἦρκει εἰπεῖν,	Πνεύματι καὶ ἡμῖν, καίτοι ἦρκει εἰπεῖν,
Τῷ ἁγίῳ Πνεύματι.	Τῷ ἁγίῳ Πνεύματι.
(It shows how credible they are,	(It shows how credible they are,
not making themselves equal	not making themselves equal,
[to God]—they are not so crazy!	it says—they are not so crazy!
But why does it put it this way?	Therefore it also adds this,
	"Persons who have dedicated their
	lives to the name of our Lord
	Jesus Christ";

Why did they add,	and why did <u>it say</u>,
"It is the decision of the Holy	"It is the decision of the Holy
Spirit and of us?"	Spirit and of us?"
It would have been sufficient	It would have been sufficient
to say "of the Holy Spirit.")	to say "of the Holy Spirit.")

Of course, "not making themselves equal [to God]" is a comment on the introduction to the apostles' declaration in Acts 15.28 ("It is the decision of the Holy Spirit and of us"). The smooth recension, however, takes Judas and Silas, mentioned in the preceding verse (Acts 15.27), rather than Paul and Barnabas, to be the subjects of ἀξιόπιστοί εἰσιν. Then, misunderstanding οὐκ ἐξισοῦντες ἑαυτούς (not making themselves equal) to refer to Judas and Silas not reckoning themselves equal to Paul and Barnabas, the later editor inserts after ἑαυτούς (themselves) the word φησίν (it says) and adds after μαίνονται (crazy) praise of Judas and Silas as persons who have dedicated their lives to Christ. Chrysostom's οὐκ ἐξισοῦντες is thus made to juxtapose Judas and Silas to Paul and Barnabas rather than the apostles to the Holy Spirit.

4. The posthumous editor also had a tendency to add sermonizing expansions to the text of the rough recension, as in the hortatory section toward the end of *Hom.* 13.4 (col. 112.9–20), which characterizes the freedom from pressure to take oaths as a benefit enjoyed by those living a life of elective poverty:

Rough Recension	Smooth Recension
Μὴ δὴ ῥαθυμῶμεν, ἀλλὰ πάλιν	Μὴ δὴ ῥαθυμῶμεν, ἀγαπητοί, ἀλλὰ πάλιν
πολλὴν ποιησώμεθα τὴν σπουδήν· οἱ μὲν	πολλὴν ποιησώμεθα τὴν σπουδήν· οἱ μὲν
κατωρθωκότες, ὥστε φυλάξαι τὸ	κατωρθωκότες, ὥστε φυλάξαι τὸ
κατορθωθέν, ὥστε μὴ εὐκόλως ἀπορροήν	κατορθωθέν, ὥστε μὴ εὐκόλως ἀπορροήν
τινα γενέσθαι καὶ παλίρροιαν	τινα γενέσθαι καὶ παλίρροιαν
εἰς τοὐπίσω.	εἰς τοὐπίσω·
	<u>οἱ δὲ ἔτι λειπόμενοι, ὥστε διαναστῆναι,</u>
	<u>ὥστε σπουδάσαι τὸ λεῖπον πληρῶσαι.</u>
Καὶ τοὺς ἐν πελάγει	<u>Καὶ τέως οἱ κατορθώσαντες τοὺς μήπω</u>
νηχομένους, τὰς χεῖρας ἐκτείνοντας,	<u>δυνηθέντας</u>, καθάπερ ἐν πελάγει
ἐν τῷ λιμένι τῆς ἀνωμοσίας δεχέσθωσαν.	νηχομέν<u>οις</u>, τὰς χεῖρας ἐκτείνοντ<u>ες</u>,
Λιμὴν γὰρ ὄντως ἀσφαλής,	ἐν τῷ λιμένι τῆς ἀνωμοσίας δεχέσθωσαν.
τὸ μὴ ὀμνύναι·	Λιμὴν γὰρ ὄντως ἀσφαλής,
	τὸ μὴ ὀμνύναι·
	<u>λιμήν</u>, πρὸς τὸ μὴ καταποντίζεσθαι ὑπὸ
καὶ πνευμάτων προσπιπτόντων	<u>τῶν</u> προσπιπτόντων πνευμάτων.
μὴ καταποντίζεσθαι.	

(Let us not be lazy,	(Let us not be lazy, beloved,
but let us again show great	but let us again show great
eagerness: those who have	eagerness: those who have
succeeded, to retain the	succeeded, to retain the
success achieved, that an ebb	success achieved, that an ebb
tide or a flood tide not	tide or a flood tide not
easily carry them in the	easily carry them in the
opposite direction.	opposite direction;
	and those who are lagging behind,
	to rise up again and strive to
	make up what is lacking. And
	meanwhile those who succeeded
And those swimming	must receive those who were
in the sea,　　reaching out	not yet able, by reaching out
their hands,	their hands
they must receive	as to people swimming in the sea,
into the harbor of not swearing.	into the harbor of not swearing.
For it is indeed a safe harbor,	For it is indeed a safe harbor,
not swearing;	not swearing;
and not to	a harbor in which one will not
be sunk by sudden storms.)	be sunk by sudden storms.)

As if to complete the thought of the first sentence, the smooth recension adds οἱ δὲ ἔτι λειπόμενοι, ὥστε διαναστῆναι, ὥστε σπουδάσαι τὸ λεῖπον πληρῶσαι (and those who are lagging behind, to rise up again and strive to make up what is lacking). Then it adds by way of exhortation Καὶ τέως οἱ κατορθώσαντες τοὺς μήπω δυνηθέντας (and meanwhile those who succeeded [must receive] those who were not yet able), before continuing with καθάπερ ἐν πελάγει νηχομένοις, τὰς χεῖρας ἐκτείνοντες, ἐν τῷ λιμένι τῆς ἀνωμοσίας δεχέσθωσαν (by reaching out their hands as to people swimming in the sea, they must receive them into the harbor of not swearing). In the rough recension, those swimming in deep water are reaching for salvation by stretching out their own hands, while in the smooth, those who have reached safety are stretching out their hands to help people swimming in the sea, *i.e.*, those who have been as yet unable to forgo taking oaths. Thus, both recensions speak to the responsibility of all Christians to avoid oaths, but the smooth gives especial emphasis to the responsibility of stronger Christians to assist the weaker who are threatened by this peril. In the final phrase, the repetition of λιμήν (harbor), the use of a preposition with articular infinitive to express purpose, and the replacement of a genitive absolute by a preposition with genitive of agent serve to simplify the grammar and clarify the thought.

There is a similar sermonizing expansion toward the beginning of the recapitulation of *Hom.* 12.2 (col. 101.28–31), where, in a discussion of the immediate judgments that befell Ananias and Sapphira (Acts 5.1–11), Chrysostom digresses on the evils of sacrilege:

Rough Recension	Smooth Recension
Μὴ γάρ, ἐπειδὴ νῦν μὴ γίνεται τοῦτο,	Μὴ γάρ, ἐπειδὴ νῦν μὴ γίνεται τοῦτο,
	καὶ ἔπεται παρὰ πόδας ἡ κόλασις,
νομίσητε ἀτιμωρητὶ ταῦτα γίνεσθαι.	νομίσητε ἀτιμωρητὶ ταῦτα γίνεσθαι
(And do not think, since this	(And do not think, since this
does not now happen,	does not now happen—
	and punishment is close at hand—
that this will go unpunished.)	that this will go unpunished.)

By adding καὶ ἔπεται παρὰ πόδας ἡ κόλασις (and punishment is close at hand), the editor adds a salutary warning that, although circumstances are now different from what they were in the days of the apostles, everyone who commits a sacrilege will soon pay for it.

5. The smooth recension especially tended to add explanations to the text of these homilies. An example is found in *Hom.* 10.2 (col. 86.45–47), where Chrysostom comments on the forcefulness of the exordium of Peter's speech before the Sanhedrin, in which he claims to be on trial for a good deed (ἐπὶ εὐεργεσίᾳ ἀνθρώπου ἀσθενοῦς, Acts 4.9):

Rough Recension	Smooth Recension
Πολλῆς βαρύτητος ἡ ἐπαγγελία γέμει,	Πολλῆς βαρύτητος ἡ ἐπαγγελία γέμει.
καὶ δείκνυσιν ὅτι αὐτοὶ	Δείκνυται δὲ ἐντεῦθεν, ὅτι αὐτοὶ
ἑαυτοὺς περιπείρουσιν.	ἑαυτοὺς περιπείρουσι τοῖς κακοῖς.
(This presentation is full of	(This presentation is full of
weight, and he [Peter] shows that	weight. Hence it is shown that
they are putting themselves	they are putting themselves
on a spit.)	on a spit by their evil deeds.)

The smooth recension begins a new sentence after γέμει (is full of). Changing the active δείκνυσιν (he shows) to the passive δείκνυται (it is shown) and adding δὲ ἐντεῦθεν (hence), it draws an explicit connection between the gravity of Peter's presentation (βαρύτητος) and the self-destructive behavior of his judges (ὅτι αὐτοὶ ἑαυτοὺς περιπείρουσι); the apostle's tone underlines the danger to the council arising from its own injustice. Finally, τοῖς κακοῖς (by their evil deeds), added to the end of the clause, specifies the means of their self-impalement.

Another example of explanation is found toward the beginning of the recapitulation in *Hom.* 21.3 (col. 167.8–12), where Chrysostom quotes Acts 9.26 describing Paul's arrival in Jerusalem and his attempt to join the apostles there.

Rough Recension	Smooth Recension
Ἐπειρᾶτο, φησί, κολλᾶσθαι τοῖς μαθηταῖς. Οὐκ ἀναισχύντως προσῆλθεν ἀλλ᾽ ὑπεσταλμένως.	Ἐπειρᾶτο, φησί, κολλᾶσθαι τοῖς μαθηταῖς. Οὐκ ἀναισχύντως προσῆλθεν, ἀλλ᾽ ὑπεσταλμένως. Μαθητὰς δὲ καλεῖ, καὶ τοὺς μὴ τελοῦντας εἰς τὸν χορὸν τῶν δώδεκα·
Μαθηταὶ πάντες ἐκαλοῦντο τότε διὰ τὴν πολλὴν ἀρετήν.	διότι μαθηταὶ πάντες ἐκαλοῦντο τότε διὰ τὴν πολλὴν ἀρετήν.
(He tried, it says, to join the disciples. He did not approach shamelessly, but modestly.	(He tried, it says, to join the disciples. He did not approach shamelessly, but modestly. He calls disciples even those who were not included in the company
All were called disciples then, because of their great virtue.)	of the twelve; because all were called disciples then, because of their great virtue.)

The smooth recension inserts, by way of explanation, μαθητὰς δὲ καλεῖ, καὶ τοὺς μὴ τελοῦντας εἰς τὸν χορὸν τῶν δώδεκα (he [the author of Acts] calls disciples even those who were not included in the company of the twelve), before giving the reason (διότι = because): the Christians of that early day excelled in virtue and were thus all entitled to be called disciples.

A similar explanatory expansion occurs at the beginning of *Hom.* 19.1 (col. 149.27–30), the comment on Acts 8.26 (Ἄγγελος δὲ κυρίου ἐλάλησεν πρὸς Φίλιππον λέγων, Ἀνάστηθι καὶ πορεύου κατὰ μεσημβρίαν). Here, the editor of the smooth recension makes more explicit what he correctly apprehends to be the meaning of the rough recension: the recipient of the angelic message was Philip the deacon rather than Philip the apostle.

Rough Recension	Smooth Recension
Ἐμοὶ δοκεῖ τῶν ἑπτὰ οὗτος ἦν· οὐ γὰρ ἂν ἀπὸ Ἱεροσολύμων πρὸς μεσημβρίαν ἀπείη, ἀλλὰ πρὸς ἄρκτον· ἀπὸ δὲ Σαμαρείας πρὸς μεσημβρίαν.	Ἐμοὶ δοκεῖ ταῦτα ὢν ἐν Σαμαρείᾳ προστάττεσθαι, ὅτι ἀπὸ Ἱεροσολύμων οὐ πρὸς μεσημβρίαν τις ἄπεισιν, ἀλλὰ πρὸς ἄρκτον· ἀπὸ δὲ Σαμαρείας πρὸς μεσημβρίαν.

(It seems to me that he was
one of the seven,
for he would not have gone toward
the south from Jerusalem, but
toward the north; but toward
the south from Samaria.)

(It seems to me that he received
this command while in Samaria,
for no one goes toward
the south from Jerusalem, but
toward the north; but toward
the south from Samaria.)

The rough text describes Philip as one of the seven (Ἐμοὶ δοκεῖ τῶν ἑπτὰ
οὗτος ἦν). To confirm that this was Philip the deacon, who was preaching
in Samaria, and not Philip the apostle, who was in Jerusalem, the smooth
recension substitutes ἐμοὶ δοκεῖ ταῦτα ὢν ἐν Σαμαρείᾳ προστάττεσθαι (It
seems to me that he received this command while in Samaria).

At other times the explanation amounts to a considerable expansion
peripheral to the point under discussion, as at the beginning of *Hom.* 26.1
(col. 197.32–40), immediately after the lemma (Acts 12.1–3):

Rough Recension	Smooth Recension
Κατ᾽ ἐκεῖνον τὸν καιρόν, φησίν. Πάντως τὸν ἐφεξῆς.	Ποῖον ἐκεῖνον λέγει καιρόν; Πάντως τὸν ἐφεξῆς. Ἀλλ᾽ ἐνταῦθα μὲν οὕτως, ἀλλαχοῦ δὲ ἑτέρως. Ὅταν γὰρ ὁ Ματθαῖος λέγη· Ἐν ταῖς ἡμέραις ἐκείναις παραγίνεται Ἰωάννης κηρύσσων, οὐ τὰς ἐφεξῆς ἡμέρας δηλῶν λέγει, ἀλλ᾽ ἐκείνας, ἐν αἷς ἔμελλε γίνεσθαι ἅπερ
Ἔθος γὰρ τοῦτο τῇ Γραφῇ.	διηγεῖται. Ἔθος γὰρ τῇ Γραφῇ τούτω κεχρῆσθαι τῷ τρόπῳ, καὶ ποτὲ μὲν τὰ ἑξῆς συμβαίνοντα ἀκολούθως ἐκτιθέναι, ποτὲ δὲ τὰ ὕστερον συμβαίνειν μέλλοντα ὡς ἐφεξῆς ἀπαγγέλλειν.

("At that time," it says.
Obviously, the time
immediately following.

(What does he mean by
"that time?"
Obviously, the time
immediately following.
But here it is meant in one way,
but elsewhere in another way.
For when Matthew says, "In those
days John appeared preaching," he
does not mean to signify the days
immediately following, but those
in which what he narrates would
take place.

For this is the custom of Scripture.)	For it is the custom of Scripture to use this turn of speech, sometimes to set forth things that happen immediately and sometimes to narrate things that would happen later as if immediately following.)

This digression on the possible meanings of κατ᾽ ἐκεῖνον τὸν καιρόν in the NT emphasizes that Herod Agrippa's persecution of the Christians and his subsequent death happened just after Barnabas and Saul were sent on their relief mission to Jerusalem (Acts 11.27–30). Thus, it insists that the phrase here indicates immediate succession while acknowledging that elsewhere it need not always signify that events contiguous in the written narrative occurred one right after the other.

6. Very often the smooth recension tries to enhance the person and role of characters in the story. An example is found at the beginning of *Hom.* 20.1 (col. 157.46–49) at the first mention of the Damascus disciple Ananias. Here Chrysostom is commenting on Acts 9.10–12:

Rough Recension	Smooth Recension
Ὅτι οὐ τῶν σφόδρα ἐπισήμων ἦν δῆλον.	Ὅτι δὲ καὶ ὁ Ἀνανίας τῶν σφόδρα ἐπισήμων ἦν, δῆλον ἐξ ὧν ἐμφανίζεται καὶ λέγει πρὸς αὐτόν, καὶ ἐξ ὧν πάλιν αὐτὸς ἀποκρίνεται, λέγων· Κύριε, ἀκήκοα.
(It is clear that he was not a very distinguished person.)	(But that Ananias was a very distinguished person is clear both because he [the Lord] appears and speaks to him and because he himself says in reply, "Lord, I have heard.")

The smooth recension here turns the statement around to mean quite the opposite of what is found in the rough recension. Then, when Chrysostom comes back to Ananias early in *Hom.* 22.1 (col. 171.37–40), the editor again omits reference to the Damascene's insignificance:

Rough Recension	Smooth Recension
Ὅτε Παῦλον προσαχθῆναι ἔδει,	Ὅτε οὖν Παῦλον προσαχθῆναι ἔδει,
οὐδαμοῦ ἄγγελος, ἀλλ᾽ αὐτὸς ὁ	οὐδαμοῦ ἄγγελος, ἀλλ᾽ αὐτὸς ὁ
Κύριος· καὶ οὐ πέμπει αὐτὸν	Κύριος φαίνεται· οὐδὲ πέμπει αὐτὸν
πρὸς μέγαν τινὰ	πρὸς ἕνα τινὰ τῶν δώδεκα,
ἀλλὰ πρὸς εὐτελῆ.	ἀλλὰ πρὸς Ἀνανίαν.
(When Paul was to be brought in,	(When Paul was to be brought in,
there was no angel, but the Lord	there was no angel, but the Lord
himself, and he did not	himself appeared, and he did not
send him to some great person	send him to one of the twelve,
but to an ordinary one.)	but to Ananias.)

Perhaps this shows that the editor of the smooth recension was sophisticated and careful enough to remember changes he had already introduced into preceding homilies.

7. On the other hand, the smooth recension sometimes removes an apparently inappropriate or unseemly detail. An example of this is found toward the beginning of *Hom.* 35.1 (col. 253.5–8) in reference to Lydia, the cloth merchant of Acts 16.13–15:

Rough Recension	Smooth Recension
Γυνὴ καὶ ταπεινὴ αὕτη, καὶ δῆλον	Γυνὴ καὶ ταπεινὴ αὕτη, καὶ δῆλον
ἀπὸ τῆς τέχνης·	ἀπὸ τῆς τέχνης·
ἀλλ᾽ ὅρα φιλόσοφον γυναῖκα.	ἀλλ᾽ ὅρα τὸ φιλόσοφον αὐτῆς.
Πρῶτον μὲν αὐτῇ ἐμαρτύρησεν	Πρῶτον μὲν γὰρ αὐτῇ ἐμαρτύρησε
τὸ τὸν Θεὸν καλέσαι αὐτήν.	τοῦτο, τὸ σέβεσθαι τὸν Θεόν, ἔπειτα
	τὸ καλέσαι τοὺς ἀποστόλους αὐτήν.
(A woman, and one of low status,	(A woman, and one of low status,
as is clear from her trade. But	as is clear from her trade. But
observe a cultured woman. First,	observe her culture. First, this
God's calling her testifies to her.)	testifies to her, revering God,
	then that the apostles called her.)

Here the smooth recension changes the description φιλόσοφον γυναῖκα (a cultured woman) to τὸ φιλόσοφον αὐτῆς (her culture) and then considerably diminishes the following commendation. Although Chrysostom was heir to a tradition in which women were generally held in lower estimation within the Christian community (*cf.* esp. 1Cor. 11.3–16 and 1Tim. 2.11f.), here he does accord Lydia the accolade of being a cultured woman called by God, an accolade that the medieval editor reduced to her revering God and being called by the apostles.

8. Countless other examples fall under the general heading of the perennial tendency of editors and scribes to try to improve the style of the author. Sometimes it is simply an attempt to smooth out the style. An example may be found toward the end of *Hom.* 18.4 (col. 147.11–14), where, in an ethical application of Peter's rebuke of Simon Magus (Acts 8.14–25), Chrysostom offers advice to the wealthy on the proper use of money for spiritual purposes:

Rough Recension	Smooth Recension
Διὸ παρακαλῶ καὶ ἀντιβολῶ καὶ χάριν αἰτῶ, καὶ νόμον τίθημι, ὥστε μηδένα ὀφθῆναι ἔρημον ἐκκλησίας χωρίον ἔχοντα.	Διὸ παρακαλῶ καὶ ἀντιβολῶ καὶ χάριν αἰτῶ, μᾶλλον δὲ καὶ νόμον τίθημι, ὥστε μηδένα ὀφθῆναι ἔρημον ἐκκλησίας χωρίον ἔχοντα.
(I beg and implore, and ask as a favor, and lay down a law, that no one who has landed property should lack a church.)	(I beg and implore and ask as a favor, or rather even lay down a law, that no one who has landed property should lack a church.)

Here the editor calls attention to the climactic tetracolon (παρακαλῶ = four syllables; ἀντιβολῶ = four syllables; χάριν αἰτῶ = four syllables; νόμον τίθημι = five syllables) by inserting μᾶλλον δὲ (or rather) before the last member of the series.

Sometimes the smooth recension provides a didactic element, as toward the beginning of *Hom.* 7.1 (col. 63.52f.). Chrysostom is commenting on Acts 2.37, where repentant Jews ask Peter what they must do to atone for the crucifixion of the Messiah.

Rough Recension	Smooth Recension
καὶ οὐδὲ ἐλπίδα σωτηρίας ἔχοντας. Οὐ γὰρ εἶπον· Πῶς σωθῶμεν; ἀλλὰ, Τί ποιήσομεν; (and having no hope of salvation.	καὶ οὐδὲ ἐλπίδα σωτηρίας ἔχοντας. Καὶ ὅρα. Οὐκ εἶπον· Πῶς σωθῶμεν; ἀλλὰ, Τί ποιήσωμεν; (and having no hope of salvation. Now mark this well!
For they did not say, "How can we be saved?" but "What shall we do?")	They did not say, "How can we be saved?" but "What are we to do?")

Sometimes the smooth recension omits a phrase that the editor may have found somewhat indelicate, as in *Hom.* 11.2 (col. 95.26–28), the comment on Acts 4.24, where the early Christian community raise their voices to God with one accord:

Rough Recension	Smooth Recension
Ὅρα πῶς οὐδὲν περιττόν φησιν, οὐδὲν γραῶδες καὶ μυθῶδες, ἀλλὰ περὶ τῆς δυνάμεως αὐτοῦ διαλέγονται.	Ὅρα πῶς οὐδὲν περιττόν, ἀλλὰ περὶ τῆς δυνάμεως αὐτοῦ διαλέγονται μόνον.
(Observe how it says nothing superfluous, no old wives' tales or stories, but they discourse about his power.)	(Observe how they say nothing superfluous, but only discourse about his power.)

Here the smooth recension omits φησιν (it says) because the editor may not have understood how this singular verb fitted the context of the group of disciples. The following γραῶδες καὶ μυθῶδες (old wives' tales and stories) may have proved offensive. This phrase, which normally refers to superstition, must be meant to qualify the sort of prayers that are not heard. The editor may have thought it improper to imagine even the possibility that the disciples might utter anything γραῶδες καὶ μυθῶδες.

I hope that these examples serve to illustrate the types of scribal revision found in Chrysostom's *Homilies on the Acts of the Apostles*. The difference between the primitive text and that of existing editions is as much as 17 percent in some homilies. This indicates clearly the need for a new critical edition based on the rough recension of these homilies.

FIFTEEN

Cassiodorus Teaches Logic through the Psalms

———————— ✢ ————————

P. G. Walsh

A S IS WELL KNOWN, the Latin Fathers were sharply divided in their attitudes toward the secular literatures of Greece and Rome. Many prided themselves on their knowledge of the pagan classics, but others sought to exclude them from their reading, for they believed that the sacred texts contained all that was necessary for the education of a Christian. Boethius in sixth-century Italy was an outstanding representative of the first group; he was such a committed student of Greek philosophy that he sought to reconcile the doctrines of Plato with those of Aristotle, and as he awaited execution, he sought the comfort of philosophy rather than that of theology. At first sight, his contemporary Cassiodorus seems equally concerned to recommend pagan learning: though the first book of his *Institutiones,* composed in his newly established monastery at Scyllacium, is devoted to guidance on sacred literature and recommends for study patristic commentaries on the Bible and other Christian texts, the second book is a systematic review of the seven liberal arts as the basis of education and incorporates reading lists of secular authors. This second book, however, is in reality ancillary to the first. Cassiodorus is suggesting that a preliminary mastery of both the *trivium* of grammar, rhetoric, and logic/dialectic and the *quadrivium* of geometry, arithmetic, music, and astronomy, is necessary to acquire a fuller understanding of the sacred texts. Thus, the study of Scripture will provide simultaneously a theological formation and a literary education based on the seven liberal arts.[1]

1. For the general background to the writings of Cassiodorus, *v.* esp. J.J. O'Donnell, *Cas-*

Among the books of the Bible, the Psalter held a distinctive place as the recommended starting point for those engaged in study of the Christian dispensation. When, about 555, Cassiodorus composed his *Institutiones* for the course of study in his newly founded monastery, he produced virtually simultaneously a revised version of his *Expositio Psalmorum.* There is a close connection between the two works, for Cassiodorus seeks to demonstrate that the psalms are not merely a prophetic anticipation of the coming of Christ and of the foundation of the Church but also a collection of sacred poems that can inculcate an understanding of the seven liberal arts and thereby provide an *enkuklios paideia* that will absolve the student from the need to have recourse to secular literature to further his education.[2] At the close of his lengthy treatise he specifically claims that the psalms contain a wealth of examples to illustrate the ramifications of the liberal arts (*Exp. Ps.* 150.6).

The study of logic held a prominent place in the secular education of the ancient world, especially as many of its precepts were incorporated into the manuals of rhetoric for the benefit of aspiring orators. Aristotle was acknowledged as the founding father of logic. His was the first and most important discussion of the syllogism, which survived as logic's most powerful tool throughout the Middle Ages. Though Cassiodorus had resided for some years at Constantinople, he seems never to have acquired the fluency in the Greek language such as would have permitted him comfortably to consult Aristotle's *Analytics* and *Topics* in the original. Fortunately, however, these works had fathered an enormous progeny of works in Latin; Cassiodorus, if his own writings are a guide, obtained his knowledge of Aristotelian theory largely from these derivative successors. Cicero's *Topica* was one obvious quarry. In his *Institutiones,* Cassiodorus himself recommended Marius Victorinus, the celebrated fourth-century convert from Neoplatonism, as an authority on the syllogism, and also the *Peri Hermeneias* of Apuleius. Boethius had translated Aristotle's *Prior Analytics,* so that this seminal work was available in Latin. Also available were the discussions of the rhetoricians, amongst whom Quintilian was especially influential.[3]

---

siodorus (Berkeley/Los Angeles 1979); for the *Institutiones,* L.W. Jones, *An Introduction to the Divine and Human Readings by Cassiodorus Senator* (New York 1966).

2. Citations of the *Exp. Ps.* will follow, with slight revision, M. Adriaen, *Magni Aurelii Cassiodori Expositio psalmorum* (Turnhout 1958) = *CChr.SL,* voll. 97f. For Cassiodorus' exploitation of the psalms for the inculcation of the seven liberal arts, *v.* R. Schlieben, *Cassiodors Psalmenexegese* (Göppingen 1979) and the introduction to *Cassiodorus: Explanation of the Psalms,* translated and annotated by P.G. Walsh, 3 voll. (New York/Mahwah, N.J. 1990–91) = *ACW,* voll. 51–53. For the clarity of this discussion, I have, on occasion, slightly modified my translation of the *Exp. Ps.*

3. Cassiodorus used Marius Victorinus' commentary on Cicero's *Topica.* For his recom-

The Categorical Syllogism

What Cassiodorus calls "the purest and chief of syllogisms" (*purissimus et princeps omnium syllogismorum, Exp. Ps.* 150.6) is the categorical, an affirmation in syllogistic form. At the very outset of his work, in his commentary on Psalm 1, he is concerned to teach its value and the nature of its presentation. "It is the reasoning," he writes, "by which from certain premises certain other conclusions necessarily follow because of those premises. It is composed of two propositions and a conclusion" (*Categoricus itaque syllogismus est ... ratio, in qua positis quibusdam, alia quaedam ex necessitate ueniunt per ea quae posita sunt. Iste ex duabus propositionibus et conclusione formatur*). He then exploits the opening words of Psalm 1 to provide a striking example: (1) *Beatus uir cuius uoluntas in lege Domini est.* (2) *Nullus cuius uoluntas in lege Domini est, abiit in consilio impiorum.* (3) *Nullus igitur beatus uir abiit in consilio impiorum.* He adds: "Serious students among you will find this feature in various places. I have thought it worthy of less frequent mention because ... I have many topics to broach" (*Hoc quidem in diuersis locis diligens tibi perscrutator inuenies, quod nos rarius ponendum esse perspeximus, quoniam nobis ... multa dicenda sunt, Exp. Ps.* 1.2). In spite of this disavowal, we find him underlining this lesson on the categorical syllogism a little later with a further example, this time from Psalm 30: (1) *Ego in Domino speraui.* (2) *Omnis sperans in Domino exsultabit et laetabitur in misericordia eius.* (3) *Ego igitur exsultabo, et laetabor in misericordia eius.* "It is indeed a fine technique," he comments, "to knit together in small compass what cannot be prised apart by any opposition" (*Pulchrum plane dicendi genus in breuitate complecti, quod nulla possit aduersitate dirumpi, Exp. Ps.* 30.8). In his commentary on the next psalm, he offers yet a further example, so that "like runaway slaves the rules for dialectic can be put to some use for the divine Scriptures" (*ut artis dialecticae regulae in quoddam diuinarum scripturarum seruitium, quasi fugacia mancipia reuocentur, Exp. Ps.* 31.11). The image of the runaway slaves seems extraordinary at first sight, until we remember that, like many earlier Christian apologists, Cassiodorus is claiming that all the techniques of rhetoric and dialectic appeared in works of Hebraic eloquence, that is, in the sacred Scriptures, before they were adopted by the Greek writers of secular literature.[4] Having cited this further example—(1) *Omnis iustus*

---

mendation of Marius Victorinus, *v. Inst.* 2.3.18; of Apuleius, *Inst.* 2.3.12, 18. For Cassiodorus' acquaintance with Quintilian and other rhetoricians, *v.* Walsh (note 2 above), *ACW,* vol. 51, p. 16.

4. At *Exp. Ps.* 15 *pf.* he quotes Aug., *Doc. christ.* 3.40 in support of this claim.

laetatur in Domino; (2) *Omnis qui laetatur in Domino recto corde est;* (3) *Omnis igitur iustus recto corde est*—he once again claims that the diligent reader can find numerous other examples in the psalms. Thus, "the divine Scriptures undoubtedly contain this facet of the arts of logic, in effect if not in form" (*inter logicas artes hanc quoque partem scripturas diuinas, etsi non specie, uirtute tamen procul dubio continere, Exp. Ps.* 31.11).

From this point onward, Cassiodorus contents himself with drawing attention to numerous similar examples of the categorical syllogism without adding further instructive comment; this is the experienced pedagogue's technique of inculcation by regular repetition. Virtually all the passages he instances occur at the initial verses, and thus reveal his eagerness to teach this lesson in logic before proceeding to the detailed interpretation of each psalm.[5] Most strikingly of all, he closes his entire commentary on the one hundred and fifty psalms by drawing attention to a final example of the categorical syllogism. "Just as we began in Psalm 1," he states "with mention of syllogisms, so we must end with a similar conclusion. We fittingly began with a categorical syllogism, the purest and chief of all syllogisms, so we now also complete our work with one" (*Nam commemoratio syllogismorum, sicut in primo psalmo coepta est, parili nobis fine claudatur. A categorico siquidem, qui est purissimus et princeps omnium syllogismorum, dedimus prout oportebat initium: nunc etiam opus nostrum in ipso concludimus*). He then assembles the syllogism: (1) *Dominum laudet omnis spiritus.* (2) *Quem debet laudare omnis spiritus, Deus uerus est.* (3) *Dominus igitur Deus uerus est* (*Exp. Ps.* 150.6). It will not escape the reader's notice that this climax to the instruction on the categorical syllogism demonstrates the importance of the art of logic in the broader aim of catechetical instruction.

The Enthymeme

A second type of syllogism in which Cassiodorus instructs his readers through the psalms is the enthymematic. Aristotle in his *Analytics* had defined the enthymeme as "a syllogism starting from probabilities" (Ἐνθύμημα δέ ἐστὶ συλλογισμὸς ἐξ εἰκότων, *Apr.* 2.27 [70a]); as such it is frequently contrasted with the categorical and labelled an imperfect syllogism. Cassiodorus aligns his view of the enthymeme with that of Quintilian, who remarks: "Some . . . call it a rhetorical syllogism, others an incomplete syllogism, because its parts are not so clearly defined or of the same number as those of the regular syllogism, since such precision is not specially

5. *V. Exp. Ps.* 36.1, 45.2, 52.2, 90.1, 120.2. He cites other examples at 60.5, 96.10.

required by the orator" (*hunc alii rhetoricum syllogismum, alii inperfectum syllogismum vocaverunt, quia nec distinctis nec totidem partibus concluderetur: quod sane non utique ab oratore desideratur, Inst. or. 5.10.3).*[6]

Cassiodorus offers half a dozen examples of the enthymeme to ensure that this distinction is thoroughly grasped. In his first example, he renders *enthymema* with the Latin term *mentis conceptio* (*Exp. Ps.* 20.8). Cassiodorus defines it as a syllogism consisting of one proposition only, followed by a conclusion: (1) *Omnis sperans in Domino exsultabit et laetabitur in misericordia eius;* (2) *ego igitur exsultabo et laetabor in misericordia eius* (*Exp. Ps.* 20.8). Because of this association with orators, the enthymeme is described by Quintilian as "the syllogism of oratory" (*rhetoricus syllogismus, Inst. or.* 9.4.57). Cassiodorus similarly labels it a rhetorical syllogism (*enthymematicus, id est rhetoricus syllogismus, Exp. Ps.* 80.3), as in this example: (1) Sumite psalmum et date tympanum; (2) Canite initio mensis tuba. It is by no means clear how the second clause can be considered a conclusion drawn from the first, until Cassiodorus explains: "It was enjoined on Israel to sing also of the judgment before the God of Jacob, and therefore they must sound forth on the trumpet at the beginning of the month" (*Canere praeceptum est in Israel, et iudicium Deo Iacob: cantandum est igitur in initio mensis tuba, Exp. Ps.* 80.3f.).

A further example of such a logical consequence to an initial proposition is more compressed and consists of a series of rhetorical questions: Qui plantauit aurem, non audiet? aut qui finxit oculum, non considerat? Qui corripit gentes, non arguet? qui docet hominem scientiam? "The dialecticians," he comments, "decided to call these brief and exceedingly clear modes of argument *enthymemata* or mental conceptions. . . . Here there is clearly a syllogism consisting of a proposition and conclusion set in opposition to each other" (*Quas argumentationes breues atque lucidissimas enthymemata, id est mentis conceptiones dialectici appellare uoluerunt. . . . Hic autem syllogismus constat ex propositione et conclusione, sibi tamen utrisque contrariis, Exp. Ps.* 93.9f). Thus Cassiodorus is claiming that "he that planted the ear" is set against the ensuing question, so that each brief rhetorical question constitutes an enthymeme.

He offers some examples in which the conclusion is implicit rather than explicit: (1) Redemptionem misit populo suo; mandauit in aeternum testamentum suum. Therefore, (2) Sanctum . . . et terribile nomen eius

---

6. W.D. Ross, *Aristotelis Analytica priora et posteriora* (Oxford 1964). All citations of Quintilian follow L. Radermacher and V. Buchheit, *M. Fabi Quintiliani Institutionis oratoriae libri XII,* 2 voll. (Leipzig 1959). I follow H.E. Butler's translation in *The Institutio oratoria of Quintilian,* vol. 2 (Cambridge, Mass./London 1921).

(*Exp. Ps.* 110.9). And again, he claims for the composer of the psalms: "His proposition is" (*Proponit enim*): (1) *Domine, ego clamaui ad te,* "and the conclusion therefore follows" (*sequitur conclusio*): (2) *exaudi . . . me.* "In this way," he concludes, "the force of the enthymematic syllogism is achieved" (*Sic uirtus illa enthymematici syllogismi . . . peracta est, Exp. Ps.* 140.1).

The *Epichirema*

A third type of syllogism in which Cassiodorus seeks to indoctrinate his monks, and, indeed, the wider world outside, is the *epichirema*, defined by Aristotle as a dialectical inference as opposed to a demonstrative syllogism (*Top.* 8.11 [162a]). Quintilian uses the word interchangeably with enthymeme (*Inst. or.* 5.14.14 and 27; *cf.* 5.10.4). It might therefore be suggested that neither is a syllogism proper, but Quintilian argues that there is no difference between the syllogism and the *epichirema*, except that the syllogism deals with true statements, whereas the *epichirema* presents statements that are plausible but not certain. Quintilian's discussion is of course set within the context of rhetorical theory: he demands a sequence of premise, reason or proof of that premise, and conclusion (*Inst. or.* 5.14.5–13). Cassiodorus offers three examples of this type. That adapted from Psalm 38 is the most extensive: (1) *Quamquam in imagine Dei ambulet homo, tamen uane conturbabitur.* This is glossed with the explanation that men preoccupied with temporal aspirations lose their integrity of mind. (2) *et nunc quae est exspectatio mea? nonne Dominus? et cetera.* [*i.e.: Ab omnibus iniquitatibus meis eripe me; opprobrium insipienti dedisti me. . . . Amoue a me plagas tuas. . . . In increpationibus propter iniquitatem corripuisti hominem*]. This allegedly minor proposition extends over four verses. But Cassiodorus reassures us about its length by stating that secular teachers later shortened such premises. He is again implicitly making the point that all the techniques of logic and rhetoric existed in sacred literature before the secular teachers appropriated them. (3) *uerumtamen uane conturbabitur omnis homo uiuens.* Thus what Cassiodorus calls the minor proposition (*assumptio*) proves the conclusion, which was initially asserted in the major premise (*Exp. Ps.* 38.12).

A regular feature of the *epichirema* as expounded by Cassiodorus is proof by example. Such exemplification is illustrated by his citation of the exordium of a celebrated psalm: (1) Dominus illuminatio mea et salus mea, quem timebo? Dominus defensor uitae meae, a quo trepidabo? (2) Dum appropiant super me nocentes, ut edant carnes meas. Qui tribulant me inimici mei, ipsi infirmati sunt et ceciderunt. Cassiodorus explains: "These three verses . . . are enclosed in the form of the great argument called by the Greeks *epichirema,* and by the Latins *exsecutiones* or *approbationes;* we employ this argument when we wish to prove a matter at issue by some example" (*Hos tres uersus paulo sollicitius audiamus, sunt enim magnae argumentationis formula comprehensi, quam Graeci epichirema, Latini exsecutiones uel approbationes uocare maluerunt. Hoc argumento utimur quoties rem de qua agitur per exemplum aliquod probare contendimus*). The premise contained in the initial statement, he continues, is then followed by the example that sustains it: there is no need for us to fear, because when wicked men sought to attack me, they were weakened and have fallen. "So the shape of the *epichirema,*" he concludes, "has been attained in small compass" (*Sic istius epichirematis breuiter forma perfecta est, Exp. Ps.* 26.1f.).

He reiterates this lesson later by a further example: (1) Noli aemulari inter malignantes, neque aemulatus fueris facientes iniquitatem. (2) Quoniam tamquam fenum uelociter arescent et sicut olera herbarum cito decident. Interestingly, Cassiodorus has just cited these verses as part of a categorical syllogism (*Exp. Ps.* 36.1), but, impressed by the image of the withering greenery, he now instances them as an example of the epichirema. "In these two verses that outstanding type of argument is used, which is called *epichirema,* or in Latin *exsecutio* or *argumentum,* which confirms by examples the validity of a doubtful case, for it is demonstrated that the wicked quickly fall by the examples cited of grass and herbs" (*In his duobus uersibus etiam illud argumentum declaratur eximium quod dicitur epichirema, latine exsecutio siue argumentum, quae rei dubiae fidem per exempla confirmat; ostensum est enim cito impios cadere per fenum et olera, Exp. Ps.* 36.2).

The Hypothetical Syllogism

The fourth type of syllogism that Cassiodorus repeatedly exemplifies is the hypothetical or conditional. Aristotle discussed it at length (*Apr.* 1.23 [40b–41b], 1.44 [50a]), and Cassiodorus recommends scrutiny of Marius Victorinus (*Inst.* 2.3.18). In his initial example, Cassiodorus goes to great lengths to explain its nature. "A hypothetical or conditional syllogism makes an inference from one or more hypothetical propositions, and deduces a conclusion. The proposition of the syllogism in the present passage is like this" (*Hypotheticus autem, id est conditionalis syllogismus est, qui ex conditionali aut conditionalibus propositionibus accipiens assumptionem, colligit conclusionem. Cuius propositio talis est, quantum ad istam pertinet dictionem*): Domine Deus meus, si feci istud, si est iniquitas in manibus meis, si reddidi retribuentibus mihi mala, decidam merito ab inimicis meis inanis. Persequatur inimicus animam meam et comprehendat eam, et conculcet in terra uitam meam et gloriam meam in puluerem deducat. Cassiodorus continues: "According to the rules of the dialecticians, the reciprocal formulation is like this" (*Istius autem propositionis secundum regulas dialecticorum reciprocatio talis est*): (1) *si non* decidam merito ab inimicis meis inanis, *si non* persequatur inimicus animam meam, et comprehendat eam, *si non* conculcet in terra uitam meam, *si non* gloriam meam in puluerem deducat, Domine Deus meus, *non* feci istud, *non* est iniquitas in manibus meis, *non* reddidi retribuentibus mihi mala. "The inference from this reciprocal statement develops like this" (*Cuius reciprocationis fit talis assumptio*): (2) *attamen non* decidam merito ab inimicis meis inanis, *attamen non* persequetur inimicus animam meam et comprehendet eam, *non* conculcabit in terra uitam meam; *non* gloriam meam in puluerem deducet. "And the conclusion drawn from this inference is" (*Hanc uero assumptionem sequitur ista conclusio*): (3) *Igitur, Domine Deus meus, non feci istud, non est iniquitas in manibus meis, non reddidi retribuentibus mihi mala* (*Exp. Ps.* 7.6).

Having offered this detailed rationale of the hypothetical syllogism, Cassiodorus is later content to offer further examples with brief comment, as at the beginning of Psalm 40, which he adapts in this formulation: (1) *Si omnis* beatus intellegit super egenum et pauperem, in die mala liberabit eum Dominus. (2) *Attamen omnis* beatus intellegit super egenum et pauperem. (3) In die *igitur* mala liberabit eum Dominus. "The hypothetical or conditional syllogism," he adds, "is that which makes an absolute assumption from conditional propositions and infers the conclusion" (*Hypotheticus autem, id est, conditionalis syllogismus est, qui ex conditionalibus propositionibus habens absolutam assumptionem, colligit conclusionem, Exp. Ps.* 40.2). And again at Psalm 62: "In these two verses a hypothetical syllogism reveals itself to us in this way" (*In isto et in inferiore versu, isto modo hypotheticus nobis syllogismus apparet*): (1) Si memor fui tui super stratum meum, et in matutinis meditabor in te: . . . *quia factus es adiutor meus et in velamento alarum tuarum exsultabo.* (2) *Attamen memor fui tui super stratum meum et in matutinis meditabor in te, quia factus es adiutor meus.* (3) *In uelamento igitur alarum tuarum exsultabo* (*Exp. Ps.* 62.7f.).

Cassiodorus offers three further examples: in his flowery language, he calls the first "the comely face of the hypothetical syllogism," which "smiles on us" (*Hic iterum hypothetici syllogismi facies nobis decora subridet, Exp.*

Ps. 70.1): (1) *Si* Deus, in te speraui, Domine, non confundar in aeternum: (2) *attamen, Deus, in te speraui.* (3) *non confundar igitur in aeternum.* The other examples are similarly self-explanatory: (1) *Si iustus perambulat in innocentia cordis in medio domus Domini, non proponit ante oculos suos rem malam;* (2) *attamen iustus perambulat in innocentia cordis in medio domus Domini;* (3) *non proponit igitur ante oculos suos rem malam* (*Exp. Ps.* 100.2). And again: (1) *Si non est exaltatum cor meum, neque elati sunt oculi mei, a superbia scilicet reddor alienus;* (2) *attamen non est exaltatum cor meum, neque elati sunt oculi mei:* (3) *a superbia igitur reddor alienus* (*Exp. Ps.* 130.1).

Conclusion

These passages denote the characteristic ways in which Cassiodorus exploits the psalms to teach the student the nature of Aristotelian syllogisms. They constitute only a fraction of his instruction in the niceties of a literary education. He is particularly anxious to inculcate the varieties of *argumenta* or proofs and of definitions and thereby to give instruction in the Aristotelian categories. He frequently halts his explanations of Scripture to explain, often fancifully, the etymologies of words. He is equally intent on explaining and illustrating every possible figure of speech and thought. For aspiring rhetoricians he supplies examples of the three genres of speeches, the deliberative, the judicial, and the demonstrative. In short, he presents the psalms as an inexhaustible source of examples for teaching the *trivium* and, to a lesser degree, the *quadrivium*. In this way he offers the most detailed model of how a Christian text might provide opportunities for a literary education similar to that based on the reading of secular texts.

SIXTEEN

Erasmus and Ancient Christian Writers

The Search for Authenticity

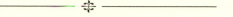

Robert Sider

ERASMUS WAS AMONG the foremost of the Renaissance humanists who devoted themselves to the task of bringing to light the literary works of antiquity. Jacques Chomarat catalogues under forty-nine entries the authors and works, both classical and patristic, in editing which Erasmus played some part.[1] If in this list one counts re-editions, one finds somewhat more than eighty publications, nearly half of them editions of early Christian authors; these include the *editiones principes* of Arnobius Minor, Basil, and Irenaeus. Whereas editions of classical authors predominated in Erasmus' work before 1520, from 1520 until his death in 1536 editions of early Christian writers outnumbered those of classical authors by more than two to one.

In the letters that preface the various editions, Erasmus clarifies for us some of the assumptions that guided him as an editor. Because an edition of an ancient literary work was in some sense a restoration of antiquity (*cf.* Allen *Ep.* 919, ll. 23–24),[2] its authenticity was a matter of primary consider-

---

1. J. Chomarat, *Grammaire et rhétorique chez Erasme* (Paris 1981) 2 voll.; *v.* vol. 1, pp. 452–76. Chomarat's list includes also the two later authors Haymo and Valla.

2. I use the following abbreviations in citing the works of Erasmus:

Allen = P.S. Allen, H.M. Allen, and H.W. Garrod, *Opus epistolarum Des. Erasmi Roterodami*, 11 voll. (Oxford 1906–47). Vol. 12, *Indices*, ed. B. Flower and E. Rosenbaum (Oxford 1958).

ASD = *Opera omnia Desiderii Erasmi Roterodami* (Amsterdam 1969–)

CWE = *Collected Works of Erasmus* (Toronto 1974–) *(continued on next page)*

ation. It was the editor's task to establish the authorship of a work, to distinguish the genuine from the spurious. It was also his task to purge the text of the accretions of scribes and other meddlers. Basil or Jerome "restored" meant that the reader had before him what in fact these authors had written.[3]

From the prefaces we can also learn much about Erasmus' methods of establishing authenticity. In determining attribution an author's style was a key indicator, but other factors were not to be overlooked: the title page might contain clues pointing to a spurious work; manifest anachronisms betrayed an inauthentic hand, as did obvious incongruencies with facts known about an author's historical context. Erasmus relied heavily on bibliographies from antiquity, above all Jerome's *De viris illustribus* and its sequel by Gennadius. An attribution not mentioned in one of these was at once suspicious. Authenticity, moreover, demanded more than correct attribution; methods had to be developed to establish the original text as well. In determining the original text, style was again important, but also the sense of what the passage, what the argument, required. Thus conjecture was of paramount importance: "No copy is so badly corrupted," said Erasmus, "that skilful divination cannot restore a great deal" (*Nullum autem tam deprauatum exemplar vnde solers coniectator non multa queat restituere*, Allen *Ep.* 919, ll. 57f.; *cf.* 1738, ll. 115f.). Yet in spite of his confidence in conjecture, Erasmus eagerly sought manuscripts. Indeed the search for manuscripts was a *venatio* that pleased him as much as a hunt in the forest pleased others (Allen *Ep.* 1790, ll. 1–3).[4]

While Erasmus saw the search for authenticity as a prerequisite to the publication of the works of the Fathers, the authenticity of the ancient writers acquired a special importance in the five editions of his New Testament.[5] For his editions of the New Testament, Erasmus published a

LB = *Desiderii Erasmi Roterodami opera omnia*, ed J. Leclerc, 10 vols. (*Lugduni Batavorum* = Leiden 1703–6; rpt. 1961–62). Unless otherwise indicated, the translations are my own.

3. The translation is that of R.A.B. Mynors, *CWE*, vol. 6 (1982). Erasmus frequently uses *restituere* in the sense of restoring the works of antiquity; *cf.* Allen *Ep.* 396, ll. 270f., 292f., 369–72, and *Ep.* 919, ll. 23–58. V. D.F.S. Thomson, "Erasmus and Textual Scholarship in the Light of Sixteenth-Century Practice," in J. Sperna Weiland and W.T.M. Frijhoff, *Erasmus of Rotterdam: The Man and the Scholar* (Leiden 1988), p. 158.

4. Erasmus' textual criticism is generally regarded today as inadequate, but for Erasmus as a textual critic v. J.H. Bentley, *Humanists and Holy Writ: New Testament Scholarship in the Renaissance* (Princeton, N.J. 1983), pp. 137–61; Chomarat (note 1 above), pp. 480–507; Thomson (note 3 above), pp. 158–71.

5. The editions were published in 1516, 1519, 1522, 1527, and 1535. When these dates are in italics, they mean the editions of 1516, etc.

Greek text from the Byzantine manuscript tradition in columns parallel to his own Latin translation, which was based on the Vulgate but radically modified to correspond to the Greek text. He justified his text and translation in notes (the *Annotations*) that became increasingly elaborate in each edition and, from the second edition on, required a separate volume. If he based his text in the first instance on the biblical manuscripts available to him, he found in the ancient Christian writers his chief supporting witnesses. His annotations, therefore, appeal extensively to the textual readings of Scripture to be found in patristic authors. Moreover, these authors constituted witnesses to an earlier understanding of biblical semantics. Finally, their authority as arbiters in matters of theological and ecclesiastical debate was recognized virtually everywhere; Erasmus, ever a reformer at heart, evoked their authority for his own contributions to the debates of the time. In these circumstances, the authority of the Fathers rested directly upon the authenticity of the texts. As we shall see, a special problem therefore emerged in the case of some authors, especially the earliest Christians, whose texts Erasmus did not have, or had only second hand, or whose words were known only through the reports of others. If reliability was the first *desideratum* in the appeal to such writers, authorial integrity might well be germane to their reliability and their authority.

In what follows I wish to bring together by way of quotation, discussion, or reference a dossier of passages that illustrate and, I trust, illuminate Erasmus' search for authenticity in his *Annotations* on the New Testament. In general we shall find expressed here the same fundamental assumptions intimated in his editions of the Fathers. It will be useful, however, to trace the search through his New Testament scholarship, first to isolate, systematize, and so make available both the fleeting notes and the more extensive discussions on authenticity that may otherwise remain obscure as incidental to the larger purpose of the *Annotations*. In doing so, we shall be able, secondly, to establish a list of the works whose authenticity appeared to be in doubt—at least in Erasmus' New Testament scholarship—for I include in this dossier all those writers and writings of the patristic period about which a question of authenticity arises in the *Annotations*. Finally, this dossier will illustrate how Erasmus articulated the problems of authenticity and will indicate the methods he used to solve them. I deem it appropriate to follow on this occasion the sequence of writers established in the four volumes of Johannes Quasten's *Patrology*. These volumes will therefore also define the patristic period for us.

The Clementine Writings

Erasmus knew well the translation of the Clementine *Recognitions* that Rufinus had made for Gaudentius, bishop of Brescia (*LB* 6, 574F; *cf. CWE* 56, p. 95).[6] In a preface to a translation of some *Lucubrations* by Athanasius, he notes the recent edition of the *Recognitions* published in Basel (1526) by Johannes Bebel (Allen *Ep.* 1790, ll. 73f.).[7] But he argues that the work is a forgery, and he bases his judgment simply on the trivial and fabulous character of the narrative. He mocks the credulity of those among the ancients who took the book seriously and contrasts the fictitious tales of the Clementine writings with the sober record of the book of Acts. He asserts that the tales found in the *Recognitions* are either composite— made up from things contained in Scripture—or entirely fictitious narratives drawing on scriptural sources (*LB* 6, 653D, 1068C, 433E).

Papias

We know Papias from later authors who have given us excerpts and reports of what he himself reported as having heard from the followers of the apostles. Erasmus understood that, in this case, the central question must be: To what extent did Papias report the authentic words of his teachers? Erasmus would have it both ways. He grants authenticity to the story of the woman taken in adultery not because it is found in the apocryphal writings (*cf.* below under "Apocrypha") but because Papias heard it from his own teacher (*LB* 6, 374E). Elsewhere, however, Erasmus believes that Papias misreported: Eusebius represents Papias as a man of small ability, who did not understand what he had heard; hence Papias "has provided many with a handle of error" (*unde et scriptis suis praebuerit multis ansam erroris, LB* 6, 433E–434A; 1056D–E).

---

6. Though Erasmus refers to the letters of Clement of Rome (*LB* 6, 1024E, and possibly 1068C), he seems to know of them only indirectly, especially through Jerome. While the spurious Latin Epistles to James have sometimes been called the Epistles of Clement, the Clementine Epistles themselves were not published until 1633, and until then were, according to J.B. Lightfoot, "a sealed book to the Western Church." *V. Apostolic Fathers*, 2nd ed., vol. 1, part 1 (London 1890): *S. Clement of Rome*, p. 146.

7. In fact, Jacques Lefèvre d'Étaples had published the pseudonymous Clementine writings including an *epistola Clementis* in 1504; *cf.* M. Schär *Das Nachleben des Origenes im Zeitalter des Humanismus* (Basel/Stuttgart 1979), note 59, p. 184, and E.F. Rice, "The Humanist Idea of Christian Antiquity: Lefèvre d'Étaples and his Circle," *StRen* 9 (1962), p. 135. But on the *epistola v.* note 6 above.

Hermas, *The Shepherd*

This work interests us only because Erasmus ridicules the credulity of Origen who attributed *The Shepherd* to the Hermas greeted in Rom. 16.14. He thus voices a certain self-confidence in his own commitment to the search for authenticity. Erasmus himself regarded it as apocryphal (*LB* 6, 653D; *cf. CWE* 56, p. 429).

The Apocrypha

Erasmus appears to have derived his knowledge of the Apocrypha from Origen, Eusebius, and Jerome.[8] He assumes that the Apocryphal Gospels were contemporary with the canonical Gospels, and while he rejects them as authoritative, he acknowledges that they may well contain authentic records such as the story of the woman caught in adultery (*LB* 6, 373F–374E). Elsewhere, Erasmus follows Jerome in giving them the authority only of pagan writings; like pagan writings they are useful for admonition, clarification, exhortation, but we are not to look to them for authentic oracles of prophecy (*LB* 6, 139F).

Dionysius of Corinth

I introduce Dionysius of Corinth primarily because Erasmus cites him as a witness in an important debate over the attribution of works that lead us beyond the period of this study to ps.-Dionysius, for Erasmus does not dispute the authenticity of the works of Dionysius of Corinth cited by Eusebius (*H. E.* 4.23). Erasmus distinguishes four men of the patristic period

---

8. In the *Annotations*, Erasmus mentions as apocryphal the *Gospel of the Nazarenes, Gospel of Thomas, Gospel of Matthias, Gospel according to the Egyptians, Gospel according to the Twelve, Gospel according to Nicodemus* (*LB* 6, 217B), and the *Gospel according to the Hebrews* (*LB* 6, 373F). Of these, the most frequently mentioned is the *Gospel of Nicodemus*. On these extracanonical works *v.* J.K. Elliott, *The Apocryphal New Testament: A Collection of Apocryphal Christian Literature in an English Translation* (Oxford 1993), pp. 3–16; for relationships among the *Gospel according to the Hebrews, the Gospel of the Nazarenes, and the Gospel of the Ebionites v. ib.*, pp. 3–6. Erasmus further mentions (*LB* 6, 139F–140F) the *Apocryphal Jeremiah or the Secrets of Jeremiah, the Book of Jamnes and Mambres,* and the *Apocrypha of Elijah (ex Heliae apocryphis),* this last described in his source, Or., on Mt. (*Com.* series 117, on 27.3–10), as the *Secrets of Elijah (in secretis Eliae prophetae; PG,* vol. 13, col. 1769C). For the apocryphal writings of Jeremiah *v.* C.A. Moore, "Jeremiah Additions To," *AncB.D,* vol. 3 (New York, *etc.* 1992), pp. 698–706. For the *Book of Jamnes and Mambres, v.* A. Pietersma, "Jannes and Jambres," *ib.,* pp. 639f.; for the *Apocalypse of Elijah,* O.S. Wintermute, "Elijah, Apocalypse Of," *ib.,* vol. 2 (New York, *etc.* 1992), pp. 466–69.

with the name of Dionysius: the Areopagite, the bishop of Corinth, the author of the Platonizing works *On Celestial Hierarchies* and *On the Divine Names,* and St. Denis, the martyr-hero and first bishop of Paris. Erasmus' efforts to distinguish Paul's convert in Athens from ps.-Dionysius aroused much opposition (*cf. Ep.* 1620, ll. 68–70 [*CWE* 11, p. 297, note 11]; *Decl. ad cen. tit.* 31, *LB* 9, 916F–917C). He debated the case earnestly, therefore, and his annotation on Acts 17.34 (*in quibus et Dionysius*) opens the window to an engaging view of Erasmus' search for authenticity.

Erasmus calls first the witness of history: an areopagite was a judge, not a philosopher of the kind implied by the books we have from Dionysius. He then argues from the bibliographies: none of the ancient authors mentions the Areopagite as a prolific writer. Jerome, it is true, lists a Dionysius more than once, but never the books in question, and Eusebius says nothing about the Areopagite's books, though he describes in detail the literary work of Dionysius of Corinth. Indeed, Eusebius reports that the latter, writing to the Athenian church, recalls the distinguished position of the Areopagite in Athens but says not a word about his writings. Finally, Erasmus appeals to predecessors who have already affirmed his view, above all, Lorenzo Valla, and more recently, William Grocyn, who, in a series of lectures on *The Celestial Hierarchies* delivered at St. Paul's in London, began by defending vigorously the attribution to the Areopagite, but, as he read the work more deeply, admitted his error before the lectures had been completed (*LB* 6, 503E–F). Scholarly consensus in itself could hardly constitute a methodology for determining authenticity, but Erasmus appreciated its persuasive value for confirming his own conclusions.

Clement of Alexandria

In the *Annotations* Erasmus generally speaks of "Clement" or "St. Clement" without further designation, and it may be that he confused the Alexandrian with the earlier bishop of Rome. Like that of the Roman Clement, the *editio princeps* of the Alexandrian Clement was published after Erasmus' death,[9] and Erasmus apparently knew the Alexandrian, as he did the Roman, primarily from Eusebius and Jerome. One passage especially invites attention: Erasmus, citing from Eusebius, appears to attribute to the Roman Clement a citation from the *Stromateis* that the historian had clearly assigned to the Alexandrian (*LB* 6, 875F–76D). But Clement of Rome had appeared in a passage earlier in the same book of the *Ecclesiasti-*

9. For the date of the *editio princeps* (1550), *v.* M. Mees, "Clemente di Alessandria," *DPAC,* vol. 1 (Casale Monferrato 1983), p. 707. For Clement of Rome *v.* note 6 above.

cal History (*cf. H. E.* 3.15f. with 29f.); if Erasmus was relying on memory, as he sometimes did in his citations, it is possible that the proximity of the two passages led to confusion. Even so, it was uncharacteristic of Erasmus to pass so lightly over the question of attribution.

Origen

Though in the *Annotations* Erasmus mentions in passing the *De principiis* and the *Contra Celsum* (*cf. LB* 6, 743C, 319C), it is the *Commentary on Matthew*, the *Homilies on Luke*, and the *Commentary on Romans* that he found particularly useful in his New Testament scholarship. In 1526 Jerome Froben found for Erasmus a Greek fragment of Origen's *Commentary on Matthew*.[10] A fragment that included some of the same text had circulated widely in a Latin version rendered by an anonymous translator, whom Erasmus believed to be Rufinus. Now the Greek fragment extended the commentary available in the Latin backward from Mt. 16.13 to Mt. 13.36. Further, with the Greek manuscript for comparison, it was possible to see in places where the texts overlapped how the translator had corrupted the original.[11] Erasmus duly noted that the translator had not only misrepresented the sense of the original exposition, but had presented the *tomoi* as *homiliae*, though they clearly had the form of a commentary (*cf.* Allen *Ep.* 1844, ll. 52–71). Yet though Erasmus criticized the falsifications of the translator, he never doubted that the fragment itself was authentic (*cf.* e.g. *LB* 6, 18C, 35C–D, 82F). In this respect the comment of André Godin is instructive. Godin observes that Erasmus deduced the authenticity of the Greek fragment not by examining the codex itself, but from its substantial identity with the old translation. So great in the eyes of the humanists was the authority of the *textus receptus*.[12]

On the other hand, Erasmus expressed repeatedly, almost constantly, his doubt about the authenticity of the *Homilies on Luke*. Curiously, the *Annotations* fail to give any rationale for his suspicions, or to show how his doubts arose from the self-conscious application of any methodology to determine authenticity. Though on one occasion he assumes the work is not Origen's (*LB* 6, 57F), for the most part he cites the *Homilies* as the work of Origen (*LB* 6, 219C) or with a simple proviso: "Origen, or whoever he was" (*Origenes, aut quisquis fuit, LB* 6, 234E; similarly 288D, 308E–F), "if

---

10. *Cf.* Allen *Epp.* 1767, 1774, and 1844. *V.* also A. Godin, *Érasme lecteur d'Origène* (Geneva 1982), p. 569.

11. *V.* Quasten, vol. 2, pp. 48f.

12. Godin, (note 10 above), p. 571.

the title is accurate" (*si verax est titulus operis, LB* 6, 236B), "[circulating] under the name of Origen" (*Homilias . . . quas habemus Origenis titulo, LB* 6, 126C; similarly 225E, 227D).[13] He expresses the same doubt in a reference to the homilies as they appeared in the *editio princeps* of the Latin *Opera* edited by Jacques Merlin (Paris 1512): "the author, whoever he was, of the *Homilies on Luke* that are ascribed to Origen in the edition of a certain Merlin" (*is, quisquis fuit, qui scripsit Homilias in Lucam, quas habemus ex Merlini cujusdam Editione, Origeni inscriptas, LB* 6, 236F). Even if the author was Origen, the translator of the Latin version has removed us some distance from the authentic work, for he was a paraphrast, not a translator (*LB* 6, 217D–E). Where authenticity failed, authority waned: "I shall not," says Erasmus, "allow myself to be burdened by the authority of this man whom no one knows" (*Verum hujus auctoritate, quem nemo novit, non patiar me premi, LB* 6, 226D).

Though Erasmus had no doubt about the Origenian authorship of the *Commentary on Romans,* he repeatedly lamented the ways in which the translator detracted from the authenticity of the *Commentary.*[14] The translator compressed Origen's original fifteen books into ten in the Latin version, and he repeatedly permitted his own voice to intrude into the translation, to explain, for example, the differences between the Greek and the Latin. Moreover, the biblical text has often been made to conform to the Vulgate. Thus we do not hear in reality the authentic voice of Origen.[15] In his discussion of Rom. 9.5 (*Christus . . . qui est in omnibus Deus*), central in debates over Arianism, Erasmus offers a fine example of his mode of reasoning: The translator here attempted to correct Origen; of this we may be confident, because he everywhere took liberties with Origen's text, because Jerome accused him at this point of correcting Origen to satisfy "Roman ears" (*quod tam insignem blasphemiam sciret Romanis auribus prorsus intolerabilem fore*), and because Origen otherwise seems to fight the Arians though the latter derived their doctrine from him (*v. LB* 6, 610F–11B).

Cyprian

Erasmus published an edition of Cyprian in 1520 (Froben, Basel). In his *Annotations* he cites frequently the *Ad Quirinum,* a useful companion for

13. Modern scholarship ascribes to Origen the thirty-nine homilies known in Jerome's translation. In Greek, only fragments of the thirty-fifth homily have been found. *V.* Quasten, vol. 2, pp. 46f.

14. For the identity of the translator, *v.* pp. 252f. below.

15. The objections frequently recur: *v. LB* 6, 554E, 586C–D, 600E, 605F, 610F (*cf. CWE* 56, p. 250), 613D, 614D, 618C, 621E–F, 623D, 631B, 631F, 647E.

the study of the New Testament text, and questions only scribal corruption (*cf. LB* 6, 335C–D, 405F; *CWE* 56, p. 251 = the *1527* version). Once he rightly questions the attribution to Cyprian of the *De singularitate clericorum,* but the *Annotations* offer no clarification of his thinking on the authenticity of this work (*cf. LB* 6, 874D).[16]

However, Erasmus' work on Cyprian becomes important to our study for the illuminating way in which he describes the path by which he discovered that the *Expositio symboli* belonged not to Cyprian but to Rufinus. In the letter dedicating his edition of the *Expositio* to Cardinal Lorenzo Pucci, Erasmus noted that the *Expositio* was found among the works of Jerome, where it was attributed to Rufinus (Allen *Ep.* 1000, ll. 34–37). Nonetheless, in all editions of his *Annotations* before *1535* he cites it as the authentic work of Cyprian (*LB* 6, 736E–F; *cf.* 1053E, 1064E).[17] His long addition in *1535* to an annotation on 1Cor. 15.22 (*ita et per Christum omnes vivificabuntur*) explains his change of mind: *Hactenus in lucubrationibus meis symboli expositionem citavi Cypriani titulo, quanquam offendebat nonnihil orationis character, et alicubi sermo loquacior, quam est Cypriani: tamen non audebam pronunciare, nec hîc animum intenderam. Et Ruffini symbolum degustaram, non perlegeram. Verum eruditi multis argumentis docent hoc opus esse Ruffini, non Cypriani. Primum quod scribitur ad Gaudentium, cui Ruffinus et alias quasdam lucubrationes suas dicavit, veluti Petri itinerarium. Praeterea quod illic commemorantur Haeretici, quos constat aetate Cypriani nondum fuisse natos, velut Arius. . . . Addunt et illud argumentum haud levis momenti, quod Ruffinus libro priore invectivarum in Hieronymum scribit hunc in modum:* Verum ad majorem rei fidem addo aliquid amplius, et calumniosorum necessitate compulsus, singulare et praecipuum Ecclesiae nostrae mysterium pando. Etenim quum omnes Ecclesiae ita sacramentum symboli tradant, ut, postquam dixerint peccatorum remissionem, addant carnis resurrectionem: nos dicimus, hujus car-

16. Erasmus is more helpful in the dedicatory letter that prefaced the 1520 edition of Cyprian (Allen *Ep.* 1000). Here he notes that he found the treatise among the works of Augustine, but attribution to Augustine was not possible both on grounds of style and the wording of the scriptural quotations. Hence, "I am not certain it is not by Cyprian" (*CWE* 7, p. 41; *is* [*i.e., liber*] *an Cypriani sit dubito,* Allen *Ep.* 1000, ll. 38f.). In the annotation Erasmus gives the title as *De clericorum vita,* but in the dedicatory letter he names it *De singularitate clericorum.*

17. *LB* is based on the 1540 *Opera omnia* published four years after Erasmus' death; it makes no attempt to distinguish the additions and changes in the five editions of the *Annotations* published between 1516 and 1535. In the references just cited, allusions to Rufinus appear first in the 1535 edition. *Symboli expositio, Ruffini symbolum,* and *Symboli apostolorum expositio* are Erasmus' titles for the work today commonly cited as the *Apologia ad Anastasium. V.* Quasten, vol. 4, p. 249.

nis resurrectionem. *Ita Ruffinus. Huic respondet, quod admonet in symbolo, idque duobus locis: in principio, ubi docet, symbolum non per omnia idem haberi in omnibus Ecclesiis: rursus in fine, tractans hanc symboli partem. In priore loco exprimit nomen Eccelsiae Aquilejensis. . . . Constat autem Ruffinum Aquilejae tinctum esse, et Presbyteri locum tenuisse: quum Cyprianus fuerit Afer, primum Presbyter, post Episcopus Carthaginensis. Porro Gennadius inter ea, quae Ruffinus non vertit e Graecis, sed suo Marte conscripsit, magna cum laude commemorat symboli Apostolorum expositionem* (LB 6, 736F–737C; Thus far in my writings I have cited the *Expositio symboli* under the name of Cyprian[18] though the character of the speech struck me rather sharply, and the language at points seemed too prolix to be Cyprian's. Yet I ventured to make no pronouncement: indeed, I had not paid much attention. Also, I had skimmed Rufinus' *Symbolum* but had not read it carefully. Scholars, however, show by many proofs that this is the work of Rufinus, not Cyprian. First, it is written to Gaudentius, to whom Rufinus dedicated some of his other writings, such as the *Itinerary of Peter*. Moreover, heretics are mentioned in this work who, it is clear, were not yet born in the time of Cyprian, such as Arius. . . . They add another argument of no small importance, that in the first book of the *Apologia contra Hieronymum* he writes thus: "But to be more convincing, I add something further and, compelled by the slanderers, I set out the unique and principal mystery of our church. For though all the churches hand down the sacred creed in a form that adds, after the clause on the forgiveness of sins, the resurrection of the flesh, we say, 'the resurrection of this flesh.'" What Rufinus points out in the *Symbolum* corresponds to this in two places: first, when he shows that the creed is not the same in all the churches, and again at the end, where he treats this part of the creed. In the former passage he explicitly mentions the church of Aquileia . . . and we know that Rufinus was baptized, and served as priest, at Aquileia, whereas Cyprian was an African, first a priest, then the bishop, of Carthage. Further, Gennadius mentions in a very laudatory way the *Exposition of the Apostle's Creed* as one of those pieces Rufinus had not translated from the Greek but had composed himself).[19]

Erasmus concludes his argument by acknowledging some differences in

---

18. *V., e.g.,* Erasmus' own exposition of the Apostles' Creed (*Explanatio symboli apostolorum*), where he frequently refers to this work as Cyprian's (*ASD*, vol. 5, part 1, pp. 187, 203, 220, 222).

19. Erasmus added this passage in the 1535 edition of the *Annotations, v.* A. Reeve and M.A. Screech, *Erasmus' Annotations on the New Testament. Acts-Romans-I and II Corinthians: Facsimile of the final Latin text with all earlier variants* (Leiden 1990), p. 512.

the text of the work circulated under the name of Cyprian and that found among the works of Jerome but ascribed to Rufinus. Nevertheless, the congruency compels the conviction that the two books are one and the same while the differences suggest a deliberate attempt to deceive the reader in the case of the text attributed to Cyprian (*LB* 6, 737C–D).

Athanasius

In his New Testament scholarship Erasmus repeatedly defended himself against the charge of Arianism (*cf.* the indices of *CWE* 42, 46, 50, 56). Though debates in which he thus engaged invited appeal to the works of Athanasius, references to this patristic author are few in the *Annotations.* As a matter of fact, in the early sixteenth century few of Athanasius' works were available even in translation (Allen *Ep.* 1790, ll. 8f.). Erasmus himself published translations of some of Athanasius' works, including the first *Letter to Serapion.* In his *Annotations* he cites the letter without demur (*cf.* *LB* 6, 337B, 601F), though, in fact, he believed it to be spurious (Allen *Ep.* 1790 intro.; *LB* 8, 405D–E).[20] Indeed, in the dedicatory letter that prefaced translations of some of Athanasius' writing, he shows how the process of translating could lead him to affirm or deny the authenticity of a work: *comperi subinde titulorum imposturas, hoc Athanasio tribuentium quod vix sani hominis videri posset. . . . In his non parum temporis et operae nobis periit, dum inter vertendum, quo longius processeramus, hoc deprehendimus absurdiora, ac tandem coepta coacti sumus abiicere* (Allen *Ep.* 1790, ll. 62–66; I frequently found the titles to be imposters, attributing work to Athanasius that could barely seem to belong to a sane man. . . . On such I lost a good deal of time and effort, inasmuch as the further I proceeded in translation, the more absurdities I detected, until finally I had to throw away what I had begun).[21]

Erasmus has left us several quite vivid accounts of his successful efforts to unmask the author (Theophylact, the eleventh-century archbishop of Ochrida) of commentaries attributed to Athanasius on the Gospels and the Pauline Epistles. In preparing his first edition of the New Testament (1516) Erasmus had used the Greek commentary of Theophylact (identified on the cover as Vulgarius, *i.e.* the Bulgarian archbishop) made available to him in Basel. But he was in Louvain in 1517 and 1518 when he was

20. Modern scholars regard the *Letter to Serapion* as authentic. *Cf.* Quasten, vol. 3, pp. 57f.

21. *V.* the similar account of Erasmus' translation of the *Commentary on Isaiah* attributed to Basil (Allen *Ep.* 229).

working on the second edition (*1519*) and had to use a Latin translation of these commentaries that purported to be by Athanasius. When he returned to Basel before the publication of the second edition, he compared the Latin translation used in Louvain and attributed to Athanasius with the Greek copy in Basel and found that the Latin was indeed a translation of Theophylact (*LB* 6, 555E). In his letter to John Longland he offers two further, very characteristic, arguments that invalidate the claim to Athanasian authorship: the author draws heavily on Chrysostom and Basil, who lived subsequent to Athanasius, and Jerome, in listing the works of Athanasius, makes no mention of these commentaries (Allen *Ep.* 1790, ll. 15–48).

It remained to report the story that explained the fabrication of false authorship: *Idque negant esse factum temeritate Librariorum, sed astutia studioque ipsius Christophori Personae, qui vertit hoc opus. Testatur id etiam codex ille, quem Christophorus Sixto Pontifici hujus nominis quarto pulchre depictum obtulit. Titulum majusculis miniatis praefixerat Athanasii, quum in praefatione nec Athanasii nec Theophylacti faciat mentionem. Videtur itaque fucum fecisse Pontifici. Haec scribunt, qui codicem in Bibliotheca Pontificia asservatum viderunt* (*LB* 6, 721F; [Certain ones] say that [the false attribution to Athanasius] occurred not through the temerity of scribes, but through the malicious cunning of Christopher Porsena himself, who translated this work.[22] This is attested by the codex itself which Christopher offered beautifully decorated to Pope Sixtus IV. He had prefixed the name of Athanasius in red capitals, though he makes no mention of either Athanasius or Theophylact in the preface. He seems to have fooled the pope. So they write who have seen the codex kept in the Pontifical Library). Erasmus notes elsewhere that his contemporary Jacques Lefèvre d'Étaples was equally fooled (*LB* 6, 988F).

Chrysostom

Erasmus' search for authenticity assumes a special interest in the case of Chrysostom because Greek manuscripts and a Greek edition of Chrysostom's *Homilies* gradually became available as he continued to re-edit his New Testament. For his first edition of *1516* Erasmus had Latin translations of Chrysostom's *Homilies* on Matthew and John and on the Epistles from 1Timothy to Hebrews. Of Greek manuscripts he had available for his first

---

22. Christopher Porsena (*ca.* 1416–85) had served as a papal librarian. His edition of Theophylact under the name of Athanasius was published in Rome in 1477; *cf. LB* 6, 768E; *CWE* 56, note 25, p. 15.

edition only the homilies on Mt. 1–15 and on 1Corinthians. These manuscripts were supplied to him from the Dominican library in Basel. For the
1522 edition he had acquired excerpts from the Greek of the *Homilies* on
Acts; by 1527 he had the Greek for all the *Homilies* on Acts, Romans, Gala-
tians, and the two Corinthians. For his final edition of 1535 he was able to
use the Verona edition of the *Homilies* in Greek on the Pauline Epistles.[23]

Perhaps surprisingly, the possession of the Greek itself did little to bol-
ster Erasmus' confidence in the authenticity of the homilies.[24] There are, in
fact, only a few sets of homilies about which Erasmus expresses no doubt
at all, in particular, the *Homilies on Matthew,* the *Homilies on John,* and the
Homilies on Romans. Even so, he notes that the "published edition" (*in
Editione vulgata*) of Anianus' translation of eighty-nine homilies on
Matthew was evidently truncated: it offered no homily on Mt. 28, though
the *catena aurea* cites Chrysostom on the last chapter, and Anianus affirms
in his preface that Chrysostom wrote ninety-one homilies on the Gospel.
Two must therefore have been lost (*cf. LB* 6, 148D).

Generally in the *Annotations* Erasmus is skeptical about the attribution
of the homilies on the other books to Chrysostom. For the most part, a
passing remark is sufficient: "the Greek commentary circulating under the
name of Chrysostom—whether true or not I do not yet say" (*Graecos
Commentarios* [*i.e., in Acta App.*] *Joannis Chrysostomi titulo, vero ne an fal-
so nondum pronuncio, LB* 6, 433D; *cf.* 435D, 471E, 473E, 536C); "in his Greek
commentary on this Epistle, if the title is correct" (*in Commentariis Graecis* [*i.e., in 1Cor.*] ... *quos in hanc scripsit Epistolam, si modo non fallit titulus, LB* 6, 661C); "in a commentary ascribed to Chrysostom, though I sus-
pect the title is false" (*Commentariis* [*i.e., in 1Cor.*] *qui Chrysostomo inscri-
buntur, sed titulo mihi suspecto, LB* 6, 686C); "a commentary on this Epistle
not by Chrysostom, but by some imitator" (*Commentarios* [*i.e., in 2Cor.*],
*qui Chrysostomi titulo feruntur ... in hanc Epistolam non ... illius, sed
simii cujuspiam, LB* 6, 762F). If we may judge from remarks added in the
edition of 1535, the appearance of the Verona edition did nothing to allevi-
ate his suspicions (*cf. LB* 6, 661C, 685B, 733E, 852F, 883E). Yet only once in
his comments on the Epistles traditionally ascribed to Paul does he explain his uncertainty: "The author [of the *Homilies on Philippians*] is more
loquacious than Chrysostom and did not achieve his deft phraseology"

---

23. V. R. Sider, "'Searching the Scriptures': John Chrysostom in the New Testament
Scholarship of Erasmus," *Within the Perfection of Christ: Essays on Peace and the Nature of the
Church in Honor of Martin H. Schrag,* ed. T.L. Brensinger and E.M. Sider (Nappanee, Ind.
1990), pp. 83–105.

24. But *cf.* (page 241 above) the comment of A. Godin on the importance—or rather the
lack of importance—of Greek manuscripts in themselves for determining authenticity.

(*Quisquis fuit, Chrysostomi* πολυλαλίαν *vincit, argutiam non est assequutus, LB* 6, 868F). In the case of the *Homilies on Hebrews,* it was the title page of his copy that raised Erasmus' suspicions, for it indicated that this work had been published after Chrysostom's death by Constantine, presbyter at Antioch, and translated by Mucianus (*LB* 6, 995D).[25] But he found support for his view in the character of the commentary. The inconsistencies, for example, in the comments on Heb. 4.3 led him to characterize the passage as a *rhapsodia* of different opinions (*LB* 6, 995F).[26]

Even in the homilies on the Gospels and Romans, whose attribution to Chrysostom he accepted, Erasmus frequently questioned the authenticity of the readings. In the case of Chrysostom, however, he was able to employ the commentaries of Theophylact as a control, for he regarded Theophylact as a borrower and imitator of Chrysostom, one who culled without embarrassment the literary flowers of the Golden-mouth for his own work. Thus where a passage of Chrysostom posed an evident contradiction between biblical text and exposition or offered an otherwise implausible reading, Erasmus would attempt to restore from Theophylact the authentic text of Chrysostom. He did so with particular frequency in his annotations on Matthew (*cf. LB* 6, 111F–112C, 112F–113D, 126C). He was not unaware of the hazards this method entailed and recognized that the readings in both authors could be wrong (*LB* 6, 846F).

Ambrosiaster

Throughout all editions of the New Testament, Erasmus identified the author of the commentaries on the Pauline Epistles (Ambrosiaster) with Ambrose of Milan, whose commentary on Luke and *Expositio in Psalmos* he knew well. The identification may surprise us, since some features of these commentaries on the Pauline Epistles puzzled him. In *1519* he noted that the author reports the reading of the Greek (*in Rom.* 12.11) from what others had told him; Erasmus queries, "And, in passing, I wonder why, when he [Ambrose] knew Greek, he did not himself consult the Greek copies" (*Atque obiter admiror, quum Graece sciret, cur non ipse potius consuluerit Graecorum exemplaria, LB* 6, 631F).[27] Again in *1519* he observed that

25. *Cf.* C. Baur, *S. Jean Chrysostome et ses oeuvres dans l'histoire littéraire* (Paris/Louvain 1907), item 4, p. 140.

26. Modern scholarship does not share Erasmus' doubts. The homilies on the Pauline Epistles and Hebrews and on Acts are regarded as authentic. *V.* Quasten, vol. 3, pp. 436–50, and *cf.* F. Gignac's remarks, p. 209 *supra.*

27. Translations from the *Ann. in Rom.* follow A. Rabil, R.D. Sider, and W.S. Smith, *CWE,* vol. 5 (1994); *v.* also note 7, p. 335.

in the *Expositio in Psalmos* Ambrose offered an interpretation of Phil. 3.8 different from that in the commentary on Philippians (*LB* 6, 873D). Indeed, in 1527 in the preface to the fifth volume of the *Opera* of Ambrose of Milan, he questioned the text of the commentaries on the Pauline Epistles: "In the commentaries themselves . . . some passages seem to have been added, others to have been mutilated" (*in ipsis commentariis alicubi videntur adiecta quaedam, alicubi decurtata; CWE* 42, p. 7, note 13).[28] Despite the difficulties, Erasmus seems not to have asserted definitively a non-Ambrosian authorship for these commentaries.

Jerome

In the *Annotations* Erasmus' search for authenticity in the writings of Jerome was directed toward (1) the biblical commentaries of Jerome, (2) the *De nominibus locorum,* a text Erasmus frequently used to identify geographical references in his New Testament scholarship, (3) the authorship of the Vulgate Bible, (4) the identification of ps.-Jerome, and (5) the translations of some of the works of Origen.[29]

1. The Biblical Commentaries of Jerome

Erasmus thought the authenticity of commentaries circulating under the name of Jerome on the Psalms, on Matthew, and on Mark, was in varying degrees, questionable. Characteristically, he dismissed the commentary on Mark with a curt affirmation of false attribution (*cf. LB* 6, 166E, 203F, 210F). His observations on the commentaries on Matthew and the Psalms are more revealing.[30] He exposes a contradiction in which the Jerome of

28. I cite Erasmus' Latin from the Froben edition *Omnia quotquot extant divi Ambrosii . . . Opera,* vol. 5 (Basel 1538), p. 2. The translation follows J.B. Payne, A. Rabil, and W.S. Smith, *CWE,* vol. 42 (1984), note 13, p. 7; the annotators of the *Paraphrase on Romans* who here refer to the preface of vol. 4 are citing the first edition of 1527.

29. For these translations, *v.* below, "Rufinus," to whom Erasmus eventually attributed them.

30. Due to his distinction as a biblical scholar, numerous works were once falsely ascribed to Jerome. For supposititious commentaries on the Gospels and on the Epistles traditionally attributed to Paul, *v. CPL,* #631, 632, 952; and for an equally inauthentic *Breviarium in Psalmos, v. CPL,* #629. For the commentary on Matthew, *v.* J.N.D. Kelly, *Jerome: His Life, Writings, and Controversies* (London 1975), pp. 222–25. Jerome translated Origen's *Homilies on Luke* but did not write commentaries on either Mark or Luke. *Cf.* J. Gribomont, "Girolamo," *DPAC,* vol. 2 (Casale Monferrato 1984), p. 1587, and R. Trevijano, "Marco (vangelo)," *ib.,* p. 2100. Jerome wrote tractates on Ps. 10–16, of which only that on Ps. 15 is extant. He also composed notes on the Psalms (*Commentarioli; cf.* Kelly, pp. 157f.), but, as the excerpt just below indicates, Erasmus' remarks on the authenticity of Jerome's commentary on the Psalms refer to the inauthentic *Brev. in Ps.* In his annotation on Mk. 15.25 Erasmus applies the title *Breviarium maius* to the commentary on the Psalms, and the title *Breviarium minus* to the commentary on Matthew (*LB* 6, 211D–E).

the commentary on Isaiah (on 42.1–4) refers the reader to his commentary on Mt. 12.18–21, where, the same Jerome claims, he has expounded the prophetic oracle "more fully" (*plenius*); in fact, Erasmus observes, the Jerome of the commentary on Matthew "barely touches" upon the prophecy (*cum . . . summis . . . digitis rem attingat*). Erasmus notes the implication, and speaks his mind also on the authorship of the commentaries on the Psalms and on Mark: *in conjecturam vocor, id quod saepenumero sum suspicatus, eos Commentarios* [on Matthew] *a fastidioso quopiam Lectore decurtatos, praetermissis in medio quae non intellexerit. . . . Idem factum arbitror in Commentariis, quos idem scripsit in Psalmos: quanquam in hos, quisquis is fuit, gemina debacchatus est injuria. Primum quod quae libuit, praemiserit. Deinde, quod compluribus locis suas nugas ceu purpurae pannum assuerit. Nam quod in Marcum habemus commentum, praeter titulum nihil habet Hieronymi* (*LB* 6, 67D–E; I have often suspected that the commentary [on Matthew] has been abridged by some fastidious reader who omitted what he did not understand. . . . I think the same thing happened in the commentary Jerome wrote on the Psalms, though the culprit, whoever he was, committed a double sin against this: first he omitted whatever he pleased; second, in a number of places he stitched on trifles of his own, like purple patches. The *Commentary on Mark* is, in name only, Jerome's).

It is the imposter of the commentary on the Psalms for whom Erasmus reserves his most bitter words: *Rem ex Hieronymo sublegit: caeterum ineptia sermonis, ridiculi διαλογισμοὶ, βαττολογία, soloecismi, caeteraeque id genus deliciae ipsius sunt* (*LB* 6, 75F; He filches the substance from Jerome, but the inept language, the ridiculous arguments, the repetitive stammering, the solecisms, and other preciosities of the same sort are his own). In his annotation on Acts 1.20, where Ps. 109.8 (*Episcopatum ejus accipiat alter*) is cited, Erasmus admits that a preliminary comment on the verse from the Psalm may indeed be Jerome's, but what follows is, he says, *ambiguum,* and he gives a specimen of the commentator's thought and style: Non solum autem in illo tempore de Juda dictum est, sed usque hodie dicitur et usque in diem judicii. Si ipse Judas Apostolatum perdidit, custodiant se Sacerdotes et Episcopi, ut non et ipsi suum sacerdotium perdant. Si Apostolus cecidit, facilius Monachus potest cadere. Erasmus promises to restrain himself from comment on the wretched syntax, but what propriety has the thought: is a monk the same as an apostle? What follows is, moreover, simply incoherent: Virtus non perit, licet homo cadat et pereat, tamen Dominus denarios suos dat sub foenore. Si ille non duplicaverit, accipitur pecunia ejus et dabitur habenti. Pecunia Domini otiosa esse non potest.[31] Erasmus asks his reader, *Quis non vidit haec esse non Hieronymi, sed hominis*

31. For this passage, *v.* ps.-Jerome, *Brev. in Ps.* 108 (*PL*, vol. 26, coll. 1157B–C).

inepte loquacis, qui similibus emblematis totum hunc Psalmum contaminav-
it, et utinam hunc solum (*LB* 6, 439C–D; *cf.* 988F)!

2. De nominibus locorum

Erasmus sometimes attributed this gazetteer of Acts to Jerome without
qualification (*cf. LB* 6, 212E, 442D). The fact, however, that the author cited
Jerome in the copy Erasmus possessed raised the suspicion that it was the
work of an educated person, but not of Jerome (*LB* 6, 433C; *cf.* 541F, and,
for qualified attribution, 535C). He also believed that the text had suffered
both abbreviation—moderns delight in brevity, Erasmus notes—and en-
largement. He had good reason for his skepticism: in his text the Forum of
Appius was located in Rome (*cf. LB* 6, 541F), although, Jerome, who had
spent some years in Rome, must have known that the Forum of Appius
was located about forty-five miles to the south. Though Erasmus recognized the similarity between the *De nominibus locorum* and Bede's list of
place names in Acts, it did not occur to him that the work might have originated with Bede, or that a manuscript foisted upon Jerome served as the
source for Bede.[32]

3. Jerome and the Vulgate Bible

Erasmus was well aware that the Bible had been translated into Latin
before the time of Jerome (*cf. LB* 6, 990A–B). He also knew that Jerome
had emended an old version (*cf. LB* 6, 850C–D), though he may well have
misunderstood the precise role Jerome played in the development of the
Vulgate Bible. Of one thing he was certain, however: that the Vulgate Bible
or Bibles of his own day could be neither the version of Jerome nor the
version emended by Jerome. He needed merely to point to the differences
between the biblical texts as given in Jerome's commentaries and the contemporary Vulgate. A single example is sufficient to illustrate. In his annotation on Eph. 4.29, Erasmus noted Jerome's report that he had emended
aedificationem fidei to *ad aedificationem opportunitatis.* He drew the inference: *Ex hoc loco colligere licet Hieronymum in hac Epistola sequi quod ipse*
emendarat, et tamen non in alia Epistola plura sunt quae discrepant a vulga-
ta lectione. Ubi sunt igitur qui coelum terrae miscent, quod aliqui dubitant,
an vulgaris Editio sit Hieronymi (*LB* 6, 850C; From this passage one can
gather that in this Epistle Jerome followed what he himself emended, and
yet in no other Epistle are there more passages that disagree with the Vulgate reading. Where then are those who turn heaven and earth upside
down because some people doubt that the Vulgate edition is Jerome's version; *cf.* also *LB* 6, 812B–C, 822E, 823C, 834F)?

---

32. These are two solutions suggested by modern critics; *cf.* M.L.W. Laistner, *Bedae Ven-*
erabilis Expositio actuum apostolorum et Retractatio (Cambridge, Mass. 1939), pp. xxxviif.

4. Ps.-Jerome

Erasmus often found a welcome support for his interpretation of Scripture in the commentaries on the Pauline Epistles that are now generally attributed to Pelagius, with interpolations by "ps.-Jerome."[33] Though Erasmus apparently did not recognize their author as Pelagius, he was aware already when he published his first edition of Jerome (1516) that the author was pseudonymous (*cf. CWE* 56, p. 155, note 22). Characteristically, in his *Annotations* he attributes the work to the "Latin scholiast" (*Scholiastes ille Latinus, LB* 6, 871E, 889F, 886F, 910D) or "the scholiast they call Jerome" (*Scholiastae, cui nomen fecerunt Hieronymo, LB* 6, 839E–F; *cf.* 870D); sometimes he speaks of the commentaries that go under the name of Jerome (*LB* 6, 777E, 876E). At two points he distinguishes between the inept writer of the preface that fastens the work upon Jerome, and the "careful scholar" responsible for the commentary: *Fateor hoc opus non esse Hieronymi, quemadmodum mentitur inepta praefatio: docti tamen hominis esse res ipsa clamitat: et qui titulis omnibus habendam fidem contendunt, nostrasque censuras rejiciunt, his certe oportet esse Hieronymi* (*LB* 6, 586C; "I acknowledge that this work is not by Jerome, as its inept preface falsely claims; but its content bespeaks the work of a learned man, and those who contend that all labels are to be trusted and reject my assessment [of pseudonymity] should certainly regard it as Jerome's"). In the annotation on 1Cor. 15.51 he again distinguishes the author of the preface from that of the commentary: *hanc puto alterius esse, quam sit ipsa collectio Commentariorum, quos apparet esse studiosi cujuspiam, nec indocti, e diversis Veterum Commentariis compendium contrahentis. Quisquis enim is fuit, qui praefatiunculam adjecit, quum sit infans ac balbus, tamen impudenter affectavit haberi Hieronymus* (*LB* 6, 741E; I think the author [of the preface] is different from that of the collection of comments, which seems to be the work of some careful and scholarly person who brought together a compendium of various comments from the ancients. Whoever added the preface shamelessly pretended to be Jerome, though his speech is infantile and hesitant).[34]

Rufinus

Just as Erasmus described in some detail the path by which he came to declare Rufinus the author of the *Expositio symboli*, so he left us also an account of his progress in discovering Rufinus as the true author of the Latin

---

33. V. A. Souter, *Pelagius's Expositions of Thirteen Epistles of St. Paul*, vol. 1 (Cambridge 1922): *Introduction*, pp. 6–34.

34. For the preface *v.* p. xiii of Souter, *ib.*, vol. 3 (Cambridge 1931): *Pseudo-Jerome Interpolations*.

translation of Origen's *Commentary on Romans*. He based his argument fundamentally on features of style and content: the style is hardly that of Jerome, though indeed the style here is "purer" ([*phrasis*] *purior*) than in Rufinus' other work. There are, moreover, clear signs that the translator was not scrupulous, specifically the practice of introducing comments whose Latin character marked them as the translator's, not Origen's; Rufinus' lack of scruples elsewhere points to him as the translator here. The same lack of scruple can be seen in the fact that there are ideas introduced into the Latin commentary that are diametrically opposed to the beliefs Origen held. Erasmus had originally accepted Hieronymian authorship because the name of Jerome appeared in the title and the concluding note. But he had discovered evidence that revealed the fraud: "[The author of the concluding note] says that he was being urged by Gaudentius to finish the translation of Clement [*ie.* the *Recognitions*] that he had begun" (*Ait enim sese a Gaudentio urgeri, ut Clementem, quem vertere instituerat, absolvat*). But we know Rufinus translated the *Recognitions* for Gaudentius. Thus the evidence suggests that, though Rufinus translated the commentary on Romans, the name of Jerome was attached to improve the sales and to deceive generations of readers (*LB* 6, 574E–F; *v. CWE* 56, pp. 95f., notes 11, 14, and 18)!

Conclusion

The passage just cited points succinctly to some of the most fundamental elements in the critical methodology Erasmus used to determine authenticity: indicators offered by title page, preface or concluding note, evidence deduced from the structural patterns and literary habits established in the uncontested work of an author, inconsistencies of thought, evident anachronisms and historical incongruencies. But perhaps no argument was more convincing than that furnished from the stylistic analysis of a passage by an expert like Erasmus. The heavy reliance on stylistic analysis we have seen in the *Annotations* finds eloquent explanation in Erasmus' Preface to Volume II Part I of his 1516 edition of Jerome, where he offers an elaborate discussion on problems of authenticity. Observing the importance of style, he says: "The surest sign [of authenticity] and truly the Lydian stone, as they say, is the character and the quality of speech."[35] Yet, and this is important to note, while Erasmus held that integrity demanded the

35. For the broader discussion *v. ib.*, pp. 73–81. The translation is that of J.F. Brady and J.C. Olin, *CWE*, vol. 61 (1992), p. 76. *LB* does not contain either Erasmus' life of Jerome or the prefaces, and no critical edition of the Latin text of the Preface to volume 2, part 1 has appeared; *cf. CWE*, vol. 61, p. xi.

scholar's uncompromising search for authenticity, he did not believe that spurious works were *ipso facto* to be rejected. They too might be worthy to be read; indeed the final volume of the Jerome edition was devoted to such writings. We might sum up his position thus: Read them we may, even should, but we must know what we are reading, for the authority of an author derives from the acknowledged authenticity of his work.

SEVENTEEN

The Training of the Hiberno-Latinist

— ✣ —

Michael W. Herren

L ET ME BEGIN by saying that it is a pleasure to contribute to this *festschrift* for Professor Halton, with whom I share an interest in the early period of Hiberno-Latin literature.[1] Before coming to the matter of how to train an Hiberno-Latinist, perhaps I owe it to readers to answer the question, "Why do it?" My answer is directed to scholars engaged in primary humanistic research who might legitimately ask whether Hiberno-Latin is sufficiently different from any other kind of late or medieval Latin to lay claim to status as a separate field. Surely one would assume that any well-trained classicist with additional background in late Latin philology would be prepared to cope with the challenges posed by the latinity of any region of Europe. Let me attempt a response.

In 1918 Paul Lehmann pointed out that the Latin written by Irish scholars in the early Middle Ages, *i.e.,* starting in the seventh century, exhibited peculiarities not found elsewhere.[2] Over the current century other scholars have developed this insight by defining the features that characterize Irish Latin. One of the most interesting works remains the doctoral dissertation of William Most written for The Catholic University of America.[3] Most

---

1. T.P. Halton, "Early Christian Ireland's Contacts with the Mediterranean World to c. 650," in *Cristianesimo e specificità regionali nel mediterraneo latino (sec. IV–VI): XXII Incontro di studiosi dell'antichità cristiana, Roma, 6–8 maggio 1993* (Rome 1994), pp. 601–18.

2. P. Lehmann, "Aufgaben und Anregungen der lateinischen Philologie des Mittelalters," *SBAW.PPH* (1918.8), pp. 38f.

3. W.G. Most, "The Syntax of the Vitae sanctorum Hiberniae" (Ph.D. diss., The Catholic University of America 1946).

was able to show that some of the syntactical features exhibited in Latin Irish saints' lives can be attributed to the influence of the Old Irish language.[4] Nearly two decades later Ludwig Bieler published an excellent study of Irish latinity in the introduction to his edition of the Irish Penitentials.[5] This was soon followed by Bengt Löfstedt's more comprehensive work in the introduction to his edition of the grammatical writings attributed to Malsachanus.[6] Löfstedt introduced a number of examples of the influence of the Irish language on Latin orthography.[7] Because many Irish and allegedly Irish Latin works are found in continental manuscripts, there has been a persistent problem, particularly in the area of orthography, of determining peculiarly Irish features. This problem was addressed, with considerable success, by J.M. Picard in 1982.[8] Picard undertook a detailed study of the orthography of Adomnán's *Life of Columba* preserved in a manuscript written in Irish script shortly after the author's lifetime.[9] His study confirmed as authentically Hiberno-Latin much of the data alleged as such in the studies of Bieler and Löfstedt. Other studies have dealt with Old Irish influence on Latin vocabulary, word usage, and idiom.[10] While vernacular influences on vocabulary and word usage occur in other regions, instances of vernacular interference with Latin syntax and orthography are rare in comparison.

Another area where Irish vernacular influence can be traced is that of meter. This can be noted particularly in examples of Hiberno-Latin heptasyllabic verse, which stands much closer in its structure to Old Irish seven-syllable verse than to any attested Latin models.[11] More work needs to be done in this and the other linguistic areas noted,[12] but I believe that since

4. *Ib.*, pp. 281–308; more critically in his summary, pp. 336–38, where Most dealt with examples of constructions that can be explained by reference to Old Irish exclusively.

5. *V.* pp. 27–47 of L. Bieler, *The Irish Penitentials*, with an appendix by D.A. Binchy (Dublin 1963; rpt. 1975) = *SLH*, vol. 5.

6. B. Löfstedt, *Der hibernolateinische Grammatiker Malsachanus* (Uppsala 1965), pp. 81–161.

7. *Ib.*, pp. 86f., *et passim*.

8. "The Schaffhausen Adomnán—A Unique Witness to Hiberno-Latin," *Peritia* 1 (1982), pp. 216–49.

9. Schaffhausen, Stadtbibliothek, MS Gen. 1.

10. *V.* M.W. Herren, "Old Irish Lexical and Semantic Influence on Hiberno-Latin," in *Irland und Europa: die Kirche im Frühmittelalter/Ireland and Europe: The Early Church*, ed. P. Ní Chatháin and M. Richter (Stuttgart 1984), pp. 197–209; rpt. in M.W. Herren, *Latin Letters in Early Christian Ireland* (Aldershot, U.K. 1996), essay 12.

11. M.W. Herren, "Hibernolateinische und irische Verskunst mit besonderer Berücksichtigung des Siebensilbers," in *Metrik und Medienwechsel/Metrics and Media*, ed. H.L.C. Tristram (Tübingen 1991), pp. 173–88; rpt. in Herren, *Latin Letters* (note 10 above), essay 16.

12. A comprehensive treatment of Hiberno-Latin meter remains to be written. This should include a study of rhyme patterns and address the question of the influence of Old

Lehmann's time a fairly solid case has been built for defining Hiberno-Latin as a specialized *Forschungsgebiet.*

Let us now look at what remains to be done. First, there are still many unedited works with known or alleged Irish origins deriving from the early medieval period, roughly 600–1000 A.D. Other works survive only in the pages of the *Patrologia Latina.* The lack of critical editions is particularly notable in the field of early medieval exegesis. Over forty years ago Bernhard Bischoff published a valuable catalogue of early medieval biblical commentaries identified as Hiberno-Latin works.[13] His basis of identification comprised not only paleographical features, but also a group of *topoi* that included the giving of terms in the three sacred languages, *i.e.,* Hebrew, Latin, and Greek; the *accessus* formulae *locus, tempus, persona;*[14] phrases such as *pauca de, ecloga de;* the use of fantastic etymologies such as those given by Virgilius Maro Grammaticus; the question "Who or what was the first?" Bischoff's criteria did not go unchallenged. Over the intervening decades, scholars have raised various criticisms of his method.[15]

It strikes me, however, that little headway can be made in resolving this interesting problem until most of the works in Bischoff's catalogue have been critically edited and examined according to the linguistic criteria that now exist for positing Irish origin or at least Irish transmission. Let me cite an example. The *Expositio IV evangeliorum,* which survives, allegedly, in three recensions, is one of the exegetical works Bischoff listed as Hiberno-Latin.[16] The second recension, represented by eighth-, ninth-, and tenth-century continental manuscripts, was recently edited as a dissertation project.[17] While this recension exhibits many of Bischoff's criteria for Irish-

---

Irish rhyme schemes on Hiberno-Latin verse. In addition, more attention should be devoted to the influence of Old Irish idiom on Hiberno-Latin constructions; *cf.* my "Old Irish" (note 10 above). For a recent treatment of the *status quaestionis* of Hiberno-Latin orthography *v.* P. Zanna, "Aspects of the Orthography of Early Hiberno-Latin Texts" (Ph. D. diss., Cambridge University 1997).

13. B. Bischoff, "Wendepunkte in der Geschichte der lateinischen Exegese im Frühmittelalter," *Mittelalterliche Studien: Ausgewählte Aufsätze zur Schriftkunde und Literaturgeschichte,* vol. 1 (Stuttgart 1966), pp. 205–73.

14. The *accessus* formulae constitute a method, dating from antiquity, of introducing the author of a work: Who wrote it? When? Where? *V.* E.A. Quain, "The Medieval Accessus Ad Auctores," *Tr.* 3 (1945), pp. 215–64.

15. E. Coccia, "La cultura irlandese precarolingia: Miracolo o mito?" *StMed,* 3rd ser., 8.1 (1967), pp. 257–420; C. Stancliffe, "Early 'Irish' Biblical Exegesis," pp. 361–70 of *StPatr* 12 = *TU* 115 (1975); and M.M. Gorman, "A Critique of Bischoff's Theory of Irish Exegesis: The Commentary on Genesis in Munich Clm 6302," *JMLat* 7 (1997), pp. 178–233.

16. "Wendepunkte" (note 13 above), #11A–C, pp. 240f.

17. A.K. Kavanagh, "The *Expositio IV Evangeliorum* (Recension II): A Critical Edition and Analysis of Text" (Ph.D. diss., Trinity College, Dublin 1996).

ness, there is nothing in the language of the text as transmitted to mark it as Hiberno-Latin. It is argued, however, that recension II derives from an as-yet-unedited recension I. It will therefore be necessary to edit this *Ur-fassung* to determine if it can be shown on linguistic grounds to be an Irish product, or at the least, to exhibit signs of an Irish transmission.

It may be worthwhile to review the criteria for assigning anonymous Latin exegetical works to Irish scholars. In my opinion, the most logical place to start is with the very few Latin works firmly assigned to writers with Irish names, such as the *Interpretatio mystica* of Aileranus Sapiens,[18] and with the *corpus* of glosses and commentaries written in the seventh, eighth, and ninth centuries in the Old Irish language,[19] or else in a mixture of Latin and Old Irish.[20] In this way, one would be working from the known to the unknown. It may well turn out that most of Bischoff's criteria will be validated by such a study. Hitherto undetermined criteria might also emerge.

In addition to works that are unedited or exist only in old editions, there are also texts now in modern editions whose origins are still disputed. Two egregious examples are the so-called *Cosmographia* of Aethicus Is-ter[21] and the grammatical writings of Virgilius Maro Grammaticus.[22] Irish origins or milieux have been claimed for both.[23] Neither work has been subjected to a detailed philological commentary. It has been claimed that the authors of both works used Irish etymologies and individual words,[24] but we still need complete studies of these phenomena. Determining the milieux of both these texts would aid greatly in our understanding of the intellectual life of the seventh and eighth centuries.

The Irish translations and adaptations of classical works, dating from

---

18. Recently edited and translated by A. Breen, *Ailerani Interpretatio mystica et moralis progenitorum domini Iesv Christi* (Dublin 1995).

19. W. Stokes and J. Strachan, *Thesaurus Palaeohibernicus: A Collection of Old-Irish Glosses Scholia Prose and Verse,* 2 voll. (Cambridge 1901–3); W. Stokes, *A Supplement to Thesaurus Palaeohibernicus* (Halle 1910; voll. 1–2 and the *Supplement* rpt. as two voll., Dublin 1975). Most of the biblical material is in vol. 1.

20. E.g. the so-called Lambeth Commentary on the Psalms; *v.* L. Bieler and J. Carney, "The Lambeth Commentary," *Ériu* 23 (1972), pp. 1–55.

21. The most recent edition is O. Prinz, *Die Kosmographie des Aethicus Ister, MGH.QG* 14 (Munich 1993); *v.* my review in *JMLat* 3 (1993), pp. 236–45.

22. The works of Virgilius were last edited by G. Polara and translated into Italian by L. Caruso and G. Polara, *Virgilio Marone grammatico, Epitomi ed Epistole* (Naples 1979).

23. For the *Cosmographia v.* esp. H. Löwe, "Ein literarischer Widersacher des Bonifatius: Virgil von Salzburg und die Kosmographie des Aethicus Ister," *AAWM* (1951.11), pp. 903–88. For the writings of Virgilius, *v.* M.W. Herren, "Some New Light on the Life of Virgilius Maro Grammaticus," *PRIA, Section C—Archaeology, Celtic Studies, History, Linguistics, Literature* 79.2 (1979), pp. 27–71; rpt. in Herren, *Latin Letters* (note 10 above), essay 7.

24. In the works cited in note 23 above.

roughly the tenth to the thirteenth century, also offer many opportunities for research. While many of these texts have been edited, they have not been deeply studied, and should provide excellent opportunities for well-trained scholars interested in the classical tradition.[25]

In addressing the need for Hiberno-Latinists, I have already given at least one clear hint about the nature of their ideal training. If we set out deliberately to create Hiberno-Latinists, let us produce young scholars who are *periti/peritae utriusque linguae,* that is, as much Hibernist as Latinist. It is not really enough to say that one is an expert in one language and can read the other for research purposes. The only true criterion of knowledge of a dead language is the ability to edit a text written in that language (and survive the reviewers!). I hold up Charles Plummer as my paragon. Because Plummer is best known as the editor of Bede's *Ecclesiastical History,* it is often forgotten that he had an expert knowledge of Old Irish and edited not only the *Vitae sanctorum Hiberniae,* but also the Irish versions of the same lives.[26]

The best place to start is with a solid undergraduate education in Classics—more Latin than Greek, but definitely some Greek as well. There is now substantial documentation of the study of Greek by Irish as well as other European scholars in the early Middle Ages.[27] One should certainly be able to read the texts written in Greek or containing Greek that were read and glossed by European, including Irish, scholars. These include the Bible; the Greek quotations in Priscian, Martianus Capella, Servius, Macrobius, and Isidore; and the complex of Greek patristic works known to John Scotus Eriugena: the writings of Maximus the Confessor, Gregory of Nyssa, and especially ps.-Dionysius.

The study of classical Latin, ideally at the undergraduate level, is the best foundation for anyone wishing to work in the field of late or medieval Latin, including Hiberno-Latin. It provides the starting point from which one gains an understanding of the historical development of Latin; it fa-

25. V. esp. W.B. Stanford, "Towards a History of Classical Influences in Ireland," *PRIA, Section C—Archaeology, Celtic Studies, History, Linguistics, Literature* 70.3 (1970), pp. 13–91.

26. C. Plummer, *Bethada náem nÉrenn: Lives of Irish Saints edited from the Original MSS. with Introduction, Translation, Notes, Glossary, and Indexes.* 2 voll. (Oxford, *etc.* 1922).

27. Beginning, of course, with the study by B. Bischoff, "Das griechische Element in der abendländischen Bildung des Mittelalters," *Mittelalterliche Studien* (note 13 above), vol. 2 (Stuttgart 1967), pp. 246–75. V. more recently *The Sacred Nectar of the Greeks: The Study of Greek in the West in the Early Middle Ages,* ed. M.W. Herren and S.A. Brown (London 1988); B.M. Kaczynski, *Greek in the Carolingian Age: The St. Gall Manuscripts* (Cambridge, Mass. 1988). For a survey of the study of Greek in western Europe from late antiquity to the end of the Middle Ages, v. W. Berschin, *Greek Letters and the Latin Middle Ages: From Jerome to Nicholas of Cusa,* revised and expanded ed., trans. J.C. Frakes (Washington 1988).

miliarizes modern scholars with the same set of rules learned by medieval scholars; it imparts a knowledge of the classical works (limited at first, but expanding by the ninth century) studied in the medieval schools of Europe.

The next phase of my ideal curriculum prescribes graduate training in late, patristic, and medieval Latin supplemented by paleography and at least one course on the methodology of editing Latin texts. I would also strongly recommend work in vulgar Latin and/or romance philology. This will aid the student of Hiberno-Latin to recognize the features of latinity that were widespread on the continent as well as in the British Isles and hence were not determiners of Hiberno-Latinity.

Since Old Irish is unavailable in North America before the postgraduate level, it is there that the training in this language must necessarily begin. To understate things, Old Irish is very hard. Its grammar is unfamiliar to anyone not already an Indo-Europeanist, its reconstructed phonology very strange, and its orthography impossibly irregular. Nonetheless, it must be thoroughly mastered. This will take even more years—an additional two, at least—than the typical graduate program allows. The training must therefore be extended with post-doctoral study at a university or institute noted for its strengths in this field.

I have neglected to say anything about the modern languages. The acquisition of a reading knowledge of French is relatively easy for English speakers, but I recommend that our ideal student go farther and learn to speak it. This will prove enormously useful for understanding the papers read at international conferences and for consulting French-speaking scholars. If anything, the acquisition of German is even more crucial. I take it as a rule of thumb that roughly fifty percent of the secondary literature in any of the traditional humanistic fields is written in German. German scholars carried out the pioneering work in Old Irish philology, and the greatest part of this work has not been, and probably never will be, translated into English. In Medieval Latin Studies the influence is even greater. The major literary histories are written in German, as are numerous important works on Latin grammar, paleography, and the history of texts. In my experience, the acquisition of a reading knowledge of this language is greatly facilitated by learning to speak it. I would recommend that our ideal Hiberno-Latinist spend at least a year at a German institute early in his or her career. This can be made possible under the auspices of a Deutscher Akademischer Austauschdienst or Alexander von Humboldt fellowship. After French and German there is still Italian to be learned. A *corso estivo* at a center such as Perugia or Florence should provide a good beginning. My roster of languages other than English has risen to six: Latin and Old Irish should be exquisite; Greek, French, German, and Italian, very solid.

To lingusitic competence must be added a knowledge of manuscripts and the skill of editing. The best dissertation as a preparation for this field consists of an edition of a text with *apparatus criticus* and *apparatus fontium,* introduction, and a linguistic commentary if needed. A competently done edition confers a double benefit: it prepares the individual scholar for almost any task ahead, and it enriches the field with new material. The edition of a Latin text, carried out in a graduate department or center with strength in late and/or medieval Latin, could well be followed by a postdoctoral project consisting of an edition of an Old Irish text or other type of assignment demonstrating philological competence in that language.

I have been hesitant to name institutions where a program like the one I have described could be carried out. One obvious difficulty in giving a list is that a move or retirement of a single scholar can change the picture completely. I have also wished to avoid the impression that I am advertising any particular program or institution. Nonetheless, to serve the needs of potential students, I shall provide an alphabetized list of universities and the relevant departments where Hiberno-Latin studies currently can be pursued up to the doctoral level. I restrict my list to Anglophone institutions: The Department of Anglo-Saxon, Norse and Celtic, The University of Cambridge; The Program in Medieval and Byzantine Studies, The Catholic University of America; The Medieval Studies Program, Cornell University; The Department of Comparative Literature and the Department of Celtic Studies, Harvard University; The Centre for Medieval Studies, University of Toronto and The Programme in Celtic Studies, St. Michael's College, University of Toronto. I should also imagine that Hiberno-Latin studies could be pursued by special arrangement at the University of Oxford and at the National University of Ireland. I would single out the Dublin Institute for Advanced Studies as an obvious venue for postdoctoral study in Irish philology.

Those who complete such a course of study will be able to envision numerous possibilities for teaching and research. In their long years of education they will have encountered many kinds of texts and documents and formed an interest in one or more fields. All the riches one finds in the standard source books are at their disposal.[28] Over the course of their

---

28. J.F. Kenney, *The Sources for the Early History of Ireland: An Introduction and Guide,* vol. 1: *Ecclesiastical* (New York 1929; rev. ed., L. Bieler, New York 1966); M. Lapidge and R. Sharpe, *A Bibliography of Celtic-Latin Literature 400–1200* (Dublin 1985).

training some scholars may decide that they are better suited to be historians or students of religion than philologists. But what excellent historians and students of religion they will be! One need not go back very far in this century to encounter a host of scholars who were as well known for their critical editions as for their monographs. Medieval Studies, which itself is a relatively new field, had to produce reliable critical editions of its source materials at virtually the same time it began to interpret them. While perhaps the majority of distinguished scholars in Hiberno-Latin Studies—Traube, Hellmann, Bischoff, Bieler, to name only some—have been primarily philologists, in more recent times, researchers whose principle interests are in history and religious studies have begun to produce critical editions. This is a welcome development. Unfortunately, there are still not enough people equally well trained as Latinists and as Celticists to handle the material still in need of editing. This deficiency in turn necessitates the inevitable postponement of any attempt to write a history of Hiberno-Latin literature. I hope that I have described the challenges of the field and how they can best be met. Any takers?

Scripta

Books

St. John Chrysostom, In Praise of St. Paul (Boston 1963).
The Church (Wilmington, De. 1985).
Theodoret of Cyrus, On Divine Providence (New York 1988) = *Ancient Christian Writers,* vol. 49.
with T.K. Carroll, *Liturgical Practice in the Fathers* (Wilmington, De. 1988).

Books Edited

with J.P. Williman, *Diakonia: Studies in Honor of Robert T. Meyer* (Washington 1986).
The Message of the Fathers of the Church (Wilmington, De. 1983–87): 20 volumes.
J.J. O'Meara, *Studies in Augustine and Eriugena* (Washington 1992).
The Fathers of the Church (Washington 1983–present): voll. 73–97.

Bibliographical Guides

with R.D. Sider, "A Decade of Patristic Scholarship, 1970–1979," *Classical World* 76 (1982–83), pp. 65–127 and 313–83.
with S. O'Leary, *Classical Scholarship: An Annotated Bibliography* (White Plains, N.Y. 1986).

Translations of Secondary Works

Baptism: Ancient Liturgies and Patristic Texts (Staten Island, N.Y. 1967). Translation of A. Hamman, *La Baptême d'après les Pères de l'Église* (Paris 1962).
The Mass: Ancient Liturgies and Patristic Texts (Staten Island, N.Y. 1967). Translation of A. Hamman *et al., La messe: liturgies anciennes et textes patristiques* (Paris 1964).
The Paschal Mystery: Ancient Liturgies and Patristic Texts (Staten Island, N.Y. 1969). Translation of A. Hamman and F. Quéré-Jaulmes, *Le Mystère de Pâques* (Paris 1965).

Journal Articles

"St. John Chrysostom on Education," *Catholic Educational Review* 61 (1963), pp. 163–75.
"St. John Chrysostom, *De Fato et Providentia:* A Study of Its Authenticity," *Traditio* 20 (1964), pp. 1–24.

"Baptism as Illumination," *Irish Theological Quarterly* 32 (1965), pp. 28–41.

"Some Images of the Church in St. John Chrysostom," *American Ecclesiastical Review* 153 (1965), pp. 96–106.

"Paschal Homily: Melito of Sardis—A New Translation," *The Furrow* 19 (1968), pp. 212–22.

"The Death of Death in Melito, *Peri Pascha*" *Irish Theological Quarterly* 36 (1969), pp. 169–73.

"Valentinian Echoes in Melito, *Peri Pascha?*" *Journal of Theological Studies,* n.s. 20 (1969), pp. 535–38.

"Stylistic Device in Melito, *Peri Pascha,*" *Kyriakon: Festschrift Johannes Quasten,* ed. P. Granfield and J.A. Jungmann, vol. 1 (Münster 1970), pp. 249–55.

"Sysiphus from Homer to Camus," *Classical Folia* 29 (1975), pp. 141–51.

"The Coming of Spring: A Patristic Motif," *Classical Folia* 30 (1976), pp. 150–64.

"Two Newly-Edited Homilies of St. John Chrysostom," *Irish Theological Quarterly* 43 (1976), pp. 133–38.

"The Early Christian Homily," *The Living Light* 17 (1980), pp. 159–63.

"Hegesippus in Eusebius," *Studia patristica* 17 (1982), pp. 688–93.

"Clement's Lyre: A Broken String, a New Song," *The Second Century* 3 (1983), pp. 177–99.

"The New Origen, *Peri Pascha,*" *Greek Orthodox Theological Review* 28 (1983), pp. 73–80.

"The Kairos of the Mass and the Deacon in John Chrysostom," *Diakonia: Studies in Honor of Robert T. Meyer,* ed. T.P. Halton and J.P. Williman (Washington 1986), pp. 53–59.

"The Five Senses in Nemesius, *De Natura Hominis* and Theodoret, *De Providentia,*" *Studia patristica* 20 (1987), pp. 94–101.

"Clement of Alexandria and Athenaeus (*Paed.* III.4,26)," *The Second Century* 6 (1987–88), pp. 193–202.

"Augustine in Translation: Achievements and Further Goals," in *Augustine: From Rhetor to Theologian,* ed. J. McWilliam *et al.* (Waterloo, Ont. 1992), pp. 207–29.

"Early Christian Ireland's Contacts with the Mediterranean World to c. 650," *Cristianesimo e specificità regionali nel mediterraneo latino (sec. IV–VI): XXII Incontro di studiosi dell'antichità cristiana, Roma, 6–8 maggio 1993* (Rome 1994), pp. 601–18 = *Studia ephemeridis Augustinianum,* vol. 46.

"Ecclesiastical War and Peace in the Letters of Isidore of Pelusium," *Peace and War in Byzantium: Essays in Honor of George T. Dennis, S.J.,* ed. T.S. Miller and J. Nesbitt (Washington 1995), pp. 41–49.

Dictionary Articles

The New Catholic Encyclopedia, ed. W.J. McDonald *et al.* (Washington 1967):
"Aeonius of Arles, St."
"Christianity and Hellenism"
"Dungal"
"Henricus Aristippus"
"John of Ravenna"
"John of Réôme, St."

"Paideia, Christian"
"Pyrrhus I, Patriarch of Constantinople"

Ib., vol. 17 (1979): *Supplement, Change in the Church:* "Deferrari, Roy J."
Ib., vol. 18 (1989): *Supplement, 1978–88:* "Patristic Studies"

Theologische Realenzyklopädie, ed. G. Müller *et al.* (Berlin/New York 1985): "Hegesipp"
Great Lives from History: Ancient and Medieval Series, ed. F.N. Magill (Pasadena, Calif. 1988):
"Saint John Chrysostom"
"Gregory of Nazianzus"

Encyclopedia of Early Christianity, ed. E. Ferguson *et al.* (New York 1990):
"Catholic Church"
"Church"
"Hegesippus"
"Providence"
 "Quasten, Johannes"
"Sign of the Cross"
"Sophia"

Works in Progress/Awaiting Publication

Bibliographic Supplement (1950–1995) to Johannes Quasten, Patrology, I–III (The Catholic University of America Press: Washington).
"The Irish Contribution to the Classical Tradition," *Aufstieg und Niedergang der römischen Welt,* ed. H. Temporini and W. Haase (Walter De Gruyter: Berlin/New York).
Theodoret of Cyrus, A Cure for Pagan Maladies (Paulist Press: New York): to appear in the series *Ancient Christian Writers.*
To Diognetus, ed. B. Norelli, trans. T.P. Halton (Figlie di S. Paolo: Milan, *etc.*).

Indices

The following *indices* are designed (1) to point out relationships between the essays of this volume and (2) to facilitate the reader's access to discussion of an ancient work or a given passage of that work. Normally, a work is cited only when a particular passage is discussed: one will find ref. to Mt. chh. 1–15 and to *Civ. dei* 1.30 but not to the Gospel of St. Matthew or to *Civ. dei* as a whole. A few exceptions are made for short and less frequently discussed works.

Plain text = ref. occurs in footnotes only.

Bold face = ref. occurs in body of paper only, or ref. to the same citation occurs both in body and in footnotes.

1f. = one citation extending over two pp. of the body of the paper.

1, 2 = two separate citations of the same passage on contiguous pp. of the body of the paper.

1, 1 = same passage cited in the body of the paper and in a footnote not dependent on that ref.

(**1f.**) = repeated ref. to a work or indicated section of a work will be found in the body of the paper or the body and the footnotes on the enclosed p. or pp.

(1f.) = repeated reff. to a work or indicated section of a work will be found in the footnotes on the enclosed p. or pp.

Index Scripturisticus

The *Ind. script.* includes (1) all biblical passages cited by the editor and the seventeen authors of these papers and (2) biblical passages to which excerpts cited from ancient and medieval works refer or on which they comment. In cases where ancient exegetical works are cited compendiously in the *Ind. loc. antiq.* (*e.g.* Chrys., *in Acta app.*), one will find here set out in detail, usually by verse(s), though occasionally by pericope, all the scriptural passages that were treated in excerpts quoted by our contributors.

Old Testament

Genesis
- 1.26: **118, 143**
- chh. 2f.: **193**
- 2.9: **131**
- 2.16f.: **131**
- 2.17: **131***bis***, 135**
- 2.23: **132**
- ch. 3: (**129**–**38**), **142**
- 3.6: **144**
- 3.7: **63**
- 3.16: **145, 174**
- chh. 7–9: **159**
- chh. 12–25: 157
- 22.13: **59**
- 28.10–17: **64**

Exodus
- 2.14: **214**
- 13.2: **45**
- 13.12: **45**
- 13.15: **45**
- 14.9–15.21: **159**
- 16.33: **106**
- 17.1–7: **106**

Leviticus
- 16.20–26: 133

Numbers
- 20.1–13: **106**
- 24.17: **46**

1 Kings
- 18.33–35: **75**

2 Kings
- 4.42–5.14: **159**

Job
- 40.25 (LXX): 106

Psalms
- 1.2: **228**
- 2.7: 159
- 7.6: **233**
- 18.11: 26
- 20.8: **230***bis*
- 22: **160**
- 26.1f.: **232**
- 30.8: **228**
- 31.11: **228f.**
- 33.6: **74, 81**
- 36.1: 229, **232**
- 36.2: **232**
- 38.12: **231**
- 40.2: **233**
- 44.3: 26
- 45.2: 229
- 50.7: **188**
- 52.2: 229
- 60.5: 229
- 62.7f.: **233**
- 70.1: **234**
- 76.14: **31**

- 78.25: **75**
- 80.2: **107**
- 80.3: **230**
- 80.3f.: **230**
- 86.8: **31**
- 90.1: 229
- 93.9f.: **230**
- 96.10: 229
- 100.2: **234**
- 103.14: 157
- 109.8: **250**
- 110.9: **231**
- 117.8f. (LXX): 31
- 120.2: 229
- 130.1: **234**
- 140.1: **231**
- 150.6: **227, 228, 229**

Proverbs
- 2.5: **17**

Ecclesiastes
- 3.1f.: **73**
- 9.17: **108**

Wisdom
- 7.25f.: 9

Sirach
- 10.15 (*Vulg.*): **136**
- 26.10: 135

New Testament

Index Locorum Antiquorum

The *Index loc. antiq.* includes reff. only to published texts. In the very few cases where no chapter, section, or page of a text is listed because no traditional system of subdivision exists, the reader will find reff. to the pp. of a modern edition *ad loc.*

For exegetical works:

in Mt. 1.1 = reference to ch. 1 of homily (*vel sim.*) 1 on Mt.

on Mt. 1.1 = reference to a comment on Mt. 1.1.

Commentaries on books of Scripture are placed in biblical order before the alphabetical listing of other works. Sermons or treatises dealing with individual texts, as opposed to complete books, of Scripture appear in the alphabetical listing.

Achilles Tatius
  Leuc. et Clit.
    2.14.5f.: 61

Acta Io(h)annis
    secc. 98–101: **54f.**
    sec. 109: 107

Ad Diognetum (Epistula)
    12.6: 14

Adrian
  Isag.
    sec. 110: **30**

Albinus
  Didask.
    chh. 8–10: 4

Ambrose
  in Lc.
    10.176: **190**
  De Abraham
    bk. 1: 157
    bk. 2: 157
  Exh. virg.
    6.36: 188
  Exp. fid.: 158*bis*
  Expl. sym.
    1: 157

Sacr. : (**156–60**)
    5.1: 75

Amphilochius of Iconium
  Or.
    8.2: 26

Anaximenes
  Ars rh.
    3.8: **23**

Anthologia palatina
    7.13.1–3: **165**
    7.712.5–8: **164f.**

Aphthonius
  Progym.
    sec. 42: 24

Apollodorus Mythographus
  Bibl.
    1.30: 167
    3.184f.: **170f.**

Apo. pat.: (**141–47**)
    Matoes 13: 129

Apuleius
  De Platone
    ch. 5: 4

Aristides
  Apol.
    sec. 11: 171
  Or.
    22.10: 163

Aristophanes
  Frogs
    341: 167

Aristotle
  APo.
    1.2: **11**
    2.19: 11, **15**
  Apr.
    1.23: **232**
    1.44: **232**
    2.27: **229**
  Ath.
    3.5: 170
  EN
    1.7: 11
    6.6: 11
  MM
    2.34.14: **11**
  Rhet.
    1.2.3–5: 94
    1.9: **23**
  Top.
    8.11: **231**